The New Regional Politics of Development

The New Regional Politics of Development

Edited by
Anthony Payne

First published 2004 by
PALGRAVE MACMILLAN
Houndmills, Basingstoke, Hampshire RG21 6XS and
175 Fifth Avenue, New York, N.Y. 10010
Companies and representatives throughout the world

PALGRAVE MACMILLAN is the global academic imprint of the Palgrave Macmillan division of St. Martin's Press, LLC and of Palgrave Macmillan Ltd. Macmillan® is a registered trademark in the United States, United Kingdom and other countries. Palgrave is a registered trademark in the European Union and other countries.

ISBN 0–333–97394–1 hardback
ISBN 0–333–97395–X paperback

This book is printed on paper suitable for recycling and made from fully managed and sustained forest sources.

A catalogue record for this book is available from the British Library.

Library of Congress Cataloging-in-Publication Data
        The new regional politics of development / edited by Anthony Payne.
            p. cm.
        Includes bibliographical references and index.
        ISBN 0–333–97394–1 (cloth) – ISBN 0–333–97395–X (paper)
            1. Economic development – Case studies. 2. Regionalism – Case studies.
        3. Globalization – Case studies. I. Payne, Anthony, 1952–
HD75.N484 2004
338.9—dc22   2004046489

10 9 8 7 6 5 4 3 2 1
13 12 11 10 09 08 07 06 05 04

Printed and bound in China

Contents

List of Tables

Preface

I began my academic career in the 1970s thinking that what I did was development studies. During the 1990s I was drawn more to the emergent field of international political economy. Over the last few years, however, I have begun to think that these two phases of my endeavours could fruitfully be brought together and that, in fact, development, as a concept and a field of study within the academy, needed urgently to be revived within the more dynamic intellectual arena of international political economy. In 1999 I published a short 'think-piece' in the *Journal of International Relations and Development* which called for a 'reframing' of the global politics of development and tried to follow up those initial arguments in a paper delivered to a stimulating conference held at Simon Fraser University in Vancouver in 2001. One can only have so many ideas and so some of the arguments contained in these two pieces of writing reappear here in fuller form in the introductory chapter to this volume.

Nevertheless, this book is conceived as the next logical step in this project to rethink development inside international political economy. I recognized the need for help and accordingly asked a number of colleagues, whose research interests also seemed to me to sit somewhere between development studies and international political economy, to prepare portraits of the politics of development in a number of the key regions of the world. The deeper thinking, such as it is, which went into the design of the book is explained in the first chapter and I will not seek to set it out here. But I would like to thank these various colleagues, all of whom responded readily to my invitation, for doing so. I trust that they will not object to the many minor ways in which, as editor, I have intervened in their chapters.

Two more people need to be mentioned by way of acknowledgement. One is Björn Hettne, whose writings over the past several years have inspired me. Amongst many conversations about development and globalization I remember in particular that conducted over fresh mushrooms and whisky on the shores of Lake Vanern at Bjorn's summer house in Sweden. The other is Nicola Phillips, one of the contributors to the book, but also, to all intents and purposes, its uncredited co-editor. She helped me shape the nature of the book and then found the time to read and comment in detail on all of the chapters. I am very grateful to Bjorn and Nicola for supporting me in their different ways in this next

ix

attempt to push forward the rethinking of development, a task which seems to me to be more necessary than ever in the context of some of the events that have already taken place in the new century.

Sheffield   ANTHONY PAYNE

List of Abbreviations

AASM	Associated African States and Madagascar (of the European Community)
AC	Andean Community
ACP	African, Caribbean and Pacific states (in association with the EU)
ACS	Association of Caribbean States
ADB	Asian Development Bank
AFTA	ASEAN Free Trade Area
AGOA	Africa Growth and Opportunity Act (of the US)
APEC	Asia-Pacific Economic Cooperation
ARF	ASEAN Regional Forum
ASEAN	Association of Southeast Asian Nations
AU	African Union
CACM	Central American Common Market
CAP	Common Agricultural Policy (of the EU)
CARICOM	Caribbean Community
CDM	Commercial defence mechanism
CEEC	Central and Eastern European country
CEFTA	Central European Free Trade Area
CFSP	Common Foreign and Security Policy (of the EU)
CIS	Commonwealth of Independent States
DG	Directorate General (of the European Commission)
DRC	Democratic Republic of the Congo
EAC	East African Community
EAEC	East Asian Economic Caucus
EBRD	European Bank for Reconstruction and Development
ECLAC	United Nations Economic Commission for Latin America and the Caribbean
ECOMOG	ECOWAS Monitoring Group
ECOWAS	Economic Community of West African States
EEA	European Economic Area
EFTA	European Free Trade Area
EMU	Economic and Monetary Union (within the EU)
EPZ	Export Processing Zone
ERDF	European Regional Development Fund
EU	European Union
FDI	Foreign direct investment

FTAA	Free Trade Area of the Americas
GATT	General Agreement on Tariffs and Trade
GDP	Gross domestic product
GNI	Gross national income
GNP	Gross national product
G7	Group of Seven
HIPC	Highly Indebted Poor Countries Initiative (of the World Bank)
IEC	Interstate Economic Council (between Ukraine, Russia and Belarus)
IFI	International financial institution
ILO	International Labour Organization
IMF	International Monetary Fund
IPE	International political economy
ISI	Import-substituting industrialization
LDP	Liberal Democratic Party (of Japan)
LPA	Lagos Plan of Action
MENA	Middle East and North Africa
MERCOSUR	Common Market of the South
MITI	Ministry of International Trade and Industry (of Japan)
MLG	Multi-level governance
NAFTA	North American Free Trade Area
NATO	North Atlantic Treaty Organization
NEPAD	New Partnership for Africa's Development
NGO	Non-governmental organization
NIEO	New International Economic Order
OAS	Organization of American States
OAU	Organization of African Unity
ODA	Overseas Development Assistance
OECD	Organisation for Economic Co-operation and Development
OPEC	Organization of Petroleum Exporting Countries
PPP	Purchasing power parity
PRC	People's Republic of China
ROC	Republic of China
SAARC	South Asian Association for Regional Co-operation
SAFTA	South Asian Free Trading Arrangement
SADC	Southern African Development Community
SAP	Structural adjustment programme
SSA	Sub-Saharan Africa
TRNC	Turkish Republic of Northern Cyprus
UK	United Kingdom

UMNO	United Malays National Organization (of Malaysia)
UN	United Nations
UNDP	United Nations Development Programme
UNECA	United Nations Economic Commission for Africa
UNP	United National Party (of Sri Lanka)
US	United States
USSR	Union of Soviet Socialist Republics
USTR	United States Trade Representative
WTO	World Trade Organization

Notes on the Contributors

Mark Beeson is Senior Lecturer in International Relations at the University of Queensland.

Shaun Breslin is Professor of Politics and International Studies at the University of Warwick.

Simon Bromley is Senior Lecturer in Government and Politics at the Open University.

Graham Harrison is Lecturer in Politics at the University of Sheffield.

Anthony Payne is Professor of Politics and Co-Director of the Political Economy Research Centre at the University of Sheffield.

Nicola Phillips is Hallsworth Research Fellow in the Department of Government at the University of Manchester.

Neil Robinson is Head of the Department of Politics and Public Administration at the University of Limerick.

Ben Rosamond is Reader in Politics and International Studies at the University of Warwick.

Andrew Wyatt is Lecturer in Politics at the University of Bristol.

Chapter 1

Rethinking Development inside International Political Economy

ANTHONY PAYNE

We used to think we knew what development meant and how to go about its study. Although the precise normative content of the term was always contested and routinely differentiated from the narrower notion of 'mere' economic growth, it was nevertheless widely agreed that development was something which select countries had already achieved but which large parts of the world still needed to experience. On that basis we distinguished knowingly between so-called 'developed countries' (the First World) and so-called 'developing countries' (the Third World). The former were to be found predominantly in North America and western Europe, the latter in Africa, Asia, the Middle East and Latin America and the Caribbean. Another category of countries, namely the Soviet Union and the various Soviet satellite states of central and eastern Europe, which were sometimes described as the Second World, were seen to have gone off down a separate socialist path, rendering them a special case. What was taken for granted in this vision was that development studies constituted a distinctive field of study devoted to the analysis of those demarcated parts of the world which remained mired in pursuit of development.

Simply put, both this map of the world and its attendant academic division of labour within the social sciences have been comprehensively overtaken by events. These 'events' refer to the seismic changes which, ever since the early 1970s, have run destructively through the economics and politics of the world order established at the end of the Second World War. Within the academy this reconfiguration of the structures of the world order gave sustenance to a new sub-discipline, that of international political economy (IPE). The field of IPE diverged fairly quickly into mainstream and critical strands of thought. The former has become somewhat fixated upon the ways in which international cooperation can, or cannot, be recreated in the context of these changes and has failed to live up to its early promise; the latter, however, has proved to be

1

highly creative. In particular, it has generated three extensive, and linked, debates about the nature of the new post-1970s world order. One concerned itself with the rise of globalization; another addressed the role of states in a putatively globalizing world order; the other emphasized the new relevance of regions. Unsurprisingly, these debates have not created a new consensus about how to envision the shape of the 'new world order' that is slowly emerging into being. Indeed, it is highly unlikely that a common vision will emerge, given both the complexity of the changes at stake and the diversity of ideological perspectives from which they can be viewed. We have therefore no choice but to take up positions in these debates in order to proceed analytically.

Yet, almost regardless of how this is done, it cannot be denied any longer that we need to think afresh about what we mean by development. To be categorical, we need to be willing to step outside the old frame of development studies and to rethink the term within the context of these wider discussions of global economic and political change taking place inside the field of IPE. The case for doing this is as yet insufficiently recognized. Some scholars working within development studies have turned out to be conservatives in radical clothing, determined to hang on to the proclaimed special nature of their field of study long after the rationale for its distinctiveness has been undermined. There is no denying that development studies has had an heroic history. Indeed in its heyday it was an exemplar of all that was best about the social sciences – interdisciplinary, focused on big questions, engaged with them, political in the most generous sense of that word. But that phase has passed and development studies, for all its continuing merits, is no longer quite such a vibrant field of enquiry and debate. This book seeks to move forward beyond the constraints of old definitions and paradigms and constitutes a first cast at mapping – within an overtly IPE framework – what we see as the contours of the new 'world of development' being created at the beginning of the twenty-first century. The remainder of this introductory chapter seeks to prepare the ground for this exercise. In turn, it reviews the classical era in development studies; it introduces the main theoretical strains within international political economy and addresses the major debates within IPE identified a few moments ago; it proposes a reconceptualization of development for the new global/regional era based on insights from development studies *and* IPE; and, finally, it describes the subsequent rationale, plan and content of the book.

The classical era in development studies

As Björn Hettne (1995: 30) has shown more elegantly than anyone else, classical development theory unfolded historically in dialectical fashion, oscillating between 'mainstream' and 'counterpoint' paradigms. In the post-1945 phase of that history, modernization theory and dependency theory proposed contrasting accounts of the problem of development. For the former, the task lay in eliminating the various internal obstacles, mostly deriving from 'tradition', which lay in the way of emulation of the path to development deemed to have been successfully blazed by modernized, Western liberal democratic states in North America and western Europe. For the latter, the challenge was to overcome the external obstacles to development, with the strongest arguments suggesting that dependent location within the international economy inevitably created *under*development. It is not clear, though, that there was ever that much actual engagement between the two perspectives. Dependency theorists typically mounted polemical attacks upon modernization orthodoxies; modernization thinkers typically ignored the attacks in the most studied of fashions. Over time what became apparent was that each body of theory had the reverse defect of the other: an excessive endogenism in the case of the modernization school, an excessive exogenism in the case of the *dependentistas*. There was created, in consequence, an 'awkward theoretical vacuum' in the field (Hettne 1995: 104). This sense that development theory had lost its way became the academic orthodoxy of the 1980s and was persuasively captured by the declaration of David Booth (1985) that an 'impasse' had been reached.

Yet, as already suggested, the reality was that classic development theory had been undone, not so much by theoretical failures, although these did exist, but by the fundamental changes that took place in the 1970s and 1980s in the structure of the world order. Although these cannot be discussed at length here, it is widely acknowledged that a series of events – including most notably the devaluation of the United States (US) dollar in 1971, the oil price shock of 1973–4 and the resulting mix of stagnation and inflation experienced in several Western economies – reflected the ending of the era of overwhelming, relatively easy, global hegemony enjoyed by the United States since 1945, as well as the attendant unwinding of the Bretton Woods system of regulated capital movements and freer international trade that had been put in place largely by the US at the beginning of the postwar period. These cumulative changes completely altered the nature of the world order in which states had to operate. As Colin Leys (1996: 41) put it, 'if the end of the Bretton Woods system spelled the end of national Keynesianism, it also spelled the end of national development as it had hitherto been conceived'. Although this new phase in the world order inevitably had a significant impact on all countries, it proved particularly destabilizing for those parts of Africa and Latin America and the Caribbean seeking to establish some limited room for manoeuvre within the international economy. The 1980s saw a swathe of such states run into intractable debt and balance of payments problems, which pushed them inexorably into the hands of the International Monetary Fund (IMF) and the World Bank. These institutions in turn used the conditionalities attached to their loans to impose 'structural adjustment programmes' (routinely involving deregulation, privatization, devaluation, removal of price controls and trade tariffs, increased indirect taxation and public-sector demanning), the declared purpose of which was to make the recipient economies ready to withstand the rigours of the international marketplace. Again to quote Leys (1996: 42), 'it is hardly too much to say that by the end of the 1980s the only development policy that was officially approved was not having one – leaving it to the market to allocate resources, not the state'. These trends angered many of those working in development studies and attention came to focus strongly on exposing the many damaging consequences for the well-being of the states and societies being 'structurally adjusted' – a task which was generally carried out with great energy and understanding.

For all the merits of this body of empirical work, the wider theoretical problem was that, in this new set of circumstances, any body of theory premised upon the possession by national state governments of a variety of policy tools which they could deploy in the pursuit of development could not but hit an impasse. Hettne (1995: 111) suggests that, as a consequence, the classical debate between modernization and dependency perspectives became transmuted from the national stage, where it had hitherto been exclusively conducted, into a global contest between what he dubbed 'world development ideologies'. In this arena there was no doubt but that neoliberalism, which was the shorthand label that came to be used to describe the case increasingly being made for a return to the values and practices of liberal market economics, moved into the ascendant during the 1980s (Toye 1987). As a body of ideas it came to dominate the thinking and policies of many governments and all the major international financial institutions (IFIs), such as the IMF and the World Bank. It also drove forward the planned extension of global free trade which the Uruguay Round of trade talks sought to effect from the middle of the decade onwards. Neoliberalism was, of course, the quintessential 'world development ideology' since its core claim was that development was a process attainable all over the world, provided that the 'market' was allowed to assert itself over the 'state'. The critical positions in this global battle of ideologies were taken by 'neoKeynesianism', exemplified by the efforts of the Brandt Commission (1980) and the Socialist International to promote belief in the notion of a fundamental interdependence binding the 'developed' and 'developing' worlds; 'neomercantilism', illustrated by the continuing interest shown by some development theorists in forms of national or regional economic protection (Hettne 1993); and the 'neopopulism' of the green movement, which called in different ways for a rejection of all forms of industrial development, irrespective of whether they were led by the market or the state (Goodin 1992). These various alternative arguments were energetically pursued both in the academic and political literatures, but they had great difficulty in shaking the ideological hold of the neoliberal counter-revolution on both development theory *and* practice. Moreover, while the arguments raged, structural adjustment proceeded apace.

In short, neoliberalism has laid effective claim to be the new mainstream development paradigm. This is not to say that it has been an unchanging paradigm. Over time some of the most fundamentalist features of 'early' structural adjustment programmes have been softened. More time for implementation has been allowed and more emphasis has been placed on social measures, in pursuit of 'adjustment with a human face'. During the 1990s, in particular, important debates have also been opened up by the World Bank about the appropriate role to be played by the state in a market economy, about corruption and about so-called 'good governance', a phrase used to catch the essence of all that was considered to be best about Western liberal state forms (Williams 1996; Doornbos 2001). Yet it is still arguable that these changes constitute no more than piecemeal additions to the core of the original neoliberal consensus in a series of attempts to rescue it from some of its inadequacies. Indeed, they make the paradigm even more all-embracing, and thus give rise to even more potential conditionalities, precisely by inserting into it a stronger social and political dimension. It is certainly striking that neoliberalism has been challenged as the 'counterpoint', not by a new, radical, post-dependency thinking or even a revival of statist social democracy, but rather by a postmodernism which has advanced what is, to all intents and purposes, an anti-development position. This body of thought deliberately turned away from political economy to emphasize culture and aggressively dismissed all existing notions of development as 'Eurocentric' by virtue of their approval of technology, innovation and growth (Esteva 1992; Said 1992; Escobar 1995). It preferred instead to laud local, non-governmental initiatives, more or less for their own sake, and certainly regardless of their likely economic or political efficacy. Although this approach still remains fashionable in some development circles, it has always been characterized by a preoccupation with its own internal debates and language and has signally failed to impact to any degree upon either mainstream ideas or policy practice. Neoliberals and postmodernists have never found a way to talk creatively to each other and in that sense, perhaps even more markedly than in the era dominated by competing modernization and dependency perspectives, there manifestly now exists no central, agreed terrain of debate within development studies.

The key organizing insight to be drawn from this last observation is not difficult to discern: if development theory has been undermined by deep shifts in the world order within which it has to argue its case, then the necessary starting point for rethinking can only be found in a better grasp of the essential features of the new order. In essence, this is what pushes us towards IPE, which as a field of study has not only taken as its *raison d'être* that very task, but derived much of its intellectual energy from the sheer extent of the post-Bretton Woods restructuring of the international economy. Accordingly, the next part of this chapter turns towards international political economy. It seeks briefly to delineate the shape of the field as it has unfolded and then moves on to survey, and evaluate, three of the central debates to have been conducted within IPE over the last few years. As indicated earlier, these are the debates about the extent to which we can sensibly now talk of globalization and the meaning that we might attach to that term; the consequences which globalization has allegedly had for the roles of states in the new global order; and the implications of the emergence of 'new regions' as both coherent political projects and ongoing processes of interaction. On the basis of lessons learned from these areas of research, we will then return to the concept of development and endeavour to suggest how we might henceforth redeploy the term and begin to use it to address the considerable complexities of the contemporary world order.

The concerns of international political economy

IPE originated in a powerful critique of the incapacity of traditional, realist international relations theory to analyse the origins and causes of the instability experienced by the international economy at the beginning of the 1970s. In a classic statement Susan Strange (1970: 304) noted the 'mutual neglect' of international economics and international relations as spheres of study and the consequent widespread ignorance and misunderstanding of important aspects of the international policy agenda beyond specific concerns with security. Two American scholars, Robert Keohane and Joseph Nye (1972 and 1977), quickly came to the forefront of the argument with arresting and original studies of the new significance of transnational relations and interdependence in world politics. However, by comparison with this lively and disputatious beginning, the theoretical evolution of mainstream IPE has since come to be characterized by a process of fertilization, and ultimately convergence, between the respective claims of dominant 'neo-realist' and 'neo-institutionalist' schools. In a thorough review of the field published in the early 1990s, George Crane and Abla Amawi (1991) argued that thinking had come to cohere around three focal points – rational action theories of the state, the theory of hegemonic stability and regime theory. In other words, mainstream IPE has become a discourse constructed around a particular view of the hegemonic state and the problems, or otherwise, variously caused by its absence or presence. Over the years the extent of the literature generated in this vein of analysis has been truly enormous. Charles Kindleberger (1973) and Robert Gilpin (1975) dominated the early debate about the need for a stabilizer to manage the world economy but did not actually use the concept of hegemony. As a result, the most-cited definition was that provided by Keohane (1984: 32), who described hegemony as a 'preponderance of material resources'. For him, the elements of hegemonic power, as they relate to the world economy, were comprised of control over raw materials, markets and capital, as well as 'competitive advantages in the production of highly valued goods...involving the use of complex or new technology' (Keohane 1984: 33). These material resources provided the means by which the hegemon could both make and enforce the rules of the world political economy. Power was thus conceived in traditional resource terms and hegemony was deployed as force.

This conception of hegemony set up a number of specific research programmes within emergent IPE. One disputed the normative manner in which hegemonic power was exercised, positions ranging from the 'benign' to the 'self-regarding'. Another concerned the impact of the loss of US hegemony on the viability of the various post-1945 regimes designed to improve international economic cooperation. A third, and logically prior, programme addressed the very matter of whether the United States had, indeed, lost its hegemonic position. A final arena of contention disputed how best to explain international cooperation – with 'neo-realists' arguing that the importance of relative gains in conditions of international anarchy inhibits cooperation, and 'neo-institutionalists' assuming that states are more concerned with absolute welfare maximization and are thus capable of learning to cooperate. However, the problem with all of this literature was that its theoretical underpinnings were marked by a number of biases which rendered many of the attendant arguments deficient (Leaver 1989). For example, the definition of the core concept of hegemony was based upon a limited range of variables, largely drawn from a selective reading of the US post-1945 experience minimally qualified by reference to nineteenth-century Britain. Other questions were also excluded from consideration, notably the matter of why some states came to accept and others resist the rule of the hegemon. Additionally, the vital issue – for an approach which believed in the measurement of power – of exactly how much power was needed to engender hegemony was never satisfactorily resolved. In the end, G. John Ikenberry (1989: 379) was right to suggest that 'the texture of hegemonic power has not been captured' in the major American texts of the IPE literature. In fact, the criticism can be widened to embrace the whole thrust of mainstream IPE theory. Richard Leaver (1994: 139) concluded his survey of recent theorizing by suggesting that Crane and Amawi's process of convergence, which he accepted had occurred, was 'evidence of involution rather than evolution'. Richard Higgott (1994: 161) noted that mainstream theory was 'no longer a self-evident way of enframing the study of power in IPE'. Susan Strange was typically the most robust of all in her call for the abandonment of both 'neo-realism' in the study of international relations and liberalism and neoclassical notions of equilibrium in the study of international economics. For IPE, she said, they were 'culs-de-sac, *strade senza uscita*, no through roads' (Strange 1995: 171). For all the force of such an injunction, it should be noted, in passing as it were, that many, of course, do still continue to seek to travel along them.

Nevertheless, within IPE, the intellectual running has now largely been taken up by 'critical' (or new, or heterodox, or counter-hegemonic) thinking. Drawing inspiration from the founding analysis of Robert Cox (1981: 129), this approach self-consciously set out to be 'critical in the sense that it stands apart from the prevailing order of the world and asks how that order came about'. In Cox's formulation, it was a theory of history concerned not just with the past but with a continuing process of change; it was directed to the social and political complex as a whole rather than to its separate parts; and it contained within its ambit the possibility of identifying the outlines of alternative distributions of power from those prevailing at any particular time. As is now well-known in the IPE field, Cox himself proposed a method of historical structures, defined as configurations of forces (material capabilities, ideas and institutions) which do not determine actions but nevertheless create opportunities and impose constraints. There is presumed 'no one-way determinism' between the three forces (Cox 1981: 136); as he later put it, 'ideas and material conditions are always bound together, mutually influencing one another, and not reducible one to the other' (Cox 1983: 168). In this spirit Cox countered the mainstream account of hegemony with a much more nuanced reading which, crucially, sees hegemony as bringing together coercive *and* consensual elements of power. This meant that 'there can be dominance without hegemony; hegemony is one possible form dominance may take' (Cox 1987: 153). His reading of the concept of hegemony has been enormously influential within critical IPE, as indeed has his work as a whole. Even so, the real significance of Cox's contribution to IPE is that he has served to inspire and legitimize both a wider and deeper range of thinking than was previously possible. Although it needs to be acknowledged that critical IPE constitutes no more than a loose college of scholars who embrace a diverse range of approaches, what binds it together – and at the same time differentiates it from the mainstream – are two commitments: first, to give due weight to both structure *and* agency in all explanations; and, second, to recognize the realities of both ideational and material definitions of power. This neatly brings us back to the three important debates within IPE mentioned earlier. Each will be examined in turn and each will be seen to draw upon these two imperatives of contemporary critical IPE.

Globalization

IPE's current preoccupation with the notion of globalization is such that the term has already been hugely overdefined, with the concept being used to launch a myriad of popular, as well as academic, analyses of the current global order. Yet it is too important to be set aside and is therefore best understood very broadly as a social process unfolding at the global level and driven forward by a mixture of forces (public and private, political and non-political) of which states (the traditional leading actors in international relations) are only one and by no means necessarily always the most influential. This sense of globalization as a very wide-ranging *process* is well-captured in the working definition adopted by David Held, Anthony McGrew, David Goldblatt and Jonathan Perraton in their commanding overview of the globalization debate. They say, specifically, that 'globalization may be thought of initially as the widening, deepening and speeding up of worldwide interconnectedness in all aspects of contemporary social life, from the cultural to the criminal, the financial to the spiritual' (Held *et al.* 1999: 2). From this conceptual starting point they then proceed to identify and distinguish three broad schools of thought within the debate which they refer to as the 'hyperglobalizers', the 'sceptics' and the 'transformationalists'.

The latter 'transformationalist' account of globalization, which Held and his co-authors derive particularly from the work of Anthony Giddens (1990), Manuel Castells (1996) and James Rosenau (1997), is much the most nuanced and persuasive and can be set out briefly as follows. It begins from the assumption that globalization as a concept draws attention to the recent emergence of what Held *et al.* (1999: 7) describe as 'a powerful transformative force' which has been 'responsible for a "massive shake-out" of societies, economies, institutions of governance and world order'. Importantly, the direction of the shake-out remains uncertain, since globalization is understood here as a long-term historical process characterized by contradictions, shaped by conjunctures and contested by increasingly aware and hostile political forces. There is thus no defined end-game, no single ideal-type of what a 'fully globalized' world would look like. Of course, certain trends can be picked out, at least up to the present point of analysis. Accordingly, 'transformationalists' generally argue that there now exist historically unprecedented levels of global interconnectedness in trade, finance, production, culture and much else. They believe that virtually all parts of the world are functionally part of a global system in one or more respects, although they do not suggest that this is bringing about global convergence or a single world society. In fact, they are struck by the force of new, emerging patterns of stratification in which some states and societies, or rather *parts* of some states and societies, are becoming enmeshed in the globalizing order even as others are being marginalized (Hoogvelt 1997). In the same uneven way the spread of global cultural forms is also having the paradoxical effect of revitalizing various highly local values and ways of living. Any sense of a clear distinction between international and domestic, external or internal, affairs also collapses in this vision of the process of change. As Rosenau (1997) puts it, politics takes place more and more 'along the domestic–foreign frontier'. In short, we are offered by these various writers 'a dynamic and open-ended conception of where globalization might be leading and the kind of world order which it might prefigure' (Held *et al.* 1999: 7).

This is an attractive way of proceeding in its own right. But, in adopting this particular formulation of globalization as the basis on which to take forward the new mapping of development undertaken in this study, it is useful too to survey quickly the essential elements of the other two widely-articulated accounts of globalization identified by Held *et al.* and to note why each offers too rigid a view of what is inevitably a highly complicated process. The problem with the 'hyperglobalist' account is mainly that it exaggerates – both in the form offered by neoliberals who effusively welcome the triumph of the market over states (Ohmae 1995) and by radicals or Marxists who bemoan what they see from their perspective as the ultimate victory of an oppressive capitalist system (Greider 1997). For all the difference of mood, they are agreed that globalization signals the arrival of a new era in human affairs which they consider to have been largely created by a technological revolution in communications which has massively accelerated the exchange of people, ideas and money. A 'borderless world' has thus been brought into being, characterized by the establishment of proliferating transnational networks of production, trade and finance which operate according to a genuinely global dynamic. More generally, the 'hyperglobalizers' share 'a conviction that economic globalization is constructing new forms of social organization that are supplanting, or that will eventually supplant, traditional nation-states as the primary economic and political units of world society' (Held *et al.* 1999: 3). Accordingly, they foresee the inexorable rise and rise of global governance, global civil society and global cultural motifs. There is no doubt that there are trends in these directions which need to be taken seriously. But they are not problematized sufficiently by the 'hyperglobalizers' and that is par for their course. The 'hyperglobalist' account of globalization is ultimately too determinist, too sweeping, too apolitical.

The 'sceptical' thesis has different faults. It is associated particularly with the critique of Paul Hirst and Grahame Thompson (1996) and has been designed explicitly to bring globalization into 'question'. Their analytical way into this debate (their 'trick', if you like) has been to propose a highly demanding definition of the end-state of globalization, namely, a perfectly integrated global economy, against which evidence relating to the contemporary period, unsurprisingly perhaps, falls short. What it reveals, according to the 'sceptics', is no more than 'heightened internationalization' – in other words, intensified interactions between predominantly national economies, the conventional units of economic analysis. Even these interactions, it is argued, do not significantly exceed the levels of economic interdependence witnessed historically at the end of the nineteenth century. In other words, globalization is more myth than new reality; the true 'global corporation' is still a rarity; national governments are far from immobilized, although they may have experienced a loss of nerve in the face of the powerful ideology of globalization; global governance, if it is anything, is merely a facade behind which the most powerful Western states continue to dominate the traditional international economic and political system. The line of argument here has been fairly trenchant and sufficed initially as a valuable counter to some of the hyperbolic (and populist) early claims about globalization. However, the globalization debate has itself unfolded in a series of waves and the 'sceptical' account has, to a considerable extent, been overtaken by events and is now in real danger of appearing as if it has an irredeemably closed mind on the matter, regardless of how much or how fast economic and political trends still seem to be moving in a globalizing direction.

In sum, it is better, as indicated, to proceed on 'transformationalist' terrain. What this interpretation offers is a strong sense of globalization as an unfolding historical process. It succeeds in identifying the main contours of the changed context within which all economic, social and political actors have now unavoidably to operate, and that is realistically perhaps as much as the analysis of globalization can hope to do for the moment. It is more than enough, though, to capture the essence of the current phase of the emergence of a global economy. As we have seen, the 'transformationalist' approach also insists methodologically on the capacity of actors to alter structures by their actions, which means that they can and do influence the process of globalization. To paraphrase Alexander Wendt (1992), as many have done, globalization is indeed 'what we make of it'; it cannot be said of itself to cause anything. Indeed, this view of globalization fully allows for the way that the ideology of globalization, understood as an all-powerful, unidirectional force, can sometimes be used by economic and political leaders to promote acquiescence in what are in reality policies they happen to favour rather than inexorable processes that cannot be gainsaid (Hay and Marsh 2000). What has been created at present is a particular sort of globalization, which many have labelled neoliberal globalization. In principle, it is possible that this current brand may be modified over time and transmute into another variant, or even that the process of globalization will itself be wound back. Nevertheless, an appreciation of the new reality of a 'globalizing' (but not yet fully globalized) liberal political economy is the first key building block to be derived from IPE towards a contemporary reconceptualization of development.

States

In a related but equally relevant debate, international political economy has also devoted great attention to the matter of the vitality and capacity of states in just such a globalizing order. Many of the arguments mounted here have, to say the least, been rather crudely made – presented as either the 'retreat or the return' of the state, as Amoore *et al.* (1997: 184) put it in a useful early review of this literature. They too set out three different schools of thought which were analogous to the three positions identified by Held *et al.* in relation to globalization. As they noted, the initially dominant conceptualization viewed globalization as 'seriously undermining the basis of the nation-state as a territorially bounded economic, political and social unit' (Amoore *et al.* 1997: 185). State authority was seen to have been variously diffused: 'upwards' to international institutions and transnational corporations, 'sideways' to global financial markets and global social movements, and 'downwards' to sub-national bodies of all shapes and sizes. In particular, states were deemed to have lost their old economic policy-making sovereignty and to have been reduced to competing with each other in the provision of the human and physical infrastructure needed to attract footloose global capital. In the strongest 'hyperglobalist' form in which this was put, the nation-state was rendered irrelevant – no longer, post-globalization, an

appropriate unit of political analysis (Ohmae 1995). Against this interpretation, others insisted, sceptically but every bit as firmly, that the
decline of the state was exaggerated. They based their reading on the
notion of 'heightened internationalization', rather than globalization,
and asserted accordingly that such global restructuring as has taken
place has been driven by the interaction of national capitalisms.
Moreover, these capitalisms, rather than necessarily converging in type,
remain characterized, as they always have been, by different institutions, processes and cultures (Zysman 1996). As a consequence, states
are held to continue to exercise considerable authority over their respective national economies and to contribute substantially still to the overall management of the global economy.

Neither of these sets of arguments was very convincing, at least when
expressed in full-blown fashion. What is required is a more perceptive
grasp of what has lately happened to the state in relation to the process
of globalization. Fortunately, a third, more nuanced, position has now
been widely advanced and is much the most subtle and interesting. In
the words of Amoore *et al.* (1997: 186) again, this suggests that 'the
usual understanding of a dichotomy between the state and globalisation
is an illusion, as the processes of global restructuring are largely embedded within state structures and institutions, politically contingent on
state policies and actions, and primarily about the reorganisation of the
state'. This last phrase is the most significant, for the point being made
is precisely that the changing nature of the state is at the very heart of
the process of globalization. *The* state is neither transcended nor unal-
tered in some overarching, all-encompassing fashion: instead *each* state
(whether located in the old First, Second or Third Worlds) is finding
that its relationship to key social forces both inside and outside of its
national space is being restructured as part and parcel of all the other
shifts to which globalization as a concept draws attention.

As indicated, the claim that the state has been reorganized has now
been taken forward in a variety of forms. Robert Cox (1981: 146) initially described the process as the 'internationalisation of the state',
understood as a process that 'gives precedence to certain state agencies –
notably ministries of finance and prime ministers' offices – which are
key points in the adjustment of domestic to international economic
policy'. More recently, Jan Aart Scholte (1997: 452) suggested that
globalization has yielded 'a different kind of state ... [which has] ... on
the whole lost sovereignty, acquired supraterritorial constituents,
retreated from interstate warfare (for the moment), frozen or reduced
social security provisions ... and lost considerable democratic potential'.
From the left, Peter Burnham (1999: 43–4) has highlighted the widespread shift in the politics of economic management in advanced

capitalist societies from 'politicised management (discretion-based)' to 'depoliticised management (rules-based)', the latter being characterized by attempts to reduce the former political nature of economic decision making and reposition it as far as possible at one remove from government. Peter Evans (1997: 85), reflecting on 'stateness' in an era of globalization, has stressed the centrality of the hegemony of Anglo-American liberal ideology in limiting belief in the efficacy of state action and charted the 'project of constructing a leaner, meaner kind of stateness' associated in particular with the 'Third Way' thinking of the Clinton, Blair and Schröder administrations in the US, the United Kingdom (UK) and Germany respectively during the late 1990s. Linda Weiss (1997: 17) in her work has similarly insisted on the variety of 'state capacities' and argued that 'adaptation is the very essence of the modern state by virtue of the fact that it is embedded in a dynamic economic and inter-state system'. Although in some states certain policy instruments, particularly those associated with macroeconomic adjustment strategies, may be enfeebled by globalization, others, such as those related to industrial policy, may and do change in all manner of creative ways. She cautions that one should therefore always look to a country's governing institutions and expect differences according to national orientation and capability.

This last point is especially well-taken. In his survey of what he called 'the rise and rise of the nation-state', Michael Mann (1997: 474) rightly insisted that states have *always* varied greatly in their degree of democracy, level of material resource, infrastructural power, national indebtedness and regional location. He asked: 'can contemporary capitalism, even if reinforced by environmental limits, "cultural postmodernity" and demilitarization, render all this variation irrelevant, and have the *same* effects on all countries?' His answer – emphatically in the negative – constitutes a warning against overgeneralization, even about the thesis of the reorganization of the state. The patterns of change and continuity are simply 'too varied and contradictory, and the future too murky, to permit us to argue simply that the nation-state and the nation-state system are *either* strengthening *or* weakening' (Mann 1997: 494). Nevertheless, what one can discern through the fog depicted by Mann is, first, that the state remains crucial to contemporary economic and political practice, but, second, that great sensitivity must always be displayed to the enormous variety of *forms of state* and, above all, to the way they are presently being reorganized in different ways in different parts of the globe in response to the differing impacts of globalization on their modes of operation.

Such an insistence is sometimes still misinterpreted by would-be critics as connoting a simplistic statism or an over-preoccupation with states, a failing with which IPE has long taxed traditional international relations analysis. On the contrary, it is only to note the obvious, which is that what is better described as the state–society relationship still remains central to any explanation in politics and political economy. Cox (1981: 127), for example, took great pains many years ago to make clear that the appropriate unit of analysis for international political economy was not states *per se*, but what he called 'state/society complexes'. It is also the case, conveniently, that state theory in political analysis (if not, sadly, in a lot of international relations analysis) has always sought to embrace a view of the varied relationships between non-state actors and states, rendering it an attractively broad-based literature. Indeed, there has lately occurred something of a convergence in thinking amongst the main extant traditions in state–society theory, namely, pluralism, elitism and Marxism (Marsh 1995). All agree that the state needs to be located socially and disaggregated institutionally. They all also accept that the interests and/or social forces which limit the autonomy of the state, and the policy networks and communities through which state and other actors exercise their relative autonomy, are as likely to be transnational as national. Finally, all strands of state–society theory further acknowledge that the structural constraints imposed on state behaviour reflect both ideational and material sources of power.

In sum, there has been forged new common ground in contemporary trends in state–society theory and hence there exists a wealth of intellectual tools with which to set about the dissection of particular state strategies and the general relationship of states to social and other forces at work within national political economies as well as within the global political economy as a whole. There is every reason to believe, too, that the notion of the state, necessarily understood as being reorganized, restructured, reengineered in conjunction with the current global shift, should remain at the centre of all political economy enquiries, viewed still as a key *political* actor on the global stage. With this point duly made, we have in place the second building block of the required rethinking of development and can now proceed to consider the debate that has taken place regarding the making of 'new regions' in global affairs.

New regions

Several observers have drawn attention to the emergence in international politics during the 1990s of a trend which they came to label the 'new regionalism' (Hettne and Inotai 1994; Fawcett and Hurrell 1995; Gamble and Payne 1996). The phenomenon was not always tightly prescribed in all its aspects, but was defined in deliberately straightforward fashion by Payne and Gamble (1996: 2) as 'a state-led or states-led project designed to reorganise a particular regional space along defined economic and political lines'. Such a theorization assumes, as above, that states and state actors are a key level of explanation in understanding the contemporary global political economy. In this way an important connection is again made to the national level of analysis since state projects (of all sorts) generally emerge as the outcome of detailed bargaining and negotiation among domestic political actors and then proceed, at least initially, via traditional mechanisms of inter-state political exchange. The calculations that state actors make of their interests and the costs and benefits they perceive to exist within alternative courses of action were thus seen as the most appropriate starting point for grasping the essence of the 'new regionalism'.

The specific issues most frequently placed at the centre of attention in this debate were the contrasting origins and natures of the European Union (EU), the North American Free Trade Area (NAFTA) and Asia-Pacific Economic Cooperation (APEC), which were generally regarded as the three major regionalist projects of the time. At first sight their emergence seemed to contradict the turn towards globalization and for a period, especially within mainstream IPE, much was made of the fear that these projects might become exclusive and protectionist (along the lines, say, of 'Fortress Europe'). But, in practice, one of the most striking common characteristics of the way that the EU, NAFTA and APEC have operated has been their commitment to 'open regionalism'. This means that policy has been directed towards the elimination of obstacles to trade within a region, while at the same time doing nothing to raise external tariff barriers to the rest of the world. The rationale for contemporary regionalism has in fact been found, not in the doctrine of protection, but rather that of strategic trade. Instead of insulating the regional economy from foreign competition the aim has actually been to expose it to that very competition while at the same time ensuring, via various measures, that regional competitiveness can be achieved and sustained. In a similar illustration of a continuing fundamental commitment to international cooperation, the leading states involved in the EU, NAFTA and APEC have still maintained their involvement in the overall management of the global political economy through membership of the Group of 7 (G7), the IMF, the World Bank and the World Trade Organization (WTO). The broader conclusion to which this pointed was that 'state projects like regionalism typically seek to accelerate, modify, or occasionally to reverse the direction of social change' associated with globalization (Gamble and Payne 1996: 250). Put differently, the key argument that came out of the debate was that the 'new regionalism', far from being in contradiction with globalization, was in fact an essential part of the politics of that process, intersecting with it in varying, inevitably quite complex, ways.

It is also necessary to insist that 'new regionalism' has been far from monolithic: the three regionalist projects were different from one another in several important respects which reflected both the varied histories of the regions and the uneven extent and impact of globalization. The US governing elite's turn to regionalism in the shape of NAFTA was born largely out of a combination of its own perception of the declining ability of the US state/society complex to continue to act as a global hegemon and its growing awareness of the closeness of some of the economic and social connections that had developed within the Americas, most notably between the US and Mexico. The end of the Cold War further facilitated the building of a new 'partnership' founded on widespread hemispheric acceptance of the basic assumptions of economic liberalism and democracy, a vision yet to be realized but set out boldly nevertheless in the final communiqué of the 1994 'Summit of the Americas' which called for the establishment of a full Free Trade Area of the Americas (FTAA) by 2005. By comparison, Europe is not dominated by a single state: indeed historically the EU has been a political construction designed to manage inter-state rivalries within Europe, notably between France and Germany. For a period from 1985 onwards the EU seemed to gain a new political momentum, marked by the creation of a single European market, the adoption of qualified majority voting as the decision rule in many policy areas and the subsequent development of plans for full economic and monetary union. Yet the EU continues to lack a fully unified political core to give overall direction to the regionalist project. Member states have never allowed the European Commission to play this role, whilst the regular heads of state summits have tended to become preoccupied with short-term decisions and necessities. For all that its operations have become routinized in a most intricate fashion the EU has remained at root a regional integration movement, subject at all times to the pressures and imperatives of inter-state bargaining. For its part, East Asia is different again, possessed of two potential regional hegemons in Japan and China and complicated by the involvement of two other major states, the US and Russia. It is still divided ideologically and there remain unresolved security issues. The state seemingly best equipped to lead a regionalist project, Japan, is characterized by a controversial modern history, weakness in decision-making and an unwillingness to assert itself politically. Japan has hitherto shied away from proposed regional bodies based on a closed Asian membership and has given priority to APEC, in large part because this body also includes the US. The main political function of APEC has thus been in effect to head off other deeper kinds of regionalist project in East Asia.

As has been seen, regionalism as an economic and political strategy has been examined primarily at what might be called the macro level, namely, the collective projects of the leading states on the world stage. But, conceptually, it can and has also been applied to 'lower' levels of regional action. In elaborations of the original Gamble and Payne volume on 'new regionalism' which considered in depth only the presenting cases of the EU, NAFTA and APEC, Hook and Kearns (1999) focused on 'subregionalism', defined as the projects embarked upon by weaker states in the global political economy in attempts to strengthen cooperation in more circumscribed spaces than the 'macro-regional' stage, and Breslin and Hook (2002) addressed 'micro-regionalism', understood as the types of regionalist project developed between national states and parts ('regions') of other states or indeed just between different parts, often adjoining, of different states. The former study thus incorporated consideration of bodies like the Central European Free Trade Area (CEFTA), the Common Market of the South (MERCOSUR), the Association of Southeast Asian Nations (ASEAN) and the East Asian Economic Caucus (EAEC) and showed how such 'sub-regionalist' projects often grew up in close interaction with, and indeed to some extent reaction against, the three larger macro-level regionalist entities. The latter study embraced schemes such as the so-called 'growth triangle' linking Singapore with the subnational economies of Johor in Malaysia and Riau in Indonesia and the Japan Sea Zone concept linking the Japan Sea prefectures with parts of the Korean peninsula, the Russian far east and China. It demonstrated that such arrangements were growing in number and significance, but argued that they should be understood more as evidence of 'micro-regionalisation' than 'micro-regionalism'.

This needs explaining. From the beginning of the debate within critical IPE about the emergence of 'new regions' it has been important to distinguish between regionalism and regionalization (Payne and Gamble 1996). Whereas the former refers to a form of statist project, regionalization can be compared with globalization: it, in turn, is best understood as a social process unfolding at the regional level and similarly driven forward by a mixture of forces of which states are only one and again by no means the most influential. In other words, regionalization refers to those processes which deepen the integration of particular regional spaces. There are many ways of measuring it, but particularly important are flows of trade, investment, aid and people. Conceptualized in this way, regionalization can thus develop prior to any cultural or political unification; it may indeed by the spur to such unification, as the neofunctionalist theory of European integration always predicted

(Haas 1958 and 1964). Regionalization may also equally occur within a region that has achieved political union *after* the event of the union. As Nicola Phillips (2003b: 232) put it:

> Regionalisation cannot be understood in the absence of a conception of regionalism ... What regionalism means, in essence, is that strategies of national economic management and the processes by which accumulation occurs (as well as the type of accumulation that is privileged) can be expected to undergo a redefinition. This redefinition involves a reconfiguration of social relations occurring over a regional, rather than a domestic, terrain and the emergence of common forms of market organisation and economic strategy.

In short, the organizing rationale of the concept of regionalization is precisely to separate out analytically the subtle and often subterranean processes by which regional interconnections are built up from the 'high politics' by which regional organizations are shaped and created.

As one might imagine, research on regionalization (and, by extension, sub-regionalization and micro-regionalization) is much more difficult and time-consuming than research on regionalism and, for that reason, there has been much less of it undertaken. Sweeping claims about what is defined here as regionalization have often been made on the flimsiest of empirical bases. Nevertheless, two tentative arguments that have been made are worth briefly highlighting. One derives from a critique of the globalization hypothesis and emanates from the 'sceptical' school of thought identified in that connection. The central argument here asserts that much of what passes for globalization in conventional analysis is, more accurately, evidence of regionalization. In particular, studies of changes in the flow of trade and of foreign direct investment (Ruigrok and Tulder 1995; Hirst and Thompson 1996) have argued that what has occurred is actually a growing concentration of these flows between the 'triad' regional economies of Europe, North America and east Asia. From this perspective the striking consequence is the exclusion of certain parts of the world (for example, Africa) from what is incorrectly dubbed globalization. The other argument concerns the fact that regionalization, like globalization, has normally proven to be uneven in its impact. This applies within regions as well as within the global political economy as a whole. Certain places and sites tend to be integrated while others are marginalized. Unless the regionalist project itself explicitly addresses the issues of inequality and unevenness, the process of deepening integration (that is, regionalization) is likely also to be a process of increasing polarization. The core areas within a process of regionalization in effect act as powerful magnets which drag other areas and societies into their orbit. In short, it should not be presumed that regionalization works automatically to bring the different parts of a region together.

There is a final dimension to the debate about regionalism and regionalization which needs to be acknowledged and fully incorporated into our thinking. This derives from the insistence of a growing number of cognitive theorists on emphasizing the impact of the process of social interaction upon the very matter of what constitutes a region. In their cognitive role, regional groupings can thus 'be seen to provide the locus in which the practices that drive them also create norms for behaviour' (Gilson 2002: 2), thereby delineating 'the social script through which institutional participants communicate and ... the basis upon which fixed and readily identifiable idea-sets for an institution's practices are founded' (Wendt and Duvall 1989: 60). Put differently, regions are always in the making, constructed, deconstructed and reconstructed through social practice and discourse. Although that was no doubt true, if for the most part unappreciated, of 'region formation' in the era of 'old' regionalism before the 1990s, it is unquestionably an insight which no attempt to discern the emergence of 'new regions' – many of which do not map on to previous, more familiar notions of region – can afford to ignore. It will play a full part in this book's endeavour to describe and analyse the new politics of development. Indeed, now that this third IPE debate about the new importance attached to regions has been explicated, we can return directly to the concept of development.

The future study of development

What does this reprise of the classical era in development studies and subsequent tour of recent debates within international political economy imply for the future study of development? From the standpoint of development studies, the good news is that, for some time now, useful insights – which can contribute to a new and broader approach to development – have begun to be thrown up. It is true that no scholar or group of scholars has had the self-confidence, or self-consciousness, to declare the birth of such a 'new' development studies in the title of a book, although Frans Schuurman (1993) did edit a collection more than a decade ago deliberately called *Beyond the Impasse*. Indeed, in the most important chapter in the book, Booth (1993) indicated that he saw signs of a 'new agenda' emerging from the enormous expansion of actual field research undertaken in different development contexts. The cumulation of this work served, in his view, to reveal the thin empirical foundations on which much early dependency theory (in particular) rested. It was all too general, too dogmatic, too pessimistic, too class-reductionist. Put the other way round, it neglected gender, ethnicity, religion and culture; deemphasized the local; and in a whole range of ways was insufficiently sensitive to the great diversity of situations in Africa, Asia and Latin America and the Caribbean. Leys (1996: 44) subsequently criticized Booth and his colleagues for viewing the transcendence of the 'impasse' in essentially idealist terms – for substituting 'development studies' for 'development theory', as he put it. However, good studies are a necessary prelude to good theory and so it was an important first step to have returned to the political economy of development a stronger sense of variety and situation.

It was on this basis that Hettne thereafter moved the agenda on a stage further. He argued in the mid-1990s that the problem for the field of development studies was that it had become 'trapped somewhere between an obsolete "nation state" approach and a premature "world" approach' (Hettne 1995: 262). A stance needed to be taken, he suggested, at a mid-point between these two extreme positions, thereby constituting a synthesis that would transcend the dichotomy of the successive endogenism and exogenism of previous modernization and dependency analyses. In his words, there were 'no countries that are completely autonomous and self-reliant, and no countries that develop (or underdevelop) merely as a reflection of what goes on beyond their national borders' (Hettne 1995: 262). This was a crucial insight because it laid the basis for a *universalization* of the study of development within which no country enjoyed more than a relative autonomy in charting its relations with the rest of the world (although manifestly the degree of that relativity varied). The key task for the future was 'to analyse development predicaments stemming from the fact that most decision makers operate in a national space but react on problems emerging in a global space over which they have only partial and often marginal control' (Hettne 1995: 263). In undertaking this analysis it was also necessary to appreciate that the decision-makers in question had to react to forms of power that were ideational as well as materialist. Development studies had in fact always been better at grasping this than some other mainstream areas of political economy – for example, dependency theory long ago incorporated discussion of cultural dependency or 'colonialism of the mind' – but it was important to give full acknowledgement to this other form of power, especially given the many emerging new means of communication and knowledge dissemination by which the battle of different development ideologies was being conducted by the end of the 1980s.

From the standpoint of IPE, on the other hand, the good news is somewhat different: it is that recent research and debate has contributed substantially to a fuller understanding of the complex interactions between globalization, states and new regions. What is disappointing is that relatively few scholars who think of themselves as 'doing' IPE seem to show much interest in those parts of the world upon which development studies has long been focused. Indeed, IPE (in its critical as much as its mainstream variant) often seems as if cannot see much at all beyond the so-called 'triad economies' of North America, western Europe and Japan. Reflecting on the three major debates reviewed earlier, it might be said that even globalization studies have centred on and emanated mainly from the advanced post-industrial countries (Mittelman 2000); that the states most scrutinized in the 'state of the state' literature are nearly all members of the self-styled club of leading Western countries, the Organisation of Economic Cooperation and Development (OECD); and that the discussion of regionalism has been dominated by comparisons of the EU and NAFTA, with other regionalist projects (and generally only APEC) used mainly to establish 'difference' from the presumed defining cases (Breslin and Higgott 2000). It is true that a few IPE scholars have tackled issues pertaining to inequality, justice, poverty and so on (Hoogvelt 1997; Hurrell and Woods 1999; Scholte 2000), but, for the most part, this literature is sparse and these concerns remain seriously understudied within IPE.

Nevertheless, from the different strengths and weaknesses of these two fields of academic endeavour, it is now just about possible to identify the main features of a new approach to the study of development. Such an approach requires 'a marriage between certain strands of development theory and certain strands of international political economy' (Hettne, Payne and Söderbaum 1999: 354). It can be assembled, as it were, in four stages. First, it rejects the 'exceptionalism' of a special category of countries deemed to be in particular need of development and endeavours to recast the whole question of development as a universal question, as 'a transnational problematic' grounded in the notion that '*all* societies are developing as part of a global process' (Pieterse 1996: 543, my emphasis). Second, it focuses attention on development strategy, principally as still pursued by a national economy, society and/or polity, albeit within a global/regional environment. Hettne (1995: 263) himself can thus describe development as no more (but also no less) than 'societal problem solving', implying that 'a society develops as it succeeds in dealing with predicaments of a structural nature, many of them emerging from the global context'. Third, it recognizes that such strategy necessarily involves the interaction, and appropriate meshing, of internal *and* external elements, even if in many cases the latter do seem to be increasingly overbearing. In this vein Philip McMichael (2000: 150) has lately noted that 'states still pursue development goals, but these goals have more to do with global positioning than with management of the national "household"'. Fourth, it insists upon due recognition of variations of time, place and history in development predicaments, something which Stuart Corbridge (1990) called for a decade or more ago and which, as pointed out earlier, was not characteristic of a lot of classical development theory in both its modernization and dependency guises.

To sum up these claims, then, development can be redefined for the contemporary era as the collective building by the constituent social and political actors of a country (or at least in the first instance a country) of a viable, functioning political economy, grounded in at least a measure of congruence between its core domestic characteristics and attributes and its location within a globalizing world order and capable on that basis of advancing the well-being of those living within its confines. It is not necessary in this conceptualization to define the moral or ethical content of development, conceived as some ultimate condition, in the way that has historically always been done by modernization, dependency and other 'alternative' bodies of theory. The merits, or otherwise, of the interim results of country development strategies will always be contested ideologically, precisely in the way that competing notions of the 'good society' have always been debated over the centuries. The point is to allow analytically for many types or forms of *actual* development. For, as Hettne (1995: 266) has repeatedly reminded us, 'the "three worlds" are disintegrating and development is becoming a global and universal problem ... too important to be left to a special discipline [development studies] with low academic status'. Redefined in this way, development is thus just as much a problem for the ex-hegemon as the smallest ex-colonial territory, for the new industrializer as much as the former communist country in 'transition'. The problems faced by some countries may in practice be much more serious and intractable than in others, but on this account they are *not* conceptually different. As the editorial in the first issue of *Progress in Development Studies*, the newest academic journal to be devoted to these questions, put it in a simple and attractive formulation, 'development is everywhere' (Potter 2001: 3).

The next stage in the rethinking being undertaken here is to specify how we are in practice to set about researching development when conceived in this way as the building by a country of a distinctive and viable political economy. As it happens, there is already a substantial amount of good work on which we can draw. Interestingly, and perhaps revealingly, it comes from both sides of the old divide between study of the 'developing' and the 'developed' worlds. We refer to the now relatively old 'models of development' literature and the much newer 'models of capitalism' literature. In its day the former strand was central to the political economy of development. It reaches right back to studies of the various state-led strategies of import-substitution industrialization pursued in Latin America in the 1960s and 1970s. Some studies emphasized institutional variation from an explicitly historicist perspective (Roxborough 1979); others, notably the highly influential work of Cardoso and Falletto (1979: 15, 172), operated within the dependency tradition, but sensitively so, seeking to deploy the concept of dependence 'to make empirical situations understandable in terms of the way internal and external structural components are linked' and yet still trying 'to demonstrate that the historical situation in which the economic transformations occur must be taken into account'. Similar analytical themes, notably the character of state institutions and their degree of autonomy *vis-à-vis* the relative strengths of domestic and external class forces, were also subsequently addressed in the African context, particularly in discussion of Tanzanian socialism and Kenyan capitalism (Randall and Theobald 1998), and then reinterpreted yet again in relation to the economic successes enjoyed by the 'newly industrializing countries' of east Asia during the 1980s. These achievements were aggressively claimed by the neoliberals as evidence of the virtues of a market-led strategy until the research of Clive Hamilton (1986), Gordon White (1987), Alice Amsden (1989), Robert Wade (1990) and others served cumulatively to undermine such an assertion. In fact, these studies demonstrated the opposite of the neoliberal argument, namely, that forceful and focused economic intervention by a strong state over a sustained period of time and in the context of a supportive social structure and a growing international economy was a necessary developmental ingredient. All in all, what this rich, but now largely quiescent, literature showed was the considerable merits of analyses of particular development strategies, in whatever preferred mode, whether institutionalist or Marxist, which sought to integrate an understanding of the domestic state–society context with a grasp of the constraints and opportunities posed by the external environment.

The latter strand of writing, that which has addressed 'models of capitalism' in the industrial world and which has been fashionable of late within what might be called comparative rather than international political economy, can in fact be dissected along much the same lines. It, too, is marked by a tension between its (dominant) institutionalist and (critical) Marxist wings. For most contributors to this literature institutions are seen as both socially embedded and nationally constrained. They are not produced randomly but reflect a 'logic in each society [which] leads institutions to coalesce into a complex social configuration' (Hollingsworth and Boyer 1997: 2). By its nature such a configuration is not easy to specify precisely, although most interpretations have lately stressed the importance of variables such as labour skills and management, systems of industrial relations, financial markets, industrial structures and political system. An interesting variation on the general theme is provided by the concept of 'embedded autonomy' which Evans (1995) identifies as the defining variable in patterns of industrial transformation in a study which focused on the computer industries of three countries conventionally deemed to be 'developing', namely, India, Brazil and South Korea. He characterized the 'developmental states' of these countries as constituted by the coexistence of a certain kind of autonomy *and* yet at the same time embeddedness in a set of social ties which allowed for continual renegotiation of policy. These institutionalist perspectives have, however, been subjected to powerful criticism from a Marxist direction by David Coates who argues that, for the most part, they lack a conception of the class underpinnings of all institutional arrangements under the capitalist system. Accordingly, in his view:

> The pattern of different performance between national capitalist economies ... is best re-specified as a set of shifting national trajectories on a map of combined but uneven development, where the spaces for catch-up and convergence were predetermined by the prior character of class relations distributed across that map by almost five centuries of class struggle, capital accumulation, production and trade (Coates 2000: 227).

Even so, his actual account of contemporary models of capitalism, which focuses on the US, the UK, West Germany, Japan and Sweden, gives only passing consideration to the way that the national basis for capitalist organization may have been seriously affected by recent globalizing trends. In this respect at least his approach is not much of an advance upon institutionalist writing.

Nevertheless, from the perspective of this study the argument to emphasize is what Phillips refers to as the essentially 'common ground' occupied by the research agendas laid out in influential strands of the development literature and in the contemporary models of capitalism debate (Phillips 2004a). What can be drawn from them is a strong sense of the key foundational components of a development *strategy* upon which analysis must necessarily focus. These are various. We need to enquire into the character of the national political economy of the country pursuing the strategy, incorporating a consideration of its core economic attributes as well as an assessment of the institutional basis of the state and the domestic forces which either sustain it or challenge it; we need to consider the impact of any regional arrangements within which the key economic, social and political actors of the country in question are enmeshed (indeed we might have to contemplate a regionalist body becoming the dominant agent charting development strategy); and we need to evaluate the positioning, actual and intended, of the national (and, as indicated, regional) political economy within the wider global order and the mechanisms available to leading actors to adjust and, conceivably, reshape that position. An additional consideration may, or may not, be the ideological claims made, or not made, on behalf of the particular strategy in question. This is a contingent political question dependent mainly on political circumstances. All these matters in combination might be said to constitute the overall development strategy within which specific policies (for example macroeconomic, industrial, educational, foreign) are then pursued as component parts. As indicated in the earlier discussion, these are also universal questions that can be asked of *all* types of strategy and country. They offer 'an authentic universalism' in marked contrast to the putative universalism of modernization theory or neoliberalism – in other words, a universalism derived from the commonality of the problem, rather than the proposed solution (Hettne 1995: 15).

A final, brief word is needed about the question of security. In recent years there has been a growing awareness that the study of security and of development cannot sensibly be kept completely separate (as largely was the case in the classical era of development studies). For obvious and compelling reasons, where there is violent conflict or civil war in a country, no coherent development strategy of any sort can be formulated, let alone implemented. The pursuit of development (of any type) requires a significant measure of security and is always affected by the nature of the security equation facing a country. The new approach to development set out here does not prioritize the security dimension, but it does acknowledge its relevance and seeks to take on board at least the simple point made above.

We suggest that the ideas set out in the last few pages constitute the most promising way forward for the analysis of development in the future. In essence, the approach proposed here embeds development, conceived essentially as strategy, within an integrated analysis of structure (conceived essentially as globalizing) and agency (conceived essentially as states, or states-societies). As we see it, this has great advantages – for two overriding reasons already highlighted. First, it endeavours to take the best from both development studies and international political economy, a line of argument that we have by now advanced often enough. Second, it tries to give due weight to both structure and agency in its approach to analysis. Fields of study which feel that they must make a choice between focusing on either structure or agency necessarily impoverish their own visions of the world by the limitations of their preferred methodology. For example, political science and international relations have traditionally been actor-oriented studies; political economy has traditionally been a structuralist undertaking. Yet the argument being made here is that the two methodologies are best held in balance, with a structuralist take on political economy seen not as an alternative to an actor-based approach to the politics of inter-state relations but rather as a logical priority to it. In a nutshell, then, what we seek to explore in this volume is the politics of the political economy of development.

The rationale and plan of this book

The practical task to which we now turn is the putting of some flesh on to the bones of these broad arguments. How to proceed? The logical first step would be to prepare an account of the country development strategies of all of the independent nation-states in the world. This would no doubt highlight very effectively the sheer variety of development predicaments and strategies that exist in the current global political economy. But obvious practical difficulties arise: in a world with no less than 190 member states of the United Nations the task would be huge and the resulting tome would have to be encyclopaedic in its reach. However, there is a satisfactory half-way house available to us. This can be built by explicitly bringing to the fore the notion of 'new regions' and attempting to map the contemporary world of development on a region-by-region basis. This both acknowledges the new significance of regions in global politics and offers at least a realistic chance of carrying off the endeavour to good effect. Yet, even for such an undertaking, the knowledge of regional experts is manifestly required. No single scholar could be expected to know enough. Accordingly there is assembled in the remainder of this book the best efforts of a group of scholars and friends – each deeply immersed in the study of a particular region but each also informed by a commitment to the notion of international political economy – to provide a portrait of the current political economy of development in eight different regions of the world.

Unavoidably, the shape of the regions chosen is contentious. We have already explained that in an important sense regions are 'constructed' by all protagonists, both in their making and, of course, their analysis. The regions examined here – namely, the Americas (that is, North, Central and South America, as well as the Caribbean); Europe (eastern, central and western Europe); Northeast Asia; Southeast Asia; South Asia; the 'post-Soviet space' represented by the Commonwealth of Independent States; the Middle East; and Sub-Saharan Africa – have been chosen by the editor with a view to identifying the key regional relationships that bear upon country development strategies. As already argued, these now routinely flow across former 'developed' and 'developing' country dividing lines, something which has been noted and deliberately taken on board in 'defining' the regions for present purposes. The book thus begins with two chapters which stretch themselves in turn over the whole of the Americas and the whole of Europe. This is deliberate: not only does it immediately confront us with the notion that countries like the US and Canada and the UK, France and Germany do actually pursue what are in our definition development strategies, but it also exposes the fact that regionalism and regionalization have reached a point in these two regions where country development can only sensibly be understood in full regional context. That point has not yet been reached in Asia: hence the need at the moment for three chapters to map development across this continent. The situation may of course be changing even as this book is being prepared, for the so-called ASEAN + 3 process (discussed in both Chapters 4 and 5) does herald the possible creation by 2020 of an effective east Asian trading bloc in the global political economy. The contours of the remaining three regions identified for scrutiny probably need less elaboration and explanation. The notion of a 'post-Soviet space' is admittedly loose, but it does neatly capture the way that the Soviet national state has disintegrated into a somewhat inchoate region. Finally, the Middle East and Sub-Saharan Africa constitute conventional regional frames of reference.

An attempt has also been made to provide some consistency of format in the ensuing analyses in that each contributor has been asked to describe and analyse the politics of development within his/her region in relation to three broad questions:

1   What are the main country development strategies currently being pursued by the component states of the region?
2   In what ways does the intra-regional politics of development affect these national strategies?
3   How are the various national (and regional) strategies carried forward into what might be called the extra-regional politics of development?

It is not expected, or desired, that a simple, neat picture of the world of development at the beginning of the twenty-first century will emerge from what follows. Nor is it presumed that an analysis of the new regional politics of development will or should suffice. But we do hope that the book will serve as a useful start in the enterprise of rethinking development inside IPE and that the ensuing chapters will succeed in presenting at least some of the complexity and subtlety of the politics of the huge, diverse world in which we all have now to live and survive.

Chapter 2

The Americas

NICOLA PHILLIPS

Locating the region of 'the Americas' is not particularly problematic. It occupies a clearly demarcated geographical continent and does not present any notable definitional difficulties relating to which pieces of land are included in it. The Americas comprises a total of 35 independent states. The legacy of colonialism is manifest in the plethora of other territorial units – almost all located in the Caribbean – that exist as the overseas territories of a range of powers: the UK (Anguilla, Bermuda, British Virgin Islands, Falkland Islands, Montserrat, Turks and Caicos Islands), the US (Puerto Rico, US Virgin Islands), the Netherlands (Aruba, Netherlands Antilles) and France (French Guiana, Guadeloupe, Martinique). These territories do not have independent statehood and will not be directly considered in this chapter. The Americas accommodates its component countries within a number of distinctive groupings, which we will classify as the Southern Cone, Andean, Caribbean, Central American and North American subregions (see Table 2.1). The first four of these, along with Mexico, are traditionally understood to comprise 'Latin America and the Caribbean', and this definition applies where this term is used in this chapter.

It is with this classification into subregions, however, that we encounter a greater number of competing definitions. The most notable case in point is the Caribbean, conventional understandings of which – as accommodating the islands located in the Caribbean sea (which we have favoured here) – jostle with those which perceive a 'wider Caribbean' or 'Caribbean Basin' subregion. The latter is taken to encompass 'all those territories whose shores are washed by the Caribbean sea' (Payne 1999: 119) – that is, including Mexico and the collection of countries that we have identified here as Central American. Similarly, Belize, which geographically would fall into the Central American orbit, is customarily classified as belonging to the Caribbean even by the narrower definition noted above, along with the three territories geographically located on the South American mainland (French Guiana, Guyana and Suriname) (Payne 1999: 119). The picture is complicated still further by the fact that both the Caribbean and the Central American subregions, as defined

29

Table 2.1 *The Americas: basic data*

Country	Population (thousands)	Total gross domestic product (GDP), 2002 (millions of US$, world ranking in brackets[a])	Gross national income (GNI) per capita, 2002 (US$)	External debt, 2001 (billions of US$)	Trade in goods as share of GDP, 2001 (%)	Aid per capita, 2001 (US$)
Southern Cone						
Argentina	37,928	102,191 (36)	4,060	148.8	17.5	4.0
Brazil	174,485	452,387 (13)	2,850	237.6	23.2	2.0
Chile	15,579	64,154 (46)	4,260	37.7	52.2	3.7
Uruguay	3,381	12,325 (80)	4,370	9.9	27.4	4.6
Paraguay	5,510	5,389 (108)	1,170	2.7	43.5	10.9
Andean region						
Bolivia	8,697	7,678 (97)	900	2.0	37.8	85.6
Colombia	43,745	82,194 (41)	1,830	37.6	30.4	8.8
Ecuador	13,112	24,347 (59)	1,450	14.5	54.5	13.3
Peru	26,749	56,901 (49)	2,050	28.1	29.1	17.1
Venezuela	25,093	94,340 (38)	4,090	37.5	36.4	1.8
Caribbean						
Antigua & Barbuda	69	710 (156)	9,390	—	49.1	125.4
Bahamas	314	4,818 (113)*	14,860*	—	58.2*	27.3
Barbados	269	2,757 (132)*	9,750*	739.3mn	54.9*	−4.3
Belize	253	843 (152)	2,960	765.0mn	71.4	86.6
Cuba	11,263	46,704 (n/a)*	—[d]	11.1[b]	—	4.5
Dominica	72	254 (173)	3,180	181.2mn	64.4	276.7

Dominican Republic	8,635	21,285 (65)	2,320	4.8	66.6	12.4
Grenada	102	414 (166)	3,500	190.2mn	56.5	114.6
Guyana	772	710 (157)	840	882.0mn	152.0	132.8
Haiti	8,286	3,590 (122)	440	817.4mn	34.5	20.4
Jamaica	2,613	8,001 (95)	2,820	5.4	58.5	20.9
Puerto Rico	3,869	67,897 (44)*	10,950*	0.0		
St Kitts-Nevis	46	340 (170)	6,370	170.3mn	59.8	235.7
St Lucia	159	660 (158)	3,840	229.2mn	48.5	103.6
St Vincent & Grenadines	117	361 (169)	2,820	155.8mn	64.3	74.6
Suriname	423	895 (151)	1,960	—	130.8	55.3
Trinidad & Tobago	1,318	9,372 (88)	6,490	2.6	93.3	-1.3
Central America						
Costa Rica	3,942	16,998 (71)	4,100	4.8	71.9	0.6
El Salvador	6,524	14,287 (77)	2,080	4.6	57.4	36.6
Guatemala	11,992	23,252 (62)	1,750	4.8	39.4	19.3
Honduras	6,755	6,594 (99)	970	3.2	66.3	102.9
Nicaragua	5,335	2,562 (n/a)*	—e	4.3	109.4c	178.4
Panama	2,940	12,296 (81)	4,020	9.0	38.1	9.7
North America						
Canada	31,414	715,692 (8)	22,300	0.0	70.1	0.0
Mexico	100,921	637,205 (10)	5,910	172.9	54.2	0.8
United States	288,369	10,416,818 (1)	35,060	0.0	19.0	0.0

Notes: *Most recent available figures, from 2000 or 2001; [a] World Bank rankings; [b] preliminary estimated figures; [c] 1997 figure (most recent available); [d] estimated to be lower middle income (US$736 to US$2,935); [e] estimated to be low income (US$735 or less).
Sources: Own elaboration. Data from World Development Indicators Database, World Bank, April 2003 and July 2003; United Nations Development Programme (UNDP), *Human Development Report 2003*; United Nations Economic Commission for Latin America and the Caribbean (ECLAC), *Statistical Yearbook for Latin America and the Caribbean 2002*.

here, are conceived as integral to a wider 'North American' political economy, arising largely from emerging economic structures and various forms of social and political interdependence in the northern part of the Americas. The two South American subregions – the Southern Cone and Andean subregions – are subject to far fewer competing definitions.

Mexico occupies a very particular position in the region. Traditionally it has been associated with Latin America, for a range of obvious historical, cultural, linguistic and social reasons. Yet, while clearly a 'Latin' country, it is usually now identified as belonging to North America, largely as a result of its participation with the US and Canada in NAFTA and its location within the political economy structures that have attended the emergence of that political project. Mexico also retains a position within the political apparatus of the 'wider' Caribbean Basin, primarily through its membership of the Association of Caribbean States (ACS), and indeed has much in common with the development model

Table 2.2   *Main regional organizations in the Americas*

MERCOSUR (Southern Common Market / Mercado Común del Sur)
Membership: Argentina, Brazil, Paraguay, Uruguay (Chile and Bolivia as associate members).
Established 1991, 'relaunched' 2000. Currently imperfect customs union; aims to establish common market.

NAFTA (North American Free Trade Agreement)
Membership: Canada, Mexico, United States.
Established 1994. Designed as free trade area (FTA).

AC (Andean Community / Comunidad Andina de Naciones)
Membership: Bolivia, Colombia, Ecuador, Peru, Venezuela.
Established 1969, 'relaunched' and reorganised 1989. Currently imperfect customs union; aims to establish common market by 2005.

CARICOM (Caribbean Community)
Membership: Antigua and Barbuda, Bahamas, Barbados, Belize, Dominica, Grenada, Guyana, Haiti, Jamaica, Montserrat, St Kitts and Nevis, St Lucia, Suriname, St Vincent and the Grenadines, Trinidad and Tobago.
Established 1973. Goals of common market, functional cooperation and foreign policy coordination.

CACM (Central American Common Market / Mercado Común Centroamericano)
Membership: Costa Rica, El Salvador, Guatemala, Nicaragua, Honduras.
Established 1960, 'redesigned' 1993. Goals of customs union and common market.

→

Table 2.2 *Continued*

ACS (Association of Caribbean States)
Membership: All CARICOM members except Montserrat, all CACM members, plus Colombia, Cuba, Dominican Republic, Mexico, Panama, Venezuela. Associate members: Aruba, France (on behalf of French Guiana, Guadeloupe and Martinique), Netherlands Antilles.
Established 1995. Aim of 'promoting consultation, cooperation and concerted action among Caribbean countries'.

OECS (Organization of Eastern Caribbean States)
Membership: Antigua and Barbuda, Dominica, Grenada, Montserrat, St Kitts and Nevis, St Lucia, St Vincent and the Grenadines (Anguilla and the British Virgin Islands as associate members).
Established 1981. Political grouping aiming to facilitate regional cooperation, 'sustainable development' and appropriate treatment of regional and international policy issues.

LAIA/ALADI (Latin American Integration Association / Asociación Latinoamericana de Integración)
Membership: All (full) MERCOSUR and AC members, Chile, Cuba, Mexico.
Established 1981. Provides loose framework for Latin American integration efforts.

FTAA/ALCA (Free Trade Area of the Americas / Area de Libre Comercio de las Américas)
Membership: All countries in the Americas, excluding Cuba.
Agreement projected for 2005.

---

prevalent in these countries. Yet, despite this, it has never been amenable to classification as Central American or Caribbean and is not a member of the Central American Common Market (CACM) or the Caribbean Community (CARICOM) (Table 2.2).

A final introductory point relates to the ways in which the study of the region has (or, more commonly, has not) been approached. In the conventional terminology of development theory and international studies, the study of development in the Americas has slotted readily into a 'North–South' framework, accommodating both – or all three – of the traditional 'Worlds' of development. The unhappy corollary has often been an assumption that the US and Canada can comfortably be excluded from the study of development, given its classic focus on those parts of the world – and indeed the Americas – traditionally demarcated as 'developing areas'. Distinct academic communities have thus arisen which rarely, if ever, rub shoulders. The theoretical and empirical remit of development studies has never been deemed to hold any relevance for the study of US or Canadian political economy, these countries not being considered to be in the process of developing, nor to be engaged in the articulation of development strategies. The aim in this chapter is thus to advance a fuller understanding of the regional politics of development in the Americas by pulling the US and North America back into the regional context and exploring the ways in which the *region* of the Americas is inserted into the 'new world of development'.

Country development strategies in the Americas

The Americas is characterized by a degree of inequality between states and subregions that is unique among the regions of the world. Indeed, it has been demonstrated statistically in the context of the negotiations for an FTAA, to which we will turn later, that the differences in size and levels of development between the 34 participating countries (Cuba being excluded) are several times larger than those found between the actual and prospective member countries of the EU (Bustillo and Ocampo 2003: 4–5). It is evident from Table 2.1 that the Americas accommodates some of the largest, richest and most populous countries of the world, alongside some of the smallest and poorest and a number of what the World Bank usually labels 'middle-income developing countries'. By extension, it also draws together the world's most powerful state with some of the weakest and most vulnerable.

This degree of diversity between states is mirrored in the wide range of national development strategies pursued in the region. At a preliminary level, one can draw a binary distinction between those that arise from so-called 'early industrialization' in the US and Canada, on the one hand, and from 'late industrialization' in the rest of the region, on the other. The former is associated with an 'Anglo-American' form of capitalism, which rests broadly on the liberal principles of individualism and the twin values of free markets and democracy. The development trajectories of Latin American and Caribbean countries have been inescapably and profoundly influenced by the liberal ideological project associated with the global hegemony of the US, but it is only recently that this form of influence has crystallized into any significant convergence on (neo)liberal forms of economic organization and democratic forms of political organization. Post-1945 development strategies in Latin America and the Caribbean rested on a set of ideas about development which were distinctly 'home grown' and nationalist in orientation, and indeed came to offer significant ideological cohesion to the vast collection of countries then taken to comprise the 'Third World'. These sets of ideas spawned the policy strategies associated with import-substituting industrialization (ISI) and evolved later into such influential development theories as that associated with the concept of dependency.

The collective postwar experimentation with inward-looking development by Latin American and Caribbean countries largely failed, particularly in the goals of reducing economies' dependence on imports and foreign capital (Baer 1972) and led, again collectively, to a turn towards neoliberalism and, indeed, to democratic government during the 1980s and 1990s. Yet this signals neither convergence on the Anglo-American development model nor the uniform adoption of a single set of development strategies by the countries of the region. Indeed, a handful of countries have remained outside or only partially engaged with these agendas. Cuba, most obviously, has been the only country in the Americas (and one of the few in the world) to remain under authoritarian socialist government, notwithstanding some movements towards greater openness to foreign investment (Pérez-López 1999). The much greater success of ISI in Brazil meant that neoliberalism was far slower to take root there than in much of the rest of the region and, indeed, the traditional priorities and structures associated with state-led industrialization came to permeate the version of neoliberalism that did emerge in the 1990s. Lukewarm adoptions of neoliberalism were characteristic also of countries like Venezuela, whilst elsewhere the progress of reform efforts was frequently faltering and politically fraught. In a nutshell, notably distinct development strategies have emerged in the region, reflecting key disparities in countries' positions in the structures and politics of trade and production, finance and debt, labour and migration, and a range of security-related issues. These various spheres are explored in turn below.

Trade and production

A key component of this generalized turn to neoliberalism has been the drastic reduction of tariff barriers to trade. Liberalization strategies have generally been pursued on a unilateral basis, in significant contrast to the emphasis on reciprocity in the post-1945 trade strategies of the US. By the end of the 1990s there remained some disparity between the low average tariff levels that prevailed in the US and Canada (4.5 per cent), the slightly higher levels in countries such as Chile, Bolivia and most of Central America (under 10 per cent), and the still higher levels across the rest of region, reaching over 14 per cent in Brazil and over 16 per cent in Mexico. Yet, in fact, by the end of the 1990s Latin American, Caribbean and Mexican economies presented very few barriers to trade flows, these remaining concentrated instead in the US economy. Simple tariff averages obscure the striking degree of sectoral variation in the US tariff structure. However, it is precisely in the sectors of most strategic interest to Latin American and Caribbean countries that market access has continued to be impeded by high tariff and non-tariff barriers. Agriculture is the most obvious case in point, along with textiles, footwear and steel, among others. Moreover, even where tariff barriers are relatively low, US trade strategies have been marked by frequent resort to specific *ad valorem* duties and contingency measures, including the notorious Section 301, and other commercial defence mechanisms (CDMs) such as safeguards, anti-dumping and countervailing duties, while their aggregate use in the rest of the region has remained fairly minimal and confined to the five largest economies (de Paiva Abreu 2002: 9–11).

Taking average tariff levels together with the customary trade openness indicators of imports and exports as a percentage of GDP, the results of trade liberalization have thus yielded a region which links some of the most 'open' economies in the world with significantly inward-looking ones. As Table 2.1 shows, the degree of trade openness – and, by extension, overall dependence on trade – is most marked in the Central American and Caribbean subregions, and least in the Southern Cone. The US, significantly, joins Argentina as the only countries where the ratio of trade to GDP was under 20 per cent. The vast majority of the countries south of the Mexico–US border have also consistently run overall trade deficits, the impact of unilateral liberalization exacerbated by a dramatic decline in the growth of world trade and prices for commodity exports from the mid-1990s onwards and the continued existence of barriers to market access. The US economy, however, has also been consistently characterized by overall deficit in the trade balance (in 2002 equivalent to about 4.2 per cent of GDP), while the Canadian economy retains a slight trade surplus (USTR 2003: annex I, 2; Canadian Department of Foreign Affairs and International Trade 2003).

Dependence on the US market characterizes the trade structures of large parts of the Americas and follows much the same pattern as the openness indicators we have just mentioned. Around 80 per cent of Canadian and Mexican trade is with the US, the figures falling to around 50 per cent for CACM, around 40 per cent for CARICOM and the Andean Community (AC), and around 20 per cent for the Southern Cone. Furthermore, the vast majority of countries are, if not dependent directly on the single US market, then highly dependent on export markets in the Americas or their particular subregion. Apart from the US, Brazil is the only country in the region that has a highly diversified trade profile – for much of the 1990s around 60 per cent of Brazil's trade flows were with the EU and the rest of the world (Tavares de Araujo 1998: 9). Chilean trade strategies over the 1990s were oriented to achieving a similar status of 'global trader' and have begun to effect some movement in this direction.

The question of which products are traded opens up discussion of the diverse production structures accommodated within the Americas. As is well-known, the restructuring of production at the global level has been characterized by two key processes: the transnationalization of production chains and so-called 'tertiarization' (Scholte 2000). These broad shifts have manifested themselves in very different ways across the Americas. US corporations have been at the forefront of transnationalization processes, with the US accounting for 16 per cent of world trade in services in 2002. Services represented 30 per cent of total US trade by 2002, such that within its overall trade deficit the US runs a surplus in respect of services (of US$47 billion in 2002) (USTR 2003: annex I, 1–2, 11). Moreover, the US is the only net exporter of services in the Americas. Across the rest of the region, including Canada, the average share of services in total trade remains at less than 15 per cent, a level inferior to the world average of 19 per cent (ECLAC 2002a, summary, 8; Canadian Department of Foreign Affairs and International Trade 2003). However, the US and Canada occupy the high-value-added, high-technology and capital intensive points of transnationalized production chains, and their exports (and by extension those of North America in aggregate) are dominated by manufactured and tertiary products of this nature.

In the rest of the region, conversely, three general models of 'export specialization' have usefully been identified (ECLAC 2002a: 12). The first rests on integration into 'vertical' flows of trade in manufactured goods – that is, assembly operations associated with the *maquiladora* (that is, assembly for export) industries in Mexico, Caribbean countries and some Central American countries – primarily with the US. This integration has meant that non-resource-based exports from these parts of the region have increased significantly, from 29.9 per cent of total exports in the mid-1980s to 71.9 per cent by 1998 (ECLAC 2001: 57). But crucially these exports are uniformly of low value added, the value added accruing once the products are exported to the US and onwards from there. It has been in order to entrench this particular type of production chain that large parts of the Caribbean and Central America (such as Jamaica, the Dominican Republic, El Salvador and Haiti) have been styled as offshore arms of the US production structure, especially in the textiles and apparel industries (Heron 2004; Robinson 1998). The economies in this model are thus inserted into the regional political economy – and specifically the transnationalized North American political economy – on the basis of their abundance of cheap and unskilled labour and, frequently, loose regulatory structures. Mexico is clearly part of this group, but is also distinctive in that it is one of the four economies of the Americas – along with Brazil, Canada and the

US – that are genuinely diversified. Certainly, its industrial base is significantly more sophisticated than those of the Central American and
Caribbean economies.

The second model, by contrast, is represented by the South American
economies' insertion into horizontal production and trade flows based
on natural resources. Notwithstanding a considerable widening of the
span of industrial activity, their overall profile is still dominated by
capital-intensive industries associated with the processing of natural
resources, such activities uniformly being of low domestic value added
(Katz 2000: 5). This profile is one of the defining features of what might
be called the 'Southern Cone model' of regional capitalist development
(Phillips 2004a), Southern Cone economies having generally made relatively slight inroads into tertiary economic activity or high value-added
manufacturing activity. Within this broad model, many Southern Cone
economies remain reliant on agriculture – Argentina and Paraguay
being the most salient examples – while raw materials and natural
resource-based manufactures dominate production and exports in Chile
and most of the Andean economies. Chile and Uruguay have come to
enjoy some distinction in the trade in services, the latter being particularly notable as the South American financial centre. Brazil, conversely,
is unique in South America for the size of its industrial base and, indeed,
for its high and mid-level technology manufactures which accounted for
a third of total exports in 1999–2001 (ECLAC 2002a: summary, 13).

The third model of export specialization overlaps with the first, rests
on the export of services and is characteristic of the Caribbean subregion, along with a number of Central American countries such as
Panama. It has been termed 'peripheral postindustrialization' in an
attempt to capture the shift from 'transnationally based, vertically integrated segments of manufacturing to transnationally based vertically
integrated segments of knowledge-intensive industries and services'
(Pantojas-García 2001: 59). This shift was occasioned primarily by the
competitive displacement of Caribbean economies by the enormous
advantage afforded to Mexican *maquiladora* industries by NAFTA, particularly in textiles and apparel (Pantojas-García 2001: 61–2). The
resulting 'service economies' were thus propelled both by Caribbean
governments seeking a niche in new transnationalized trade and production structures and by transnational corporations seeking to capital-
ize on the supply of cheap labour, skilled *and* unskilled. By 2001 services
accounted for over 50 per cent of total Caribbean trade and in some
cases, particularly in the eastern Caribbean micro states, nearer to 80 per
cent (ECLAC 2002a: summary, 8). The predominant sectors are tourism
and entertainment, along with a range of commercial and financial
services, both legal and illegal.

Finance and debt

As with production structures, there is a clear distinction between the US and Canada, as net exporters of capital, and the rest of the region's countries, as net importers. Financial deregulation removed most of the barriers to investment, as well as trade, during the 1980s and 1990s. Taken as a whole, Latin America and the Caribbean (including Mexico) accounted for 29 per cent of total capital flows in 1995 to what the international financial institutions classify as 'developing countries' and 37 per cent of this total by 2000, annual average flows in 2000 having tripled from their average levels for 1990–94 (ECLAC 2001: 35–6). Within these patterns, the dominance of Mexico and Brazil as destinations for foreign direct investment (FDI) is striking, each accounting for nearly 40 per cent of total flows in 2001.

The consequent, pronounced vulnerability of many of the region's economies to financial volatility, and in particular capital flight, was highlighted by three key crises – Mexico 1994–95, Brazil 1999 and then Argentina 2001–02. However, the difference with the Asian countries, which also suffered financial crisis in the late 1990s, was that some two-thirds of the capital flows to Latin America and the Caribbean in 1997 constituted long-term direct investment and, consequently, the recovery from the Brazilian devaluation, in particular, was relatively rapid. Susceptibility to the vagaries of global finance has also been exacerbated by the widespread absence of regulatory structures in banking and financial systems, in contrast with the extensive webs of financial regulation that are intrinsic to US and Canadian development strategies. It is notable that Chile has been the only country in Latin America and the Caribbean to impose a system of controls on capital flows (albeit amounting to no more than the levels maintained in the US), but even in this case the government felt obliged to relax these restrictions at the time of the Asian financial crises in order to shore up investor confidence. Uruguay and Mexico are examples of other countries in which banking supervision and regulatory management are fairly effective, while Argentina and, of course, many of the region's smaller economies occupy the other end of the spectrum.

Turning to patterns of debt, the basic distinction lies again between the US and Canada, as key creditors, and the rest of the countries of the region, as some of the world's most indebted states. In a number of cases, the external debt matches or substantially exceeds total GDP, as for example in Guyana and Nicaragua, and these two countries join Bolivia and Honduras as the four members from the Americas of the World Bank's Highly Indebted Poor Countries (HIPC) initiative (the others being concentrated overwhelmingly in Africa). Among 'large' debtor nations, external debt frequently exceeds 50 per cent of GDP, as in the Brazilian case, and in some cases exceeds total GDP by some margin, as in the Argentine case by the start of the 2000s. The latter's catastrophic economic collapse in 2001 was marked by both a devaluation of the currency and a default on external debt payments, which at the time represented a value equivalent to about 500 per cent of exports.

Labour and migration

Flexible labour markets are intrinsic to the neoliberal development model which, as a result, has been associated with comparatively high levels of unemployment. Labour flexibilization strategies have been key facets of neoliberal reform in the majority of Latin American and Caribbean countries and Mexico, involving a shift to flexible workforms and employment practices which allow for a significant reduction of firms' employment costs. The impact of flexibilization is manifest in such trends as falling real wages and high levels of unemployment – as illustrations: urban unemployment levels in 2001 of 17.4 per cent in Argentina, 18.2 per cent in Colombia and 16.2 per cent in Panama; and national levels for the same year of 9.9 per cent for Barbados, 15 per cent for Jamaica and 13.4 per cent for Venezuela (ECLAC 2002b). Even where urban unemployment figures are relatively more modest (as in Mexico at 2.5 per cent in 2001), across the region rural unemployment levels are often very significant. The US economy is also characterized by comparatively high unemployment in comparison with other Organisation for Economic Cooperation and Development (OECD) countries, the comparatively modest official statistics being made possible, interestingly, by the statistical omission of the incarcerated proportion of the population which is very significantly higher in the US than in most other parts of the world (Coates 2000: 50).

More salient still are the phenomena of underemployment and informalization, which have been particularly conspicuous in Latin America and the Caribbean (including Mexico) as a consequence of both the particular challenges of competitiveness in these countries, the relative abundance of labour and, in many cases, the demography of a very young population. In Paraguay, for example, only about 30 per cent of the economically active population has paid employment in the formal sector (Klein 2000: 155), whilst for Brazil it was estimated in 2001 that around 60 per cent of the workforce was 'informal', double the 1991 level (*Financial Times* 6 June 2001). Informalization has been particularly evident in sectors such as textiles and footwear and in the numbers of manual workers that are hired daily, weekly or seasonally, mainly in the construction and agricultural sectors. These patterns also correlate strongly with the use of migrant labour. A significant percentage of those hired on a daily or seasonal basis (legally and illegally) in the large Southern Cone economies, particularly Chile, are migrant workers from the smaller Southern Cone countries and the Andean region. Migration in these parts of the region, however, is political as well as economic. Costa Rica represents the other major destination for migrants, most notably from Nicaragua but also increasingly from Colombia; Colombian migration to Venezuela is also significant.

Yet these links between migration, underemployment and informalization are perhaps most salient in North America, and most of all in the US–Mexico context. The most arresting fact is noted by Domínguez and Fernández de Castro (2001: 149): 'Mexico is the world's major country of emigration; the United States is the world's major country of immigration'. Thirty-eight per cent of legal immigrants to the US in 2002 arrived from other countries in the Americas, with the 219,380 Mexicans that legally entered the US in this year accounting for by far the largest group within this number (US Department of Homeland Security 2002: 5). Estimates indicate that over 400,000 new illegal immigrants entered the US each year over the 1990s, and again it is likely that at least half were Mexican. During the 1980s, however, Central Americans came to displace Cubans as the dominant 'refugee' migrants, with large-scale emigration taking place from such war-torn countries as El Salvador, Nicaragua and Guatemala (Suárez-Orozco 1999: 229). According to 2002 figures, the Hispanic population in the US represents about 13.3 per cent of the total population, 66.9 per cent of which are Mexican (US Census Bureau 2002). This population is concentrated in five key states (and cities) – New York (New York City), Florida (Miami), California (Los Angeles), Illinois (Chicago) and Texas (Houston).

The implications of these trends are considerable for the US, but they are just as important for the 'home' countries from which emigrants depart, especially in relation to the loss of (particularly skilled) labour and professionals, the impact on the position of women in labour markets and the extent of their reliance on remittances from migrant workers. The latter enter both the formal and informal economies and often represent the key source of foreign exchange. For instance, in 1996 remittances from Mexican workers totalled around US$4–5 billion (Domínguez and Fernández de Castro 2001: 152), causing the administration of President Vicente Fox to take steps from 2000 onwards to ease the extensive restrictions on remittances imposed by financial intermediaries (Rozental 2003: 13). To give another example, remittances from El Salvadoreans totalled around US$1.1 billion in 1995, approximately half the value of total Salvadorean exports and around a ninth of GDP (Fernández de Castro and Rosales 2000: 239).

Security issues

It hardly needs saying that the US occupies a very particular position in the global security arena by virtue of its superpower status, and thus its development strategy is much more intimately bound up than those of the rest of the region with interests in the Middle East and Asia (as discussed in other chapters). The Americas as a whole has remained largely immune from the threat of territorial invasion (apart from US-led incursions into 'problem states') and inter-state warfare within the region has been infrequent. Border disputes run on between Peru and Ecuador, El Salvador and Honduras (drawing in Nicaragua and Belize), Guyana and Suriname, and Guyana and Venezuela, but for the most part conflict has been concentrated within the borders of states, largely associated with terrorism and insurgency and concentrated in the Andean region. The ongoing civil conflict in Colombia is by far the most obvious current example – the economic costs of the extraordinary levels of violence being estimated at around 25 per cent of GDP (Marcella 2003: 13) – along with El Salvador (with similar economic cost levels) and Peru in the 1980s. Terrorist incidents have also been important in Venezuela, Argentina and Central America (Griffith 2000). The direct significance of terrorism for the US increased dramatically over the 1990s, culminating, of course, in the attacks of 11 September 2001. Like these new threats from transnational terrorism, the majority of security-related development challenges in the Americas are of the 'non-traditional' variety. They include the migration question, as already discussed, and the variety of issues associated with the drugs trade, energy and the environment.

The narcotics issue in the Americas bears some resemblance to migration in that drugs, like migrants, originate from Latin America and the Caribbean and move northwards to the US. There is also the similarly striking distinction of the US enjoying the 'dubious distinction' of being the world's largest consumer of drugs (Griffith 2000: 67) and Latin America and the Caribbean being by far the world's largest producer of cocaine and marijuana. The big South American producer countries are concentrated overwhelmingly in the Andean region – Colombia (by far the largest), Bolivia and Peru – with enclaves also in countries like Mexico. Mexico and much of Central America and the Caribbean (notably the Dominican Republic, Jamaica and Puerto Rico) are integrated into the narcotics trade mainly as what the US State Department calls 'transit zones'. Again, like migration, narcotics is particularly salient as a US–Mexico issue and the drugs trade is crucial to the economies of the producer countries, accounting for a very significant part of their GDP and the livelihoods of a sizeable part of their populations.

Energy-related security issues gather around the key fact that the US is a net importer of energy and consequently secure supplies are of fundamental importance. Most of the rest of the region's countries are also importers (despite sizeable oil and gas industries in, for instance, Mexico, Brazil, Argentina and Trinidad and Tobago), with the notable exception of Venezuela, which is one of the world's major oil producing countries and a member of the Organization of Petroleum Exporting Countries (OPEC). Its economy is highly dependent on this single resource, which accounted for some 78 per cent of exports in 1997 (Kelly and Romero 2002: 44) and its development trajectory from its time as 'Saudi Venezuela' in the early 1970s to the present day has been overwhelmingly conditioned by this dependence and the concomitant economic and socio-political dislocations generally associated with oil economies.

Finally, security issues relating to the environment stem in the first instance from the region's vulnerability to natural phenomena associated with weather and geography, a significant part of the Americas being located in earthquake and hurricane belts, the former running along the Pacific coast of the region, and the latter affecting most parts of Central America and the Caribbean, as well as parts of the US. Other instances of natural environmental phenomena are the flooding associated with El Niño (affecting particularly Peru and the southern US) and the cyclical drought affecting parts of the region such as northeast Brazil (Barton 1999: 188). However, many of the region's environmental security challenges have been induced by human activity, much of it associated with the shift to large-scale industrial activity in North America and export-led growth across the rest of the region. A number of problems of a 'global' nature have been particularly acute for parts of the Americas, such as the perforation of the ozone layer over southern Chile and the problems associated with the exacerbation of natural phenomena by climate change. Global issues in respect of 'differential responsibility' have obviously been mirrored in the Americas. Problems of more 'local' dimensions have included deforestation, depletion of marine stocks and the erosion of biodiversity. These 'green' issues are accompanied by the full gamut of so-called 'brown' issues relating to urban matters such as air pollution, water quality, sanitation and sewage and waste management. These are of perhaps greater concern than traditional green issues in North America and are particularly salient as 'transborder' issues in the US–Mexican relationship.

The intra-regional politics of development in the Americas

The presence of the US in the Americas implies a close and unique over-lap between the intra-regional and the global politics of development. In a sense there is little distinction for the bulk of the countries of the Americas between the arenas and the power structures associated with their region and the global political economy. Not surprisingly, intra-regional politics in the Americas has traditionally been dominated by the US and shaped primarily by its policies. During the Cold War, US power was asserted mainly through repeated direct and covert interventions in Latin America and the Caribbean, ostensibly in the interests of the containment of communism, and was marked by an overwhelmingly unilateral approach to the region. In the post-Cold War era, however, the changing nature of US hegemony and the embrace across the Americas of neoliberalism and democracy have led, as one observer has interpreted it (Muñoz 2001), to a 'relational delinking' in which, on the one hand, regional relations are no longer characterized by dependence on and domination by the US, and, on the other, the political and diplomatic interest of the US in the rest of the Americas has markedly diminished. Both of these trends are certainly in evidence in patterns of intra-regional relations over the 1990s, and perhaps have been sharpened since 11 September 2001. The Clinton administration's 'benign neglect' of the Americas in the 1990s was offered substantial redress in the early days of the George W. Bush administration, the President's feeling of particular affinity with Mexico leading him to place the Americas at the heart of his 'foreign' policy and diplomatic agenda. Since that time, however, the war on terrorism and the focus on the Middle East has increasingly rendered Latin America and the Caribbean the 'forgotten relationship' for the US (Castañeda 2003).

Nevertheless, the US unquestionably retains its position of regional hegemony (Phillips 2003a) and the intra-regional politics of development is still extensively conditioned by the strategies pursued, or not pursued, by the US. A notion of 'de-linking' is misleading if it is taken to suggest a dilution of the importance of the relationship with the US, which remains pivotal both at the bilateral level and in the regional context. The decline in the intensity of the relationship has been widely lamented, with moves towards market reform and democratization creating the conditions in which 'what would have been seen as imperialism in earlier decades' now has 'the promise of reinforcing development aspirations' (Fauriol and Weintraub 2001: 144). Perhaps the most important dynamic in this respect has been increased recognition of the 'intermestic' character of key regional relationships, signifying the close

linkage between foreign policy and domestic issues and diluting traditional notions of the US as an 'external' power and of the rest of the
region as targets of 'foreign' policy. While it remains the case that much
of the region is not especially crucial to US interests in economic terms,
the importance of issues such as security, migration and drugs and the
regional relationships engendered by them is not to be underestimated.
The most striking 'intermestic' relationship exists between the US and
Mexico, as well as the Caribbean, and is perhaps nowhere more amply
illustrated than in President Fox's unprecedented conduct of parts of his
electoral campaign in the US (Fernández de Castro and Rozental 2003)
and the enormous importance of the 'Hispanic vote' in US electoral politics. Certainly, the extent of such relationships suggests that, for the US,
intra-regional politics has become considerably more, rather than less,
pivotal to its development strategy.

What has been particularly interesting in this light is that the changing nature of the position and engagement of the US in its region has
given rise to a set of strategies that not only rely upon the continuing
management of key bilateral relationships, but also revolve around
a novel turn to regionalism. This regionalist impetus derived largely
from perceptions within the US political elite of its declining global
hegemony at the end of the 1980s, combined with progressive frustration with the ponderous advance of multilateral liberalization in the
WTO (Payne 1996; Phillips 2003a), and signified an important abandonment of its traditional reticence in matters of regionalism. Prior even to
the signing of NAFTA in 1994, the US had initiated a wider Enterprise
for the Americas Initiative (EAI) in 1990, which subsequently mutated
into negotiations for an FTAA from 1994 onwards. This trade project
came to be the cornerstone of the emerging 'Summitry of the Americas'
process, which enjoys a broad mandate to oversee regional cooperation
across the economic and social development, security and democratization agendas. While active US political leadership of these projects has
been lamented for its absence, and overall neglect of the Americas has
been characteristic of successive post-Cold War administrations, there is
nevertheless an important sense in which these initiatives represented
a concrete turning point in the evolution of the regional dimension of
US development strategy.

The implications of all of this for the autonomy and sovereignty of
countries in all of the subregions of the Americas have necessarily
become a matter of concern: indeed, the key theme of contemporary
intra-regional politics has come to be the mitigation of the unilateral
assertion of US hegemony across a range of key relationships and issue
areas. In part, this has issued from (and been served by) increasing
leadership exercised within Latin America and the Caribbean by such

countries as Mexico and, more recently, Brazil. The contemporary strategies of these two states have been somewhat different, the former having sought a role primarily as a bridge or interlocutor between the northern and southern parts of the region, and the latter having sought to position itself as the primary counterweight to US power. Brazil's increasing assertiveness in the South American arena – most significantly (particularly for the US) in its interactions with Colombia, Cuba and Venezuela – has generated an array of tensions with Washington. Likewise, Mexican positions on Cuba, for example, and its opposition in the UN Security Council to the war on Iraq in 2002–3 reveal important – if often incipient – shifts in the international relations and power structures of the Americas. The key handmaiden of this gradual restructuring has, however, been the revival of political interest in regionalism across the region, not just in North America. Along with a complex web of bilateral trade agreements, the establishment of the MERCOSUR and the 'relaunching' of CARICOM, CACM and the AC over the course of the 1990s were in the first instance conceived as strategic responses to the challenges posed by globalization – means by which national governments could 'lock in' and further neoliberal reform strategies. In addition, of course, they have served as strategic platforms from which to engage with the US and other partners in the region and from which to address other relevant matters of subregional, and regional, interest.

These shifting patterns are reflected in the contemporary management of a number of key issues on the regional agenda. Migration, first of all, has been addressed largely within the US–Mexico relationship, but it was only towards the end of the 1990s – and even then only briefly – that this issue received high-level diplomatic attention and, in so doing, moved substantially beyond the traditionally dominant focus on border control. This culminated in proposals laid out by President Fox at the White House in September 2001 for what Mexican foreign minister Jorge Castañeda famously dubbed the 'whole enchilada' – that is, for an encompassing agreement to 'regularize' the status of the estimated four million Mexicans illegally resident in the US based on a recognition of their centrality to the US economy, the benefits of mitigating the welfare consequences of their illegal status and the continuing costs of border enforcement policies (Ewing 2003; Rozental 2003; contrast Martin and Teitelbaum 2001). The strength of domestic anti-immigration lobbies in the US was always likely to constitute a significant challenge for such an agreement, along with longstanding political biases – indeed, it is interesting in this latter respect that US governments never granted formal refugee status to the majority of Central American migrants but, at least until the end of the 1990s, did so almost automatically for Cuban refugees from the Castro regime (Suárez-Orozco 1999: 231). Yet, in the event, the Mexican initiative floundered on the shift of US preoccupations after 11 September, at which point border security again became of pivotal – and misplaced – importance in high-level deliberations in the US on national defence. Tensions on the issue were further exacerbated in 2003 when the US House of Representatives passed a 'sense of Congress' amendment to make further progress on a migration agreement conditional upon the opening to US investment of the Mexican state oil company Pemex, ostensibly in the interests of stimulating the economic growth in Mexico necessary to stem the tide of migrants to the US and ensuring adequate oil supplies for both Mexico and the US – a proposal received with uproar in Mexico and roundly rejected by Fox (*El Universal* 10, 11, 12 May 2003).

The drugs issue, by contrast, has prompted much more committed and interventionist strategies on the part of the US, with significant consequences for 'target' countries such as Bolivia, Colombia, Mexico and a range of Central American and Caribbean points in trafficking chains. The strikingly consistent element of US drug policy has been the emphasis on controlling supply rather than demand, particularly through the so-called 'interdiction' of shipments and direct crop eradication (Smith 2000: 289–91; US Department of State 2001). The key policy mechanism for securing cooperation has been the annual 'certification' process, in place since 1986, in which countries are 'decertified' for their failure adequately to fulfil commitments to drug control. While this is a strategy of international scope, around three-quarters of the budget of the Bureau for International Narcotics and Law Enforcement Affairs (INL) is directed at the Latin American and Caribbean region (Joyce 1999: 209), with the proportion of the federal budget directed to the anti-drug strategy also increasing each year over the 1990s. The certification process, moreover, has become highly politicized. For example, the decision to decertify Colombia but not Mexico in the mid-1990s was made on the grounds of the importance of the relationship with Mexico in US domestic politics (Joyce 1999: 215–16).

All of these dimensions of US strategy on narcotics have generated significant tensions in the region, exacerbated by its progressive conflation of drugs with issues of terrorism and insurgency. The term 'narco-guerrilla' entered US discourse in the 1980s in order to establish drugs as a 'national security' issue and legitimize the shift to a highly militarized approach (Serrano 2000: 97–9). However, this 'militarization' of US engagement in the region can be seen to have carried significant developmental consequences for target countries, notably in its strengthening of national militaries at the expense of civilian political institutions, its encouragement of activities by both governments and

armed forces that would be illegal in both US and international law, and
its significantly negative consequences for human rights in already fragile democracies (Evans 2001; Isacson 2001). More recent US initiatives
such as the Plan Colombia and the overall sharpening of the perceived
connection between terrorism and drugs in the Bush administration's
post-September 11 phase (US Department of State 2003) have created
further unease on this issue between the US and key countries such as
Brazil and Venezuela. Nevertheless, certain steps have been taken to
diminish US unilateralism and strengthen regional mechanisms for dealing with narcotics, notably the Inter-American Drug Abuse Control
Commission, set up by the Organization of American States (OAS) and
headed by Canada and Chile, which propelled the establishment of the
'Multilateral Evaluation Mechanism' at the 1998 Summit of the
Americas. The US government also softened the certification process in
2001 (US White House 2002). At the same time regionalist strategies
have at least gained some rhetorical status, with Andean and Caribbean
countries indicating their intentions to develop joint strategies through
the AC and CARICOM for addressing the range of security problems
(particularly drugs) afflicting both regions.

For all this, the FTAA and Summitry processes are perhaps the arenas
in which the changing architecture and substance of contemporary
intra-regional politics are most easily discerned. As noted earlier, the
emerging multilateralism in the Americas has been marked by the lack
of active political leadership, with the result that during the 1990s the
process left little mark on political debate in the US (Phillips 2004b).
Just as it was the Mexican government that made the initial running for
a NAFTA, so the impetus to the hemispheric trade project has come
almost entirely from Latin American and Caribbean participants and an
array of regional business interests. Yet the substance of the negotiations
has systematically been moulded to reflect the key economic interests of
the US – namely, the opportunity it presents to push forward a range of
new trade disciplines, notably in services, investment rules and property
rights, in which successive US governments have perceived inadequate
progress at the multilateral level. This thinking underpins the concept of
WTO-plus (whereby the substance of an FTAA agreement would exceed
existing multilateral provisions) around which the FTAA negotiations
have come to congeal, despite initial opposition from Latin American
and Caribbean representatives. The structure of nine technical working
groups also explicitly reflects the negotiating areas of key concern to the
US (agriculture having been included only at the behest of Latin
American and Caribbean negotiators) and facilitates significant US
leverage over the agenda in that precedent, expertise and existing internal arrangements in many of the nine key areas are notably

underdeveloped in most of the subregional blocs (Phillips 2003a: 272–3). Moreover, the WTO-plus concept is directly tied to an attempt by US negotiators to establish a 'spiral of precedents' (VanGrasstek 1998: 169), which would then form the basis for subsequent negotiations at the multilateral level and with extra-regional partners. US interest in an FTAA is thus fundamentally connected with its construction of a world trading order consistent with its economic and ideological interests.

Nevertheless, the US has not been able to dictate all aspects of the hemispheric agenda nor to retain absolute control over the negotiations. It was established early in the FTAA negotiations that US preferences for a format of NAFTA enlargement was unacceptable to the majority of other participants. Since 1998 the negotiations have instead formally been conducted according to the principle of bloc bargaining by existing subregional units, except the North American countries. This strategic articulation of subregionalism has been envisaged as a means of bolstering the respective regionalist projects against absorption into a putative FTAA, but also of strengthening bargaining power within the negotiations. The AC has been the most effective in pursuing this strategy, given the comparative greater cohesion of its member countries and the more intensive institutionalization of the bloc. CARICOM and CACM have also participated in largely coordinated fashion, facilitated by their focus on the single issue of special and differential treatment for smaller and poorer economies and, in the case of the former, by the existence of a specific Regional Negotiating Machinery. Their weight in negotiations, however, has remained slight and, in general, the heavy dependence of Caribbean and Central American economies on the US imposes obvious restrictions on the strategies available to their governments.

The MERCOSUR, conversely, has been the least effective instance of coordinated negotiation, but at the same time represents the most influential set of participants outside North America by virtue of both the size of the member economies and the distinctive presence of Brazil. It is the US–Brazil relationship that has largely defined the progress and structure of the FTAA process and these two countries which have jointly held the presidency of the final stages of the process since late 2002. Brazilian positions have explicitly sought to retain control over the shape of an integrated Americas and avoid the possibility that the FTAA would come to represent, in then presidential candidate 'Lula' da Silva's words, 'a process of the economic annexation of the continent by the United States' (*La Nación* 23 October 2002). Parallel strategies have consequently emerged of strengthening the MERCOSUR and constructing a solid 'South America' agenda, largely through AC–MERCOSUR integration, under Brazilian leadership. Brazilian governments have also taken a hard line in negotiations with the US on certain key issues. Most notably, Brazil has insisted that the principle of 'WTO-plus' must be genuine and encompassing – that is, including the areas of agriculture and CDMs which the US has consistently refused to open for negotiation.

By the end of the 1990s, however, bloc strategies to mitigate US hegemony in the hemispheric process were starting to buckle under pressures from the continuing preference of the US for bilateral trade agreements, such as that concluded with Chile in December 2002. Their apparently greater utility in serving key US priorities has meant that the strategies of the United States Trade Representative (USTR) have given far more time and attention to bilateral market access agreements than more encompassing hemispheric arrangements of the sort envisaged within an FTAA. Yet the pursuit of bilateral agreements is also useful as a mechanism for increasing the incentives of other partners (notably Brazil) to engage in similar negotiations, or else for increasing their interests in the success of the FTAA negotiations and thus encouraging a softening of negotiating positions. To some extent, this strategy has already been successful inasmuch as it has combined with a growing reticence about the FTAA in various parts of the region. Mexico, possessed of an existing and effective bilateral agreement with the US, has always been the most lukewarm about a putative hemispheric agreement and has lately found a greater coincidence of concern with Brazil. This general reticence among many of the most influential figures in the political elite has shown signs of hardening into opposition as the 2000s have progressed. Furthermore, in the face of overtures from the US to negotiate bilaterally with the MERCOSUR and a number of individual countries, incentives to engage fully in encompassing hemispheric negotiations have diminished. For their part, the interest of the MERCOSUR countries in an FTAA has always been rather less pronounced, given that their more diversified trade structures and export destinations make them the ones with most at stake in the multilateral system. Indeed, Brazilian hesitancy has stemmed specifically from the trade-off an FTAA would represent against its more significant multilateral interests (de Paiva Abreu 2003: 23–4). The Lula government has also ushered in an important redefinition of Brazilian negotiating strategies in the FTAA context, according to which the key issues of market access, services and investment will be negotiated in a bilateral 4 + 1 (MERCOSUR–US) format, leaving only 'basic elements', such as dispute settlement, trade facilitation and special and differential treatment, on the hemispheric negotiating table (Amorim 2003). Uruguay has been engaged since 2001 in bilateral negotiations with the US and Argentina has made little secret of its preference for a similar arrangement.

In sum, the ongoing nature of US hegemony in the Americas does not obscure key changes in the landscape and substance of the intra-regional politics of development. In the contemporary period they have been delineated in striking ways by strategies designed to mitigate US unilateralism in key areas of the regional agenda. These have not always borne fruit and the US hegemonic imprint remains indelible on both intra-regional politics and national development trajectories across the region. It is worth noting, too, that this has been further facilitated by the lack of any robust system of regional institutions across the Americas as a whole: indeed the absence of such a system owes much historically to the dominance of the US. The 'inter-American system', such as it is, has the OAS at its helm, the other two key institutions being the Inter-American Development Bank (IDB) and the United Nations Economic Commission for Latin America and the Caribbean (ECLAC). The OAS was established in 1948 and gradually broadened to include all the independent states of the region, except Cuba. Yet cooperation under its aegis has historically been hampered by divergent visions of its purpose, Latin American perspectives seeing it as a shield against US intervention, and the US seeing it as a vehicle for the pursuit of its foreign policy interests. In the 1990s, the OAS was revitalized primarily by its protagonism of the new regional democratization agenda (Cooper and Legler 2001; Boniface 2002) – Canada joining the organization in 1990 and taking the lead in this issue area – and also, as we have seen, by its strong presence in the FTAA and Summitry processes (Salazar-Xirinachs 2001). As pressures for multilateral solutions to regional problems have mounted, so the potential mandate for regional or hemispheric institutions has strengthened. Yet the OAS remains a spectacularly underresourced institution and in its key actual and potential areas of competence (such as drugs) the US continues to resist a full devolution of control over the regional agenda.

The extra-regional politics of development in the Americas

The US, clearly, occupies a category entirely of its own in relation to the insertion of the countries of the region into the global politics of development, the extent of its power and the depth of contemporary unipolarity being widely accepted as being without historical precedent. Throughout the post-1945 period, its development strategy has been closely tied to a multilateralist thrust in its international engagement and, as a result, it has been unquestionably pivotal to the construction of all the multilateral organizations currently in existence. This historically close link between US development and multilateralism has, however, been characterized by a notable ambivalence on the part of both governments and public opinion towards the multilateral institutions and the rules they have established, albeit largely through the impetus of the US (Luck 1999). This reached something of an apogee in the aggressive unilateralism of the George W. Bush administration. Recent US engagement with multilateral institutions has been marked by its withdrawal from or refusal to ratify such conventions as the Anti-Ballistic Missile Treaty, the Kyoto Protocol on Global Climate Change, the International Criminal Court and the Germ Weapons Ban, and in 2003 by its decision ultimately to bypass the UN altogether in its actions in Iraq. We have noted already the increasing US frustration with the ponderous progress of WTO negotiations, and its record of compliance with its rules and procedures since the 1980s has consequently been an unhappy one (Tussie 1998).

At the same time, the US retains a position of considerable dominance across the spectrum of multilateral institutions. Historically, there has been no inclination in US policy to grant these institutions significant independent powers (Ruggie 1996: 21) and it remains the most powerful political force within them. Indeed, the US has systematically adapted its strategies and the institutional structures themselves to perpetuate this position. In the UN, its dominance is facilitated by the fact that multilateral engagement in large-scale military or humanitarian operations remains largely unfeasible without US participation. But it is also significant that, as membership of the UN has expanded, the US undertook from the organization's early days to make the Security Council, rather than the General Assembly, its 'forum of choice', in that there it wields a veto by virtue of its permanent membership (Malone 2003: 73). Similar patterns have prevailed in its interactions with the IFIs. In both the leading bodies, the share of votes accruing to the US – 17.1 per cent in the IMF and 16.4 per cent in the International Bank for Reconstruction and Development (the principal agency in the World Bank structure) – implies a unique veto power in that major decisions require an 85 per cent majority. Yet the IMF's need to supplement its resources in recent years has also meant a certain political and financial dependence on the US, which has used the IMF's quota reviews as opportunities to exercise considerable pressure. Indeed, even as the relative quota of the US declined, the relevant articles were revised so that its veto was retained (Woods 2003: 99).

US dominance of the WTO agenda has operated likewise through the structures of the organization which, while premised on consensual decision-making, does remain extensively imbued with the political power of the US (along with other powerful trading states). The WTO thus tends to reflect a negotiating agenda particularly in line with the preferences of the USTR. The so-called 'green room' consultations convened by the Director-General among a select number of powerful countries (primarily the EU and US) have effectively served to lend a 'closed-door' character to most of the major WTO negotiations and decisions of recent years and have accordingly been the focus of many of the complaints about the exclusionary character of WTO processes. The US has also been strikingly adept at using the legal mechanisms of the WTO to influence both the agenda and the policies of other trading states, although it has itself been the subject of successful major appeals by, in particular, the EU within WTO dispute-settlement channels. Recent examples include the appeal against the quotas on steel imports imposed by the Bush administration in 2002.

The rest of the countries of the Americas occupy much weaker positions in the global politics of development. For much of the post-1945 period, the region was largely absent from many of the new multilateral forums, even from the General Agreement on Tariffs and Trade (GATT) system. While Brazil, Chile and Cuba were among the first members in 1948 and membership spread across the region in the next 50 years, the prevailing development model and nationalist ideological trends meant that trade issues lay at the heart of the 'North–South' tensions of the time (Tussie 2002: 4). The result was that Latin American and Caribbean countries were on the whole drawn more towards participation in political movements such as Third-Worldism and the New International Economic Order (NIEO), in which countries like Brazil and Mexico were especially pivotal. From the mid-1980s, however, the situation changed to one in which the region as a whole engaged in much more active participation in the multilateral system, facilitated by economic reform and the restructuring of attendant foreign policy and global strategies. The interesting facet of this increased participation has been that the influence of many of the region's countries (notably the smaller and poorer ones) has remained slight, while the profile and weight of others (notably Brazil, Mexico and several of the other larger countries) has been notably enhanced.

By 2003, all the countries of the Americas had become members of the WTO, with the exception of the Bahamas which has observer status and made application in 2001 to initiate the process for full accession. The consequence of this growing membership and engagement in the multilateral trading system was a particularly active participation in the Uruguay Round and the attainment of some real gains, such as the inclusion of agriculture, commitments on the elimination of tariffs on textiles and the establishment of more robust dispute-settlement mechanisms. These gains were eroded, however, by the unfavourable concessions required of the countries themselves on matters of special and differential treatment, intellectual property, services and subsidies, among others (Tussie 2002: 5). The first of these was of special developmental significance for the smaller and poorer countries of the region, while the others were of particular concern to some of the larger economies, particularly in the Southern Cone. Patchy implementation of commitments on market access and agricultural liberalization by the most powerful trading states led by the end of the 1990s to a widespread disillusion among poorer countries. Many Latin American and Caribbean governments were amongst those which pressed for more complete compliance with Uruguay Round commitments before they were willing to countenance new negotiations.

The loudest such noise from within the region has come from Brazil, positioned increasingly, together with India, in a leadership role among 'developing countries'. These two governments led the opposition to a new round after the failure of the WTO meeting in December 1999 in Seattle, but interestingly Argentina, Chile and Uruguay participated in the so-called 'Friends of the Round' group formed at Seattle to support its launching, even though Argentine actors were also at the forefront of a motion to veto a subsequent round in the absence of a satisfactory agreement on agriculture at the next meeting in Doha (Phillips 2004a). The growing Brazilian role in global trade politics has also been facilitated by its comparatively effective negotiating team which, in conjunction with Indian colleagues, achieved some major concessions in Doha on intellectual property and medicines. Other countries in the region have found their participation hampered by lack of technical capacity and expertise (as highlighted also in the FTAA context), as well as the exclusionary characteristics of the WTO process itself. Nevertheless, Latin American and Caribbean countries as a whole, along with Canada, have played a significant role in global trade politics primarily through their dominance of the influential 'Cairns Group' of the world's major agricultural exporters, 10 of the 17 members being drawn from the region – Argentina, Bolivia, Brazil, Canada, Chile, Colombia, Costa Rica, Guatemala, Paraguay and Uruguay. Agriculture has unquestionably been the dominant preoccupation of the countries of the Americas in the WTO negotiations, although the interests of countries such as Brazil, Mexico and Chile have also been tied closely to trade in manufactured and industrial goods, along with services and intellectual property, and those of smaller and poorer countries have focused on special and differential treatment.

In the UN system, the US is the only country of the Americas to hold a permanent seat on the Security Council, but both Mexico and Chile successfully applied for non-permanent seats (occupied for two-year terms) in 2001 and 2002 respectively. Mexican and Chilean influence in the UN was brought to bear most visibly in their opposition to the war on Iraq in 2003: indeed, it was interesting in this respect that the two Latin American countries with the closest economic (and in the Mexican case political) relationships with the US were the ones which most stridently challenged its policy and enjoyed the institutional platform from which to do so. It is not yet clear what sort of imprint will be left on intra-regional politics by the global political ramifications of the Anglo-American intervention in Iraq. Mexico's application to the UN Security Council was the centrepiece of the priority attached by the Fox administration to the enhancement of the country's international profile and engagement. This built upon important steps taken in the 1990s with this end in mind. The NAFTA was one; another was Mexico's application for membership of the OECD, agreed in mid-1994, as a result of which it joined the US and Canada as the three member countries from the Americas.

At various points over the last decade both the Argentine and Brazilian governments have expressed similar aspirations as part and parcel of their respective – and very different – reworkings of their positions in the global politics of development. Argentina, furthermore, has been a particularly salient participant in multilateral military and humanitarian efforts (such as in the first Gulf War, Bosnia and Kosovo) and was granted the status of non-member NATO ally during the 1990s. This was opposed by Brazil and Chile at the time, but then also criticized by the new Argentine government in 2000 for its 'unilateral' character. Brazilian strategies, conversely, have emphasized a leadership role not only on the global stage, as already mentioned, but also among the non-North American parts of its own region. We have already mentioned its protagonism in the South America project (for some time largely an exercise in rhetoric), but under Lula this has been taken forward on to the global stage and the President has positioned himself increasingly assertively as the regional 'spokesperson' in various global arenas – notably at the 2003 G7 summit and in the forums relating to international trade.

The arenas in which Latin American and Caribbean roles have changed little over time have been their interactions with the IFIs. Their voting shares in the IMF and the World Bank are negligible and, in this respect, the disparities between the various parts of the Americas are substantial. Moreover, given the continuing scale of debt and widespread dependence on multilateral funds from the IMF and the World Bank, the majority continue to interact with these institutions from a position of weakness, many of them directly, and negatively, affected by the aforementioned US ambivalence towards multilateral institutions that has been equally evident in the area of finance and lending. The Clinton administration was much criticized by Republican opponents for its willingness to act as a 'firefighter' – that is, to bail out economies in financial distress at considerable expense. By comparison, the Bush administration's handling of the Argentine economic crisis at the start of the 2000s was perfectly indicative of both the influence of the US over the IFIs and the progressively pronounced reticence in public opinion and in the structures of the US state to indulge in financial crisis management – particularly when the country concerned is not immediately visible on the political or security-related radar screens of US policy-makers.

Indeed, the IMF and the World Bank were widely criticized for their failure to respond adequately to the burgeoning crisis in Brazil in the late 1990s and later in Argentina, and have been widely held to have contributed to many of the contemporary development problems experienced by Latin American and Caribbean countries. While neoliberal reform might have constructed a more cooperative interaction between some governments and the IFIs in the 1990s, the conditionalities attached to loans have been ineffective in producing the anticipated growth and improvement in social conditions across the region and the so-called 'good governance' agenda has, as elsewhere, proved to be neither responsive to the institutional realities of the countries in which it has been forcefully pushed nor effective in dealing with some of the key issues of concern, such as corruption and judicial independence (Philip 1999). Questions relating to debt management, in addition, have been notably neglected by IFI strategies for the region, provisions for debt restructuring being woefully inadequate in the eventual agreement signed with Argentina in the early 2000s and few serious initiatives (bar HIPC) having emerged to deal with the developmental consequences of high levels of indebtedness.

Conclusion

The hallmark of the Americas is the sheer extent of the diversity and inequality accommodated within the region. Our discussion has highlighted the ways in which these are manifested across, and moulded by, the three levels of the contemporary politics of development. What has emerged with some force is that a serious reconsideration is required of the manner in which we conceptualize the region of the Americas and the categories we deploy in order to understand its architecture. The traditionally rigid division of the region into two parts – the US and Canada on the one hand, and 'Latin America and the Caribbean' on the other – is manifestly inadequate as a way of understanding the politics of development in the region. It has severe limitations inasmuch as it usually correlates with traditional rich–poor, strong–weak, developed–developing distinctions seen here to be both misleading and unhelpful. It has become increasingly customary to locate Mexico within a new 'North America' in the light of the restructuring of the North American political economy, which has both compelled and reflected Mexico's gradual repositioning within the regional architecture. Moreover, the patterns and substance of contemporary intra-regional and global politics in the Americas indicate that traditional North–South understandings of the Americas, reflected in definitions of the region as consisting of two distinct parts best 'cordonned off' from each other, have little remaining meaning beyond a certain acknowl-edgement of the preponderant weight of the US and the still striking dis-parities in trajectories and levels of economic activity between the US and Canada, on the one hand, and the 'Latin American and Caribbean' parts of the region, on the other.

The term 'Latin America and the Caribbean', in turn, has become both outdated and largely meaningless. Perhaps unfortunately, it remains somewhat useful as a shorthand term to connote the parts of the Americas outside the US and Canada and it has been used on occasion in this chapter largely for reasons of convenience. It is also important to note the ongoing deployment of the term in official discourse – inside and outside the region – to denote a specified group of countries. Yet, while it had both coherence and utility in the era of Third-Worldism and the NIEO, our discussion here has suggested that the way we need to think about development in the context of the contemporary architecture and politics of the Americas has rendered it anachronistic. While there may still be some cultural, social and historical validity to the conception of 'Latin America and the Caribbean', there is no longer a sufficiently coherent or cohesive political economy of the countries conventionally covered by this term to make it sensible to think of them as a single region. There is a large question mark over Mexico's inclusion in a grouping which is customarily intended to mean 'non-North America', and indeed a notion of a wider North American political economy raises similar questions about the position of Caribbean and Central American parts of the region (Payne 1998). Contemporary processes of regional-ization, and regionalist projects, have straddled and dismantled tradi-tional boundaries between the northern and southern parts of the region. At least as much divergence and inequality exists between the parts of the region traditionally classified as 'Latin America and the Caribbean' as between 'north' and 'south', and indeed we have seen that the politics of development at all three levels has produced a situation in which the weight in the global and regional arenas of the smaller and poorer economies has, if anything, diminished further, while that of certain other countries – notably Brazil, Mexico and Chile – has steadily been enhanced.

The most profitable way of proceeding is therefore to abandon traditional categories in favour of a mode of analysis which seeks to advance an integrated understanding of the Americas *as a region*, the various parts of which are best disaggregated into the five distinctive but interlocking subregions identified at the outset. A subregional approach of this sort allows us to step away from the continuing influence of outdated terminologies and frameworks and to understand better the widely disparate development strategies articulated by *all* the countries of the region in national, intra-regional and extra-regional arenas.

Further reading

Bulmer-Thomas, V. and Dunkerley, J. (1999) *The United States and Latin America: The New Agenda* (London: Institute for Latin American Studies).

Domínguez, J. I. (ed.) (2000) *The Future of Inter-American Relations* (New York: Routledge).

Foot, R., MacFarlane, N. and Mastanduno, M. (eds) (2003) *US Hegemony and International Organizations* (Oxford: Oxford University Press).

Mace, G., Bélanger, L. and contributors (1999) *The Americas in Transition: The Contours of Regionalism* (Boulder CO: Lynne Rienner).

Payne, A. and Sutton, P. (eds) (2001) *Charting Caribbean Development* (London: Macmillan–now Palgrave Macmillan).

Phillips, N. (2004) *The Southern Cone Model: The Political Economy of Regional Capitalist Development in Latin America* (London: Routledge).

Tussie, D. (2002) *Trade Negotiations in Latin America: Problems and Prospects* (London: Palgrave Macmillan).

Chapter 3

Europe

BEN ROSAMOND*

Europe is – of course – a region of the world where there exist inequalities between countries and thus relationships that might be characterized in terms of power or dependency. For want of a better phrase, the dominant model of political economy on the continent is now capitalist liberal democracy and the magnetic force exercised by the European Union in this regard can hardly be exaggerated. It is easy too to forget that this movement constitutes a drastic alteration to the organization of the continent, which for nearly half a century was characterized by a deep division between two radically different forms of socio-economic organization. Europe (in its various guises) also has relationships of various kinds with countries and regions in all other parts of the world – in Africa, the Americas, Asia and the Middle East. As suggested, the EU looms large in both dimensions. It seems that the EU has become 'the only game in town' for emerging liberal democracies within the European region, as the long list of candidate countries testifies. Indeed, the relationship between EU and non-EU Europe is a source of great discussion about the region's existing and potential political economy. Yet this discussion is rendered difficult by the fact that membership of the two categories remains unfixed. Indeed, we must not neglect issues of inequality *within* EU Europe itself. A lot of this points to the key matter of definition – what is 'Europe' and where lie its boundaries? And to what extent is Europe to be thought of as simply coterminous with the EU?

This fuzziness also applies to how we think about Europe as a global player in the politics of development, albeit in a slightly different way. The EU is constituted in various ways as an actor in the global polity and as such plays a role (often self-consciously) in both the normative and distributive politics of development. But the EU's status as a coherent and unitary actor within the global political economy is simultaneously variable, ambiguous and contested. Much of the analytical

* Research informing this chapter was funded by the Economic and Social Research Council's 'One Europe or Several?' programme (Award number L213 252 024).

59

discussion here attempts to shoe-horn the EU into conventional 'statist' notions of actorness (Knodt and Princen 2003). If the EU is an 'in-between' or an entirely novel phenomenon (perhaps even being the harbinger of a world order or mode of governance yet to come), then such a move is likely to be mistaken. At the same time, however, the global polity contains embedded 'rules of recognition' that require an entity to appear state-like in order to become a legitimate player in the international system (Jørgensen and Rosamond 2002). In other words, the reality is that both the intra-regional and extra-European politics of development are characterized by multi-level and multi-actor interactions. This picture stands at variance with the largely state-centred discourse of most development theory, both old and new. That said, the European politics of development sheds interesting light on some of the more recent attempts to conceptualize development in a globalized world. If it is the case that we are witnessing not so much the marginalization of the state, but its reorganization, then the EU can be read as part of this process. The supranationalization of its various aid policy instruments might be thought of as an organizational consequence of the reorientation of state strategies in the light of globalization.

These complexities need to be borne in mind, although this chapter concentrates quite explicitly upon the EU as a focal point for the framing of development strategies both within and beyond the region. It poses essentially two questions. The first considers the extent to which an 'EU model' of development is hegemonic within the European region. The second asks about the developmental footprint which the EU makes upon the rest of the world. With these considerations in mind, the chapter proceeds in three steps. The first section offers an overview of the national politics of development in Europe. The purpose here is to illustrate the heterogeneity of the continent and to suggest that discussions of development are entirely relevant to the post-Cold War political economy of the European region. This section further suggests that the fault lines within the European political economy are far from straightforward. This feeds into the second section, which focuses on the first question raised above. The argument here points to the existence of strong pressures for convergence on a model of development based upon EU norms. However, at the same time there is evidence of quite distinct national pathways being retained, plus some ambivalence in terms of the 'model' represented by the EU. The third section describes the role of the EU in the global politics of development. The analysis shows how this is a complex policy area and once again suggests that a singular conception of Europe's developmental footprint is misconceived.

Country development strategies in Europe

Europe (which, for present purposes, excludes Russia and those parts of the former Union of Soviet Socialist Republics (USSR) not conventionally thought to be European) consists of some 44 members of the United Nations. The region also includes a handful of quasi-states, such as the semi-autonomous UK crown dependencies of Guernsey, Jersey and the Isle of Man as well as the Danish self-governing overseas administration of the Faeroe Islands plus the rather peculiar case of the Vatican City. These entities are not considered. Each of the states under scrutiny here is constitutionally self-governing and free from occupation, with two partial exceptions. In Serbia and Montenegro (formerly the Republic of Yugoslavia) the southern province of Kosovo has been governed by a UN interim administration since June 1999. Meanwhile the island of Cyprus has been divided since the Turkish invasion of 1974. The self-declared Turkish Republic of Northern Cyprus (TRNC) has existed since 1983, but is not recognized by the United Nations (indeed only Turkey offers diplomatic recognition to the TRNC). Despite recent attempts to deliver a peace settlement to both parts of Cyprus, Nicosia remains the only divided city in Europe.

There has been considerable turbulence in the region since 1989 when the fall of the Berlin wall signalled the beginning of the end for communist rule in the central and eastern European satellite states of the former USSR. The former German Democratic Republic was incorporated into a reunified Germany in 1990. The USSR broke up into 15 independent republics in 1991, while Czechoslovakia was separated into two separate states by the so-called 'velvet divorce' of 1993. The former Yugoslavia has since the early 1990s fragmented into five states, a process accompanied by a particularly bloody civil war. The most significant regional grouping among former communist countries is the Commonwealth of Independent States (CIS), an organization created in 1991 that now seeks to facilitate the creation of a common economic space among the former constituent units of the USSR minus the Baltic Republics of Estonia, Latvia and Lithuania.

The territorial integrity of states in western Europe has remained intact during the post-1945 period. The key change in this part of the region has been the emergence of the European Union, which had its origins in the creation by six countries of the European Coal and Steel Community in 1951. The organization has undergone three successful waves of enlargement and at the time of writing comprises some 15 member-states. The EU is set to enlarge once more to include 10 Central and Eastern European countries (CEECs) along with the small

Mediterranean island states of Cyprus and Malta by 2007 (European Commission 2002). The current candidate countries (including Turkey, which will not join in the current enlargement round) constitute collectively the second largest trading partner of the EU 15 (behind the United States). In a similar vein, the EU is the leading trade partner of the candidate countries as a group (Allen 2001). Four of the western European states (Iceland, Norway, Liechtenstein and Switzerland) that – for various reasons – have not joined the European Union constitute the European Free Trade Association (EFTA) founded in 1960. Of these, only Switzerland does not participate in the European Economic Area (EEA), an agreement designed to extend the operation of the EU's single market to partner countries without binding them to the other obligations of EU membership. Indeed, more generally, as recent scholarship has shown, economic boundaries in post-Cold War Europe are rather more 'fuzzy', not least in 'micro-regions' such as Transcarpathia, an area that includes parts of Poland, Ukraine, Hungary, Slovakia and Romania (Batt 2002a and 2002b), and within the EU, where an integral part of European integration has been the growth of trans-border economic interaction (O'Dowd 2002; Van Houtum 2002).

Table 3.1 gives a general overview of the 44 European states in terms of population, per capita gross national income, net inflows of foreign direct investment and the extent to which high-technology exports form a proportion of manufactured exports. The table also describes the nature of each country's relationship with the European Union. Europe is perhaps most frequently divided into two categories in terms of economic development: so-called 'developed economies' and so-called 'transition economies'. Yet the economic inequalities across Europe are perhaps better shown in Table 3.2, which collates the World Bank's classifications of the 44 countries. While such data may in good part reproduce conventional and analytically not especially useful understandings of development, they do help to emphasize two points. First, the table makes it clear that, in terms of income and indebtedness, Europe is a very diverse region, with some very apparent inequalities. Second, it is a useful reminder of how European policy-makers might themselves conceptualize the region and its sub-divisions. While projects such as the present volume deliberately seek to transcend conventional discourses of development, it remains the case that policy actors remain largely wedded to those notions of development propagated by international institutions, both in terms of how it is conceptualized and how it is quantified and measured. Accordingly, we must be cognisant at least of the prevailing European policy discourse on development. With the above in mind, Table 3.3 again uses World Bank data to show which states are net recipients of aid. These data simply underline the point that Europe

Table 3.1 *Europe: basic data*

	Population 2001 (000s)[1]	Gross national income per capita 2001 (US$)[2]	Foreign direct investment, net inflows 2000 (US$m)[3]	High-technology exports (% of manufactured exports), 2000[4]	EU status	Euro zone
Albania	3,164	1,340	143	1	SAP	
Andorra	70	*	n.d.	n.d.		
Austria	8,132	23,940	3,008	14	M	Y
Belarus	9,970	1,290	444	4		
Belgium	10,286	23,850	12,013	10	M	Y
Bosnia-Herzegovina	4,060	1,240	0	n.d.	SAP	
Bulgaria	8,020	1,650	1,002	4 (1997)	C (2007)[a]	
Croatia	4,381	4,550	926	8	SAP	
Cyprus	761	12,320	160	2	C (2004)[a]	
Czech Republic	10,224	5,310	4,583	8	C (2004)[a]	
Denmark	5,359	30,600	34,192	21	M	
Estonia	1,364	3,870	387	30	C (2004)[a]	
Finland	5,188	23,780	9,125	27	M	Y
France	59,191	22,730[b]	43,173	24	M	Y
Georgia	5,279	590	131	n.d.		
Germany	82,333	23,560	189,178	18	M	Y
Greece	10,591	11,430	1,083	9 (1999)	M	Y
Hungary	10,187	4,830	1,692	26	C (2004)[a]	
Iceland	282	28,910	145	12	EEA	
Ireland	3,839	22,850	22,778	48	M	Y

continued overleaf

Table 3.1 Continued

	Population 2001 (000s)[1]	Gross national income per capita 2001 (US$)[2]	Foreign direct investment, net inflows 2000 (US$m)[3]	High-technology exports (% of manufactured exports), 2000[4]	EU status	Euro zone
Italy	57,948	19,390	13,175	9	M	Y
Latvia	2,359	3,300	407	4	C (2004)[a]	
Liechtenstein	30	**	n.d.	n.d.		
Lithuania	3,482	3,350	379	4	C (2004)[a]	
Luxembourg	441	39,840	n.d.	17	M	Y
FYR Macedonia	2,044	1,690	176	1 (1999)	SAP	
Malta	395	9,210	631	72	C (2004)[a]	
Moldova	4,270	400	128	3		
Monaco	30	***	n.d.	n.d.		
Netherlands	16,039	24,330	54,138	35	M	Y
Norway	4,513	35,630	5,882	17	EEA	
Poland	38,641	4,230	9,342	3	C (2004)[a]	
Portugal	10,024	10,900	6,227	5 (1999)	M	Y
Romania	22,408	1,720	1,025	6	C (2007)[a]	
San Marino	30	****	n.d.	n.d.		
Serbia-Montenegro	10,651	930	0	n.d.	SAP	
Slovak Republic	5,404	3,760	2,052	4 (1999)	C (2004)[a]	
Slovenia	1,992	9,760	176	5	C (2004)[a]	
Spain	41,117	14,300	36,023	8	M	Y

Sweden	8,894	25,400	22,125	22	M
Switzerland	7,231	38,330	17,902	19	A
Turkey	66,229	2,530	982	5	
Ukraine	49,093	720	595	n.d.	
United Kingdom	58,800	25,120	133,974	32	M
EU15 average		22,571			
Euro-zone average		21,453			
EU candidates average[†]		5,066			
Non-EU candidates average[#]		1,417			

Notes: * No comparable data available. The World Bank makes no estimate of Andorra's global ranking in terms of GNI per capita. ** No comparable data available. The World Bank estimates Liechentstein to rank 2nd globally in terms of GNI per capita. *** No comparable data available. The World Bank estimates Monaco to rank 15th globally in terms of GNI per capita. **** No comparable data available. The World Bank estimates San Marino to rank 11th globally in terms of GNI per capita. A = applicant for EU membership; C = candidate for EU membership; M = EU member-state; EEA = part of the European Economic Area; SAP = Stabilization and Association Process. [a] likely date of accession according to the European Commission (2000); [b] includes the overseas departments of French Guiana, Guadeloupe, Martinique and Reunion; † including Turkey; # excluding Andorra, Iceland, Liechtenstein, Monaco, Norway, San Marino and Switzerland; n.d. no data available.

Sources: Derived from [1] World Bank at http://www.worldbank.org/data/databytopic/POP.pdf; [2] World Bank (Atlas method of calculation) at http://www.worldbank.org; [3] World Bank at http://www.devdata.worldbank.org/data-query/; [4] World Bank at http://www.devdata.worldbank.org/data-query/

Table 3.2 Classification of European countries by the World Bank

Country	Developing	High-income[1]	Upper-middle income[1]	Lower-middle income[1]	Low-income[1]	Severely indebted[2]	Moderately indebted[2]	Less-indebted[2]
Albania	✓			✓				✓
Andorra		✓						✓
Austria		✓						✓
Belgium	✓	✓						
Belarus	✓			✓				
Bosnia-Herzegovina	✓			✓				
Bulgaria	✓			✓			✓	
Croatia	✓		✓				✓	
Cyprus	✓	✓	✓					
Czech Republic	✓	✓	✓					✓
Denmark		✓	✓				✓	
Estonia	✓	✓						
Finland		✓						
France	✓	✓						
Georgia	✓		✓		✓			✓
Germany		✓						
Greece	✓	✓	✓					
Hungary	✓	✓	✓				✓	
Iceland		✓	✓					
Ireland		✓						
Italy		✓	✓					
Latvia	✓	✓	✓					
Liechtenstein	✓	✓		✓				✓
Lithuania	✓		✓					
Luxembourg		✓						
FYR Macedonia	✓		✓					✓
Malta			✓					✓

Moldova	✓						
Monaco		✓					
Netherlands		✓					
Norway	✓	✓					
Poland	✓	✓			✓		
Portugal	✓			✓			✓
Romania	✓		✓		✓		✓
San Marino	✓		✓				
Serbia-Montenegro				✓		✓	
Slovak Republic		✓					
Slovenia		✓					
Spain		✓					
Sweden	✓	✓					
Switzerland	✓						
Turkey		✓	✓	✓	✓	✓	✓
Ukraine							
United Kingdom							

Notes: [1] A lengthy explanation of these income classifications is available at http://www.worldbank.org/data/countryclass/history.htm;
[2] '*Severely indebted* means either of the two key ratios is above critical levels: present value of debt service to GNP (80 per cent) and present value of debt service to exports (220 per cent). *Moderately indebted* means either of the two key ratios exceeds 60 per cent of, but does not reach, the critical levels. For economies that do not report detailed debt statistics to the World Bank Debtor Reporting System (DRS), present-value calculation is not possible. Instead, the following methodology is used to classify the non-DRS economies. *Severely indebted* means three of four key ratios (averaged over 1994–6) are above critical levels: debt to GNP (50 per cent); debt to exports (275 per cent); debt service to exports (30 per cent); and interest to exports (20 per cent). *Moderately indebted* means three of the four key ratios exceed 60 per cent of, but do not reach, the critical levels. All other classified low- and middle-income economies are listed as *less-indebted*. See http:// www.worldbank.org/data/archive/wdi/class.htm

Source: Derived from the World Bank at http://www.worldbank.org/data/countryclass/classgroups.htm

Table 3.3   *European recipients of aid: aid per capita (current US$)*

Country	1997	1998	1999	2000
Albania	50	77	144	93
Belarus	5	4	4	4
Bosnia-Herzegovina	236	240	278	185
Bulgaria	26	29	33	38
Croatia	9	9	11	15
Cyprus	57	46	71	72
Czech Republic	11	44	32	43
Estonia	46	65	60	47
Georgia	45	31	49	34
Hungary	18	23	24	25
Latvia	33	40	41	38
Lithuania	29	38	38	28
FYR Macedonia	49	46	137	124
Malta	58	57	65	54
Moldova	15	9	25	29
Poland	22	23	31	36
Romania	10	16	17	19
Serbia-Montenegro	9	10	60	107
Slovak Republic	13	29	59	21
Slovenia	50	21	16	31
Turkey	0	0	0	5
Ukraine	5	9	11	11

Source: Derived from http://www.worldbank.org/

is a highly diverse region. None of the countries featured in Table 3.3 is a member of the EU at the time of writing, which suggests that the pre-enlargement EU is also divided between donors and recipients of aid (of which more later).

This conventional mapping of the region into two distinct categories is, however, not the only way of looking at the national politics of development in Europe. This is perhaps better addressed by reference to the well-established comparative political economy literature on European models of capitalism. Such an approach has the decided advantage of looking beyond the arguably over-simplistic bifurcation of Europe and exploring the nature of and the interaction between the different styles of capitalism that prevail on the continent (Hall and Soskice 2001; Schmidt 2002). In general this literature pays attention to the extent of institutional variation between regimes of accumulation. Institutions are understood as historical and social phenomena that shape, *inter alia*, patterns of authority and legitimacy in political economies, styles of industrial relations, systems of government and corporate finance, structures of education and training, and norms of inter-firm relations. Such an approach brings two issues immediately to the fore. The first is a qualitative question about extant variations among established capitalist economies in Europe. By and large, this question is most frequently applied to the cases of existing EU member-states (the established Western European liberal democracies), although the transformation of former state-socialist regimes pushes us to think more seriously about pan-European similarities and differences. This leads naturally to the second question: how much does the existence of the EU represent a convergence amongst these preexisting models? Or, put differently, to what extent and degree are the 'emerging' economies within Europe seeking to forge development strategies along the lines of a singular model as prescribed by the EU?

These questions are addressed in the next section of this chapter. For now it is worth noting that scholars have long flagged the variability of capitalist models within (western) Europe, with much attention being paid to the differentiation, evolution and transformation of welfare regimes (Esping-Andersen 1990; Goodin *et al.* 1999). The debate about the sustainability of European welfare capitalism has been given added impetus by recent discussions about the extent to which the EU represents a departure from or a rescue of the 'European social model'. As an analytical category, the latter concept is no doubt fairly vacuous, but it has acquired considerable cachet of late in European Commission discourse. In this the term is used to describe the way in which EU capitalism is differentiated from the US free-market variant (for example, Diamantopolou 2000 and 2002) and seems to refer to a long-term commitment to preserve solidaristic institutions in a new globalizing knowledge economy context. In this respect it is interesting to note how (somewhat bowdlerized) 'models of capitalism' ideas have entered European policy discourse to the extent that EU policy-makers are beginning to be attentive to some of the analytical questions posed in this volume.

The political economy literature tends to trade in the exploration of variations in capitalism with reference to ideal types. Thus Hall and Soskice (2001) set up a contrast between liberal and coordinated market economies, with the UK and Germany representing the respective archetypes in Europe. Vivien Schmidt (2002) identifies three ideal typical models of capitalism within the EU: market capitalism (UK), managed capitalism (Germany, the Netherlands, Sweden) and state capitalism (France, Italy). In both studies, the emphasis is upon both the path-dependent continuity of national models in the face of external change, and the distinctive national strategies used to intercept and manage that change. This general discussion has also now been extended to analyses of the anatomy of the political economy of post-communist Europe. While there have been obvious external pressures placed upon 'transition' economies that have necessitated reconstruction along capitalist lines, some studies point to the emergence of considerable variety among the CEECs, with evident variation in indicators such as property regimes, privatization methodologies and the size of the state sector (Bandelj 2003). Others have even gone so far as to argue that a distinctive CEEC model of capitalism has been added to the repertoire of extant European varieties. Thus Stark's (1996) discussion of the Hungarian case claims that the transformation of the property-rights regime has yielded a highly distinctive pattern of inter-enterprise ownership that can only be explained with reference to the legacies of pre-transition state-socialist norms.

The intra-regional politics of development in Europe

The pull exercised by the EU on Europe writ large extends to the problem of defining the European region. This poses three principal issues that touch directly upon the politics of development in the region. The first is the question of the boundaries of Europe. In many ways this has been dissolved into a question of the ultimate geographical and cultural borders of the EU. In terms of geography, the western border of Russia is often considered as the easternmost frontier of a pan-European EU. Meanwhile, the question of Turkish membership has been a longstanding issue that raises the difficult question of European cultural and religious identity. The question of geographical and cultural boundaries is central to the definition of what constitutes the intra- and extra-European politics of development. If the potential extent of the EU is taken to be coterminous with the European inside, then it might be possible to provide a clear cut-off point for discussions of development strategies. Important here is the emergence of intersubjective understandings about the nature and extent of 'Europe' (Jönsson, Tägil and Törnqvist 2000: 13).

The second related issue is the normative significance of Europe. As Rose (1996: 1) writes, 'locating Europe on a map is a test of political values. Where we look depends upon what we are looking for.' The EU quite clearly exercises a normative influence over the character of Europe (Manners 2002). EU enlargement is premised upon the fulfillment of the so-called 'Copenhagen criteria' by potential member states.

The Copenhagen European Council of June 1993 provided a clear endorsement of the candidacy of a clutch of post-communist central and eastern European states. To this was added a set of conditions of membership: (a) the existence of stable institutions (to underwrite democracy, the rule of law, human rights and minority rights); (b) the existence of a functioning market economy and the capacity to deal with the competitive pressures associated with EU membership; (c) the ability to adopt the consolidated body of European Community law (the *acquis communautaire*); and (d) the willingness to accept the aims of political, economic and monetary union. In other words, the EU's enlargement project might be read as an attempt to spread particular economic (market economy), political (liberal democracy, rule of law, human rights) and affiliational (EU membership) norms across the continent. Beyond the immediate enlargement round that is set to occur between 2004 and 2007 (see below), a parallel strategy is evident with regard to the embryonic states of southeastern Europe (including the former Yugoslavia). For example, the Commission insists that 'the EU aims to bring the former Yugoslav Republic of Macedonia closer to EU standards and principles' (European Commission 2001: 1). The June 2000 European Council meeting in Santa Maria da Fiera (Portugal) declared that, with regard to the western Balkans, the EU was committed to 'the fullest possible integration of the countries of the region into the political and economic mainstream of Europe' (European Council 2000: 12). Arguably, this exercise of normative influence has a telling effect upon the developmental trajectory of the EU's neighbouring states. It suggests a convergent trend to a particular model of capitalism as espoused by the EU.

The third issue concerns the various subregions within Europe. The (pre-2004) 15 member states of the EU form one such subregion. Of the large high-income economies of Europe, only Norway and Switzerland remain outside of the EU. With the accession of some eight CEECs in 2004 and two more in 2007, the old Cold War category of 'Eastern Europe' (a term coterminous with the communist bloc) will cease to have real meaning when it comes to defining sub-parts of the European continent. Meanwhile, and as suggested already, the EU itself contributes to the demarcation (and thus the construction) of subregions within the broader European region. Thus the EU organizes external relations with its 'near abroad' by dividing the neighbourhood into a series of (occasionally overlapping) subregions. These are shown schematically in Table 3.4, together with an indication of stated EU policy objectives in each subregion and a note of the EU policy instruments deployed in each case.

An examination of these broad policy objectives suggests a three-pronged strategy by the EU in relation to non-EU Europe and its

Table 3.4 *External relations with the EU's 'near abroad' by subregion*

Subregion	Balkans/South-Eastern Europe	Eastern Europe (candidate states)	Eastern Europe and Central Asia	Northern dimension	Mediterranean (candidate states)
Component states	Albania Bosnia-Herzegovina Croatia FYR Macedonia Serbia and Montenegro	Bulgaria Czech Rep. Estonia Latvia Lithuania Poland Romania Slovak Rep. Slovenia	*Armenia* *Azerbaijan* Belarus Georgia *Kazakhstan* *Kyrgyzstan* Moldova *Mongolia* *Russia* *Tajikistan* *Turkmenistan* Ukraine *Uzbekistan*	Estonia Iceland Latvia Lithuania Norway *Poland* *Russia*	Cyprus Malta Turkey
EU policy objectives	Preparation of states for new forms of contractual relationship with the EU	Accession to the EU	Support for transition to market economies Building strong trading links with the EU	Increase cooperation between the EU member states, the EU applicant countries and Russia	Accession to EU

Strengthening democratic institutions Strengthening links of the region with the single European market	Foster enduring political, economic and cultural links with the EU so as to ensure peace and security	Address issues of environment, nuclear safety, energy cooperation, Kaliningrad, infrastructure, business cooperation, Justice and Home Affairs, social development.	
Policy instruments	Stabilization and Association Process Europe Agreements Enlargement negotiations	Tacis Programme (technical assistance) Partnership and Cooperation Agreements	Phare Programme Tacis Programme Interreg Programme	Barcelona Process

Note: Italicization indicates states not considered part of Europe for the purposes of this chapter.

adjacent subregions. First, there is clearly adherence to a commercial liberal argument about the benefits of closer economic interaction between the EU and neighbouring groups of states. This relates to the second element of strategy, namely, the aspiration to use 'external' policy instruments as a device for the supply of pan-European security. This is especially apparent with regard to relations with the non-candidate states of the former USSR and central Asia as well as the 'Mediterranean partners' identified by the Barcelona process. Finally, there is a clear aspiration to make the EU the central hub of (intra-European) development strategy. The EU is here 'imagined', or discursively constructed, as an entity with which other subregions have economic relations and which is itself more or less secure. Such a strategy not only has real effects in terms of the creation and deployment of policy instruments, the initiation of dialogue and the provision of resources. It also contributes to the identification of the EU as a unitary space and as a significant (perhaps even the key) actor that contributes to the developmental shaping of the region as a whole (Rosamond 2002).

This begs further questions that refer us back to the discussion of European capitalist models raised earlier in the chapter. Here the question becomes: what (if any) is the model of capitalism being spread across Europe by the EU? If the EU can be seen as an attempt to propagate a particular capitalist model within EU states, then it might follow that the EU acts as an agency for the spread of that model across the continent as a whole. Two empirical pathways appear to offer promise in pursuit of answers to this question. The first explores the hypothesis that EU membership produces a convergence among member-state political economies upon a common model of capitalist organization. The second pushes us to address the issue of whether the EU does indeed represent a singular model in its own right. The evidence would seem to suggest: (a) that strict convergence is not happening within the confines of the EU; (b) that the EU has become an arena for contestation between rival models; and (c) that national economic models operate within a complex pattern of (real or imagined) external imperatives that embrace regional (EU) as well as global pressures for adjustment.

The general expectation has been that European integration induces pressures for member-state political economies to converge upon an Anglo-American model of market capitalism characterized by the likes of marketized business relations, flexible labour markets and 'night-watchman' states. Yet Schmidt's (2002) comparative study of France, Germany and the UK in the light of globalization reveals quite distinct adjustment pathways involving differential interactions with financial markets, particular national production profiles and continuing differences in the role of the state. These, she argues, are driven by national path dependencies rather than by tangible external pressures. Further studies (for example, Hay 2000) have tended to reinforce the idea that developed European states have not converged upon an Anglo-American model of capitalism characterized by an across-the-board adherence to neoliberal policies. Other work has emphasized the distinctiveness of national discourses about the nature and implications of external imperatives (Hay and Rosamond 2002). Such work has tended to place emphasis upon national responses to globalization, but a similar pattern emerges in work that analyses national adjustment in light of the context supplied by 'Europeanization'. For example, O'Donnell's (1997) work on the Irish case describes not so much the breakdown of a national model in the 1990s, but its reformulation in light of European integration. In this analysis Ireland's remarkable economic growth during that decade was a function of a redesigned repertoire of post-corporatist macroeconomic instruments that reflected the successful strategic engagement of the Irish state with its new global and European environments. In short, what external change seems to supply is less pressures for convergence and more an altered set of opportunity structures within which national models adapt.

A more nuanced reading might be that the EU is seen as an arena for struggles between alternative models of capitalist organization. At the level of discourse it is very clear that there is considerable ambivalence in this question. For example, Commission discourse on the relationship between globalization and European integration reveals quite distinctive narratives about what the EU represents. To simplify, there is a clear contrast between neoliberal narratives and 'European social model' narratives about the EU-globalization interface. In the former, economic globalization is conceived as an unequivocal normative good and the EU as a vehicle for both (a) the supply of 'sound' policies to member-state economies and (b) the bolstering of global institutions. In contrast, the 'European social model' discourse emphasizes that the EU exists to protect Europe's distinctive solidaristic and managed model of capitalism from the onslaught of global market forces. This discourse also has an external dimension, with the EU conceived as a force for pushing the 'social dimension' of globalization through the development of international labour standards, corporate social responsibility and so on (Rosamond 2004).

The existence of rival narratives about the nature and purposes of the European integration project reflects the complex institutionalization of the EU, which, in turn, creates the space for multiple subject positions to become embedded. It also echoes analytical confusion about the function of the EU: whether it exists to facilitate or capture the effects of globalization. For the purposes of this section the key question is whether a definitive EU development strategy (for Europe) is discernible. The broad Copenhagen criteria described above outline a general commitment to a functioning market economy emanating from the EU. The Maastricht Treaty on European Union (1992) specified a set of 'convergence criteria' for admission to economic and monetary union (EMU). These stipulated performance targets for government deficits, inflation, exchange-rate fluctuation and long-term interest rates and were reinforced by the Stability and Growth Pact. The latter was, in effect, an agreement designed to underwrite and give substance to the neoliberal economic orthodoxy at the heart of the EMU project. One noticeable consequence of the instigation of this 'stability culture' (Underhill 2002) was the pursuit of the convergence targets by member states, even those such as the UK that had negotiated an opt-out from the formal timetable for monetary union laid down at Maastricht (Rosamond 2003). The convergence criteria and the Stability and Growth Pact appeared to compromise the macroeconomic autonomy of both member and candidate states. Governments facing economic problems could, in theory at least, use fiscal policy instruments to raise finances, but the electoral consequences of raising taxation effectively ruled out such strategies.

The former communist states of central and eastern Europe have been required to subscribe to the norms of the EU's stability culture if they wish realistically to aspire to membership. But the 'transition' process has also been overseen by international institutions such as the IMF. Indeed, it ought to be remembered that the pattern of capitalist reconstruction in this area has been guided principally by IMF conditionalities (Weber 2001: 276). For many observers the EU's role in guiding European 'transition economies' through the shift from communism to neoliberal orthodoxy was largely secondary. That said, the 'Europe Agreements' signed in 1991 by Poland, Hungary and (what was then) Czechoslovakia required the 'transition economies' to produce competition regimes and trade policies that would be compatible with future EU membership (Sedelmeier and Wallace 2000). One interpretation would be that these embryonic EU conditionalities simply dovetailed with the development trajectory prescribed by global institutions (Campbell 2001: 114). However, this would seem to be a simplistic judgement. Global institutions (notably the IMF and the World Bank) have tended to burrow much deeper into the structure of the domestic political economies of the transition states. The EU's export of a stability culture may have implications for, say, domestic welfare expenditure, but there is nothing to compare with the seemingly harsh judgements on such matters supplied by the global institutions. For example, Therborn cites World Bank strictures from the mid-1990s that recommend the dismantling of

Hungary's embryonic and relatively generous (even by OECD standards) pension and welfare system (Therborn 2001: 243). This broadly neoliberal view of transition has been used as a template by global institutions and credit-rating agencies in their evaluation of diverse CEECs. The basic model imagines 'sound' transition as a scenario where 'tight monetary policy, restricted fiscal policy and export-led growth necessitate low social security expenditures and privileging price control beyond wage growth' (Bandelj 2003: 10). What is revealing is that the World Bank chooses to portray its intervention in candidate countries as helping to deliver the conditions for the adoption of the EU's *acquis communautaire*, along with assistance in areas such as 'education, health, social services and pension reform which form essential elements of EU candidate countries' comprehensive efforts at poverty reduction' (World Bank Group n.d.).

Even so, within the CEECs, there seems to have been substantial room for manoeuvre for national policy-makers to retain a measure of autonomy in their developmental pathways. Thus Campbell's (2001) study of the development of fiscal policy in the CEECs finds common global (IMF) and European (EU) impulses for neoliberal convergence in national taxation regimes in the Czech Republic, Hungary and Poland. Yet, echoing studies of western Europe cited above, he also finds institutional mediation and refraction in each national case that has yielded significant divergences in the conduct of fiscal policy. Booth's (2002) study of the implementation of various training programmes organized by the European Commission and the British Council in Poland similarly finds evidence of the 'stickiness' of communist administrative norms that has had a significant mediating effect upon the ways in which officials interpret and understand the operation and functioning of a civil service within a capitalist liberal democracy. This suggests that the capacities of the CEECs to engage in the autonomous construction of a political economy is constrained and shaped by external forces (including the EU), but it also indicates that the exact convergence upon a neoliberal model is far from evident, thanks largely to the ways in which institutional refraction and cultural mediation remain important determinants of the precise outcomes of the transition process. The adoption of neoliberal reforms in the CEECs is further explained by Bockman and Eyal (2002) whose study points to evidence of longstanding dialogic networks involving western and eastern European economists that assisted the diffusion of neoliberal economic knowledge in the region.

This discussion of the EU's handling of the CEECs should not deflect attention away from the intra-EU politics of development. In part, this can be explored through a discussion of the convergence pressures that have accompanied the creation of the euro-zone. A substantial portion of the EU's budget is geared towards so-called 'cohesion' policy. The redistribution of resources to poorer areas of the EU has been an integral part of the integration project since the 1957 Treaty of Rome. Indeed, the creation of the Common Agricultural Policy (CAP) is often read as a side payment designed to secure the allegiance of rural communities to economic integration. The Guidance Section of the European Agricultural Guidance and Guarantee Fund (EAGGF) forms part of the EU's structural funds, together with instruments such as the European Social Fund (ESF) and the European Regional Development Fund (ERDF). As Allen (2000: 244) shows, the various structural funds have grown dramatically in importance – from less than 5 per cent of the Community budget in 1975 to a projected 39 per cent by 2006. This increase is explained in part by the appearance of a formal treaty commitment to 'cohesion' in the Single European Act (1986), which gave the Communities a formal competence in the area of internal development.

The stated aims of EU cohesion policy reveal a concern to supply infrastructural resources to 'regions whose development is lagging behind' (European Commission 2000b: 2), which means in turn that 'not all Europeans have the same advantages and chances of success when faced with the challenges of globalisation' (European Commission 2000b: 3). According to the European Commission, this definition applies to some 50 regions within the EU that together account for some 22 per cent of the EU's total population (European Commission 2000b). In addition, structural funding is designated for the 'revitalization' of areas facing high structural unemployment and for the 'modernization' of training and employment promotion instruments. A special 'cohesion fund' targeted at the four least prosperous member states (Greece, Ireland, Spain and Portugal) has existed since 1993.

Structural funding and cohesion policy is often thought of in terms of side-payments and transfers from the prosperous to the least prosperous member states in the context of inter-governmental bargains. In this interpretation EU regional development funding becomes a 'second-order' policy instigated to facilitate the process of (neoliberal) market deepening that follows from the preferences of the dominant member states. Reforms to 'cohesion' policy might appear to have strengthened the redistributive capacity of the EU. However, this inter-governmentalist interpretation suggests that the wealthier member states have simply ensured that rigorous tracing mechanisms are in place to confirm that their net transfers are being used in a 'value for money' way (Pollack 1995). This view dovetails with assessments of EU regional policy that question the developmental value of these internal transfer mechanisms (Scott 1995; de Rynck and McAleavy 2001).

The counter-argument about cohesion policy has two strands. In the first, the inter-governmentalist thesis is challenged by Borràs and Johansen (2001) who argue that the existence of cohesion policy reflects a genuine contest between models of political economy within the EU. Here the very existence of structural funding instruments is indicative of redistributive impulses that counter some of the main neoliberal tendencies within the EU polity. The second strand identifies the altered opportunity structures that have emerged as a result of the deepening of cohesion policy competence. Most attention has been paid to the mobilization of sub-national activism within member states, which in turn is often taken to be one of the most obvious manifestations of 'multi-level governance' (MLG) within the EU (Marks 1993; Smith 1998; Hooghe and Marks 2001). The literature on MLG describes a multi-tiered, multi-actor political economy of redistribution within the EU which undoubtedly takes us somewhat beyond the image of development politics as a matter of *national* development strategies. Indeed, various Commission initiatives seem to be deliberately designed to bring about the loosening of national-territorial control of the development process. For example, the Interreg programmes (funded through the ERDF) are explicitly designed to instigate 'cross-border, transnational and interregional co-operation, i.e. the creation of partnerships across borders to encourage the balanced development of multi-regional areas' (European Commission 2000b). This process is being expanded under the third phase of Interreg to facilitate the integration of the candidate countries.

The extra-regional politics of development in Europe

Following the 2004–07 enlargement the EU will account for approximately one-fifth of total world trade. In addition, the European Commission estimates that the enlarged EU will account for around half of global outward foreign direct investment. Meanwhile, if the EU is thought of as a unitary entity, then it becomes the single largest source of official development assistance (ODA) in the world, contributing more than 50 per cent of global ODA. Some 22 per cent of this is managed at the EU level (Richelle 2003). These bald facts alone suggest that the EU is an important presence in the global politics of development. Yet we need also to consider the extent to which the EU represents an attempt to export a particular model of capitalism/development beyond its immediate environs. To that end, it is worth focusing on three facets of the EU's presence in the present world order: its participation in global institutions and international negotiations, its normative capacities and its status as an exemplar for the governance of globalization.

First, the EU's status as a customs union ensures that the member states constitute themselves as a unitary actor within the WTO, with the Commission acting as chief negotiator. A complex inter-governmental commercial policy process sits beneath this collective presence (Woolcock 2000). While cooperation among member states in trade matters is far from assured, Young (2002) finds an institutionalized propensity to cooperate in pursuit of common positions among member governments, particularly where the EU is participating within the WTO framework. Other trade-related issues, such as the ill-fated Multilateral Agreement on Investment (MAI), which took place under the auspices of the OECD, reveal a much-reduced likelihood of EU member states engaging in cooperative behaviour. Such cases reveal the continued existence of liberal (e.g. the UK) and protectionist (e.g. France) preferences among European governments (Young 2002: 85–108). This bifurcation of elite opinion impacts on EU policy. Official EU rhetoric routinely extols orthodox arguments about the virtues of liberalized free trade and the value of the global multilateral system (European Commission 2003). Indeed, some have argued that the EU acts as the most consistent advocate of multilateralism, especially given the tendency of the US to defend multilateralism only when domestic expediency allows (Woolcock 2000: 375). On the other hand, there is widespread criticism that the CAP continues seriously to disadvantage producers from Africa, Asia and Latin America and the Caribbean (*Guardian* 19 February 2003), while 'anti-globalization' movements maintain that the EU's actions within the WTO simply favour powerful transnational companies (Manet 2001).

As indicated, then, the EU's deliberate presence is easiest to discern within the global trade regime. At the same time it has been noted that it has not been able to assert itself meaningfully – as the EU – in discussions about the post-Asian crisis financial architecture. This stems in part from the continued dominance of the IMF in the global financial regime and the excessive leverage therein of the G7 countries (of which, of course, four members – France, Germany, Italy and the UK – are European) (Gavin 2003). On the other hand, echoing points raised earlier and again in the third point below, Gavin (2003: 3) argues that:

> The EU offers an alternative to the rapid-fire liberalisation model of the IMF. The EU has now pioneered a successful model of regional monetary integration to follow regional trade integration…A common regional currency offers an alternative to the existing set of regimes – all of which have led to currency misalignment and currency crises.

Second, recent work has begun to assess the normative influence of the EU in the post-Cold War world. The pioneering work of Manners (2002) has assessed in detail the ways in which the EU has constituted itself as an agent seeking to shape conceptions of 'the normal' in world politics. The norms that Manners identifies are all integral to the project of the EU in that they follow from either the conditions of its foundation in post-1945 Europe or aspects of its subsequent evolution. These include notions of liberty and democracy, respect for human rights and fundamental freedoms, the rule of law, social solidarity, anti-discrimination and sustainable development. The fact that these norms are integral to the internal development of the EU means that they spill over as guiding principles of EU external action.

Within this broad argument Manners has paid particular attention to the ways in which the EU has come to argue strongly – often in quite extraordinary ways – for the spread of universal conceptions of human rights. Perhaps the most striking case has been the campaign, sponsored by successive national presidencies of the Council of Ministers, for the international abolition of the death penalty. This has involved consistent pressuring of the US government regarding its continued endorsement of judicial executions within its borders. The increasing visibility of such ideational instruments of soft diplomacy adds nuance to long-established discussions of the presence of 'Europe' in the international arena. Often this has been portrayed in terms of the EU's relative strength as a 'civilian power', perceived as standing in marked contrast to its manifest weakness as a 'military power' (Whitman 2002). The general point is that the influence of 'Europe' upon the global political economy needs to be rethought in post-Westphalian terms. The existence of deep integration among European states has had the effect of constituting 'Europe' as an actor in global development, but its power operates in ways that conventional state-centric conceptions of world order have difficulty assimilating. While it acquires a unitary presence in some aspects of foreign economic policy (notably commercial policy), perhaps its most significant impacts are less the consequence of deliberate interventions as the product of external spillovers from the creation of an integrated market space among the member states.

The third important element in the EU's role in the global politics of development is the idea that the European region offers a general model for economic governance in globalizing times. A central theme in Commission discourse since 1999, when Romano Prodi became president of the Commission, has been the idea that the 'EU model' represents an exemplar for the rest of the world:

Our European model of integration is the most developed in the world. Imperfect though it still is, it nevertheless works on a continental scale. Given the necessary institutional reforms, it should continue to work well after enlargement, and I believe we can make a convincing case that it would also work globally (Prodi 2000: 4).

This notion of the viability of the EU as a model of post-national governance has much to do with the familiar ways in which the Commission's discourse seeks to justify and legitimize the continued Europeanization of governance capacity (Rosamond 2004). However, there is some (global) policy substance to such rhetoric. It has less to do with the idea that other regional organizations might emulate the particular institutional configuration of the EU – a notion that has long dissipated in analytical and policy discussions of comparative regionalism (Breslin, Higgott and Rosamond 2002). Rather, the EU represents a model of internationalization and transnational governance for a world where international economic interaction has gone far beyond the traditional agenda of trade in goods and the application or removal of tariffs. The ways in which the WTO agenda has altered over the past decade has persuaded some analysts that the EU offers a kind of 'off-the-shelf' demonstration of how the governance of 'deep internationalization' might be achieved (Laffan, O'Donnell and Smith 2000: 208). So, rather than focusing on either the classical 'Monnet method' of partnership between authoritative supranational and inter-governmental institutions or the substance of EU policy, this approach considers the methodologies of economic governance that the EU has spawned. As Helen Wallace (2000) has noted, these include: (a) a style of regulatory governance premised on neoliberal conceptions of the removal of restraints of the free movement of factors of production; (b) a post-national, multi-level politics of redistribution found in areas such as cohesion policy; (c) the extensive use of benchmarking methods to develop conceptions of 'best practice'; and (d) the deep 'transgovernmental' inter-penetration of member-state executives to facilitate positive sum bargains in areas of high politics such as security and monetary policy (Jørgensen and Rosamond 2002). The common element to these policy methodologies found in the laboratory of the EU is the compromise of autonomous member-state jurisdiction in the area of economic governance. But, in a context where national capacities to manage domestic political economies are widely thought to be under threat from emergent forms of transnational market power, the variety of European governance styles may be read as devices through which public authority might be reconfigured to take account of the challenges of globalization.

What is more, all of this can be said before we return to the most obvious, practical demonstration of the EU's involvement in the support of other countries' development strategies, which is its contribution to

Table 3.5 *European Union and EU official aid and official development assistance, 2000–01*

	Net ODA (US$m)		Net ODA as a % of gross national income		Net official aid (US$m)	
	2000	2001	2000	2001	2000	2001
Austria	423	533	0.23	0.29	187	212
Belgium	820	867	0.36	0.37	74	88
Denmark	1,664	1,634	1.06	1.03	189	181
Finland	371	389	0.31	0.32	58	61
France	4,105	4,198	0.32	0.32	1,657	1,334
Germany	5,030	4,990	0.27	0.27	647	687
Greece	226	202	0.20	0.17	12	9
Ireland	235	287	0.30	0.33	0	0.16
Italy	1,376	1,627	0.13	0.15	406	281
Luxembourg	123	141	0.71	0.82	7	9
Netherlands	3,135	3,172	0.84	0.82	206	214
Portugal	271	268	0.26	0.25	27	28
Spain	1,195	1,737	0.22	0.30	12	14
Sweden	1,799	1,666	0.80	0.81	122	119
United Kingdom	4,501	4,579	0.32	0.32	439	461
European Union	4,912	5,961	–	–	2,808	2,689

Source: Adapted from data at http://www.oecd.org/

global ODA. The data assembled in Table 3.5 show not only that the EU is an important presence in aid provision as a collective actor, but that individual European states also still remain significant participants in bilateral aid processes. In fact, the figures reveal distinctive national priorities in terms of where aid is directed. This is – more often than not – a function of each state's individual 'colonial footprint'. Thus, of the top ten recipients of gross ODA and official assistance from the UK in 2001, nine were Commonwealth member states (the tenth is China). The top two destinations of French ODA were French Polynesia and New Caledonia, while Spanish ODA was heavily targeted at Spanish-speaking Latin American countries (OECD 2002).

Four specific points are worthy of note in relation to these figures. First, while national strategies clearly remain important in the global politics of development, there have been concerted attempts at the EU level to coordinate the levels of development assistance sourced from the member states. Member states have agreed in principle that a minimum of 0.39 per cent of gross national income should be committed to ODA by 2006 (Richelle 2003). The current member-state average is 0.44 per cent of GNI (calculated from Table 3.5 above). This commitment to the achievement of a coordinated budgetary contribution has been in place formally since the Maastricht Treaty on European Union and has since been factored into the negotiations with the accession countries. However, the coordination of member and candidate state policy making is about rather more than setting norms for levels of ODA. Each European country has a distinctive aid policy process. For example, not all EU member states possess a national ministry of development such as the UK's Department for International Development (DfID). In many domestic polities, aid falls within the remit of the foreign affairs ministry, while the complexity is somewhat exacerbated by the fact that a number of the candidate countries do not have a tradition of aid policy competence at all. Moreover, national policy communities in this area remain quite distinct in terms of both consultation procedures and bodies and involved NGO communities.

Second, this overview throws up the inevitable question of the extent to which the EU is an appropriate policy actor in relation to ODA provision. Holland (2002b: 6) places this issue in the context of internal EU debates about 'subsidiarity':

> The onus is on the EU to demonstrate that the EU is better at conducting and delivering development policy to the Developing World than are the member states. If this cannot be demonstrated a renationalisation of development policy could emerge ... The challenge, then, is to what extent can the EU demonstrate both a *distinct* development role for itself as well as a *superior* one to that of member-states? (Emphasis in the original)

Holland notes that there is little in the way of an agreed formula to demarcate national and EU competences in the area of aid and overseas assistance. Others have thought about this question less as an issue of 'subsidiarity' and more as a problem of complementarity and coordination (Box and Goodison 1994), an issue that evidently preoccupies policy-makers within the EU institutions (European Commission 2000a). Thus, if EU aid policy instruments are to coexist alongside national ones, then a degree of convergence would seem to be in order. Alternatively, the EU might be seen as an agency for the disbursement of aid to *particular* parts of the world. OECD data does in fact indicate that EU-level ODA priorities seem to be targeted most at the EU's 'near abroad', as discussed in the previous section. While between a quarter and a third of EU ODA is targeted at Sub-Saharan Africa and, more generally, at what the World Bank defines as the Least Developed Countries, the largest group of recipients is classified (again by the Bank) as low–middle income countries. The top ten recipients of gross ODA and official assistance from the EU are states falling into the 'near abroad' categories portrayed in Table 3.4 (above) (OECD 2002).

Third, and notwithstanding these last two points, EU-level aid policy can be read as a derivative of the political interests of the member states. For example, Stevens (2000) describes the Yaoundé and Lomé Conventions – the pillars of pre-1989 European Community aid and trade policy – as 'descendants' of the European colonial period. He meant that the primary geographical targets of the European Community's evolving policy were those regions of the world most affected by the history of member-state colonialism. Post-colonial economic relations had seen the establishment of particular trading patterns between the ex-colonies and the former imperial powers of Europe. In particular, states in the Caribbean and Sub-Saharan Africa had discovered receptive and stable markets for the export of (sometimes otherwise unprofitable) primary products, while the pattern of manufacturing exports from European countries reflected colonial legacies. The two Yaoundé Conventions that operated between 1964 and 1975 were based upon (qualified) preferential trading arrangements between the Community member states and 18 Associated African States and Madagascar (AASM). The conventions largely waived the application of the Community's common external tariff for industrial exports from AASM states. However, preferential access to Community markets was rather more limited when it came to agricultural products. The system of internal Community preferences gathered together in the CAP ensured that member states were neither willing nor able to extend the Yaoundé regime meaningfully into the domain of primary production. The four Lomé Conventions (1975–99) emerged largely as a consequence of the UK's accession to the European Communities. Lomé extended the qualified free trade and aid regime to the UK's numerous Commonwealth associates and also built in a number of compensations for African, Caribbean and Pacific (ACP) states in instances where the CAP was held to penalize export income in primary goods. That the Lomé regime was a path-dependent outcome of European colonial history was given credence by the criticism that this main plank of supranational European policy simply helped to reproduce and modernize relations of dependency within the world economy (Holland 2003). It is also clear that the particular form of integration chosen by European states from the 1950s onwards influenced the ways in which they engaged in collective interaction with their former colonial associates.

The Lomé system of preferences came to an end for a variety of reasons, not least of which was the glaring incompatibility between the regime and WTO rules (Stevens 2000). Meanwhile, the end of the Cold War created imperatives for a re-focusing of the EU's aid-giving strategies to its 'near abroad', while external trade data reveal a steep decline in the significance of ACP trade for the EU compared to emerging markets elsewhere (Stevens 2000: 405). Indeed, formal EU aid to ACP states (financed through the European Development Fund) fell from 67 per cent of the total between 1986 and 1990 to 29 per cent during 1996–98 (Petiteville 2003: 129). The new Cotonou Agreement of 2000 projects the abolition of ACP trade advantages by 2020. In their place, the agreement envisages the progressive creation of free trade areas between the EU and various regional sub-groups of ACP countries (Holland 2003). While such an arrangement clearly brings the EU's relationship with ACP countries into line with existing WTO rules, the new regime has been criticized as an attempt on the part of the EU to sabotage the recent efforts of African states to develop continent-wide economic integration (Hormeku n.d.).

Fourth, while the EU possesses a so-called 'development policy' managed by a particular Directorate General of the European Commission (DG Development – formerly DG VIII), most observers agree that it is not an isolated policy domain. Indeed, DG Development conceptualizes its strategy as part of a policy triangle that also includes trade and the Common Foreign and Security Policy (CFSP) (Richelle 2003), while the formal organization of the EU policy process places DG Development as part of a Commission triumvirate that also includes DG External Relations and DG Trade. In addition, the European Commission Humanitarian Aid Office (ECHO) exists to 'provide emergency assistance and relief to the victims of natural disasters or armed conflict outside the European Union' (http://europa.eu.int/comm/echo/presentation/mandate_en.htm). Despite the existence of a complex 'development policy' apparatus within the Commission, key decisions in this domain remain the responsibility of the member states and are made through inter-governmental negotiation in the Council of Ministers. Here recent reorganization has confirmed the connections between aid and foreign and security policy. There have been moves to abolish the (inter-governmental) Development Council with the issues it has hitherto handled tending to fall increasingly within the purview of the General Affairs Council, whose remit includes external political relations.

The overall relationship between aid policy and the other external instruments is made clear by Holland (2002a, 2002b, 2003) in his various studies of the interaction between the EU and the 'Third World' (his phrase). For example, the traditional style of relations between the EU and ACP states has been re-calibrated to take account of the growing interest of the WTO in preferential trade agreements (Stevens 2000): hence the replacement of the Lomé Conventions with the Cotonou Agreement. Holland also notes that the main CFSP policy instruments – 'common positions' and 'joint actions' – have been used in ways indicating that 'developing countries have become the EU's major foreign policy focus outside of the Balkans and Eastern Europe' (Holland 2002b: 4). In sum, perhaps the best way to capture the current place of ODA in the EU's external agenda is to think of it in terms of the rather patchy and uneven foreign economic policy that has emerged in light of the new security and trade environments that characterize the post-Cold War world (Young 2002). The EU regime has evolved within the context of changing global rules on the conduct of trade and in the light of shifting, perceived security challenges.

Conclusion

This chapter has focused on the EU, but this is not necessarily intended to suggest that national actions in the area of development have diminished in significance in Europe. Indeed, there is considerable ambivalence in the EU's development strategy and part of the explanation for this resides in the continued importance of distinct national perspectives on development amongst the member states. Contests over the merits of different national models of political economy themselves offer ample evidence of this.

This ambivalence is also clearly apparent in terms of the EU's role in the intra-European politics of development. The enlargement process is suggestive of the emergence of a common European neoliberal model centred on the disciplines necessary to achieve monetary union and – to a lesser extent – the adoption of the *acquis communautaire*. At the same time, there are clearly attempts to assert 'core' European values of democracy and human rights promotion in the European region. There is certainly much evidence within the EU and its candidate countries to counter the notion that national, sub-national and even supranational development strategies are converging upon a simplistic neoliberal model. Even if this can be described as a model of liberalization, it represents, at the very least, an alternative notion of liberalization to that propagated by the global institutions. Within the EU institutions, there are identifiable struggles over the place of redistributive politics and the role of social protection as a central pillar of the way in which Europeans are to engage with globalization.

The distinction between intra- and extra-European development strategies has become increasingly blurred for the reasons described above. Global systems of rules, such as those supplied by the WTO, have induced modifications to the ways in which EU member states have interacted with the poorer countries of the world. But once again this does not necessarily signify the straightforward triumph of a singular model of political economy. Rather, the expanding external role of the EU, which has come, in good part, to be expressed through the various instruments of 'soft diplomacy', identifies the EU as a distinctive – if often contradictory – normative presence in the new global political economy.

Further reading

Holland, M. (2002) *The European Union and the Third World* (London: Palgrave).

Rosamond, B. (2004) *Globalization and the European Union* (London: Palgrave).

Schmidt, V. A. (2002) *The Futures of European Capitalism* (Oxford: Oxford University Press).

Wallace, H. and Wallace, W. (eds) (2000) *Policy-Making in the European Union*, 4th edn (Oxford: Oxford University Press).

Young, A. R. (2002) *Extending European Cooperation: The European Union and the 'New' International Trade Agenda* (Manchester: Manchester University Press).

Chapter 4

Northeast Asia

SHAUN BRESLIN

Identifying what we mean by the Northeast Asian region is not as easy as it sounds. An assessment based on cartography would lead to the inclusion of at least parts of Russia and all of Mongolia. But, notwithstanding the growing economic linkages between the Russian far east and northeast China (Kerr 1996), economic analyses tend to exclude Russia and the study of Mongolia's political economy remains largely confined to domestic issues (Bruun and Odgaard 1997). In economic terms, the notion of region would suggest a wider definition that moved southwards to include the member states of the Association of Southeast Asian Nations to constitute a wider definition of 'East Asia' (or ASEAN + 3). Yet, when strategic considerations are brought to the fore, it is impossible to consider the region without including and focusing on the most powerful relevant actor – which is the United States, an extra-regional state.

Taking all this into account, Northeast Asia is best defined as encompassing the People's Republic of China (PRC) (including what are now described as the two Special Administrative Regions of Hong Kong and Macao), the Republic of China (ROC) (more commonly now referred to simply as Taiwan), North and South Korea, and Japan. This region (with the occasional inclusion of what became Vietnam) corresponds to the 'sinitic' zone in the traditional Chinese world order which predated the statist era. This zone was considered by the Chinese to encompass those neighbouring territories which had similar cultures to China and accepted Chinese supremacy through formal tribute relations. However, this is not to suggest that the contemporary region should be conceived as a culturally homogeneous one – far from it. Even during the 'sinitic' era, the concept of Confucianism as philosophy and guide to political action took various forms in China and Japan and, in general, the course of history can be said to have defined the region more by division than by union.

Country development strategies in Northeast Asia

For this reason, if for no other, it is impossible to consider the national politics of development in Northeast Asia without considering the historical geopolitical context. It is a region where mutual suspicion and downright hostility continue to impact on national strategies and bilateral relations. Not least amongst these issues are the contemporary political implications of Japanese colonialism in the first half of the twentieth century. In China and Korea, there remains deep hostility towards Japan for war crimes – something which is not just historical resentment but is often manifest in hostility towards the contemporary Japanese state. As Rose (1998) notes, while issues of history are not usually the cause of serious bilateral disputes, they are nevertheless utilized by governments as a tool for legitimating action in disputes that emerge for other reasons.

There are also a host of new rivalries. Rising nationalism in China and Japan, although partly built on historical considerations, is also a consequence of each state's current self-image and ambitions. Both see themselves as great powers which have overcome adversity and economic collapse in the twentieth century to re-emerge as major powers on the regional and global scene. Moreover, in the view of Austin and Harris (2001), both want to increase their power further (albeit in different ways) in the present century. Both countries are keen to ensure that the other does not dominate the region, to the point where studies of international relations within Northeast Asia sometimes look like a game of 'spot the hegemon' (and the policies of individual states a process of 'stop the hegemon'). In this environment, the rise of popular nationalism in each state is in large part inspired by fears of the implications of the rise of nationalism in the other (Rose 2000).

The region is also politically divided. The demilitarized zone in Korea is manifestation of the continued division of the peninsular and remains the major focus of regional policy in both Seoul and Pyongyang. In addition, more than half a century after the end of the Chinese civil war, the PRC still claims sovereignty over Taiwan, and not only refuses to recognize the Republic of China as a legitimate entity, but also insists that other states do not do so either. The PRC allows Taiwan to participate in economic forums that are not based on statehood. Thus Taiwan can join the WTO as a customs union, but is debarred from participating in political organizations such as the United Nations (UN). Accordingly, the WTO currently has four Chinese entities as members – the PRC (joined 2001), Hong Kong (1986), Macao (1991) and the rather inelegantly titled Separate Customs Territory of Taiwan, Penghu, Kinmen and Matsu (2002) – while the UN only has one. As such, Beijing's claim to be the sole legitimate government of all China, notwithstanding the evolution of a democratic regime in Taiwan, makes it impossible to establish a regional *political* dialogue to deal with security and development issues.

At first sight, these divisions appear to be residual hangovers of the Cold War and, on one level, they clearly are. But in many respects they also derive from the pre-Cold War phenomenon of incomplete state building in the region. The rapid collapse of Japanese colonial rule after the US dropped atomic bombs on Hiroshima and Nagasaki in 1945 created a vacuum in which competing groups sought to set up new national entities. In both China and Korea the process of building genuine and comprehensive national entities has not (yet) been finished, with the division of the Korean peninsular and the Korean War resulting in the inclusion of Taiwan within the US strategic defence perimeter, thereby also effectively ensuring the continued existence of the ROC. In short, incomplete decolonization both led to, and was reinforced by, the emergence of Cold War hostilities in Northeast Asia and provides one of the reasons for the continuation of political divisions after the Cold War has been concluded.

The Cold War era itself provides much of the basis for the contemporary context of uneven national development in the region. In China and North Korea the combination of a policy of isolation by the US-led capitalist world and self-imposed rejection of engagement with the capitalists (Zhang 1998) resulted in the pursuit of largely autarkic development strategies. Both states initially adopted and then adapted a Soviet model of development and international contacts were confined in the main to the socialist bloc. From a contemporary perspective, and in light of the collapse of communist rule in the Soviet Union and eastern Europe, it is easy to forget how successful this model proved to be in reinvigorating economies that had been ravaged by decline, colonization and war. In fact, in the 1950s and 1960s, it was North Korea that was one of the fastest growing economies in the world and South Korea that was relatively poor. Nevertheless, whilst this strategy proved highly successful in building new heavy industrial bases, the relative economic fortunes of China and North Korea began to decline once reconstruction was complete and over time both states became ever more inward-looking.

Although the non-communist states of the region began to outperform China and North Korea from the 1960s and 1970s onwards, this did not reflect a stark communist versus capitalist or state-planned versus free market dichotomy. Japan, South Korea and Taiwan all deployed considerable elements of planning and guidance in generating their economic 'miracles', as well as defending domestic producers with considerable barriers to trade. Indeed, there were a number of 'socialist' elements within the industrial strategy of these 'capitalist developmental states' (Johnson 1982 and 1987; Leftwich 1995; Deans 2000) – not only heavy state involvement in planning and guidance, but also state ownership of enterprises and the financial sector (Amsden 1989; Haggard 1990; Chowdhury and Islam 1993; Cotton 1994; Evans 1995; Wade 1990). For Johnson (1987: 152) this mix of plan and market – what we might call market-conforming guidance planning – was facilitated by the 'relative state autonomy' of elite bureaucrats. By this, Johnson meant that economic development strategy was not influenced by pressure for specific policies from interest groups outside the business–government–bureaucracy triangle. Even though there was a competitive electoral system in Japan, this impacted mainly on the geographic distribution of rewards, rather than challenging the overall direction of national economic policy *per se* – in effect, 'politicians reign[ed] but bureaucrats rule[d]' (Zysman 1983). In Japan developmental authority lay in the hands of MITI – the Ministry of International Trade and Industry. By inviting key business elites to participate in industrial planning through MITI's industrial bureaux, developmental strategies were designed in conjunction with business interests, and then supported by state investment under the banner of restoring Japan to its rightful position in the world.

In Korea Japanese occupation resulted in the formation of weak societal and interest groups, many of which were tainted because of perceived collaboration with the Japanese. In order to fill the political vacuum, the US supported the claims of Syngman Rhee, who became the president of South Korea in 1948. Rhee was the self-professed representative of the Korean right who had been previously acted for a short period as leader of the exiled Korean Provisional Government in Washington. A committed anti-communist, he mobilized the country against the threat of communism from the north and used the political climate he had created to suppress opposition. Although Korea flirted with democratization on a number of occasions, military coups (in 1961 and 1980) and the election of the General Noh Tae-woo meant that it was not until the election of Kim Young-sam in 1992 that a civilian ruler led South Korea (Oh 1999). The Korean economy, which had boomed in the 1970s and 1980s under authoritarian rule, began to face problems during Kim's tenure, not least due to external pressure to open up the domestic market and liberalize the economy generally.

In Taiwan, following the collapse of Japanese imperial power, the incoming Guomindang regime eliminated indigenous local interests and power-holders in the 28 February 'massacre' of 1947. By taking control of land and residual Japanese industrial complexes, the Guomindang acquired a tight hold on the Taiwanese economy. It also implemented a Leninist party-state control of society and economy and prevented opposition via the imposition of martial law until as late as 1987. As with South Korea (and to a lesser extent Japan), the Taiwanese state was emboldened by proclaimed strategies of national renewal and determined to defend its new statist identity in the face of possible communist aggression in the region (Cumings 1987).

In this Cold War context, being authoritarian, but anti-communist authoritarian, was often enough to win considerable US economic aid and tolerance of the lack of democratic forms. With US support, Japan was rehabilitated into the international system, with its war record overlooked, if not forgotten. The US also provided a 'strategic defence parameter' for the anti-communist states of the region, as well as massive financial inputs. US aid to Japan ran at an average of US$500 million a year in the two decades from 1950 (Borden 1984). Cumings (1984) also argues that the US decision to use Japanese products in the Korean War was a key spur in Japan's subsequent industrialization. Between 1949 and 1979 South Korea similarly received US$13 billion (US$600 per capita) of economic and military aid, while Taiwan was given US$5.6 billion (US$425 per capita). An indication of the relative significance of these sums is that, during the same period, all of Africa and Latin America combined received only some US$21 billion, whilst US aid to Korea was only marginally less than all Soviet economic aid to all countries between 1954 and 1978 (Cumings 1987: 67). In the understated turn of phrase of Giovanni Arrighi (2002: 30), such facts help to explain 'the discrepancy between the developmental potentials' of east Asia and Sub-Saharan Africa.

Equally importantly, these Northeast Asian states also gained preferential access to the benefits of the global economy, primarily through advantageous trading relations with the United States. This entailed both toleration of the maintenance of barriers to imports to protect emerging industries in the region and privileged entry to the US market for regional exporters. In other words, they were permitted to benefit from export-led strategies and the opportunities offered by a newly globalizing economy without being subject to its reciprocal impact on domestic producers. As Cumings (1987: 68) put it:

> The three Northeast Asian political economies had in the 1950s a rare breathing space, an incubation period allowed to few other peoples in the world. The period set the stage for the breakthroughs of the 1960s, and it may be a capitalist analogue to the radical tonic of withdrawal and reorientation by socialist state machineries and societies.

Of course, the developmental successes of the Northeast Asian 'Three' cannot wholly be attributed to their relationship with the US and Cold War politics. But it is undeniable that this favourable external context facilitated their achievements – and it is an issue to which we shall return later in the chapter.

The astonishing economic growth of Japan, Taiwan, South Korea and Hong Kong (combined with the growth of the Southeast Asian countries discussed in the next chapter of this book) led the World Bank (1993) to produce a report explaining the 'East Asian Miracle'. It commended the 'sound development policies' of regional states, which had not only seen rapid economic growth, but equitable growth, increased educational levels, technological upgrading and an expansion of 'human and physical capital'. For many observers, the report's concluding recommendation that that 'most countries should not use government interventions in today's changing global economy' was counter-intuitive, as such government intervention was seen as in large part explaining why the 'miracle' had actually occurred. Nevertheless, the argument that there had been an east Asian developmental miracle did chime with a widely held acceptance of the dynamism of the Asian model (Chan 1993; United Nations 1997) and even seemed to point towards the twenty-first century emerging as 'the Pacific Century' (Linder 1986; McCord 1996; Simon 1997). Add the growth experienced by China in the 1990s in particular and the notion of east Asia's rise to global dominance arguably became even more convincing (Berger and Borer 1997). The date of all these publications is, however, instructive: all were written (if not published) before the east Asian financial crises of 1997. Thereafter the dominant theme in the literature on the region changed from explaining the miracle to explaining the crisis (Godement 1998; Pempel 1999; Haggard 2000; Woo, Sachs and Schwab 2000). By 2001, rather than accounting for the Asian success story, the World Bank was producing a report under the editorship of Joseph Stiglitz and Shahid Yusuf (2001) which sought to understand why the miracle had faltered and yet at the same time accepted that the evidence of recovery from the crisis suggested that it had by no means run its course.

This last point needs exploring. A cursory examination of the literature on the contemporary region could give the impression that the miracle states are now mired and that China is the new model of miraculous development. On the one side, deflation in Japan, Hong Kong and Macao, combined with the impact of financial crises on Korea (and, to a lesser extent, their secondary impact on Taiwan), paints a picture of decline and weakness. On the other side, near double-digit growth in China for the best part of two decades and a phenomenal increase in exports create the image of a newly rich and powerful regional force. Indeed, for some more hyperbolic interpreters, primarily located in the United States, economic reform is turning China into the next superpower (Overholt 1994; Weidenbaum and Hughes 1996). It is, of course, true that the Chinese economy has grown very rapidly and it is also true that other regional states are facing economic problems. Nevertheless, there are still large variations in the economic and social record of the region. Only North Korea faces more developmental problems than China. The reality is that Japan is a rich country facing problems of post-industrialization but with large financial reserves to support developmental projects. China remains a relatively poor country, seeking to industrialize and 'modernize' with over half its population dependent on the rural sector and funding development strategies by increasing government and banking debt. The implications of high growth figures from a very low starting point should not therefore be exaggerated. If a country produces one tractor one year, and two tractors in the following year, it may have achieved 100 per cent growth, but it still has only three tractors!

It is difficult to find acceptable comparable statistics for a number of reasons. First, the lack of international recognition of Taiwan in political organizations means that it is often precluded from data sets, such as the most recent World Bank development indicators. Second, information from North Korea is at best patchy and often not available. Third, different means of calculation, of national income in particular, generate widely differing figures. For example, purchasing power parity (PPP) calculations of per capita GDP in China generate a figure that is close to four times the official Chinese calculation. With this caveat in mind, Table 4.1 provides a comparison of key economic indicators for the

Table 4.1   *Northeast Asia: basic data*

	Population (millions, 2002 estimate)	GDP PPP (US$ billions)	Per capita GDP (US$, PPP)	Composition of GDP by sector (per cent)[1]
China	1,280.9	5,560	4,300	18, 49, 33
Hong Kong	7.3	180	25,000	0, 14, 86
Japan	126.9	3,450	27,300	2, 36, 62
Korea North	22.2	22	1,000	36, 64, 0
Korea South	48.3	865	18,000	5, 44, 51
Macao	0.5	8	17,600	1, 25, 74
Taiwan	22.5	386	17,200	2, 32, 66

[1] Agriculture, Industry, Services. Figures are rounded to nearest whole, so figure for agriculture in Hong Kong is reported as 0 rather than the real figure of 0.1 per cent. Note that in China, although agriculture accounts for only 18 per cent of GDP, it employs 50 per cent of the workforce.
Source: Compiled from online data sets provided by the World Bank, the OECD and the Central Intelligence Agency at http://www.worldbank.org/, http://www.oecd.org/ and http:// www.cia. gov/

regional states of Northeast Asia. It should be remembered that these data generate the highest possible interpretation of Chinese income and should be viewed with some scepticism.

Table 4.2 provides an alternative comparative overview of the region, namely, of the challenges, responses and potential to meet these challenges of regional states. Perhaps the main conclusion suggested by this table is that all regional states face problems of domestic economic stagnation to greater or lesser extents and that the global economic environment, which had previously been such an important support for growth in previous eras, can no longer be relied upon to meet domestic development goals. Certainly in Japan the domestic economy has remained stubbornly flat for a decade. Japanese interest rates have been below 1 per cent since 1995, yet real GDP growth and the domestic price index have both been negative since 1994 (with the exception of just one year). All that prevents further deflation is massive government spending funded by the traditionally high rate of domestic savings, which provides the Japanese government with a bulwark against inclement economic climates. In South Korea, Taiwan and Hong Kong, too, recession is impacting on the middle classes for the first time in generations, giving rise to awkward new political pressures on the respective leaderships.

This matter of political demands brings us back to the issue of relative state autonomy and state legitimacy outlined earlier. On one level, we have witnessed key political transitions in three regional states – Japan, South Korea and Taiwan. In Japan the previous structure of consensual factionalism contained within the dominant party, the Liberal Democratic Party (LDP), has been replaced by a system of conflictual factionalism and political fragmentation in post-LDP coalition governments, creating new challenges for democratic politicians. In South Korea and Taiwan authoritarian rule under military control has given way to systems where transfers of power via the ballot box have become an accepted feature of political life. In the case of Taiwan the end of martial law and a transition from Guomindang single-party rule to the presidency of Chen Shui-bian of the Democratic Progressive Party has occurred in little over a decade. What this suggests is that the relative state autonomy of planners in these capitalist developmental states has been eroded by political changes that have reduced their ability to pursue national development strategies unhindered by sectoral and other pressures for preferential treatment. On another level, the legitimacy of governing elites in many regional states was in large part maintained by successful economic management. Authoritarian politics was tolerated for as long as the government, through successful management of the economy, provided increased wealth and economic opportunity. To achieve this, many regional states followed a path of capital accumulation and wealth

Table 4.2 *Development challenges and responses in Northeast Asia*

Country	Development challenges	Level of commitment to a response	Ability to deliver
China	Domestic recession as consumers prepare for increasing market cost of services previously provided by the state. Large-scale unemployment in former state-owned enterprises. Comparatively low rural incomes and large-scale migration from rural areas. Massive inequalities between coast and interior and between rural and urban population. Endemic corruption. Severe environmental degradation.	Moderate to high. Fear of social consequences of increased unemployment – particularly in wake of WTO entry. Strong political pressure from inside the party from representatives of areas and sectors perceived to have lost, or not gained sufficiently, from economic reform.	Moderate. Massive government investment in infrastructure and other projects funded by fiscal deficit. Banking system used to provide para-fiscal investment, but returns on investment extremely low. Very high level of debts and non-performing loans threatens stability of financial system. Heavy reliance on exports as engine of growth.
Hong Kong	Migration of manufacturing capacity to China. Concerns that traditional role as gateway to China will decline as China develops its own service and transportation sectors. Heavily trade dependent and suffering from global economic downturn. Increasing unemployment, declining wages and contracting domestic economy.	Moderate. Chinese government is keen to ensure that the transition of sovereignty from UK is not associated with economic decline. Limited democratic freedoms but considerable domestic pressure from middle classes to increase confidence and overcome economic downturn. Increased need for welfare payments to unemployed conflicts with proposals to cut welfare spending to reduce budget deficit.	Moderate. Deficit spending to fund growing welfare demands, while domestic recession and reduced exports have led to declining fiscal resources. Double dependence on the global economy and on the continued growth of China's Pearl River Delta. Massive civil service pay cut in 2002 only produced half of expected savings.

continued overleaf

Table 4.2 *Continued*

Country	Development challenges	Level of commitment to a response	Ability to deliver
Japan	Decade-long domestic recession. Erosion of traditional lifetime employment system, with a growth in unemployment to around 5 per cent. Global economic downturn impacted on export growth. Ageing population poses welfare challenges. External pressure to reduce subsidies to rural producers. Financial system in need of restructuring.	High – although the structure of the electoral and political system means that politicians are often concerned with lobbying for local interests. Heavy commitment to subsidising agricultural producers and rural society.	Moderate to high. Technological innovation and advancement continue to be a spur to growth. Interest rates virtually nil in an attempt to boost domestic economy. But massive government expenditure supported by high rate of domestic savings. Financial reform 'stalemated' by LDP opposition.
Korea, North	Potential famine for most years since 1995. Economy close to collapsing.	Low. Emphasis on channelling what funds are available to large military sector.	Low. Dependent on food aid to prevent famine. Attempt to introduce Chinese-style economic reforms yet to have much positive impact. Very low levels of investment.
Korea, South	Slow recovery in wake of Asian financial crises. Need for financial and *chaebol* reform. Domestic demand low, with cuts in overtime and bonus payments resulting in lower incomes. Unemployment increasing – still relatively low by international comparison at around 3 per cent, but large increases in public sector.	Moderate to high. Increased domestic pressure from middle classes suffering from impact of financial crisis. Commitment to reforms as part of IMF support package of 1997, but perceived to be modified by strong domestic industrial interests.	Moderate. Limited available domestic credit. Public funds pumped in to support 'viable' financial institutions. Inflow of funds from IMF in 1997 helped currency stabilization. Investment in small and medium enterprises to reduce dependence on *chaebols* as engine of growth. Continued emphasis on export growth.

Macao	Economic contraction as a result of reduced exports to US and EU. Domestic deflation and historically high unemployment rate of over 6 per cent. Heavily dependent on taxes on gambling for 60 per cent of all government revenue.	High. Chinese government is keen to ensure that the transition of sovereignty from Portugal is not associated with economic decline.	Moderate to low. Deficit-based public spending initiatives combined with tax cuts to boost consumption. Reforms to gambling structure to break monopolies to increase revenues. Need to diversify from casino-based capitalism.
Taiwan	Heavily trade dependent, and suffering from global economic downturn. Migration of low-tech production to China and Southeast Asia. Domestic recession in 2001, and negative growth for the first time since 1947. Growing unemployment to levels of 4–5 per cent, not seen since the early 1970s. Increasing problem of bad debts in the financial system. Fear of dependence on the Chinese economy.	Moderate to high. Government policy might be dominated by relations with Beijing, but the transition to democracy has increased the significance of domestic social issues for competing politicians, particularly in local elections.	Moderate. Very high level of trade dependency and emphasis on reinvigorating export growth. Twelve interest rate cuts in 2001–02 to record low of just over 2 per cent in an attempt to boost consumption with only minor effect. Ongoing structural reform of financial system.

creation that resulted in a heavy trade dependency, ignoring slower, but also potentially more sustainable, processes which had a stronger domestic bias.

By contrast, legitimacy through rapid economic growth remains important – if not crucial – in China. Yet even in this case an excessive focus on growth alone can mislead. After a recession lasting a decade, Japan still has one of the highest figures for per capita income in the world. Conversely, after years of rapid economic growth, China remains essentially a poor country – even using PPP figures, China's per capita GDP still comes out at about half that of Russia's. Furthermore, growth does not necessarily bring benefits for all. High national growth rates hide massive geographic and sectoral differences. In China the decline of the old industrial heartlands of state planning is hidden by the growth of export-oriented production primarily along the coast. In the countryside the provision of health, education and welfare through the collectives has all but disappeared, impacting most severely on women. In addition, although China's external debt remains relatively low, it has experienced growing internal debt generated through budgetary deficits and the extension of bank loans, many of which will never be repaid. It is difficult, in fact, to come to an accurate assessment of the extent of bad loans in China's four major state banks. The figures emanating from the People's Bank of China are widely regarded as being politically constructed to present a positive confidence-building image, rather than being based on firm accounting. The real extent of non-performing loans in the big four banks in 2002 ranged somewhere between the official figure of 25 per cent and the most pessimistic calculation of 50 per cent (Chang 2003). Although we cannot get accurate figures, we can nevertheless say that the domestic Chinese economy, despite impressive overall growth rates, is characterized by an increase in government spending, bank loans and money supply with simultaneous deflation and unemployment growth (Breslin 2003).

Even these problems are relative. The difficulties facing the North Korean regime dwarf those that face the Chinese leadership. Here the challenge is not so much the pursuit of development, but rather the prevention of economic collapse. Shortages of fertilizer, fuel and industrial spare parts have combined with major droughts to threaten mass starvation during virtually every year since 1995. Such investment as there has been has largely been focused on military projects, even though keeping the military fed further undermines the state's ability to follow any development strategy on behalf of the wider population. The irony is that, while North Korea still espouses the ideology of *Juche*, or self-reliance, famine has only been averted through massive international food aid.

Finally, in this first section we should consider the environment as an important developmental challenge for all of the countries of Northeast

Asia. In many respects, Japan's experience of dealing with environmental issues has created a problematic paradigm in the region. Its experience has been summarized as one of polluting, getting rich, then cleaning up. However, this ignores the extent to which Japan has simply exported its environmental problems to other states. The first real shift in Japanese policy came in the 1960s in response to the growth of environmentally related health problems. Perhaps the most important of these was Minamata disease, first discovered in 1956 after the fish in Minimata Bay ingested chemicals (particularly mercury) found in waste dumped into the sea without treatment by the nearby Nippon Chisso plant and poisoned those who subsequently ate them (Ui 1992). In response, much of Japan's polluting heavy industry was relocated into Southeast Asian states that were actively seeking foreign direct investment to spur growth at the time. The problem simply moved to become another country's concern. To be fair to the Japanese, its regional environmental initiatives of the 1990s did take on a new significance and Japan is now the most important state in terms of environmental aid and technological transfer in the region. The Japanese experience is also worrying in that it provides a justification, or excuse, for other regional states not to worry about current environmental threats in the belief that they can be taken care of once growth and wealth have been achieved.

Taiwan and South Korea suffered similar severe environmental problems during their years of rapid economic growth. In Taiwan industrialization has resulted in land, air and water pollution and a loss of fishing grounds. Per capita carbon emissions more than doubled in Taiwan in the 1980s and 1990s. South Korea faced similar issues, with particularly severe acid rain problems. In both states environmental issues became more important after the transition to democracy, with South Korea now officially committed to becoming the 'model environment country' in the world. Nevertheless, air pollution in major cities in particular has yet to be seriously addressed. By comparison, North Korea's environmental problem is the reverse: its issues relate to the absence of economic growth. Lack of cars, petrol shortages and a low level of industrialization (combined with an emphasis on electricity rather than fossil fuels) at least mean that air pollution is not a serious matter, although the inefficiency of many industrial enterprises does lead to localized problems. There are, however, serious shortages of water both for domestic consumption and agricultural irrigation.

By far the biggest cause of environmental hazard in the region is China. Urban air quality is appalling; most water sources are polluted; land is being lost to urbanization, industrialization and pollution; greenhouse gas emissions increase year on year; and coastal waters are heavily polluted. It is important to note here that this record is not just a consequence of an expanding population, but also a reflection of land usage and availability. Nor is it purely a domestic issue, as Chinese sea- and air-borne pollution refuses to recognize sovereign political borders. Betke and Küchler point out that across the globe a decline in agricultural land has historically accompanied economic growth as a result of the expansion of construction activities, pollution and inadequate or inappropriate land use (wind and water erosion, loss of nutrients, salinisation and so on). But, while these are common concerns for all fast-growing countries, they note that China is 'one of the few countries in which *all* these problems exist simultaneously within the same political and economic framework' (Betke and Küchler 1987: 86–7, emphasis in the original). This devastating combination is largely a consequence of the simultaneous existence of environmental problems associated with market forces *and* state planning. It is also a consequence of the simultaneous existence of both rapid growth and poverty. As Qu (1990: 103) observes, 'China's environmental problems are two-sided: (1) modern industrial growth has given rise to pollution, and (2) economic stagnation or slow development in large remote areas has resulted in ecological destruction'. It is not that environmental concerns are ignored in China. Indeed, there exists an impressive array of environmental legislation. The obstacle is that the legislation is not enforced at the local level, where officials have to weigh up the potential conflict between environmental enforcement and local wealth creation and employment. There does, however, exist a strong sentiment among the Chinese elites that, at the international level, environmental issues are used as a tool to prevent Chinese development. If it was acceptable for industrialized countries to pollute when they were industrializing, then why is it not legitimate for China to do the same today?

Within this single region, then, we can see almost all of the schisms that exist in the world. It is possible to take virtually any dichotomy of choice and point to examples within Northeast Asia – North–South, East–West, poor–prosperous, authoritarian–democratic, large–small, internationalized–autarkic, industrializing–post-industrial, polluting–clean and probably many more as well. Not surprisingly, these schisms have played significant roles in influencing the trajectory of intra-regional relations in Northeast Asia.

The intra-regional politics of development in Northeast Asia

As noted already, there are a number of key obstacles to the establishment of formal intra-regional organizations and dialogue and three issues warrant initial attention. First, there is the question of the coherence of the region. Economically, with the exception of North Korea, there is considerable regional integration, even though a strong argument can be made for suggesting that in this respect Northeast Asia is but a subregion of east Asia; in security terms it remains divided on what remain essentially Cold War lines; politically it is also divided between the residual authoritarian communist party states of China and North Korea, on the one hand, and the parliamentary democracies of Japan, South Korea and Taiwan, on the other. Second, there is the fact that mistrust and suspicion about the motives of key regional states – effectively Japan and China – mean that other regional states are fearful of one or the other using regional organizations to impose hegemony. Third, there is the key issue of divided states and the diplomatic 'mess' that all but defines intra-regional politics as a consequence. The first two points have already been made, but the last needs some elaboration.

The reality is that North and South Korea remain nominally still at war, although since the accession to the presidency of Kim Dae-jung there has been a move towards reducing tension. Both Koreas joined the United Nations simultaneously in 1991 and each allows other states to recognize the other diplomatically. However, within the region only China has fully normalized relations with both North and South Korea. Japan recognizes the *de facto* existence of two Korean states, but despite a series of bilateral discussions normalization has yet to occur and there is therefore no *de jure* diplomatic relationship. However, although the concept of 'two Koreas' is now accepted within the region, the same is not the case for China. The PRC will not allow other countries to recognize both itself and the ROC as separate political entities, insisting that there is only one China and that the PRC is the government of that China. Although the Guomindang also initially pursued a 'one China' doctrine, its approach is now to seek recognition as the government of Taiwan only – in effect, either a 'two China' policy or a 'one China, one Taiwan' policy. The problem for Taiwan is that, even though it has changed its position and other countries may indeed want to recognize it as a separate state, the PRC simply will not permit dual recognition. If any country recognized Taiwan, then the PRC would immediately break off diplomatic and other relations with that country. The PRC further maintains that, if Taiwan should ever declare itself to be an independent state, then the People's Liberation Army would invade. Japan, which originally recognized the ROC as the sole government of China, switched diplomatic recognition to the PRC in 1972, South Korea following suit in 1992. As the PRC is responsible for the diplomatic relations of both Macao and Hong Kong, and North Korea has always recognized the PRC, the upshot is that none of the other regional states have diplomatic relations with the ROC on Taiwan. Indeed, any sign of political recognition of Taiwan invokes nothing less than diplomatic fury from Beijing. Such a convoluted diplomatic situation makes the establishment of inclusive regional organizations impossible. North Korea could participate diplomatically, but largely does not want to; Taiwan wants to participate, but is diplomatically isolated.

As a result, as Table 4.3 shows, while the states of Northeast Asia are members of a number of regional organizations, there is no regional organization where *all* regional states are represented. Furthermore, the overwhelming majority of these organizations are built on a conception of region that is much broader than Northeast Asia. A partial way round this diplomatic maze has been found in the separation of politics and economics. Such a separation was at the heart of Japanese policy towards the PRC before the normalization of relations in 1972. *Seikei bunri*, as it is called in Japanese, was intended to allow increased economic relations with the PRC, notwithstanding the retention of formal diplomatic relations between Tokyo and Taibei. Whilst the PRC argued formally that the two forms of relationship should not be distinguished, a strategy of separation has in fact been pursued by Beijing and other regional states in the contemporary period. Thus we have a situation where the PRC receives substantial inward investment from a state whose existence it refuses to recognize! By means of this façade Taiwan does have some quasi-official relationships with other regional states – for example, its Economic and Cultural Representation Office in Tokyo performs some of the functions of a diplomatic agency, although it is not meant to deal with overtly political issues. South Korea and Japan similarly have economic offices in Taibei that provide for some form of formal link. Under the name of Chinese Taipei, Taiwan can attend APEC meetings since APEC is an organization for economies, not nation-states; but it cannot attend the Asia Pacific Parliamentary Forum as this is a political organization for national legislatures.

The separation of politics and economics is also a useful tool on the Korean peninsular. President Kim Dae-jung's 'Sunshine Policy' was built on such an approach, aiming at the creation of a more peaceful environment through multiple forms of cross border non-political engagement – almost a classic example of liberal international relations theory in practice. By taking the politics out of business relations, the policy was in part designed to allow South Korean companies to invest in North Korea, contributing to economic growth but also promoting friendly exchange. Despite the existence of a number of organizations aimed at encouraging cooperation in East Asia and the Pacific, this example highlights the fact that, in large part, multilateralism in Northeast Asia means no more than multiple bilateral relations.

Table 4.3 *Main regional organizations in Northeast Asia*

Organization	Aims	Regional members	Extra-regional members
ASEAN Regional Forum (ARF)	Promote security through confidence-building mechanisms and preventative diplomacy.	China, Japan, South Korea, North Korea.	19 from South Asia, Southeast Asia, European Union, North America and Oceania.
Asia Pacific Economic Cooperation (APEC)	Promotion of investment and trade through economic liberalization. A form of 'open regionalism' as any reforms (i.e. tariff reductions) also apply to non-members.	China, Hong Kong, Taiwan (as Chinese Taipei), Japan, South Korea.	16 from East Asia, Oceania and the Pacific coastline states of the Americas.
Asia Pacific Parliamentary Forum (APPF)	Forum of national parliamentarians to identify and discuss matters of common concern and interest and promote a sense of regional cohesion.	China, Japan, South Korea.	21 from Mongolia, East Asia, Oceania and the Pacific coastline states of the Americas.
East Asia Economic Caucus (EAEC) – formerly East Asian Economic Group (EAEG)	Originally to enhance economic cooperation, in Asia to the exclusion of the non-Asian states of APEC. Has become a discussion group within APEC.	China, Japan, South Korea.	10 members of ASEAN.

Continued overleaf

Table 4.3 *Continued*

Organization	Aims	Regional members	Extra-regional members
Pacific Basin Economic Council (PBEC)	Association of senior business leaders dedicated to expanding trade and investment through open markets.	China, Hong Kong, Taiwan (as Chinese Taipei), Japan, South Korea.	Australia, Canada, Chile, Colombia, Ecuador, Indonesia, Malaysia, Mexico, New Zealand, Peru, the Philippines, Russia, Singapore, Thailand and the US.
Asian Development Bank (ADB)	Multilateral development finance institution dedicated to reducing poverty in Asia and the Pacific.	China, Hong Kong, Taiwan (as Chinese Taipei), Japan, South Korea.	39 from Asia and the Pacific, 16 from Europe, and the US.
Pacific Economic Cooperation Council (PECC)	Combines business, government and academic representatives to discuss developmental issues and promote economic policy coordination.	China, Hong Kong, Taiwan (as Chinese Taipei), Japan, South Korea.	20 from Asia, Oceania and the Pacific coastline states of the Americas, Russia, Mongolia and France (Pacific territories).
ASEAN + 3 (APT)	Mechanism for encouraging dialogue between ASEAN and Northeast Asia. Aim of building a comprehensive partnership, particularly in financial affairs.	China, Japan, South Korea.	10 members of ASEAN.

Chiang Mai Initiative	Emerged from the APT. Aims to strengthen regional policy dialogue, monitor capital flows and provide early warning system for financial crises. Establishment of a network of bilateral swap arrangements to protect regional currencies from speculative attacks.	China, Japan, South Korea.	10 members of ASEAN with technical support from the Asian Development Bank.
Asia–Europe Meeting (ASEM)	Mechanism for dialogue between the EU and east Asia. High profile biannual summits with regular 'track-two' diplomacy.	China, Japan, South Korea.	Brunei, Indonesia, Malaysia, the Philippines, Singapore, Thailand and Vietnam and the EU member states.
Tumen River Area Development Programme (TRADP)	UNDP-sponsored attempt to bring development to the Russia–Mongolia–Korea–China borders.	China, Japan, South Korea North Korea.	Mongolia, Russia.
Korean Peninsula Energy Development Organization (KEDO)	Mechanism to prevent the development of a nuclear programme in North Korea by providing aid for alternative sources of energy.	Japan, South Korea.	US, Uzbekistan, EU, New Zealand, Australia, Canada, Indonesia, Chile, Argentina, Poland, Czech Republic.
Tripartite Environment Ministers Meeting (TEMM)	Mechanism to discuss transnational environmental issues.	China, Japan, South Korea.	None.

As the wealthiest country in the region, Japan has also been the main regional source of aid. Initially taking the form of 'reparations' to countries occupied by Japan during the Second World War, this has continued subsequently as Official Development Assistance. Whilst being welcomed by other regional states, the policy was not divorced from Japan's own developmental needs:

> Reparations and ODA were designed to forge new economic links between Japan and the region, as they were made mainly in the form of the transfer of machinery and loans, which led the states of the region to become dependent on Japanese corporations for their spare parts, related products and technical assistance (Hook *et al.* 2001: 184).

Japan has also been at the core of the informal regional economic integration which Cumings argues has been a defining characteristic of development in Northeast Asia over the last century. As he put it, 'it is misleading to assess the industrialization pattern in any one of these countries: such an approach misses, through a fallacy of disaggregation, the fundamental unity and integrity of the regional effort in this century' (Cumings 1987: 46). For the first half of the twentieth century the 'regional effort' was accomplished by Japanese military force and occupation. Subsequently, 'largely to bypass import restrictions, although [also] to take advantage of their skilled and inexpensive labor forces' (Altbach 1998), Japanese investment in Korea and Taiwan helped to generate heavily interdependent economic growth. Following Akamatsu (1962), Cumings (1984) explained this process by deploying the 'flying-geese' model of regional development. This suggests that, as the lead goose (Japan) industrializes, it will shed outdated and unprofitable industries to neighbouring states with lower production costs. Thanks to the influx of investment, these lower-cost states will subsequently industrialize to the point where they in turn cast off unprofitable industries to states with even lower costs. The whole cycle then repeats itself, leading eventually to growth for all (Kwan 1994: 93).

It was the promised benefits for all that made the model so attractive – if not for academic analysts, then at least for regional policy-makers. In this respect, it represented something like the promise of the 'trickle-down' theory writ large and justified the emphasis on low-cost production for 'foreigners' by the state elites of the region. The 'model', especially as applied to Korean and Taiwanese development, had a strong pull for other leaders in the region, notably in China, but also for many of the member states of ASEAN. It was not unimportant either that it also provided a strong justification for the actions of the leaders of the core states (essentially Japan). Yet, for Hollerman (1991), Crone (1993), Bernard and Ravenhill (1995) and perhaps most forcefully Hatch and Yamamura (1996), while this process unquestionably generated growth in the region, it simultaneously created asymmetric interdependence. Indeed, Hatch (1998: 3) argues that official enthusiasm for the flying-geese model has become the quasi-official ideology of the Japanese government, 'justifying Japan's ongoing role as the economic hegemon of Asia'. This is because whole industries have not been passed down the chain as 'should' be the case in the ideal-type model. Japanese companies have instead offloaded the labour intensive (that is, not profitable in Japan) element of production and kept the production of profitable high-tech components, control over brand naming, marketing and 'research and development' within Japan. Hollerman (1991) has referred to this as Japan's 'headquarters economy'. In other words, rather than creating a unified regional economy with gains for all, the pattern of investment and trade has perhaps instead created a structure of 'technological dependence' on Japan.

As normally construed, the model emphasizes push factors in regional economic relations – rising land and labour costs, appreciating currencies, tighter labour and environmental legislation are seen to push production out of countries at certain points in their growth trajectory. But we should also think about the pull factors – those policies adopted by regional states to attract investment. Regional states have invested millions of dollars in creating both the hard infrastructure (roads, ports, railways) and soft infrastructure (tax breaks, subsidized land and so on) to attract investment. Furthermore, there has been a clear regional learning process. For example, China's Special Economic Zones (SEZs), established to pull investment away from the rest of the region, are very similar in both intention and policy to the Export Processing Zones (EPZs) established earlier in Taiwan at Gaoxiong and in South Korea at Masan. Indeed, what is striking is the extent to which investment in the region largely comes from other regional states. As there are very strong linkages between investment and trade, the region (with the exception of North Korea) thus displays a high degree of informal economic integration which, as already highlighted, stands in stark contrast to the fragmentation and disunity in formal regional political integration.

In particular, the extent of investment from Hong Kong and Taiwan into China has led many to talk about the creation of a 'Greater China' economic space (Shambaugh 1995; Khanna 1995; Rowley and Lewis 1996). Trade and investment flows between these different Chinese political entities, according to this argument, have been so intense that the three economies have become intertwined into a single entity. While there is some value in considering the way in which political borders do not always correspond with functioning economic spaces, the Greater China concept has to be modified in two key ways. First, the export industries built on FDI are heavily concentrated along China's coastal provinces. It is therefore incorrect to think in terms of all of China forming part of this Greater China economic space. Indeed, the Chinese example suggests that state-led projects aimed at internationalizing part of the national economic space can also simultaneously denationalize the national economic space. Second, Taiwanese investment into China (often through Hong Kong) is itself either dependent on, or a consequence of, Japanese investment into Taiwan. In this context Naughton (1997) provides the most penetrating understanding of how subregional economic integration interacts with wider regional integration – primarily because he deploys a fluid multi-level approach at the expense of seeking to be definitive. He suggests that there are in fact three levels of integration: at the lowest level, a Greater China circle which covers the most intense level of integration – that between Hong Kong and the Pearl River Delta of Guangdong (which accounts for over half of all investment in the province); at the intermediate level, the most internationalized provinces of China (Guangdong and Fujian), Hong Kong and Taiwan; and at the highest level, which has certainly not yet seen full integration, the three Chinese economies in total. The major benefit of this approach over other 'Greater China' conceptions is that it recognizes the significance of Japanese economic interests – not only direct Japanese investment into China, but also the role played by Japanese interests in investment from Hong Kong, Taiwan and elsewhere into China.

There is no doubt that the majority of the literature on the Northeast Asian economy emphasizes the developmental benefits of regional integration. But, while it is possible to construct a 'win–win' scenario when looking at the region as a whole, such an argument is less sustainable if we examine the distribution of benefits within individual countries. For example, although China's re-engagement with the global and regional economy has resulted in overall national growth, the spatial and sectoral distribution of this growth within China has been highly uneven. Rapid growth fuelled by the FDI–trade linkage has been heavily concentrated in eight coastal provinces, which together account for 95 per cent of all national exports by foreign-funded companies. Recognizing the uneven spatial impact of FDI, the Chinese government has launched a 'look West' strategy aimed at encouraging more investment (both domestic and international) into non-coastal areas. This strategy is part of a wider attempt by China's new generation of leaders to try to deal with the perceived disadvantages of the move away from socialism and, specifically, to do something for the 'underprivileged areas and people left behind in the breakneck transition to free markets' (Hutzler 2002: 1).

There are problems, too, in other countries. In Hong Kong the fear is that the transfer of manufacturing production has led to the domestic economy becoming 'hollowed out', contributing to growing unemployment (Phar Kim Beng 2002; Hornik 2002). There are similar anxieties in Japan that some industries – notably textiles – are being damaged as production moves to China where wages are just 4 per cent of comparable Japanese manufacturing wages (Hiranuma 2002). But the biggest concerns are in Taiwan, where alarm has grown at the prospect of over-dependence on China as a production site for Taiwanese manufacturers. In 1993 Taiwan's economic minister, Chiang Pin-Kung, announced a 'Go South' policy to encourage investors to look at Southeast Asia rather than China, while in 1996 a new policy of 'No Haste, Be Patient' was introduced in an attempt to slow the rate of investment on the mainland. Neither of these strategies has had a significant influence on the flow of investment from Taiwan to the PRC – quite simply because, as with Hong Kong and Japan, producing in China makes more economic sense than either producing at home or in other regional states. The issue is in essence quite straightforward – what is good for the investor might not be as beneficial for the 'national interest'. While China matters in one respect for workers who are fearful that their jobs will migrate to lower-cost production sites, it matters in a very different way for investors seeking to maximize profits.

For all these qualifications, the extent of regional integration in terms of investment and trade is clearly of great significance. Perhaps the most extreme explanation is found in Hou (2002: 1) who argues that:

Much like the tropical forests of the Amazon River Basin, Asia is almost a complete ecosystem economically speaking...Just as it is hopeless for any individual biologist to unravel the interdependencies of the Amazon ecosystem, it is impossible for any economist to fully characterize the multilateral trade/investment relationship between the Asian economies.

But, in rightly emphasizing regional integration, there is a concomitant danger that we ignore the significance of extra-regional actors. As noted earlier, the rapid growth achieved in Japan, Taiwan and South Korea was heavily dependent on these states' relationship with the US. The increase in intra-regional trade has meant a decreased reliance on the extra-region and in particular the US. But much of the intra-regional trade is in components. The final good still has to be sold somewhere; and still, as much as ever, the US remains the major market for these goods. In divesting productive capacity to lower-cost sites in the region, the intention was primarily to reduce the cost of exporting to the US.

Although Japan has been and still is an important market, access to major extra-regional markets – primarily the US, but also the EU – remains essential for exporters in other regional states. Furthermore, much intra-regional investment has extra-regional origins. On one level, the development of the computer industry in Taiwan has been predicated on Original Equipment Manufacturer contracting with not only Japanese but also US companies (Sasuga 2002), and much of this manufacturing has now been divested to China. On another level, many companies from Europe and North America use intermediaries in Hong Kong and Taiwan to manage their investments in China. In other words, while the bilateral trade and investment figures show intra-regional integration, it remains a form of regional integration that is heavily dependent on wider processes of global economic change.

The extra-regional politics of development in Northeast Asia

As the discussion in the previous section has demonstrated, the region as a whole does not possess a coherent voice. There is also massive diversity in the way in which regional states are involved in global politics. Since the reversion to Chinese sovereignty, the diplomatic affairs of Macao and Hong Kong both fall under Chinese control, though they retain local control of international economic relations. Thus both are independent members of the WTO, but are represented by China in economic organizations such as the World Bank where membership is limited to sovereign states. Similarly, although both subscribe to the IMF and accept its standards, unlike China they do not have formal membership voting rights.

As with regional organizations, Taiwan's ability to participate in global political forums is seriously constrained by its lack of diplomatic recognition. Although Taiwan has joined the WTO, its desire to join political organizations remains frustrated by Beijing's insistence on a 'one-China' policy. Thus Taiwan is not a member of the UN, the World Bank, the IMF or the International Labour Organisation (ILO). As a 'non-state', it cannot send representatives to formal political meetings about the environment held under UN auspices, although non-governmental agencies such as the International Energy and Research Laboratory in Taibei can participate in non-governmental environmental forums.

North Korea also has a low level of participation, but, in contrast to Taiwan, this is self-imposed (although North Korea is also not recognized diplomatically by many states). Although it is a member of the UN, North Korea is not a member of the Asian Development Bank

(ADB), the IMF, the World Bank, the ILO or the WTO. With annual famines in recent years, the country has become dependent on food aid not so much to boost development, but to prevent economic collapse and humanitarian crisis. But, even in this connection, North Korea's position has been highly defensive, compromised by external opposition to its nuclear missile programme. Despite its desperate need for international aid, it refuses to respond to what it considers to be the bullying tactics of an arrogant West led by the US. Witness, for example, the expulsion of UN inspectors and the restarting of the Yongbyon nuclear reactor (which had been dormant since a deal with the US in 1994) in response to criticisms of its nuclear programme in 2002.

Japan, on the other hand, does play an important role in world institutions, courtesy of its combination of rapid rehabilitation into the Western family of states after the Second World War and sustained economic growth thereafter. However, Japan's economic strength has not been reflected in the acquisition of real power. This is partly because other countries are wary of Japan's hegemonic ambitions, and partly because, in recognition of this, Japan itself has been cautious in pushing itself forward as a leader, either regionally or globally. The former is illustrated by Japan's role in the UN. Although it provides around 16 per cent of all the UN funding, and despite years of diplomatic initiatives, it has no permanent seat on the Security Council (Drifte 1999). What is more, its chances of achieving this are virtually nil for as long as China, as a permanent member, has a right of veto. The latter is revealed in Japan's self-imposed pacifism since 1945, although it should be acknowledged that since the late 1980s there has been considerable debate within Japan as to whether the time is right for it to take on a greater leadership role in world politics and for that role to be accepted as legitimate and non-threatening by other states (Wanner 1999).

Nevertheless, although Japan has not always taken a visible leadership role, it has played important roles in shaping the way that global politics works. First, it is not only the biggest source of funds at the ADB and, through the Tokyo financial markets, the World Bank, but is also an important source of bilateral aid. Its initial attempt in the wake of the Asian financial crises to create an Asian Monetary Fund – either to supplement or compete with the IMF, according to point of view – came to nothing in the face of Chinese and US opposition. Nevertheless, Japan did play a key role in helping regional states through the crises via the Miyazawa Initiative – a US$30 billion package of financial support to Asian countries to provide bail-out loans and support debt restructuring more generally (Hughes 2000). The Japanese Ministry of Finance also claimed to have exerted influence on both the World Bank and the ADB to listen to the pleas of the crisis-hit states (Ministry of Finance 1998).

Second, Japan does seek to exert influence on international organizations. In referring to the manner in which Japan helped shape the emergence of east Asian regional forums, Rix (1993: 62) termed its habit of establishing initiatives, and then letting other states pursue them, as 'leading from behind'. In relation to the IMF, its current managing director, Horst Köhler (2002), has argued that:

> Japan has shown leadership in shaping the Fund's policies, especially on relations with low-income countries, crisis management, and measures to strengthen the international financial architecture ... Moreover, Japan is the largest provider of resources for lending by the IMF's Poverty Reduction and Growth Facility, and for technical assistance and training through its Administered Account with the Fund.

Moreover, since 1975, Japan has been a member of the G7 post-industrial states and, perhaps more importantly, belongs to the 'Quad' (Japan, Canada, the US and the EU) at the WTO. This group of countries is widely considered to be the real agenda-setting forum within the WTO, providing Japan with the opportunity to help shape the rules of world trade. Perhaps Japan is not so much leading from behind as increasingly taking a more normal proactive role, albeit in forums where decision-making processes are somewhat opaque.

One policy area in which Japan has been more able and prepared to take a leadership role is that relating to the environment. Again, this is in no small part based on Japanese financial resources. The transition of the Global Environmental Facility from a pilot project into a fully functioning aid organization to promote environmental protection would not have occurred without significant Japanese financial inputs – around 20 per cent of the required funding, and second only in quantity to the US contribution. Japanese ODA has been increasingly linked to environmental projects since the United Nations Conference on Environment and Development in 1992 and Japan manifestly felt a real sense of responsibility to bring to fruition the protocol to the UN Framework Convention on Climate Change, given that the key meeting was held in Kyoto in Japan (Grubb with Vrolijk and Brack 1999). Japanese companies are also amongst the world leaders in the promotion of clean technology. Yet there is more to Japanese environmental leadership than simply money and technology. Not only is it an arena in which Japan can promote its leadership without appearing to be seeking hegemony – although some Japanese environmental ODA is tied to the purchase of its environmental technology – but it is also an issue-area where global philanthropy can be deployed effectively and where organizations such as the United Nations Development Programme (UNDP) actually want Japanese leadership. In sum, the environment is one area where politically Japan appears to be gaining a global comparative advantage.

For South Korea, the financial crisis of 1997 proved to be a key turning point in its relations with the IFIs, most notably the IMF. The decision to ask the Fund for help was a response to two spectacular collapses: one in the value of the Korean won – an almost 50 per cent depreciation between July and December 1997 – and the other in the value of the stockmarket. In some respects the Korean crisis can be seen as an outcome of earlier crises elsewhere – as foreign investors moved their money from the whole region, thereby triggering the economic collapse they feared. It is also true, however, that many Korean companies had relied very heavily on bank loans that were only rarely based on prudent credit and risk analysis (Balino and Ubide 1999). At the time of the crisis, the combined debt of the South Korean government and major South Korean corporations (*chaebols*) was in the region of US$200 billion. As such, the US$60 billion provided by the G7 states, the IMF, the World Bank and the ADB, and administered through the IMF, only provided short-term temporary support. In order to solve what it perceived to be the underlying domestic structural causes of the crisis, the IMF required the Korean government to undertake a number of key policy changes. These involved raising interest rates to help support the won, increasing 'labour flexibility', restructuring the financial system to ensure that loans were only made after prudent financial analysis, liberalizing the capital account, removing government restrictions on foreign purchasing and further opening up the domestic economy to facilitate greater foreign ownership and access to the domestic market. Assessments of the efficacy of this programme have thus far been mixed. Analysts from the IFIs point to economic recovery since the turn of the century (despite a global turndown) as evidence of success. Others are more sceptical. The cover of Francois Godement's (1998) *The Downsizing of Asia* has the picture of a South Korean demonstrator holding a banner with the words 'IMFired', indicating the discontent of many Korean workers at the consequence of restructuring. Walden Bello simply thinks that IMF policy is wrong and that such growth as it generates will be at the cost of increased unemployment and a decline in social welfare provision. These debates remain to be resolved. What is manifest in relation to development is that the distinctive domestic attributes of the South Korean political economy, and its place in the globalizing world, have been changed as a result of IMF-inspired reforms.

A similar change has also taken place within the Chinese political economy through entry into the WTO at the Doha Ministerial Conference in 2001. In seeking foreign investment to boost growth in the 1990s the

Chinese leadership had followed a very simple and logical strategy. Foreign investment was welcomed if it was likely to produce exports, but domestic producers were insulated from international competition. The Chinese economy thus became distinctly dualistic in nature – a very liberal export-oriented economy alongside a heavily protected domestic economy. In its initial negotiations within the then General Agreement on Tariffs and Trade (GATT) over membership, the Chinese negotiating position reflected this dualism. It wanted to join on terms that allowed China to retain as far as possible its defence of domestic producers from international competition, while simultaneously assuring access to markets in the industrialized world for its exporters. However, the deal, as finally signed, was in some ways a mirror image of these motivations, in that it entailed market opening that threatens the interests of many domestic producers while providing other states with considerable protection (in theory at least) from a rise in Chinese imports (Breslin 2003).

How is this breach between intention and outcome to be explained? A partial answer can be found in the WTO's membership criteria. Quite simply, key WTO members – notably the EU and the US – would not allow China to join unless it agreed to these changes. But, as China did not have to join the WTO – it had after all been doing quite well outside – this cannot be the full answer. It is true that China wanted to stabilize access to major markets in the West and that joining the WTO was a key means of assuring this. But the real answer to the question is to be found in the changing view of the Chinese leadership as to whether the existing domestic political economy was working and, more tellingly, could provide the basis for sustainable long-term growth. In particular, the then premier, Zhu Rongji, decided that maintaining the existing system – particularly the ailing state-owned sector – was no longer viable. Faced with considerable domestic opposition to change, he turned to an international coalition and the conditions imposed by WTO membership to force through domestic change. As with the case of South Korea and the IMF, China's interaction with international financial institutions can be seen to have led to a key change in development strategy, except that, in this case, the international institution in question has been used to promote what was otherwise desired, rather than force what would otherwise have been rejected.

This fundamental shift in policy has created a new era in China's relationship with global institutions. But, for different reasons, China is not unique within the Northeast Asian region in undergoing this transition. For much of the post-1945 era global institutions were not significant actors in the development policies of regional states. Nor were regional states significant actors in global institutions – with the important exception of China's role as a permanent member of the UN Security

Council. Much more important in this period were bilateral relations with the US. Since the end of the Cold War this has begun to change. Although the 1997 financial crisis clearly had a huge impact on South Korea's relations with the IMF, it is tempting to speculate as to whether the US would have bailed out South Korea on a bilateral basis if the crisis had occurred at the height of the Cold War. We can conclude that the increasing importance of geo-economic relative to geo-strategic considerations in the region has had a considerable impact on its role in the global politics of development.

Conclusion

The conclusion can be brief. Despite the impact of the financial crisis, Northeast Asia (with the exception of North Korea) does display a high level of economic interdependence – albeit asymmetrical interdependence with wide divergences in levels of prosperity between regional states. Uneven development has thus been a dominant characteristic of the region in the post-1945 era: not only does this unevenness persist between regional states, but it is also now a key concern *within* many of the states themselves. An outline case can be made for saying that Northeast Asia does possess elements of common identity and some of the bases from which more cooperative problem-solving could be attempted. But continuing political divisions and ensuing mutual distrust are problems and will ensure that attempts at building effective regional organizations will come to little, unless and until divided regional states can reconcile their differences and, above all, China and Japan can engineer an accommodation of each other's regional aspirations. For the moment, the prospect of Northeast Asia finding region-wide solutions to developmental issues does not look especially rosy.

Further reading

Borrus, M., Ernst, D. and Haggard, S. (eds) (2000) *International Production Networks in Asia: Rivalry or Riches?* (London: Routledge).

Deyo, F. C. (ed.) (1987) *The Political Economy of the New East Asian Industrialism* (New York NY: Cornell University Press).

Foong Wai Fong (2000) *The New Asian Way: Rebuilding Asia through Self-reliance* (Subang Jaya: Pelanduk Publications).

Katzenstein, P. and Takashi, S. (eds) (1997) *Network Power: Japan and Asia* (New York NY: Cornell University Press).

Richter, F.-J. (ed.) (2000) *The East Asian Development Model: Economic Growth, Institutional Failure and the Aftermath of the Crisis* (London: Palgrave Macmillan).

Chapter 5

Southeast Asia

MARK BEESON

One of the most striking qualities of the Southeast Asian region is its heterogeneity. Indeed, so diverse are the cultural traditions, social practices and levels of economic activity across Southeast Asia that it is debatable whether it makes sense to think of it as a region at all. The very notion of a distinct Southeast Asian region only came into being during the Second World War, when the British established a South-East Asia Command to coordinate the war effort against the Japanese (Korhonen 1997: 356). At the very least, the Southeast Asian region stands as a warning against extensive generalizations based on sheer geographical propinquity or common historical provenance. Yet amidst all this diversity there have been a number of sustained attempts to carve out a distinct regional identity via the elaboration of indigenous institutions and agreements. The fate of such ventures tells us much about the forces that have constrained and facilitated development within the region. More than most areas, Southeast Asia's recent fortunes have also been shaped by external influences and long-run changes in the international system that have exerted a powerful influence over weaker, emerging economies. What is becoming increasingly apparent, however, is that some states and institutions have been able to accommodate such influences more successfully than others. This has potentially major implications for both intra-regional cooperation and the region's place in the increasingly integrated global order.

This chapter provides an initial overview of the very different countries that make up Southeast Asia. It then considers how this diversity has manifested itself and been managed at the level of intra-regional politics, particularly in the Association of Southeast Asian Nations. Finally, it examines how the region has been incorporated into the global political economy – an international order dominated by the established industrialized powers and key agencies that have the capacity to influence the course and content of public policy in the countries of the region, as the recent economic crisis and its aftermath illustrated all too vividly. Although the region has produced some noteworthy challenges to the existent orthodoxy, Southeast Asia's capacity to develop a distinctive and

118

coherent response to increased global integration is limited by a number of factors – internal and external, as well as economic and political – that continue to militate against a unified regional position. At a time when even the limited capacities of Southeast Asian states are being actively discouraged from greater involvement in the developmental process, and when the possibility of carving out a niche in the upper echelons of the global production hierarchy looks increasingly remote, the prospects for much of Southeast Asia look significantly diminished.

Country development strategies in Southeast Asia

Three historical factors have been especially influential in shaping contemporary Southeast Asia: the colonial experience; the incorporation of the region into a global capitalist economy; and the expansion and adoption of the 'Western' states system. Although these issues cannot be treated in detail here, it is important to remember that the very territorial demarcation of modern, post-colonial nations like Indonesia and Malaysia was a reflection of a European, rather than an indigenous, logic. Although European colonization in places like Java may not have overturned preexisting patterns of cultural activity (Osborne 2000), the borders of contemporary Indonesia are testimony to the colonial experience and encompass groups of people with no obvious affinity or allegiance. The continuing ethnic tensions across much of the Indonesian archipelago are an ample reminder of how artificial a creation Indonesia is and just what a challenge maintaining stability can be, especially at moments of economic dislocation.

The impact of that complex interplay of economic, political and social forces subsumed under the rubric of colonialism is evident at a number of levels, from the physical transformation of Southeast Asian geography to the creation of the region's distinctive and occasionally volatile ethnic mix. The intensification of rice growing throughout Southeast Asia, particularly in the Mekong River delta in Vietnam, and the rapid expansion of rubber plantations across the region were dramatic, highly visible expressions of the impact of colonial economic priorities (Elson 1992). Indeed, in general, the colonial experience and the subsequent withdrawal of the imperial powers left a number of the newly independent countries of Southeast Asia with the dual handicap of narrow, resource-based economic profiles that were vulnerable to price fluctuations in global markets and complex social relations that made the task of nation building extraordinarily difficult. Yet there was one aspect of the interaction with Europe which Asia's emergent political elites embraced with significantly greater enthusiasm, namely, state sovereignty. The integration of the region's newly independent states into the norms of the external states system conferred a juridical framework within which the process of nation building could occur. It also provided a convenient shell for the emergence of authoritarian rule across much of the region as economic growth and political stability were often privileged above democratic accountability.

In thinking about the current economic order in Southeast Asia it is useful to divide the countries of the region into groups, largely reflecting living standards and the nature of their respective incorporation into the global division of labour. Table 5.1 provides basic data for all of the countries in the region and the subsequent parts of this section of the chapter briefly discuss the national political economies of the countries by reference to these groups.

Singapore, Brunei and the Philippines

One group of Southeast Asian countries is most noteworthy for the fact that, even within a region characterized by diversity, they are remarkably different from other countries in the region. Of the three countries in this diverse group – Singapore, Brunei Darussalam and the Philippines – Singapore is distinguished by its extremely high GDP per head (at nearly US$21,0000, greater than that of the United Kingdom, its former colonial master) and by its relatively early and highly successful integration into the global economy. While its position as a former British colony allowed it to consolidate its role as a regional *entrepôt* within an imperial trading system, what is striking about Singapore is the fact that it has reinforced its 'natural' advantages through highly interventionist government policies designed to attract foreign investment and carve out an export-oriented niche in electronics industries in particular (Rodan 1989). Significantly, Singapore industrialized earlier than its immediate Southeast Asian neighbours, using multinational capital to spur development from the mid-1960s onwards, and is consequently generally associated with the original 'tiger' economies of east Asia such as South Korea and Taiwan. Singapore is also distinguished from some of its neighbours in having a relatively small (about 4.1 million), highly educated population, and a generally competent and corruption-free government. True, Singapore is also noted for the intrusive, not to say authoritarian, nature of its political leadership, but this elite is generally considered to have successfully overseen Singapore's remarkably rapid economic rise and the creation of a sophisticated economy supported by a highly effective infrastructure. Brunei, by contrast, has an even smaller population (0.3 million), constitutes a

Table 5.1 *Southeast Asia: basic data*

	Total population	Per capita GDP US$	GDP per capita in PPP US$	Percentage of GDP		
				Agriculture	Industry	Goods & services
Brunei	344,000	12,245	18,357	–	–	–
Cambodia	12,265,220	270	1,414	37	22	41
Indonesia	208,981,088	711	3,521	16	47	37
Lao PDR	5,403,170	329	1,573	51	23	26
Malaysia	23,802,360	3,696	8,614	9	49	42
Myanmar	48,320,440	142	1,269	–	–	–
Philippines	78,317,032	914	3,994	15	31	54
Singapore	4,131,000	20,847	25,990	0	32	68
Thailand	61,183,900	1,822	6,898	10	–	–
Vietnam	79,526,048	420	2,282	24	38	39

Sources: Compiled from World Bank Development Indicators and ASEAN Secretariat. All data refer to 2001.

comparatively limited geographical area, and has been almost entirely reliant on oil revenues to underpin its – by regional standards – relatively high living standards. It remains, however, essentially a *rentier* state with limited regional influence, most notable for the conspicuous consumption of its royal family and its failure to build a more diversified economic structure (Cleary and Wong 1994).

The reason for including the Philippines in this anomalous group is that, although it has much in common with some of the other founders of ASEAN, its cultural heritage, distinctive economic structures and longstanding historical relationship with the United States give it a profile unlike any of its neighbours. Indeed, the Philippines was frequently referred to as the 'sick man of Asia' because of its failure to take part in the remarkable economic boom enjoyed by much of the region in the 1980s and early 1990s. The Philippines has also had the misfortune to experience authoritarian rule, but, in marked contrast with Singapore, Filipino elites have frequently used their position to loot the country on a systematic basis, rather than seek to ensure its economic growth (Hutchcroft 1998). Adding to the Philippines' problems have been endless ideologically and ethnically inspired rebel movements, something that has made the establishment of stability, let alone the pursuit of widespread development, fundamentally problematic. In the context of the Cold War and the perceived threat of communist expansion, repressive leaders like Fidel Marcos (president from 1966–86) were allowed to exploit the country with little external interference. As a consequence, a system of patronage politics, in which a handful of powerful landowning families dominate economic activity and political power, continues to characterize the Philippine political economy, even though the Marcos era has long since ended.

The installation in 2001 of the supposedly reformist and 'clean' administration of new President Gloria Arroyo has been described as a ' "soft revolution" that ejected an elected president in order to return the old, wealthy political and business elite to power' (Sheean 2001). Although democracy has been reinstated in the Philippines and the country enjoys, by regional standards, a highly liberal press, a generally vibrant civil society and an effective legal system, this has proved of little assistance in addressing the entrenched poverty and limited range of activities that continue to characterize the Philippine economy. Crucially, the symbiotic relationship established in the Marcos era between the local privileged elite and the multinational corporations of the former colonial power has meant that the Philippines has become trapped in what Neher (1994) called a cycle of underdevelopment. The continued reliance of the Philippine economy on primary product exports and the limited success of import-substitution policies during the 1950s and 1960s have caused Philippine living standards to remain significantly lower than those of neighbouring Thailand, Malaysia and even Indonesia.

Thailand, Malaysia and Indonesia

These countries constitute another distinct grouping, united by their founding position in ASEAN and, more significantly in the longer term, their comparatively successful economic record over the last couple of decades. Of these countries Malaysia has been the most successful and, as we shall see later, a prominent advocate of developmental strategies that have often been at odds with the orthodox economic wisdom of the day. The point to make at this stage, however, is that Malaysia has achieved its noteworthy rise in living standards (some US$3,696 GDP per head in 2001), and rapid shift from a predominantly resource-dependent economy to one in which manufacturing accounted for 33 per cent of GDP by the mid-1990s, through policies that have been consciously modelled on the Japanese 'interventionist' model of economic development (Jomo 1997). Not only were such policies designed to accelerate the structural transformation of the Malaysian economy, and thus overcome the limitations and resource dependency of the inherited colonial model, but they also allowed the Malaysian government, especially under the authoritarian leadership of Mahathir Mohamad, who became prime minister as long ago as 1981, to promote policies of racially based positive discrimination. This strategy was triggered by another colonial inheritance – an ethnically divided population with large Chinese and significant Indian minority elements – something that meant sophisticated social engineering was deemed an essential part of the overall development strategy.

A significant consequence of this distinctive Malaysian development strategy has been to blur the distinctions between the economic and political spheres. The dominant political grouping – the United Malays National Organization (UMNO) – has also come to be a major stakeholder in the domestic economy, meaning that 'economic' and 'political' actors are often either the same people, or intimately connected through mutually supportive and rewarding relationships (Gomez and Jomo 1999). It is precisely such relationships that have been at the centre of allegations about 'crony capitalism' in the region – relationships which, as we shall see, powerful external agencies have been intent on abolishing. Whatever the merits of such arguments, the New Economic Policy developed under Mahathir has generally been successful in alleviating poverty and encouraging the creation of a more diversified economy. Furthermore, Malaysia's attempts to maintain a degree of economic autonomy meant that it was not badly exposed to overseas lenders when the recent economic crisis began in 1997, something that helped insulate it from both the demands of external creditors *and* the attentions of organizations like the IMF (Beeson 2000). In this respect the contrast with Indonesia, which also experienced significant economic growth prior to the crisis, is especially revealing.

Indonesia's very large population (almost 209 million in 2001), its strategically pivotal position across some of the region's major trade routes and the prominent role it has played in supporting the region's institutional structures all mean that it has an importance that transcends its relatively modest economic status. Indonesia has an average GDP of only US$711 per head and a total GDP of US$221 billion – the latter a little more than double that of Singapore, which has a fraction of Indonesia's population. Yet, for nearly three decades prior to the crisis in 1997, Indonesia regularly posted annual economic growth rates of around 6–7 per cent and attracted widespread plaudits and attention in the process. As we now know, such figures concealed continuing structural vulnerabilities and tensions over the style and direction of policy. Not only has Indonesia come to be highly dependent on global commodity prices because of the dominance of oil and gas in its export profile, but such fluctuations have directly affected domestic policy: whenever oil prices are high Indonesian governments have generally been much less willing to follow the market-centred orthodoxy espoused by US-trained 'technocrats' (Winters 1996). One of the reasons that Indonesia has been so badly affected by the regional crisis was that its financial position generally, and massive accumulated debt burden in particular, left it vulnerable to the demands of external creditors and agencies.

When times were good, however, Indonesia under long-time President Suharto (president from 1968–98) used oil revenues to encourage the building of a more diversified economy and successfully carved out a competitive niche in the labour-intensive manufacturing of clothing, furniture and the like (Hill 1996). Despite the existence of some notoriously repressive labour conditions (Hadiz 1997), Indonesia enjoyed a steady rise in overall living standards. There was, however, a dark side to Indonesia's development experience. Elaborate networks of patronage and favouritism developed under Suharto, which saw his family assume a prominent position in key sectors of the national economy – relationships which came in for remarkably little internal or external criticism for most of his presidency. As in Malaysia, political and economic power was often fused, rendering the reluctance to relinquish control of the economy the more understandable as a consequence. As in the Philippines, ruling elites used their position to obtain significant private wealth. Indeed a feature of the Indonesian experience is that some Indonesians were able to take advantage of both their crucially important political and economic connections, as well as the evolving international economic order, to borrow money from obliging foreign financial institutions. One of the most serious long-term problems that emerged from this interplay between the local and the global was a massive foreign debt that continues to limit the available policy options of Indonesian governments. The country's external debt to GNP ratio reached more than 170 per cent in 1998 and, currently, its spending on debt servicing, including to the World Bank, is six times greater than combined spending on education and health care (*Asia Times OnLine* 22 August 2001). Adding to these problems is the fact that the economy contracted by a massive 15 per cent in 1998, the largest such fall experienced by any country of Indonesia's economic size in the post-1945 period (Case 2001: 104). In these circumstances, which placed the hard-won prosperity of the new middle class in jeopardy, the legitimacy of the Suharto regime began to unravel, culminating in his resignation in 1998.

Thailand was also battered by economic problems and ultimately experienced similar political problems as a consequence of the general financial crisis. In Thailand's case this was more surprising, as its higher living standards (US$1,822 GDP per head in 2001) and the apparent consolidation of democratic rule after years of military coups and instability suggested it was better placed to ride out the storm. Indeed, for all its political difficulties, Thailand had, like Indonesia, enjoyed steady economic growth from the 1960s onwards. Again, like Indonesia and Malaysia, Thailand also saw a long-run change in the structure of the domestic economy as agriculture declined in importance (down from 40 per cent of GDP in 1960 to just 10 per cent in the 1990s), with manufacturing experiencing steady expansion in the same period. Significantly, by the end of the 1990s manufacturing accounted for around 75 per cent of exports, up from a mere 1 per cent in 1960 (Hewison 1997: 105), fundamentally transforming the way the Thai economy is articulated with the global economy. Not only is Thailand now plugged in to global markets and transregional production structures, but its dependence on, and potential exposure to, external forces is heightened by the high levels of foreign investment – up to a third of the total between the 1960s and the 1990s – that have underpinned the industrialization process in Thailand (Hewison 1997: 108). As with other parts of the region, however, integration with the global economy has been accompanied by increasingly divergent patterns of wealth and income distribution, especially between urban and rural areas, a factor that helps to account for the strength of the anti-globalization movement that has emerged in Thailand in the wake of the crisis (Hewison 2000). Compounding Thailand's problems are a number of environmental and social issues that flow from the rapid exploitation of its natural resources and its unenviable reputation as a centre for sex tourism.

Burma and Indochina

The final group of countries in Southeast Asia lack even Thailand's modest capacities. Like the Philippines, Singapore and Brunei, Burma (which is also known as Myanmar, a name chosen by the current military leadership but not widely recognized by the international community) is also something of an anomaly. It merits inclusion in this group on the basis of its overall poverty and the fact that it is amongst the most recent of countries to join ASEAN's expanded membership. It is hard to know just how poor Burma actually is, as its military government – the State Law and Order Restoration Council, recently 'rebadged' for public relations purposes as the State Peace and Development Council – maintains tight control over such 'sensitive' information as part of a more general policy of political repression. What is clear, however, is that Burma has failed to grow economically to anything like the same extent as some of its immediate neighbours in Southeast Asia, despite some potentially significant natural advantages. Like the Philippines and more recently Indonesia, Burma's leaders face a number of continuing challenges to their authority from political opponents like Aung San Suu Kyi and from armed independence movements like that of the Karen people. One of the key issues at stake here is not simply the integrity of the state itself, but control of the lucrative narcotics trade which has become such a major export industry – some estimates suggest that Burma accounts for 70 per cent of the global supply of heroin and opium (Neher 2001: 161). Other, more legitimate, forms of economic development have been less successful. One of the more bizarre claims made by the country's military leaders in the wake of the regional economic crisis of the late 1990s was that Burma had been only mildly affected because of their policy of isolation from the international economy. The reality is that its economy remains overwhelmingly agriculture-based, with 70 per cent of the population barely even eking out a tenuous existence off the land. The prospects for either rapid economic or political change continue to look bleak under the current regime – which thus poses an awkward challenge for its ASEAN partners. Burma not only lacks the basic institutional capacity to be an effective member of ASEAN, but also attracts widespread international criticism because of the nature of its current governing regime. The effect has been to undermine ASEAN's overall credibility (Henderson 1999).

The incorporation of the countries of Indochina into ASEAN has also been difficult, chiefly because of the gap that exists between the economic level reached by the founding states and that of Vietnam, Laos and Cambodia. With some 79 million people, Vietnam has the second largest population in Southeast Asia. Although it is more ethnically homogenous than many of its neighbours, it remains grindingly poor

(US$420 per head in 2001). However, even in Vietnam, as in Indonesia, Malaysia, the Philippines and Thailand, the so-called 'overseas Chinese' – the 50 million or so ethnic Chinese who live outside 'Greater China', especially in Southeast Asia (Dirlik 1997; Wai-chung Yeung 1999) – assume a prominent place in economic activity, especially in Ho Chi Minh City in the south. The prominent role and economic power of Chinese business people has been something to which political elites across the region have had to respond, but in Vietnam this situation is complicated by the fact that they are often successful capitalists in what remains, nominally at least, a socialist country. Transforming the structure of the Vietnamese economy remains a challenge for what is still, despite increasingly rapid urbanization, a predominantly rural population. Given that some of Vietnam's ruling elite still has reservations about the wisdom of fully embracing a market-based economy, the difficulties of economic management are compounded (Kolko 1997). Nevertheless, the economic reform programme tentatively initiated under the banner of *doi moi* in 1986 has unleashed what looks like an unstoppable pattern of change as the agricultural sector is increasingly privatized, enterprise actively encouraged, the economy opened and the currency floated (Nugent 1996).

It is worthy of note that Vietnam's history has been more directly shaped by the actions of powerful external actors than most countries, even within Southeast Asia. China has long exerted a profound influence, but the more recent interventions of France and the US have also been of immense significance. Plainly, Vietnam's position and prospects must be read in the context of unfolding 'great power' contestation, of which the ending of the Cold War and the collapse of communism as a viable alternative to capitalism is but the latest chapter. One of the most important consequences of these more recent events has been to shift Vietnam's economic orientation away from the Soviet Union and its former allies and towards its immediate neighbours in Asia. Creating a significant manufacturing capacity, especially on the back of inefficient state-owned enterprises, remains a daunting challenge, however, one that has been exacerbated by a recent decline in foreign investment, which dropped by half in the wake of the regional financial crisis (Hussain 2001: 130). Vietnam's apparently chronic balance of payments problems suggest, in short, that there will be no easy escape from its difficult and impoverished position.

The last two countries in this group are Cambodia and Laos, which share with Vietnam similar historical influences and contemporary problems. In the recent past Cambodia is best known as a site of great power contestation that had the ultimate effect of unleashing the Khmer Rouge under Pol Pot to wreak havoc on the Cambodian people themselves for a traumatic period between 1975 and 1978 when Vietnam invaded and drove the regime from power. The complex history behind this tragedy (Chandler 2000) is beyond the scope of the discussion here, but the impact of this period saw perhaps one million Cambodians, or one-sixth of the population, killed, the country's modest infrastructure destroyed and its indigenous intelligentsia and potential leadership cadre virtually eliminated. When order was eventually restored during the 1990s, initially under UN auspices and subsequently under a coalition government elected in 1993, it rapidly became clear that many of those entering government lacked the competence to run the country. Compounding these problems was the fact that 20 per cent less land was under cultivation in 1992 than in 1967, of which fully 30 per cent was affected by the planting of landmines (Downie 2001: 139). Add to this high levels of illiteracy (possibly 65 per cent) and infant mortality, as well as poor health and social infrastructure, and Cambodia's problems seem of another order of desperation when compared to the likes of Indonesia and even Vietnam. Unsurprisingly, Cambodia remains dependent on assistance from the World Bank, the IMF and sundry external aid agencies. Of the aid that is provided something like a third is lost through corruption, which fundamentally undermines the capacity of this still fragile state. While the emergence of a textile and clothing industry is beginning to make a significant contribution to Cambodian exports, the general Asian crisis also had a major impact on Cambodia, forcing the government to make further reductions in spending on education, health and rural development.

Like Vietnam, Laos remains a nominally communist country, but it has not assumed anything like the same prominence in international affairs. Although not as obviously affected by former superpower contestation as Cambodia, the Laotian economy was dominated by French and US business interests before the inauguration of the Lao People's Democratic Republic in 1975, and was so undeveloped literally that its principal export was postage stamps. The key challenge for the new government was actually to secure national sovereignty and create a nation-wide economic structure in a country devastated by years of civil war during which it lost up to 50 per cent of its population and, like Cambodia, suffered the decimation of the educated portion (Fry and Faming 2001: 147). The inauguration of the so-called New Economic Mechanism (1986–92) marked the beginning of an adjustment to the new political and economic realities that were emerging toward the end of the Cold War and an attempt to shift from central planning to a market economy. Despite these efforts to chart a development strategy, the Laotian economy remains heavily dependent on foreign aid and its external economic relations are dominated by its larger neighbour,

Thailand. Thai goods accounted for an estimated 45 per cent of Laos' total imports and 37 per cent of exports in the 1980s and 1990s (Lintner 2001: 178). Unfortunately, Thailand's own post-crisis economic problems caused a significant drop in investment and led to the cancellation of plans to develop much-needed electricity-generating power plants (Lintner 2001). More generally, Laos continues to experience civil strife which may be as much linked to the country's remarkably diverse ethnic groups as the sorts of ideological issues that characterized the earlier civil war. Whatever the cause of such instability, it adds to the country's economic difficulties, causing bouts of hyperinflation and falling foreign investment, factors which have seen Laos become increasingly dependent on remittances from the estimated 10 per cent of the population that has left the country since the communist takeover in 1975.

The intra-regional politics of development in Southeast Asia

Even this brief survey of the disparate countries of Southeast Asia suggests that future economic and political development at either the national or regional levels in Southeast Asia is likely to be fraught with continuing difficulties. This is striking because as recently as five years ago many of these problems seemed at least to be in the process of being overcome. At one level, the difficulties are undoubtedly compounded by indigenous factors: different political systems and levels of economic activity, to say nothing of cultural and ethnic diversity, make greater regional economic integration or political cooperation inherently problematic. At the same time at the international level, Southeast Asia's future, and the potential for more regionally based responses to collective developmental challenges, continue to be powerfully influenced by external forces. This is where regional organizations (Table 5.2) matter and, despite such constraints, Southeast Asia can boast in ASEAN one of the most enduring institutional bodies outside of Europe or North America with a declaratory agenda dedicated to greater economic integration and political cooperation. Indeed, ASEAN's very survival is noteworthy in an area with little history of successful transnational institutionalization.

ASEAN's vitality and effectiveness at different moments are in fact important measures of the prospects for greater regional economic and political autonomy. Created in 1967, ASEAN was a product of the Cold War. Its original members – Indonesia, the Philippines, Singapore, Thailand and Malaysia – shared a number of concerns about external

Table 5.2 *Main regional organizations in Southeast Asia*

	Full name	Date of foundation	Members	Aims
ASEAN	Association of Southeast Asian Nations	1967	Brunei Darussalam, Cambodia, Indonesia, Lao PDR, Malaysia, Myanmar, Philippines, Singapore, Thailand, Vietnam.	• To accelerate economic growth, social progress and cultural development in the region through joint endeavours in the spirit of equality and partnership in order to strengthen the foundation for a prosperous and peaceful community of Southeast Asian nations. • To promote regional peace and stability through abiding respect for justice and the rule of law in the relationship among countries in the region and adherence to the principles of the UN Charter.
ASEAN +3			ASEAN states + People's Republic of China, Japan, Republic of Korea.	• Increasingly formalized grouping that includes the major Northeast Asian countries in addition to the ASEAN states. • Beginning in 1997, heads of government meetings have occurred in conjunction with ASEAN summits. • Agenda still evolving, but discussions about regional free trade area and monetary cooperation.

ARF	ASEAN Regional Forum	• To foster constructive dialogue and consultation on political and security issues of common interest and concern. • To make significant contributions to efforts towards confidence-building and preventive diplomacy in the Asia-Pacific region.	1994	Australia, Brunei, Darussalam, Cambodia, Canada, China, European Union, India, Indonesia, Japan, Democratic People's Republic of Korea, Republic of Korea, Malaysia, Myanmar, Mongolia, New Zealand, Papua New Guinea, Philippines, Russian Federation, Singapore, Thailand, United States, Vietnam.
AFTA	ASEAN Free Trade Area	• Designed to increase ASEAN region's competitive advantage as a production base geared for the world market. Elimination of tariffs and non-tariff barriers among the ASEAN members seen as crucial part of this process. • Originally intended to achieve trade liberalization by 2008, but this was accelerated to 2003, despite wide-spread scepticism about feasibility.	1992	

continued overleaf

Table 5.2 *Continued*

	Full name	Aims	Date of foundation	Members
APEC	Asia-Pacific Economic Cooperation	• APEC has a membership of 21 economic jurisdictions, a population of over 2.5 billion and a combined GDP of 19 trillion US dollars accounting for 47% of world trade. • Dedicated to promoting trade and investment and 'practical' economic cooperation. • APEC is working to achieve what are referred to as the 'Bogor Goals' of free and open trade and investment in the Asia-Pacific by 2010 for 'developed' economies and 2020 for 'developing' economies. • APEC has identified three specific areas that are crucial to achieving the Bogor Goals: trade and investment liberalizaton; business facilitation; and economic and technical cooperation.	1989	Australia, Brunei Darussalam, Canada, Chile, People's Republic of China, Hong Kong, China, Indonesia, Japan, Korea, Malaysia, Mexico, New Zealand, Papua New Guinea, Peru, Philippines, Russia, Singapore, Chinese Taipei, Thailand, United States, Vietnam.

and internal security threats. Not only were they preoccupied by the superpower contestation that threatened to engulf Southeast Asia; they were equally concerned to shore up their own domestic structures of power. The protection of sovereignty during the process of nation building has been a continuing preoccupation of many post-colonial states (Jackson 1990), but in ASEAN's case the principle of non-interference in the domestic affairs of member countries was elevated to foundational status (Frost 1990). The privileging of national independence and the reluctance to impinge on national autonomy have thereby placed major constraints on what ASEAN can actually do – something that was highlighted by its inability to play a more effective role in the management of the post-1997 regional financial crisis. As a consequence, critics of ASEAN have argued that it is, in fact, an 'issue avoidance organization', in that it has been defined more by what it does *not* do than what it actually does (Smith and Jones 1997: 147).

Although, plainly, there is some substance to these criticisms, the fact remains that ASEAN has had to cope with some formidable challenges. While the Cold War spurred ASEAN's formation, its abrupt end raised fundamental questions about the organization's future. Although it is important to acknowledge that ASEAN had played a role in maintaining peace in a region not previously noted for stability (Kivimäki 2001), and in which a series of major potential flashpoints continue to exist (Tan 2000), the ending of the Cold War created a new security environment to which the ASEAN states had to respond. Significantly, the inauguration of the ASEAN Regional Forum (ARF) in 1994 was designed to institutionalize a regional security order that not only incorporated key strategic actors like the US, Japan and China, but was based explicitly on the sort of informal, consensus-based 'Asian way' of decision-making that had characterized ASEAN itself (Leifer 1996: 25). In the security sphere, at least, ASEAN was thus able to play a significant role in creating a new forum in which intra- and inter-regional relationships between the major powers could be conducted.

There is a good deal of debate about how significant this process has been and what it means for ASEAN itself. Narine (1998) argues that ASEAN's own institutional frailties and inability to act decisively, or in opposition to the major powers, makes it even less influential than it was during the Cold War when it enjoyed an enhanced strategic importance. Acharya (2001: 184), by contrast, suggests that, while progress may be slow, the ARF's consensual, non-legalistic *process* is playing an important role in 'shap[ing] the balance of power by providing norms of restraint and avenues of confidence building among the major powers. In the long term, the ARF may even enable states to transcend the balance of power approach.' Clearly, in the security context, ASEAN's influence and independence hinge on an absence of conflict in the region and – crucially – a continuing coincidence of interest between Southeast Asian countries and the infinitely more powerful strategic actors outside. Not only was the region ideologically divided for most of the post-1945 period when the constituent countries were attempting to consolidate their own political structures and economic modes, but the dominance of the US and its predilection for bilateral, rather than multilateral, strategic arrangements meant that security relations were generally externally rather than internally oriented. Paradoxically enough, the enhanced stability of the post-Cold War environment has been the precondition for a range of even more direct and indirect challenges to the autonomy of ASEAN's members.

One of the most important changes in Southeast Asia over the last two decades has been the increased integration of the region's economies into global and regional production structures. Southeast Asia has come to occupy a pivotal position as part of a triangular trade relationship between east Asia and North America, in which Japan has provided manufactures, capital and technology to Southeast Asia, and Southeast Asia has been a source of primary products for Japan and labour-intensive manufactures for North America (Gangopadhyay 1998). The industrialization process in Southeast Asia has undoubtedly been accelerated by Japanese investment and the establishment of subsidiary operations that often cross national borders throughout the region, although two qualifications must be entered. First, Japanese companies and the array of aid and assistance packages provided by the Japanese government have left the countries of the region in a somewhat dependent position. Second, the extent of the industrialization has often been limited because of a reluctance to transfer technology (Beeson 2001). This picture has, of late, become even more complex as Japanese capital flows have diminished as a consequence of its own economic problems and as other regional countries, like Korea, Taiwan and Singapore, have become more significant providers of investment capital (Pempel 2000). This has had implications for the emergence of subregional production zones and 'growth triangles' (Chen and Kwan 1997). Nevertheless, the Southeast Asian industrialization process remains partial and concentrated in a number of sectors – something that reflects the dependent nature of the regional economy and the sheer difficulty of breaking into highly competitive economic sectors experiencing diminishing returns (Kaplinsky 2000). One of the reasons why it has failed to 'deepen' is because of the use of export-processing zones that tend to reflect the needs of transnational corporations and consequently do not build up strong linkages with the rest of the domestic economy (Amirahmadi and Wu 1995). In the longer term this intermediate role in global production structures and concomitant dependence on key North American markets leaves the region highly vulnerable to downturns in the global economy. The importance of electronics exports in the region's export profile generally, together with reliance on the US market in particular, meant that even Singapore fell into recession in the late 1990s (*Far Eastern Economic Review* 9 August 2001). Compounding these problems from a Southeast Asian perspective is the rise of China as both a competing producer of labour-intensive manufactured goods and an alternative regional investment location (Ho 2001).

This regional economic evolution provided the backdrop for an important ASEAN initiative: the creation of the ASEAN Free Trade Area (AFTA). When inaugurated in 1994, AFTA offered a potential new *raison d'être* for the ASEAN group generally in an era in which security issues had come to be accorded less priority. In the same way that ASEAN had earlier held out the promise of increasing the political importance of the Southeast Asian countries, an expanded ASEAN economic area promised to provide the region with greater weight at a time when international influence in institutions like the WTO depended greatly on market size (Oman 1994: 29). Simultaneously, AFTA and its trade liberalization agenda offered a way of increasing the level of intra-ASEAN trade, which had remained much less important than ASEAN's trade with Japan, the US and the EU during the rapid economic expansion of the 1980s and 1990s. Indeed, if the Singaporean *entrepôt* is excluded, intra-ASEAN trade falls to about 5 per cent of the region's total trade relations (Chia Siow Yue 1998). At one level, this attempt to reduce intra-regional trade barriers reflected the widely promulgated and dominant international view that liberalization was the route to economic growth and prosperity. At another level, the creation of AFTA marked a pragmatic attempt to make Southeast Asia a larger, more attractive and increasingly coherent investment location at a time of heightened competition for mobile flows of foreign direct investment (Bowles and MacLean 1996).

It is important to recognize, however, that not only are some prominent regional leaders like Malaysia's Mahathir still keen to protect politically sensitive and economically strategic sectors of their respective economies, but that the AFTA programme itself has had discriminatory elements and been envisaged as a way of encouraging domestic capital formation. The ASEAN Investment Area, as initially proposed in 1998, differentiated between domestic investors from within ASEAN, who would enjoy full market access and national privileges by 2010, and foreign investors, who would not enjoy the same treatment until 2020 (Nesadurai 2002). In Malaysia and Indonesia concerns about the possible impact that unregulated foreign investment might have on domestic manufacturing, and the limitations this might place on the capacity of domestic governments to assist 'national champions', made them wary of wholesale investment liberalization. Significantly, in September 2001, the disparity between domestic and foreign investors was removed as a consequence of a general desire in the region to stimulate growth in the aftermath of the financial crisis.

What is interesting and noteworthy about this change of tack is that, despite entrenched opposition by vested interests that might be expected to lose from a wholesale reduction of protective trade barriers, the continuing integration of the region's economies into the wider international system is changing the balance of political forces within national jurisdictions. In Malaysia, for example, there has been significant resistance to the trade liberalization timetable in cases where such initiatives are expected to have a major impact on Malaysia's national car project, the Proton (*Asiaweek.com* 2000). Yet the position of economic nationalists in both Malaysia and Indonesia is being undermined by the increased influence of liberal reformers who stand to benefit from entrenching precisely the sorts of measures conventionally advocated by external organizations bent on changing the region's economic structures and political practices (Soesastro 1995; Stubbs 2000). In this regard, as Bowles (2000: 438) observes, regional trade and investment agreements like AFTA 'offered another way to signal to foreign investors that the move towards investor-friendly neoliberal policies was permanent since the costs of reneging on them were significantly increased'.

In another telling indication of Southeast Asia's readiness to try and come to terms with its somewhat dependent position within the global political economy generally and within the east Asian region in particular, ASEAN has responded positively to China's suggestion that a larger free trade area should be created between itself and Southeast Asia 'within a decade' (*Japan Times* 8 January 2002). Given the long-term historical significance of the expansion of China's economy, its rapid integration with the world economy and the fact that China directly competes with ASEAN for foreign investment and markets, this is a potentially major initiative. It remains to be seen whether it will be realized effectively or how it will be integrated into the wider economic architecture that increasingly governs international commerce, but it is indicative of ASEAN's willingness – whether enthusiastic or not – to accommodate the realities of the contemporary international political and economic order that a framework trade agreement is emerging, along with a raft of other agreements that China has played a similar key role in driving (*Far Eastern Economic Review* 14 November 2002).

In the absence of an effective region-wide grouping that includes countries like Japan and China that are actually prepared to champion alternative economic and political visions, it seems as if neoliberal policies of the sort advocated by powerful external agencies like the IMF are being 'locked in' as part of Southeast Asia's increasingly dense institutional architecture. Given the importance of state intervention and economic regulation in the region's earlier, comparatively successful, strategy of development, this is a significant and major departure from established policy frameworks. Not only is there no guarantee that this new strategy will prove successful in the long term, but it is likely to further erode national policy autonomy in the short term. The possible dangers of closer integration with the wider global economy were vividly revealed in the Asian crisis of the late 1990s. It is, therefore, helpful to consider briefly the genesis, management and aftermath of this crisis in its Southeast Asian manifestation as a point of entry into a discussion of the region's role in the wider global politics of development.

The extra-regional politics of development in Southeast Asia

If one event highlighted just how integrated with, and vulnerable to, the international economic system Southeast Asia has become, it was the economic and concomitant political crisis that swept through the region from 1997 onwards. Indeed, the whole affair served as a powerful reminder of the inextricable nature of the links between economic and political processes – and not just within countries. For if one lesson became, often painfully, apparent, it was the extent of the vulnerability of less-powerful countries and economies to the interventions and interests of external powers. As the following examination of the crisis makes clear, while there have been a number of important indigenous initiatives designed to advance Southeast Asian interests, the region remains highly exposed to the actions of more powerful external actors. That such obstacles to development have not simply reappeared, but continue to limit the options available to regional policy-makers testifies to the enduring asymmetries of power embedded in the structure of global relations.

The economic crisis that developed in Thailand, and which ultimately affected most of east Asia, had an especially devastating impact on the countries of Southeast Asia. The remarkable growth and social progress that had characterized the region for several decades not only came to an abrupt stop, but actually went into reverse as living standards generally, but especially those of the poor, went into decline. Indonesia, Thailand and Malaysia were particularly badly affected as they had been the principal beneficiaries of the earlier high growth period and their respective governments had gained a good deal of legitimacy from their claims to superior economic management. In the wake of the crisis the governments of Thailand and Indonesia fell, and Malaysia was plunged into a protracted leadership struggle which has still not been definitively resolved, although Mahathir's resignation may help to clarify the situation. There is no need to provide a detailed analysis of the crisis here, as there is already a proliferation of accounts and the general pattern of events is by now quite well-known (Beeson and Robison 2000). The purpose is to highlight issues that are of importance to the region's overall position as a collective economic and political entity and its capacity to play a role in wider global affairs.

Perhaps the key point to emphasize is that Southeast Asia's 'image' has been profoundly changed, and not just in the minds of those controllers of mobile capital who, notwithstanding the many genuine problems that attach to corruption, 'cronyism' and governance more generally within the region, were arguably deeply implicated in establishing the initial preconditions for the crisis itself (Beeson 1998; Winters 2000). Peter Hartcher (2001: 77) captures this change in sentiment when he suggests that when, five years after the crisis:

> Southeast Asia is compared to the Balkans, it is not to draw a contrast but a parallel. Most regional economies are in disarray. They have emerged from the Asian economic crisis of 1997–98 not improved but enduringly impaired. The collective Southeast Asian economy is smaller today that it was before the crisis. Many dormant ethnic and religious resentments have exploded into violence. Democratic systems are under tremendous stress and a stinking tide of corruption is on the rise ... The ASEAN grouping has lost the power of action and degenerated to the brink of meaninglessness.

The region's change in circumstances has certainly been marked. Not only have a number of countries been left with large debt burdens, but flows of capital into Southeast Asia have also diminished (World Bank 2001b: 35). Moreover, where foreign direct investment has continued, it has often been of a significantly different type, directed more toward the acquisition of existing, extremely cheap, assets in the region, rather than constituting genuinely new investment (Mody and Negishi 2001). At a time when perceptions have become increasingly important determinants of interest rates, investment flows and the like (Van Ham 2001), the region's capacity to attract only the 'bottom feeders' of global capitalism is clearly of concern.

It is this transformation in the region's fortunes, especially when combined with what has been seen by many as the intrusive, even opportunistic, nature of the externally organized crisis-management strategies forced on regional governments, that has fuelled what Richard Higgott (2000) described as the 'politics of resentment'. The most prominent expression of this phenomenon has come from Mahathir, especially in his fulminations against the activities of the 'West' generally and unscrupulous financial speculators in particular (*Australian* 10 October 1999). Although he is invariably dismissed or demonized by commentators from outside the region, he identifies a number of issues that are particularly important in a Southeast Asian context. Moreover, Mahathir has been at the centre of efforts to develop authentically regional responses to the challenge of economic development and political management. Central to Mahathir's critique are two interlinked contentions: not only that the countries of Southeast Asia confront major structural obstacles when trying to break out of their dependent positions in a global economic order dominated by Japan, North America and western Europe, but also that the institutions charged with managing the global economy systematically privilege the interests and entrench the dominance of these parts of the post-industrial world. In this vision the case for countering such external political pressures and the constraining influence of an increasingly powerful international financial system is the rhetorical justification for Malaysia's attempts to flout the conventional policy wisdom and retain a degree of economic autonomy (Beeson 2000). Manifestly, there is much that is self-serving in Mahathir's position, given the deeply interconnected nature of political and economic activity in Malaysia and the threat posed to this system by greater liberalization. Nevertheless, whatever his motivations might be, he articulates a widely held perception in Southeast Asia that the activities of the key international financial institutions, working in tandem with the post-industrial countries, make the sustained pursuit of autonomous development especially difficult.

Regional non-governmental organizations (NGOs) have consistently drawn attention to what they see as the non-transparent, discriminatory activities of the WTO, which they claim are designed to impose a regulatory regime that advances the economic interests of transnational corporations from the 'Western' world (Khor 2001; Kwa 2001). The difficulty the Thai government has experienced in producing cheaper, generic versions of HIV/AIDS treatments to counter the epidemic sweeping the country in the face of resistance from patent-owning foreign pharmaceutical companies is but one of the more glaring examples of the potential clash of interests which the WTO encapsulates. What is less obvious, however, is that the manner in which the WTO itself operates has the effect of entrenching particular interests and perspectives. Despite that fact that it has a more democratic organizational basis than the World Bank or the IMF, the sheer inability of poorer countries from Southeast Asia to have their interests effectively represented within the

WTO's decision-making bodies means that their positions are frequently underrepresented; it is simply not possible for poorer countries to cover all the issues with the requisite expertise, or always to resist the threats and blandishments of the richer members in the back-room negotiations that precede many WTO deals (Michalopoulos 1998).

ASEAN's overall attitude to trade liberalization is, consequently, somewhat ambivalent. Although the grouping has offered rhetorical support for a new WTO-sponsored round of multilateral trade negotiations, and despite its own continuing commitment to AFTA, there is overall disappointment with the impact that trade liberalization has had on the region thus far. The reluctance of the richer post-industrial countries to dismantle quota-based systems that limit the access of key ASEAN exports like clothing and textiles has induced widespread scepticism about the benefits of such processes and entrenched the idea that the WTO reflects only the interests of these rich economies. Similarly, countries like Thailand, which have attempted to reduce support for domestic agriculture in the spirit of WTO reforms, have seen farm-based incomes fall significantly, debt increase and the natural environment continue to suffer (*Bangkok Post* 20 August 2000). One of the consequences of the WTO's failure, thus far, to carry through a new round of trade liberalization that will actually address the specific concerns of Southeast Asia has been an increase in bilateral, rather than multilateral, trade deals, as countries like Singapore have lost faith in both the WTO and the pace of ASEAN-led reform. Although Singapore is more completely integrated into international trade and investment circuits than most countries, the fact that it has attempted to strike bilateral deals with Japan, Mexico, New Zealand, Australia and Chile not only undermines the WTO's multilateral approach, but may encourage others in the region to follow suit (Ravenhill 2003).

The activities of the other IFIs have frequently been even more intrusive and threatening to Southeast Asian sovereignty. The IMF's role in the management of the crisis was widely and frequently criticized for its inability to adjust its standard policy response to the actual needs of the region (Sachs 1997). Even more significant in retrospect, however, was the extent of the reforms it demanded in return for financial assistance. In Indonesia, for example, the IMF presented a blueprint for the virtual reconstitution of Indonesia's political economy (*Jakarta Post* 17 January 1988). Whatever the merits of such policies, the point to emphasize here is that they undermined the authority of the Indonesian state, sparking a political crisis that continues to reverberate. Moreover, the actions of the IMF were widely seen as intimately connected with the goals of US foreign policy, allowing the US to pursue the long-term goal of trade liberalization in Asia with an effectiveness that years of trade negotiations within organizations like APEC had been unable to achieve (Beeson 1999). Even where the IFIs may be thought to have provided a useful role in precipitating the downfall of an authoritarian leader like Suharto, any credit that may have been obtained from such pressure was compromised by revelations about the World Bank's lending policies. Not only did the Bank effectively legitimize the Suharto regime, but it also facilitated the corruption that was central to its patronage politics and encouraged inflows of speculative capital of precisely the sort that ultimately undid the Indonesian economy (*Asian Wall Street Journal* 15 July 1998). Given such a history it is perhaps unsurprising that the new leader of Indonesia, Megawati Sukarnoputri, appears to share much of Mahathir's misgivings about the influence of the IFIs and the post-industrial world more generally (*AFP* 31 May 2000).

The IFIs, then, have effectively been arms of US foreign policy, using structural adjustment policies to try and impose specific forms of public policy throughout the world (Caufield 1996). In keeping with the overarching logic of the Cold War, the World Bank and the IMF were prepared either to ignore or actively encourage the predations of dictators like Marcos in the Philippines and actually establish the preconditions for the sort of 'crony capitalism' they now decry (Hutchcroft 1998: 114). Even though the strategic calculus and thus the goals of the IFIs may now have changed, the reality for the countries of Southeast Asia – demonstrated all too vividly by the crisis and its aftermath – is that they remain highly vulnerable to an external order over which they have little control. It is in this context that one of the potentially most important initiatives of the whole post-1945 period in Asia has emerged: the so-called ASEAN + 3 grouping.

The ASEAN + 3 proposal rapidly gathered momentum in the late 1990s and culminated in the holding of the third ASEAN + 3 summit in Manila in 1999 – the first one in which all the leaders of participating countries attended. Although it is too soon to know whether the proposed grouping – which includes Japan, China and South Korea in addition to the ASEAN states – will continue to develop and become a major part of the region's institutional infrastructure (Beeson 2003), it highlights a number of issues about Southeast Asia and its links to the rest of east Asia, as well as the wider international system, that merit emphasis. The fundamental point to make about this grouping is that it exists at all, given that it is essentially the same as an earlier proposal by Mahathir that was swiftly derailed by US opposition and Japanese ambivalence (Hook 1999). Yet the east Asian crisis highlighted just how vulnerable *all* the countries of east Asia were to external forces, be it at the political level of the IFIs or the more narrowly economic level of global financial markets. Consequently, interest was reignited in the idea of an unambiguously 'Asian' body that might permit more independent regional responses to similar future crises. The great potential attraction of such an organization to the Southeast Asian countries, of course, was that it might prove less intrusive and politically demanding than the IFIs. Indeed, one of the attractions of the Asian Monetary Fund, originally proposed by Japan in 1997, was that it would probably have attached far less onerous conditions for potential borrowers. The rapid squashing of this proposal by the US provided an early and important insight into the practical difficulties of developing an authentically east Asian order in the face of US opposition (Mastanundo 2000).

Yet, in the words of former Indonesian foreign minister Ali Alatas (2001), 'the ASEAN + 3 forum is an idea whose time has come'. Whether its advocates' hopes will be realized, or whether the smaller ASEAN states will be able to maintain a prominent position amongst such regional giants, are moot points. What is clear, however, is that there is a determination to develop a self-consciously 'Asian' grouping in line with what has been described as the 'Asianization of Asia' (Funabashi 1993). Although one of the most distinctive manifestations of this impulse – the proclamation of so-called 'Asian values' – has become less prominent following the crisis, the emergence of such a debate was indicative of the region's capacity for generating indigenous discourses that challenge the ruling orthodoxy and the ideational dominance of the US in general and the IFIs in particular (Bauer and Bell 1999).

Finally, it needs to be recognized that, even if a more effective political architecture and framework for international economic integration could be developed, the region faces acute environmental problems that make any strategy of development inherently problematic. Ironically, the boom obscured the extent of problems that were actually exacerbated by economic growth. By now, 90 per cent of the Asia-Pacific's wildlife habitats have been destroyed, 13 of the world's 15 most polluted countries are found there, and one in three people do not have access to clean drinking water (*BBC* 18 June 2001). The relatively immature nature of civil society, the paucity of effective environmental NGOs and the continuing importance of close, mutually enriching relationships between government and business leaders in Southeast Asia mean that the environment generally continues to be ruthlessly exploited within national borders (Hirsch and Warren 1998). Despite the fact that influential IFIs like the World Bank are now encouraging aid recipients in Southeast Asia to take environmental issues seriously, ASEAN has been revealed to be incapable of dealing with the increasingly acute transboundary pollution problems that flow from the continuing exploitation of natural resources (Cotton 1999). This is not simply a manifestation of the pernicious effects of 'crony capitalism'. The continuing dependence of more than half of

Southeast Asia's population on subsistence lifestyles, which of necessity exploit the environment, makes the sort of technocratic, growth-led neoliberal response to the environmental challenge problematic, to say the least. As Bankoff (2001: 189) observes:

> The WTO and regional trading accords such as AFTA are supposed to promote more rational use of resources, and greater economies of scale between countries, but the policies they embody may just as easily promote the further erosion of environmental standards and encourage inappropriate shifting of resource pressures from one part of the world to another. Any approach that does not recognise that poverty is a root cause of environmental degradation and that fails to integrate resource considerations fully into development programmes is likely to exacerbate the present discouraging state of affairs.

If noble intentions and worthy rhetoric were the key to successful environmental management, ASEAN would have few problems. The 'Hanoi Plan of Action', enunciated in 1998 and intended to help realize ASEAN's 'Vision 2020', contains no less than 15 specific initiatives designed to improve the region's natural environment (ASEAN 1998). However, as Elliott (2001: 79) observes, without the requisite investment in environmentally friendly infrastructure, and without an adequate human and administrative capacity to implement and manage such initiatives, the region's significant environmental challenges are likely to become more acute.

Conclusion

Southeast Asia remains a highly diverse part of the world, marked by continuing differences in levels of economic activity, political practices and social values. Yet it shares a number of common factors that may, despite some formidable obstacles, provide a basis for a more enduring sense of regional identity. Whether it is the experience of colonization and decolonization, the incorporation of the region into a global capitalist order, the Cold War, the preoccupation with sovereignty and internal security, or the economic crisis that devastated the region in the late 1990s, there are a number of issues which may over time generate, if not solidarity, then at least a perception of common problems. True, Singapore's remarkable economic growth may eventually undermine ties with its ASEAN partners, whilst major cultural, political and even economic divisions continue to distinguish the ASEAN countries. But, important as such differences clearly are, they are being inexorably blurred by powerful forces of political and economic integration. Indeed, when seen in a longer historical perspective it is remarkable how much 'convergence' has already occurred as global capitalism and the powerful IFIs that attempt to regulate its operations steadily permeate every part of the planet (Beeson 2002). That does not of course mean, as we have seen here, that there are not also enduring, distinctive qualities that distinguish the Southeast Asian region and will continue to shape its overall trajectory for the foreseeable future.

Despite the dominance of the IFIs and the influential discourse of economic reform they champion, major questions remain about the efficacy of the neoliberal project generally and its appropriateness for Southeast Asia in particular. Thus far only Singapore has decisively graduated to the front rank of high-income economies and even it remains highly vulnerable to external circumstances beyond its control. Significantly, Singapore's transition was facilitated by favourable historical timing and effective state intervention – fortuitous circumstances that have become rarer as a consequence of global economic downturn, an ideational orthodoxy that discourages an active state and a notably less effective state capacity in the rest of the region. This is not intended as a ringing endorsement of Singapore's notoriously authoritarian brand of 'developmental state', but simply to emphasize how difficult – and rare – sustained and successful pursuit of development has been in a part of the world that has generally been integrated with the global capitalist economy on unfavourable terms. In retrospect, the economic growth that occurred throughout the 1980s and 1990s looks all the more remarkable. Until external economic circumstances improve significantly, and unless the US and the IFIs take a more accommodating, less doctrinaire attitude to the needs and capacities of Southeast Asian countries, such an achievement is unlikely to be easily repeated.

Further reading

Beeson, M. (ed.) (2002) *Reconfiguring East Asia: Regional Institutions and Organizations After the Crisis* (London: Curzon Press).

Heenan, P. and Lamontagne, M. (eds) (2001) *The Southeast Asia Handbook* (Chicago IL: Fitzroy Dearborn).

Osborne, M. (2000) *Southeast Asia: An Introductory History*, 8th edn (London: Allen & Unwin).

Robison, R. *et al.* (eds) (2000) *Politics and Markets in the Wake of the Asian Crisis* (London: Routledge).

Rodan, G. *et al.* (eds) (2001) *The Political Economy of South-East Asia: An Introduction*, 2nd edn (Melbourne: Oxford University Press).

Singh, D. and Smith, A. (eds) (2001) *Southeast Asian Affairs 2001* (Singapore: Institute for Southeast Asian Studies).

Chapter 6

South Asia

ANDREW WYATT

South Asia is an asymmetrically constituted region prone to conflict. India is far and away the largest state in the region, whilst the small states of Nepal, Bhutan and the Maldive Islands lie at the other extremity of size and influence. The major states of the region also constitute some of the poorest in world. South Asia lags in terms of regional integration, which contributes to its ongoing poverty. The region is also characterized by considerable internal diversity, being marked by significant linguistic differences as well as a range of distinctive political systems. At the same time there do exist forces that draw the countries of the region together. There are remarkable cultural affinities. Languages, religious traditions, musical tastes and cinema audiences cross national boundaries. It is possible to speak genuinely of a common South Asian history as the sub-continent was home to the various states and empires that formed part of an Indian civilization that extended well beyond the borders of contemporary India. Finally, the region has a shared colonial experience as the geographical area now occupied by India, Pakistan and Bangladesh was ruled by the British as one unit before 1947. Ceylon was ruled separately as a British colony while Nepal and Bhutan were British protectorates. There is much, in short, that should create a real sense of regional identity. Yet, in spite of all of this, the region still lacks political and economic cohesion.

Country development strategies in South Asia

The South Asian region is defined here as comprising the following countries: Bangladesh, Bhutan, India, the Maldive Islands, Nepal, Pakistan and Sri Lanka. This definition matches the membership of the South Asian Association for Regional Cooperation (SAARC). As Table 6.1 shows, India dominates the region with a population of over one billion, the largest economy and significant military power. In spite of this the smaller states in the region have, for the most part, been able to preserve their autonomy since Britain gave up its imperial possessions. The colonial

Table 6.1   *South Asia: basic data*

	Area (1,000 sq. km)	Population (millions)	Total GNI (US$ billions)	GNI per capita (US$)
Bangladesh	144	133.3	46.7	360
Bhutan	47	0.83	0.53	640
India	3,300	1,000.0	477.4	460
Maldives	0.3	0.28	0.56	2,000
Nepal	147	23.6	5.8	250
Pakistan	796	141.5	60.0	420
Sri Lanka	65	18.7	16.4	880

Sources: Compiled from Census of India (2001) *Provisional Population Totals: India, Census of India 2001, Series 1, Paper 1 of 2001* at http://www/census india.net/results/webed.html; and World Bank (2003) *World Development Indicators Database, June 2003* at http://www.worldbank.org/

interlude had a profound impact on South Asia's position in the international political economy, with the British colonial administrations reorienting the economies of India and Ceylon to ensure a closer fit with broader imperial designs (Washbrook 1990).

The timing and nature of the British departure had important consequences for the structure of the region's political economy. Ceylon, renamed Sri Lanka, achieved its independence in 1948. The Indian political elite was unable to achieve a consensus and in 1947 the British, anxious to leave, created two new states by partition: India and Pakistan. The latter was formed out of two separate areas at the eastern and western extremities of British India. However, the idea of a two-winged state eventually proved to be unworkable and in 1971 East Pakistan seceded and formed the new state of Bangladesh. The initial act of partition had created two states with competing objectives and a good deal of unfinished business between them. The hostility generated by partition meant that the newly created states were disinclined to cooperate and the previously integrated economy of British India was reorganized into the distinctive national economies of India and Pakistan. Nationalism has consequently been the strongest motivating idea in the politics of modern South Asia. India's freedom struggle was driven in part by economic issues, the nationalist movement basing some of its campaigns around economic symbols such as the import of

Lancashire cottons and the salt tax. This same nationalism encouraged India to disengage from the global economy after 1947 (Wyatt 2002).

India

The ruling Congress elite was extremely keen to establish India's economic independence in the new world system shaped by the twin forces of decolonization and the Cold War. The objective of India's economic nationalism was to build a strong industrial infrastructure and avoid undue reliance on external capital. The method preferred was a system of planning in which the private sector would be regulated by the state to ensure socially optimal industrialization. In return the state would invest heavily in the physical infrastructure and capital goods industries and refrain from aggressive nationalization. This mixed economy model had a significant but uneven impact on the Indian economy. India now has a diverse manufacturing industry with a degree of technological capacity unusual for a poor country. Another outcome was a thicket of bureaucratic regulation that constrained the private sector and contributed to modest levels of economic growth. Most large-scale industry, much of it loss-making, was established and owned by the state.

These policies of economic nationalism certainly did not result in the complete structural transformation of the economy. Barbara Harriss-White (2003: 1–3) argues that the metropolitan economy currently involves only a small fraction (12 per cent) of the working population, while the majority of the population (74 per cent) still lives in the countryside and works in agriculture or the agricultural service sector. The balance of the population lives and works in the largely informal economies of the smaller towns of India. Corporate capitalism thus remains a distant force for the majority of the population. The informal Indian economy itself sustains a high degree of inequality and keeps the rural poor in an extremely vulnerable position. The operation of India's democratic political system gives influence to powerful interests in the countryside (Varshney 1995). However, it is a testament to the relative autonomy of the Indian state that the rural middle classes have not directly dominated the national politics of development. Accusations of urban bias can be plausibly made and the substantial state investment in industry demonstrates the limits of rural power. Only in the 1980s did state intervention have a significant impact on poverty. Yet this was more the consequence of applying improvements in farming technology and direct spending on rural development than industrialization motivated by economic nationalism (Corbridge and Harriss 2000: 148). Following a major balance of payments crisis in 1991 the ruling Congress Party shifted policy towards liberalization. The new aim was to reduce the role of the state and remove the obstacles in the path of the private sector.

As implied above, India has a particular geography of development and inequality. As well as the urban–rural divide, there are also significant differences between India's states and within those states important variations between districts. Those states that have better educated populations, higher levels of urbanization and more industry tend to be wealthier. The state of Punjab has, for example, done very well out of the extensive irrigation works initiated during the colonial period (Brass 1994: 283–5). The 'green revolution' of the 1960s involved the application of new technology by private farmers in receipt of state subsidies. High yielding variety seeds and fertilisers were supplied at below market prices and cheap credit was made available. However, these schemes were only applied selectively, which has meant that favoured districts, especially those able to grow wheat, have built up much stronger local economies (Sharma 1999: 144–7). As India reintegrates with the global economy this regional inequality has persisted and taken on new forms. Foreign direct investment has clustered around established cities, with such investors showing a marked preference for locations in southern and western India.

India's exports reflect the preference for inward-looking economic nationalism; they accounted for only 8.5 per cent of GDP in 1999–2000 (Mahbub ul Haq Human Development Centre (HDC) 2001: 71). The global comparison is also sobering – India contributed only 0.6 per cent of the volume of world trade in 1998 (Government of India 2003). On the positive side, the exports are themselves diverse and in some notable cases the products, such as software and pharmaceuticals, are technology-based and can compete on the basis of innovation. Nevertheless, the majority of exports lack sophistication and are vulnerable to competition (Lall 1999). Textiles and the cutting of precious stones are among the largest earners.

In many ways India's size compensates for its lack of economic dynamism. Import substitution was viable given the size of the Indian market and the central government has a tax base large enough in absolute terms to be able to concentrate resources and use them to meet strategic priorities, although, of course, there was never enough to fund development projects fully. Some of the strategic choices, such as the pursuit of a space programme and the relative neglect of primary in favour of higher education, have been criticized. In relative terms the tax base is too narrow because sizeable groups, such as farmers, have not been required to pay income tax and others have been remarkably adept at avoiding business taxes. The expansion of subsidies, mostly to wealthy farmers, over the last two decades has obliged the Indian government to borrow heavily. This external debt was implicated in the balance of payments crisis which, as indicated, befell the economy in 1991. Since then the Indian government has continued to spend heavily on subsidies and has not substantially improved its tax-raising ability. The debt continues to pile up, with India's debt-to-GDP ratio currently standing at 84 per cent (Wolf and Luce 2003: 15), and interest payments eat ever deeper into government spending. Significantly, very little of this money is owed to overseas lenders. Most of the debt is owed to Indian banks and savers. This domestic borrowing helps to keep interest rates high, making it expensive for Indian businesses to invest and thereby slowing economic growth. Attempts to control the fiscal deficit have resulted in spending cuts on capital projects, such as roads and power generation, that are necessary for economic growth. Cuts have also been made in areas vital for the poor. Food subsidies have come under similar pressure and funds available for long-term development projects have been curtailed.

Pakistan

The process of partition disrupted the political economy of Pakistan. The cotton and jute growing areas of Pakistan were cut off from their markets in the industrialized areas of India. Rather than continuing these links it was decided that Pakistan should build its own processing industries and the state took on the role of directing this reconstruction (Noman 1990: 15–16). It was decided that the agricultural sector should be used to provide resources to fund industrialization. Within this strategy two controversial methods stand out. First, a strong rupee policy meant that exports were more expensive and imports of industrial equipment were cheaper than if the rupee had been exchanged at a market rate. This had both a sectoral and a regional bias: whilst favoured industrial houses had access to cheaper inputs, agriculture faced an export disincentive. Furthermore, the jute exporting regions of East Pakistan struggled to compete, whereas new industrial projects in West Pakistan found it easier to invest (Ali 2001: 111–13). It was only in 1982 that a managed floating exchange rate was adopted (Mahbub ul Haq HDC 2001: 77). Second, the price of cotton was controlled so that the textile industry had access to cheap raw materials. This policy continued to benefit industry and disadvantage cotton growers until the 1990s (Ali 2001: 113, 177).

The chaos of 1947 contributed to a fear that India might seek to undo the process of partition by military means (Jalal 1990: 265–6). The military elite carefully nurtured this anxiety, with the result that defence spending has always been given priority and economic planning subordinated to security needs. The bias towards military security also strengthened the role of the army in national politics. Even in the periods of civilian rule the army has always been remarkably powerful and the defence budget has remained off limits even during periods of economic austerity. Pakistan's economic record has been mixed. On the one hand, growth figures for the first 40 years after independence were more impressive than those of neighbouring India. A discernible manufacturing base has been established and following the 'green revolution' of the 1960s agriculture has improved its productivity. On the other hand, the manufacturing sector lacks breadth and ownership has been concentrated among a small number of politically well-connected industrial houses. This concentration of ownership was so marked that, by the late 1960s, 22 families owned two-thirds of industry (Noman 1990: 41). After the fiasco of the 1971 war civilian rule was established and Prime Minister Zulfikar Ali Bhutto exploited popular resentment against these families to settle scores with political enemies among the business elite. His government followed a policy of aggressive nationalization that has not been fully reversed (Ali 2001: 114–18). Maintaining close links with the political and bureaucratic-military elites thus remains critical for large business houses that wish to be successful.

Unlike India, where it was taken for granted that equality was an important objective, concentration of wealth was assumed to be a vital part of Pakistan's route to economic development (Candland 2001: 272–4). Land reform has never been implemented effectively, with the result that a small landowning class accrued most of the benefits of agricultural modernization (Husain 1999: 52–64). The concentration of government spending in urban areas has accentuated this inequality. Pakistan has a very poor record in terms of human development; there is an acute gender bias against women in the provision of healthcare and education, and levels of literacy are low even when compared to other poor countries in the region (Candland 2001). The weak performance of the economy in the 1990s meant that poverty increased by nearly half to 32.6 per cent of all households by 1998 (Mahbub ul Haq HDC 2001: 82). The failure to tax the sources of industrial and agricultural wealth contributed to heavy government indebtedness, reliance on US aid and inadequate spending on the basic social and physical infrastructure (Weinbaum 1999: 93). In addition to exhausting the good will of international lenders the government made desperate appeals to the Pakistani diaspora and borrowed so heavily from domestic banks that many were functionally bankrupt by the mid-1990s. In the late 1980s Pakistan began a process of economic liberalization that faltered as a series of civilian governments were not able, or willing, to implement reforms agreed with the World Bank and the IMF.

Bangladesh

The path towards industrialization in East Pakistan after 1947 was even more convoluted than that described above for West Pakistan. Prior to partition the area of Bengal province that became East Pakistan served as the hinterland to the metropolitan economy centred on Calcutta (Kochanek 1993: 22–4). Partition divided East Pakistan from this industrial hub. Deteriorating relations between India and Pakistan necessitated the restructuring of the regional economy of Bengal. The Bengali middle class had to contend with competition from the politically favoured entrepreneurs of West Pakistan, and those that succeeded were seen as clients of the detested West Pakistani regime. Political and economic resentment combined to create an atmosphere in which the wholesale nationalization of industry proved popular after Bangladesh gained its independence from Pakistan (Kochanek 1993: 28–9). Thus the state assumed a leading role in an *ad hoc* manner. The government took over control of industries that had been abandoned by their owners in West Pakistan, and shortly afterwards the banks and the jute industry were nationalized so that by the end of 1972 the government owned 92 per cent of Bangladesh's modern industry (Hossain *et al.* 1999: 10). The constitution of the new state declared that socialism was to be a key principle informing policy. This commitment was gradually reversed following the assassination of President Mujib in 1975, with the result that by 1988 only 40 per cent of industry was state-owned (Kochanek 1996: 711). The industrial sector has expanded since the late 1970s and the garment industry has contributed to export growth. Export processing zones have been established to encourage foreign direct investment. Generous tax breaks and convenient locations have helped to attract investment and create some jobs, but in general international investors remain coy (Mahbub ul Haq HDC 2001: 86). The dominance of the garment industry proved problematic when exports to the US declined sharply after 11 September 2001 (Jahan 2003: 227). The overall objective has been to expand the industrial sector, create employment and reduce rural poverty indirectly by facilitating migration to the cities. That said, agriculture remains a core part of the Bangladeshi economy, with the majority of the population living in the countryside. The high population density puts heavy pressure on the land to support the livelihood of the population. The application of technology and improved agricultural practice has helped to increase productivity and reduce the need for food imports. The practice of double and triple cropping has also contributed to keeping the rural economy growing (Baxter *et al.* 1998: 292–3). However, the issues of individual food security and the availability of employment have not been adequately addressed. Although poverty levels are falling in

Bangladesh, the head count ratio was still distressingly high at 44.9 per cent of the population in 1999 (Mahbub ul Haq HDC 2001: 92–4).

Sri Lanka

Sri Lanka is something of an exceptional case in South Asia. It achieved very impressive improvements in social development indicators as spending on welfare projects was accorded a high priority as early as the 1940s. Poverty levels are lower than the rest of the region, and Sri Lanka also leads in terms of life expectancy and high rates of literacy. Yet this developmental model was built on weak foundations. First, the British bequeathed an economy dependent on the export of tea, rubber and coconut. Second, the ethnic divisions between the Sinhala-speaking majority and the Tamil minority were not adequately addressed in the process of decolonization. Sri Lanka struggled to maintain its export earnings from plantation exports at the same time as those very exports forced it to import a large amount of rice to feed its population (Herring 1994: 260). Investment was needed to maintain and improve the plantation economy, while at the same time the state was trying to invest in domestic agriculture to create jobs and increase the amount of home-produced food. These were both costly projects. To increase employment the area under cultivation was extended into the 'dry areas'. This was a long-term project because irrigation had to be provided and people resettled, which required the extension of the physical infrastructure and the provision of new social services (Wilson 1979: 70–1). There were persistent concerns among professional economists about the imbalance between the long-term investment required to diversify the economy and the high levels of actual spending on welfare (Wickremeratne 1977: 150–1). In 1977 the United National Party (UNP) government broke with the state-oriented development strategy and, supported by the World Bank, began a process of liberalization (Moore 1990). Ironically, the government chose this moment to accelerate the massive Mahaweli project that used dams to feed large irrigation works and develop agriculture in the north and west of the country in the style described above. This public investment was mostly paid for by overseas aid and loans. The project has increased agricultural output, 20 per cent of Sri Lanka's rice is now grown on this land and half of the island's electricity is generated by the hydropower scheme (Baxter *et al.* 1998: 354).

However, the overall outcome was a mixed blessing. The economy in the Tamil areas was weak and unemployment, a general problem across the island, was particularly marked amongst young Tamils. The Mahaweli resettlement symbolized this ethnic divide. Almost all of the land was allocated to Sinhalese farmers. This material exclusion was accompanied by the symbolic alienation of the Tamils as:

> the Mahaweli touched chords deep in the Sinhalese psyche, reflecting an almost mystical connection between blood and soil ... the Mahaweli replicated the irrigation networks built so spectacularly by the Sinhalese kings of old ... in some cases, the new irrigation works ... us[ed] the very same canals and tanks that had carried water to fertile paddies more than a thousand years before (McGowan 1993: 166–7).

Uneasy relations between the Sinhala-speaking majority and the minority Tamil population eventually deteriorated into civil war in 1983. This long war, which has only just been concluded, held back economic growth and created a climate of inter-ethnic tension inimical to a broad conception of successful human development. Only the growth of the garment trade and other market-friendly reforms have helped Sri Lanka to improve its trade profile and keep its exports buoyant.

Nepal, Bhutan and the Maldives

The physical environment shapes the economic possibilities open to the three smaller states of the region. Nepal and Bhutan are landlocked mountain states and, while both have borders with India and China, the only practical transport links for the passage of trade run through India. This helps to explain why, in contrast to the other countries of South Asia, both economies trade so heavily with India. Nepal's currency is also linked to the Indian rupee. Nepal has a largely agricultural economy, with most of the population relying on agriculture for their livelihoods. The unequal distribution of assets in the countryside has not been conducive to reducing poverty. This sector has lacked dynamism and many can only find seasonal employment. Cuts in fertiliser subsidies in the late 1990s slowed growth and exacerbated rural poverty (Mahbub ul Haq HDC 2001: 92–4). The state depends heavily on overseas aid and loans to support its annual budget, yet various state interventions to promote development undertaken since the 1950s have not been especially successful (Khadka 1998). By contrast, Bhutan has enjoyed relative success. The Bhutanese state has been keen to protect its cultural heritage while cautiously seeking to promote the growth of its economy (Mathou 2001). The economy is intimately linked with India through trade ties and the provision of Indian financial and technical assistance. Bhutan earns a substantial income from carefully regulated tourism and the export of hydropower to India, and also receives substantial amounts of aid and concessional loans which fund development projects and enable the state to meet its import bill while keeping its current account in surplus (Mathou 2001: 131). The Maldive Islands, finally, are a group of tiny islands located in the Indian Ocean south-west of India and west of Sri Lanka. This microstate has a population of only 300,000 and its economy is dominated by tourism and fishing, although the export of textiles does reflect some recent diversification of economic activity.

Summary

State-sponsored modernization projects have generally fallen far short of expectations in South Asia. The states themselves struggle to mobilize resources and high levels of debt, poor tax collection and fiscal deficits are common features of the region's economies. Agriculture still dominates the life experience of the population of the region. In terms of trade and foreign direct investment South Asia has mostly been bypassed, other regions experiencing on the whole more intense integration with the global economy. Attempts have been made to improve export performance across the region, but the countries of South Asia still do not produce the high value-added goods and services that underwrite the prosperity of the post-industrial economies of North America, western Europe and Japan. The import of oil makes a heavy contribution to the ubiquitous trade deficits which exist across the region, rendering the economies constantly vulnerable to balance of payments problems. Such crises present opportunities for the World Bank and the IMF to sponsor structural adjustment programmes. The migration of labour is another common pattern across South Asia. Movement takes place within states, between the regional states (usually illegally) and internationally. Although the social cost is high, the remittances paid by these workers make an important contribution to the localities in which their families live. Nationally these payments help to reduce the balance of payments deficits of the sending countries (Hossain *et al.* 1999: 130–2). However, international migration takes place on the terms of the receiving countries and global inequalities are reflected in patterns of employment. Working conditions can be extremely poor and labour legislation in the host countries is routinely ineffective. Even the much-vaunted Indian software engineers are frequently employed on contracts reminiscent of the indentured labour system of the colonial period (Xiang 2002).

Trade within the South Asia region constitutes less than 5 per cent of the region's recorded trade. It is inhibited by the similarity of the economies of the region. The frequency of political conflict between

India and Pakistan further limits trade between the region's two largest economies. States also keep in place protectionist measures to control trade within the region, although this is not completely successful as a large amount of 'informal trade' does take place. This smuggling avoids official controls and reduces state income from customs duties (Taneja 2001: 960). Across the region as a whole such little trade as takes place is dominated by India. This can partly be explained by geography; India lies at the centre of the region, whereas the other states are located on its periphery and have poor communication links with each other. Accordingly, India, with both the largest and most diverse economy in the region, has little difficulty maintaining an export surplus with the other states.

The intra-regional politics of development in South Asia

In what follows it will become clear that concerns about security have inhibited moves towards political and economic integration in South Asia. A number of general observations need to be made to sustain this claim. Security tends to be understood in the region in realist terms with issues of territorial integrity and relative military strength at the fore. Tense relations between India and Pakistan also spill over into intra-regional politics generally. For example, regional summits have often been delayed because the two states have been in dispute. The smaller states are also fearful that India will use its dominant status to influence the process of regional integration to its advantage. Nor can discussion of security in South Asia escape the historical legacy of partition. India's first prime minister, Jawaharlal Nehru, recognized the nexus between security and development, arguing that India should avoid military entanglements and keep defence spending to a minimum in order to allow for the maximum possible development expenditure across the region. However, his aspirations were only partially achieved. Military conflict between India and Pakistan occurred as early as 1947. The war between China and India in 1962 caused India's modest defence spending to be further increased, with inevitable consequences again for spending on economic and social matters. In similar fashion Pakistan's developmental aspirations have been profoundly undermined by military dominance of its political system. As noted earlier, senior military leaders in Pakistan have successfully argued for large defence outlays to meet the ever present 'Indian threat'. They portrayed India's involvement in the liberation of East Pakistan and subsequent formation of Bangladesh in 1971 as ample confirmation that India's ultimate ambition was, and remains, the dismemberment of Pakistan.

Sri Lanka has also suffered the negative consequences of the defence/development trade-off. The civil war has resulted in the death of over 64,000 people since 1983 and skewed spending towards the military. In 2001 the government spent as much as 22 per cent of its budget on defence, with spending expected to reach US$1bn in 2002 (Bullion 2001: 16). For its part India has long been concerned that the conflict in Sri Lanka does not spill over into its southern state of Tamil Nadu. The failure of the Indian peacekeeping operation in the late 1980s and the subsequent assassination of Rajiv Gandhi in 1991 encouraged the political establishment in Delhi to overlook events in Sri Lanka. Direct Indian involvement in Sri Lanka's affairs appears an unlikely prospect at present, although India's regional dominance remains an ongoing concern among the Sinhalese elite.

Bangladesh also has a security outlook dominated by concerns about India. Relations were initially positive, given that India intervened to enable the eastern wing of Pakistan to achieve independence. However, Bangladesh's fundamental geopolitical position is weak and it has experienced difficulties with India over the issues of water and refugees. Apart from a short border with Myanmar, it is surrounded by India. Furthermore, several rivers, including the Ganges, rise in India but flow out to the sea through Bangladesh. In the monsoon they threaten to flood the low-lying areas of Bangladesh; yet at other times of the year the free flow of water is vital for agriculture and fishing. India has constructed an upstream barrage at Farraka to regulate flows into the Ganges and Bangladesh has complained that this barrage has been operated without regard to its needs and with devastating consequences for its economy and environment (Iftekharuzzaman 1998). It claims that water has been kept in short supply during the drier times of the year and that floods have been exacerbated during the monsoon. India's dilatory response to these concerns has encouraged popular resentment in Bangladesh against its dominant neighbour.

India considers itself to be an important world power even though its military and economic capabilities are somewhat at odds with this self-perception. India's size and military strength is the source of some discomfort among the other states of South Asia, especially as India has intervened in crises beyond its borders in the region. India has attempted to allay these fears by offering defence treaties and promoting cooperation through the SAARC (Bajpai 1998: 179). This regional foreign policy, sometimes described as the 'Indira Gandhi doctrine', has, however, been given a less charitable interpretation. According to this line of argument, India 'has increasingly sought to tie up its regional primacy through a series of regional, bilateral accords covering defence, trade and technical co-operation' (Hewitt 1997: 74). A number of factors have nevertheless enabled most of the smaller states to avoid succumbing to Indian hegemony. The regional security complex does not exclude the influence of powers external to the region, which has limited India's military dominance. Pakistan has sought close relations with China and the United States to counter India's dominant status, and Bangladesh has actively cultivated China and other Islamic states for the same reason. Nor do most of the smaller states depend on India for their trade and finance. With the exceptions of the Himalayan kingdoms of Nepal and Bhutan, both of which are closely tied to India, the economies of the region are not well-integrated and this has undermined Indian influence.

India considers its security to be linked to the security of South Asia as a whole. According to this view, any military attack on the states surrounding India would require an Indian response. Bhutan and Nepal, in particular, are of great strategic importance because they share borders with India and China. A striking interpretation of India's attitude was offered in 1996 by a former maker of Indian foreign policy:

> India has a responsibility to ensure that socio-political changes in Bhutan occur in an orderly and gradual manner. We must be supportive of the king and his government. Any abrupt destabilisation of Bhutan or disruption of its institutions would constitute a serious strategic threat to India's security (Dixit 1996: 94).

India has used a number of devices to keep the Himalayan kingdoms within its sphere of influence. It contributes generous amounts of aid to both countries and, following the tradition established in the British colonial period, continues to 'advise' Bhutan on certain foreign policy matters. Bhutan's development policy was also heavily influenced by Indian expertise in the 1970s and 1980s. Bhutan's policy-makers are resigned to the structural constraints of size and geography and have accepted India's hegemony (Hewitt 1997: 61–6, 228–30). Relations between India and Nepal are largely determined by the 1950 treaty of Peace and Friendship between the two countries, but many Nepalis feel the treaty undermines the independence of their state and that India has not treated Nepal fairly. In 1989 India imposed a punishing trade embargo at a time when it was perceived that Nepal was allowing China to extend its influence. Tensions continue to mark the relationship between India and Nepal. In spite of a democratic transition in 1990 the monarchy maintains considerable influence in Nepal and has at times shown an interest in deepening relations with China (Cherian 2001). The recent intensification of the Maoist insurgency in Nepal raises further concerns as India is keen that its bordering states are politically stable and do not provide opportunities for external intervention. Accordingly, India has given aid to the Royal Nepal Army in recent years (Navlakha 2003).

The regional definition of India's security also extends to the Maldive Islands. As the same senior policy-maker quoted earlier put it, 'good relations with that country are important to safeguard India's security interests in the northern reaches of the Indian Ocean' (Dixit 1996: 94–5). In 1987 the Indian military was used to prevent a coup attempt against the incumbent government and India has also been keen to neutralize Pakistan's attempts to enlist the Maldives as an ally in its intrigues against India. For its part, the Maldives, in common with other states in the region, has sought to build up extra-regional links to counter the possibility of Indian hegemony. In particular, along with Bangladesh, it has tried to strengthen links with other members of the Organization of Islamic Conference (Hewitt 1997: 128–9).

It was in these unpromising circumstances that a formal process of regional cooperation was launched. The SAARC held the first of its biennial summits in 1985. However, the institution has not been particularly successful. It bears the strong imprint of the realist concerns of its member states and has not, accordingly, become the basis of successful collective action in the global political economy. Its very design is revealing. India was unwilling to be a member of an organization in which it could be outvoted by its smaller neighbours. At the same time, as we have seen, the rest of the region has long been suspicious of possible Indian hegemony and keen to bring collective pressure to bear on India. The SAARC is further limited by the security problems noted above and also by articles of association that keep contentious issues off the agenda at summits. In 1991, for example, it was decided to work towards a South Asian Free Trading Arrangement (SAFTA), but progress on this project has been extremely limited. More has been achieved in bilateral agreements signed between different countries of the region. In other words, institutional obstacles and mutual suspicion have made the process of creating the SAFTA a protracted one. The smaller states fear that regional liberalization will allow India to dominate their economies and, in turn, India fears that the smaller states will be used as staging posts by transnational corporations and other states determined to gain access to India's large market. Overall, the SAARC record probably merits a negative assessment, but that judgement does need at least partially to be qualified. It does provide a forum for diplomacy and helps to reassure the smaller South Asian states which remain nervous of India's ultimate ambitions. It is also a step in the direction of regional cooperation and promotes institutional interaction. In short, the SAARC needs to be seen as the start of a larger process of regional integration. Its limitations do not generally stem from tensions integral to the institution itself but tend to flow instead from the unresolved inter-state conflict at its core.

The tense relationship between India and Pakistan is the leading explanation for the limited success of the SAARC project. The causes of mistrust between India and Pakistan are numerous and can be traced back to political developments in the colonial period. The Kashmir dispute is the major cause, and symbol, of the poor relations between the two states. Given that Pakistan was established as a homeland for the Muslims of India, Kashmir, which has a Muslim majority, has always been coveted by the Pakistani political elite. The Congress nationalists made the counter-claim that their secular version of Indian nationalism could accommodate all faiths. They were therefore anxious to claim Kashmir and prove that a Muslim majority state could function satisfactorily inside a secular India. The Hindu prince, Hari Singh, vacillated as the British left India in August 1947. When Kashmir was invaded by a group of 'rebellious tribesmen' supported by Pakistan the area was hurriedly incorporated into India and the Indian army was used to keep Pakistan at bay. Thereafter Kashmir was formally integrated into the Indian federal system as a state with special privileges. However, a significant part of the state is still occupied by Pakistan and the final status of Kashmir remains hotly disputed. Wars were fought over the issue in 1947 and 1965, and border skirmishes occur with such frequency that they have almost ceased to be newsworthy. In the late 1980s insurgents seeking an independent Kashmir took up arms against the Indian government. India has routinely denounced Pakistan for arming and training the militants and insists that Kashmir is a bilateral issue, which, as such, should not be subject to third-party mediation. Pakistan takes a contrary view and has attempted at various points to internationalize the whole question. One interpretation of the undeclared Kargil war in 1999 was that Pakistan was hoping to put the issue of Kashmir on the international agenda. Following the military coup in Islamabad in 1999 the Indian government worked assiduously to isolate Pakistan. The US seemed sympathetic to the view that India, an economically prosperous democracy, would be a safer ally than Pakistan, ruled by an undemocratic regime and in possession of an weak economy. The relative diplomatic gain thereby achieved by India was, however, nullified by the events following the attack on the World Trade Center in New York in 2001. Pakistan was able to demonstrate that it could become a loyal ally of the United States in the 'war against terrorism', and in return it was rewarded by the US with generous bilateral aid and given broad diplomatic support by Western powers previously reluctant to associate with a regime that lacked democratic legitimacy.

It is frequently assumed that the May 1998 nuclear tests carried out by India and Pakistan were a product of this longstanding hostility between the two countries. It is certainly the case that Pakistan developed its nuclear programme in response to India's 'peaceful nuclear explosion' in 1974; however, India has had broader objectives. First, it was frustrated at the functioning of a nuclear non-proliferation regime that served the interests of the existing nuclear powers, in particular the US. Following the tests, some Indian commentators proclaimed that India's security concerns would henceforth have to be taken more seriously by the United States. Second, India had long been concerned about the threat posed to its security by China. China was seen as an existing nuclear power, with nuclear facilities in Tibet, extending its interests into the region in a hostile manner. The tests served to remove some of the ambiguity over the level of India and Pakistan's nuclear preparedness. They also created a new (and for some more threatening) security environment. The concept of deterrence was introduced to South Asia and in the view of some analysts diplomacy was henceforth likely to be supplemented by new calculations about relative military power (Kapur 2001: 338–44). There was certainly added a new global dimension to the region's security as external powers reconsidered their relationships with India and Pakistan. The regional dynamics of development became increasingly linked to the larger context of global politics, with the efficacy, or otherwise, of the SAARC *per se* perceived as a relatively minor consideration.

The extra-regional politics of development in South Asia

As in other regions, the end of the Cold War was the cause of considerable uncertainty in South Asia. The collapse of the Soviet Union deprived India of a superpower ally, and the Non-Aligned Movement, which India had promoted so energetically, lost relevance in the absence of superpower conflict. The United States became more difficult to ignore as a consequence of these changes and India in particular moved to strengthen its troubled relationship with the sole remaining superpower. This relationship became particularly important as states in the region have had only moderate success in integrating themselves within the global economy. Pakistan was placed in a more exposed position at the end of the Cold War because it had been a key ally of the United States. During the Soviet occupation of Afghanistan the US had given Pakistan large amounts of aid as part of its strategy of supporting the anti-Soviet militias. It reduced the level of this support in the early 1990s and was not strongly engaged with the various civilian governments of that decade.

The nuclear tests in 1998 drew attention to a region often overlooked by larger powers. The initial sanctions and condemnations have slowly given way to recognition that India and Pakistan are significant military powers, but the full extent of this change has yet to be worked through. India, for example, continues to argue that the structure of the United Nations ossifies a hierarchy of states that is no longer relevant (Hewitt 1997: 115). In its eyes the inclusion of Britain and France as permanent members of the Security Council is difficult to justify as a number of other medium-sized powers that have achieved a similar economic and military standing are excluded. India would like the membership of the Security Council to be expanded to include other middle-ranking powers such as itself (Cohen 2001: 34). The states of South Asia have all been active in the UN, although India, with its principled resistance to *apartheid*, has unquestionably achieved the highest profile. Pakistan has repeatedly tried to involve the UN in the Kashmir dispute and, although India has successfully resisted this proposal, Pakistan has relished the opportunity to give the issue international publicity. Nepal, Bangladesh and Bhutan have at times voted the opposite way to India in the UN General Assembly as a way of asserting their independent status in the region (Hewitt 1997: 112).

As regards their approach to global environmental issues, the states of South Asia have much in common with the rest of the non-industrialized world. Many policy-makers in the region consider the eradication of poverty to be a higher priority than the preservation of the environment, and leaders are wary of international environmental agreements that seem to embed Western values and run contrary to the needs of poorer countries. India did sign all of the agreements at the Earth Summit in Rio in spite of concerns that the biodiversity and patents agreements overlooked its interests (Dixit 1998: 271). But, even though the states of South Asia were excluded from the emissions targets outlined in the Kyoto Protocol, India has headed the opposition of the Group of 77 (the alliance of former colonial countries within the UN) to proposals to enable permits to be traded (Anonymous 2000). However, it would be wrong to suggest that attitudes towards environmental action are uniformly sceptical across the region. Numerous civil society activists argue that the environment should indeed be protected at the local and global levels. Some countries are more affected than others and are anxious for effective action to be taken. The Maldives, for example, is threatened by the looming prospect of global warming; the islands rise only a few feet above sea level and are highly vulnerable to climate change. The president of the Maldives raised the issue of global warming at the Commonwealth heads of government meeting in 1987 and has continued to argue for strong action to reduce emissions since then (Paterson 1996: 34). Bangladesh is also commonly cited as a country that is vulnerable to the effects of climate change and, although some doubts have been expressed about the empirical basis for this claim (Bradnock and Saunders 2002), the perception has given strength to calls for additional financial aid and for reductions in emissions.

The states in the region are marginal players in terms of their contributions and thus their voting rights in the World Bank and the IMF. On the other hand, the World Bank has a large stake in the region as a consequence of heavy lending in South Asia (Guhan 1995). In the late 1970s the two institutions began to encourage externally oriented development policies in the region. As elsewhere, lending was linked to policy reforms; the World Bank was keen that markets should be freed from state control and that the economies of South Asia become export-oriented (Hossain *et al.* 1999: 89–90). The World Bank played a critical role in coordinating support for the liberalization of the Sri Lankan economy, and other donors were encouraged to join the World Bank and the IMF in underwriting the turn away from a statist model. It was hoped that Sri Lanka could be used as a model for others to emulate. However, the reform agenda in that country proved difficult to sustain and the liberalization did not immediately result in the slimmed-down public sector that had been predicted (Moore 1990: 353–7). The liberalization of trade was partially reversed in the 1980s and foreign investment fell away under the combined impact of regulation and the civil war. In July 1989, with the encouragement of the World Bank and the IMF, the strategy was resumed. Controls on foreign investors were relaxed and a process of privatization was begun, with over 60 enterprises being sold off between 1989 and 1995 (Athukorala and Rajapatirana 2000: 39–42, 56–7). Following an economic crisis Sri Lanka agreed to a standby loan from the IMF in early 2001. The conditions attached to the loan required the vigorous further implementation of privatization, the restructuring of the banking sector and some changes in labour laws (Kelegama 2001: 2671).

Trade liberalization in South Asia accelerated in the late 1990s following the formation of the WTO, although it should be noted that tariffs on imports remain at approximately 30 per cent across the region. Linked to the issue of trade was the matter of exchange rates. Rates tended to be set high to enable the cheap import of investment goods. Exports were relatively more expensive and used in effect to subsidize domestic industries that relied on capital imports. In order to maintain high fixed exchange rates capital controls were used to limit the flow of funds and to protect what would otherwise have been an unsustainable balance of payments situation. The neglect of exports meant that only limited funds were available to buy imports and pay the interest on overseas loans, and import controls were required to protect the balance of payments against a rush of cheap imports. So, again with encouragement from the World Bank and the IMF, currencies were devalued and moved to flexible systems in order to make exports more competitive. The effect of this change was especially notable in the Indian case, with exports surging following the devaluation of the rupee.

Governments were also encouraged to remove price controls and reduce subsidies. Cutting red tape was thought to be one way of encouraging the private sector and increasing the flow of foreign direct investment, whereas removing subsidies was deemed to help the market function, as prices would convey accurate information about the state of the market. Privatization was similarly encouraged because it would help free up public resources where these enterprises were loss-making and would also fit the free-market template preferred by the IFIs. The World Bank and the IMF also wanted governments to get their finances on an even keel by reducing the fiscal deficits generally created by spending on subsidies. This has been the area where the reforms have been least successful; fiscal deficits have remained stubbornly high, as governments have been reluctant to confront powerful domestic interests.

Within this framework India enjoys a degree of autonomy in its dealings with the World Bank and the IMF. It was obliged to call on assistance from the IMF in 1991 following the balance of payments crisis mentioned earlier, but quickly moved to reduce its external debt and bolster its foreign exchange reserves in order to remove the risk of becoming dependent on external agencies. The World Bank has also recognized India's status as a major regional power and has been anxious not to be seen to be dictating terms to its client. As a consequence India's programme of structural reforms has been gradual and measured by comparison with countries outside of the region. Beginning in 1991 the state relinquished many of the policy tools associated with the term 'economic nationalism'. Licensing controls were relaxed and investment in new public-sector enterprises has ceased, foreign exchange controls have been eased, and rules on foreign direct investment have been successively liberalized. However, many reforms have yet to occur. Outright privatization has been avoided and labour laws still favour workers. Capital controls remain in place and government spending on subsidies increased during the 1990s. Yet perhaps the most important aspect of the reforms has been ideological; planned development in India has been abandoned in favour of a rather ill-defined model in which high rates of growth are the main objective. This does not represent a conversion to outright neoliberalism. Instead, India's political economy is now a rather messy halfway house in which a chastened state retains important residual powers in a market economy. While external lenders, such as the World Bank, appear disappointed with the pace of reforms, it is widely recognized that structural adjustment has to be consistent with domestic political imperatives. Resistance to the reforms has been widespread and has come from a number of sources, including cabinet ministers, backbench politicians of all parties, senior civil servants and trade unions. This resistance does not derive solely from progressive quarters. Influential organizations that support the ruling Hindu nationalist Bharatiya Janata Party have also protested against the reforms and remain deeply uneasy about the impact of globalization on Indian culture. One result of this political constraint has been an increased interaction since 1991 between the World Bank and the state governments of India's federal system. The central government has been reluctant to engage in a comprehensive programme of national reform. Instead, the process of externally influenced structural adjustment has been uneven, and difficult to monitor, with individual state governments mostly taking out the conditional loans from the World Bank.

Pakistan agreed structural adjustment programmes with the IMF in 1988, 1993 and 1996. Significantly, these agreements were signed by technocratic caretaker governments backed by the military and the responsibility for implementing the agreements fell on subsequent civilian governments (Candland 2001: 274). Benazir Bhutto made some effort to liberalize the economy and reduce state controls during her first period in office (1988–90); these reforms included a new exchange rate policy and cuts in agricultural subsidies. Government spending on development projects was cut, while the defence budget was increased. Nawaz Sharif promised to extend the reforms, encourage private investment and relinquish government-administered price controls. However, Sharif's period in office (1990–93) was more memorable for poor economic management and a sharp increase in public debt. The interim government of Moeen Qureshi committed Pakistan to a new structural adjustment programme that cut government spending, increased taxes and devalued the rupee. The next elected government, under the leadership again of Benazir Bhutto, promised to meet the IMF conditionalities, liberalize trade and privatize a large number of state-owned enterprises. However, it failed to meet the IMF targets and was dismissed in late 1996 as a consequence, among other things, of its economic failings (Weinbaum 1999: 93–5). The new Sharif government thus inherited an economy in crisis. In 1997 the IMF temporarily suspended assistance because of the failure to meet earlier targets and a new agreement was reached on the basis of new undertakings to increase taxes and liberalize the economy. Yet Sharif also failed to fulfil these promises, valuing domestic popularity more than the approbation of the IMF. The Pakistani economy was thrown into further crisis with the sanctions imposed as a result of the nuclear tests of May 1998. As in other parts of the world, the World Bank and the IMF have not always been able to resist the starker imperatives of US foreign policy (Woods 2000: 138–9). Following the nuclear tests loans to both India and Pakistan were delayed because the US representative on the board of the World Bank voted against new lending. However, Pakistan's support for the US-led 'war on terrorism' meant that in late 2001 the Bank and the Fund were persuaded to overlook their earlier misgivings about Pakistan's wayward economic performance and increase their lending. The military–civilian dichotomy has been sustained since 1999 as General Musharraf has demonstrated an appetite for liberalizing economic reform.

Five of the states in the region have ratified the WTO treaty and have begun to avail themselves of the opportunities offered by the organization's dispute-settlement mechanism. Of the remaining two, Bhutan and Nepal, the latter is preparing to join. Conforming to the WTO norms will require a difficult process of adjustment and it still remains to be seen how the economies of South Asia will respond to this change. The WTO introduces a new dimension to the regulatory order of the region; this was traditionally provided by states at the national level, but from now on much of this regulation will be shaped by the WTO. The South Asian countries played an active role in the WTO negotiations held in Doha during November 2001. Prior to the meeting the SAARC member states set out a common position opposing a new round of negotiations for as long as commitments made during the previous Uruguay Round remained unimplemented. There was a consensus around opposition to the Agreement on Agriculture and resistance to linking trade to labour standards and environmental issues. However, Bangladesh demonstrated the limits of SAARC unity by declaring itself in favour of a new round of trade talks (Business Line 2001). During the course of the Doha discussions the general principle of agreeing to a new round of trade negotiations was conceded in return for a number of concessions. India adopted a strong position and secured the postponement of negotiations in the areas of competition policy, investment and government procurement. By virtue of its size and determination India has been able to position itself as a leading representative of the poorer countries in global trade negotiations.

In sum, South Asia has increasingly experienced the pull of global trends in development. The end of the Cold War has given international institutions greater influence in the region and economic liberalization undoubtedly picked up pace in the 1990s. However, the prevailing assumptions of these Western-dominated institutions are not accepted uncritically in South Asia; there is a degree of scepticism about Western views on the environment, nuclear proliferation and trade liberalization. It is also the case that regional disputes affect the interaction of South Asia states with the institutions of global politics.

Conclusion

In common with other regions, South Asia has witnessed a shift away from state-led development strategies. International institutions and market forces have a greater structural significance in the region than at any time since the colonial era. Yet it must be said that, whilst they have become an important constraint on elite agency, they have not yet completely eliminated this agency in determining development outcomes. The reality is that the conversion to more market-oriented economic policies across the region has been more pragmatic than ideological. Some leading bureaucrats favour reforms for principled reasons, but neoliberal ideologues are rare among the political classes of South Asia. It is therefore too early to assume that there will be a simple transition to a fully fledged neoliberal political economy in the region. There are powerful interests that favour a continuing role for the state, for the statist model is one way of ensuring a distribution of resources whereby the poor get at least the minimum share required to ensure political stability. State control of the economy also provides politicians with resources they can use to reward their supporters. The slow process of privatization illustrates their reluctance to give up this opportunity. Jobs in public companies are a valuable form of patronage that political leaders are keen to monopolize and the large-scale (and unpopular) redundancies that follow privatization are a political liability. It is true that the traditional development paradigm did not produce dramatic reductions in poverty within the region, although some scholars argue that the achievements of state-led development have been overlooked (Corbridge and Harriss 2000). On the other hand, South Asia did not fare well during the 'reforming' decade of the 1990s. Pakistan, Bangladesh and Sri Lanka experienced economic crises of varying degrees of severity, even as economic growth remained positive. India has enjoyed respectable economic growth since 1991, but it is far from clear that this has had a significant impact on poverty. Some groups, including elements of the urban middle class, have clearly prospered under the reforms, suggesting that inequality may have been worsened by measures that have given the greatest assistance to competitive industries and foreign investors. The eradication of poverty is an urgent problem in the region and this requires reform. The key question is: what kind of reform? Leaders in the region appear, by default, to be accepting the notion that rapid economic growth will solve the problem of poverty, rather than considering the possibility that creative state intervention may still have something to offer.

Inequality in the region is undoubtedly further exacerbated by the difficult regional dynamic. India harbours the suspicion that Pakistan has been conducting a proxy war against it by supporting militants in the states of Kashmir, Punjab and Assam. For its part Pakistan suspects India of supporting militant groupings in its domestic politics. Similarly, Bangladesh felt India did little to stop the Chakma separatists from establishing bases in India. Sri Lanka has never been fully comfortable with India's attitude towards the Tamil rebels. Aside from the direct casualties, these conflicts have caused local economic difficulties and created significant numbers of refugees. Security is all too often construed in terms of realist concerns with protecting the territorial integrity of the nation-state (Vanaik 1998). The irony is that none of the major states in the region has arrived at a satisfactory definition of the nation around which political institutions can be constructed. These unresolved issues have contributed to the conflicts discussed above. Defence spending is consequently too high at a time when the various countries have to borrow to cover the substantial gap in their budgets. Finally, it bears repeating that the persistence of conflict prevents the formation of an effective regional organization that could promote economic integration.

South Asia's position in the global politics of development is in the end somewhat ambiguous. The countries of the region are among the poorest in the world and this is reflected in their exclusion from positions of influence in global institutions. There is common frustration at the functioning of international treaties and regimes, and the perceived failure of the WTO to recognize the interests of the non-industrialized countries is just the latest source of irritation. Nevertheless, the states of the region have been able to carve out a certain space for themselves by careful use of the rules and procedures of these institutions. Canny alliance-building has also helped South Asian policy-makers to further their objectives in the general conduct of foreign policy. India's absolute size enables it to pursue a fairly independent course in global politics and there is no doubt that an effective regional organization, with India at its core, would increase the overall influence of the region. The detrimental impact of politics at the state and regional level is felt here. Global institutions also provide an arena in which local conflicts have been played out. In relative terms South Asia's development experience can be viewed more positively than is the case in some other regions.

Structural adjustment has not dampened economic growth too excessively; the region enjoys a fair degree of political stability; and major inter-state wars have been avoided since 1971. The most urgent problem of South Asia – which cannot be ignored for much longer by national, regional or global policy-makers – remains the distressing extent of the concentration of poverty.

Further reading

Alagappa, M. (ed.) (1998) *Asian Security Practice: Material and Ideational Influences* (Stanford CA: Stanford University Press).

Bradnock, R.W. and Williams, G. (eds) (2001) *South Asia in a Globalising World* (Harlow: Pearson).

Corbridge, S. and Harriss, J. (2000) *Reinventing India: Liberalization, Hindu Nationalism and Popular Democracy* (Cambridge: Polity Press).

Hewitt, V.M. (1997) *The New International Politics of South Asia* (Manchester: Manchester University Press).

Shastri, A. and Wilson, A.J. (eds) (2001) *The Postcolonial States of South Asia: Democracy, Identity, Development and Security* (London: Curzon Press).

Chapter 7

The Post-Soviet Space

NEIL ROBINSON

The post-Soviet space occupies a land mass that stretches from the Pacific Ocean in the east to Europe in the west. It comprises the states of Armenia, Azerbaijan, Belarus, Georgia, Moldova, Kazakhstan, Kyrgyzstan, Russia, Tajikistan, Turkmenistan, Ukraine and Uzbekistan, which were formerly republics of the Union of Soviet Socialist Republics (USSR) and are now loosely joined within the Commonwealth of Independent States (CIS). Estonia, Latvia and Lithuania are not included here in this definition of the post-Soviet space because they have been drawn towards involvement in European regional structures and membership of the North American Treaty Organization (NATO). This has made their post-Soviet fate very different to that of the CIS countries. What we describe as the post-Soviet space is sometimes referred to as Eurasia. However, this term can be used to refer to parts of the Middle East and in some usages to eastern Europe and for these reasons it will not be used here. The notion of a post-Soviet space is preferable because it refers to a specific common property of the countries under examination.

However described, this is a huge territory. The USSR not only accounted for roughly one-sixth of the world's land mass, but physical conditions within it varied enormously since it stretched from the Arctic Circle in the north to desert in the south. Notwithstanding these differences, a single issue has dominated the regional politics of development in the post-Soviet space: how to deal with Soviet collapse. This cataclysmic change presented three problems to the elites that took power at the USSR's demise: how to cope with the legacy of central planning and economic decline, how to build new and stable political regimes and states, and how far to resolve questions of economic and political reconstruction collectively or as independent actors in the global community of states. The reality is that post-Soviet leaders have generally failed to deal with these problems. They failed because at root they headed weak states with two major deficiencies, each of which reinforced the other. On the one hand, they did not possess the economic resources to support the construction of market economies or modernize state institutions to the point where they could lead economic transformation; on the other, they did not enjoy sufficient political legitimacy to compensate for economic weakness, given that weak traditions of statehood in a region where loyalty to the state is often weaker than fidelity to clan, family or area mean that there have long been limits to what rulers can ask of their populations. In other words, Soviet legacies constituted a powerful ongoing structure within which successor leaders and elites made choices after 1991 about economic and political strategy, but, in doing so, succeeded only in creating different varieties of weak post-Soviet state. In some cases, these choices have perpetuated Soviet legacies; in others they have begun to change them, but only slowly and uncertainly.

Nevertheless, the mechanics of failure have varied across the region because of the vast disparities that existed in the post-Soviet space at the moment of independence from the USSR (Bremmer and Taras 1997; Dawisha and Parrott 1997a, 1997b; Smith 1999). All post-Soviet states were faced with economic collapse and were uncompetitive in the global economy, but some, most notably the Central Asian states of Kyrgyzstan, Tajikistan, Turkmenistan and Uzbekistan, possessed only the most basic of infrastructures and industry. All lacked administrative capacity to reform their economies, but some – Georgia, Moldova and Tajikistan – also faced civil war. All post-Soviet leaders have had to chart a path between economic reforms, the political reconstruction needed to support them and the perpetuation of personal rule. But when confronted with this choice they have moved in different directions: some saw they could avoid reform and stay in power from the onset of independence; others embarked on reform, but were subsequently forced to change course. All of the post-Soviet states were, however, faced with the issue of how to deal with Russia's regional hegemony. For its part Russia had to decide whether it would act to secure its own interests above those of its new neighbours; for their part the other post-Soviet states had to decide how far cooperation with Russia, to which they remain closely tied militarily and economically, could either be pursued to their advantage or might compromise their newly won sovereignty and threaten their leaders' hold on power.

This chapter will examine how Soviet legacies and post-Soviet choices have shaped the development of weak states by looking, first, at how and why these various countries have not been able rapidly to overcome Soviet economic legacies. This failure means that regional inequalities have been perpetuated and that there has been a general failure to build up the capacity needed to manage domestic transition or international cooperation. We will then look at the creation of the CIS and suggest that it has proved to be a weak vehicle for the resolution of problems in the area. For the most part, the post-Soviet states have chosen not to cooperate with one another to resolve problems, but to work together in a piecemeal fashion, with the result that there have been few general gains in the region from collective problem solving. Finally, we will consider the relationship between the region and the rest of the world. Russia's concerns about losing influence in the region, the difficulties Western powers have had in managing their relations with Russia, and international indifference have meant that most of the post-Soviet space has had either limited or ineffectual, and sometimes harmful, relations with the outside world. Both the failure of the CIS and of international action in the region make the same essential point: the post-Soviet space is not very unified, except in that it is a contiguous zone of weak states tied to a large state, Russia, that is weak globally but strong regionally. This imbalance distorts relations within the region and between it and the rest of the world.

Country development strategies in the post-Soviet space

Post-Soviet political leaders faced a common and immediate economic problem at independence, namely, how to cope with economic decline caused by Soviet collapse. This economic decline had been in the making for several decades as Soviet growth slowed and the Soviet economic system proved impervious to reform (Goldman 1983). Gorbachev's economic and political reforms accelerated this downturn by disrupting the political management of the Soviet economy. The last two years of Soviet power saw a collapse of industrial production and growing budget deficits, external debt and inflation (Ellman and Kontorovich 1992). The ability of post-Soviet leaders to deal with these problems was complicated by four factors.

First, the Soviet state was not able to ensure equitable economic progress across the country over which it presided. Soviet planners were infatuated with economies of scale and 'gigantism', the construction of huge industrial complexes that frequently monopolized a sector of production (Kornai 1992: 399–402). This produced a peculiar form of economic interdependence and economic inequality amongst Soviet republics, and hence amongst post-Soviet states. Republics often specialized in some aspect of economic activity. Sometimes this was because of size and the possession of natural resources – for example, Russia's predominance as an energy producer and its large share of industrial and agricultural production. However, differences were often planned. Production of new high-value goods – like television sets – was based in areas, such as Russia and the Ukraine, that already had well-established industries, rather than in areas of low industrial activity. These latter areas were often commanded to concentrate on agricultural production to service industries based elsewhere. The most notable case of this was the decision made in the 1930s to concentrate cotton production in central Asia, whilst the manufacture of cotton cloth was concentrated in Russia. The concentration of production in one Soviet republic or plant created a forced interdependence since republics often had no native industries producing essential goods. For example, Kazakhstan produced only 27 per cent of the finished goods its economy needed at the end of the Soviet period (Kalinichenko and Semenova 2001: 55).

Second, all of the post-Soviet states were technologically backward and produced goods that were uncompetitive on world markets. The USSR's economy was modern in that it was largely industrialized and supported a welfare state, but it increasingly had the foreign trade structure of a non-industrialized country. The USSR's exports were predominantly raw materials, rather than industrial goods to which value had been added in the process of their transformation from raw materials into manufactured objects. This became more marked over time as technological advances in the rest of the world left the USSR behind; only 4 per cent of Soviet plant was on a technological level equivalent to world standards by 1991 (Kuzin 1993: 33). In 1960 only 16 per cent of the USSR's exports were oil, gas and electricity; by 1987 46 per cent of Soviet exports were from the energy sector (Goskomstat SSSR 1987: 32). The chief reason for this was that Soviet goods were unsaleable on world markets because of their low quality and high cost. Soviet production often created 'negative value-added goods', manufactured objects worth less on world markets than the raw materials used to produce them (McKinnon 1993; Gaddy and Ickes 1998). Only about 7–8 per cent of Soviet production was of 'world standard', that is, exportable to the West by the late 1980s (Åslund 1989: 17). The extent to which the post-Soviet states have been affected by these problems has varied. Russian industry, for example, had a slightly better technological base than average, with 16 per cent of its plant equivalent to world standards (Abelin 1996: 4–5). These problems have been compounded by the fact that access to external markets was not a priority in the Soviet era, which has meant that transport and communications infrastructures have long been very weak. This is a particular problem in central Asia: Uzbekistan, for example, has only one road, to Afghanistan, that leads to a non-Soviet successor state (Vassiliev 2001: 15). Poor transport links and low-quality production have further meant that there has been little to draw foreign investment to the area and consequently little prospect of export-led economic growth being achieved (an issue to which we will return).

Third, no post-Soviet state had either the public or the private infrastructure to run a market economy successfully. The Soviet planning system had no need for institutions, such as commercial banks, insurance companies and the like, which support market activity. Some such institutions began to develop in the late 1980s, but they did not engage in activities that would have supported marketization. Instead, they took advantage of the arbitrage opportunities afforded them by the coexistence of market and plan to make large profits at the expense of the society as a whole. The public infrastructure necessary for a market did not exist because the Soviet state had never fostered services such as commercial law or arbitration. It was in any case in the advanced stages of financial collapse by its last years, with the state running a yearly budget deficit of about 9 per cent of GDP in the late 1980s (Economist Intelligence Unit 1991: 37). This deficit, caused by a collapse of economic activity under Gorbachev which shrank the tax base and by the appropriation of state property and resources by bureaucratic entrepreneurs (Solnick 1997), meant that the governments of the republics were often faced with declining revenue sources on attaining power. As a result, they did not have the money with which they could have reformed state administrations in line with economic needs and, moreover, had little prospect of acquiring it from new sources. Some leaders calculated that it was in fact best to avoid reform and to keep hold of the revenues that state property brought in. This was the case in Belarus, Uzbekistan and Turkmenistan, where political change under Gorbachev had been minimal (Bremmer and Taras 1997).

Fourth, the efforts made by post-Soviet leaders at controlling economic collapse were complicated by the fact that the largest economy in the region – Russia's – did not recover sufficiently to help the rest of the area in its reconstruction. The problem was that Russia could not avoid radical reform in the same way that some other states did – and reform did not work. The collapse of the Soviet state budget and the fact that so much state property had been transferred into the hands of Soviet-era economic managers led the Russian government under Boris Yeltsin to calculate that radical reform was the best option available to it. Reform, it was hoped, would change the balance of power in the Russian economy by weakening Soviet-era managers, creating the basis for the state to take tax from the economy through commercialization and currency stabilization and generally opening up the Russian economy to investment from abroad. The state would thereby accumulate resources to manage the market economy and the Yeltsin regime would not face political competition from the remnants of the Soviet elite and would instead gain support from new capitalist groups (Woodruff 1999; Robinson 1999a: 533–8). It is a matter of debate as to whether radical reform could ever have worked; what is certain, however, is that political conditions did not favour it. Economic and political reconstruction became viciously intertwined and Russia was plunged into a contest over power between Yeltsin and the Soviet parliament in 1992–93. Yeltsin's political survival depended on his compromising on economic reform and he accordingly sacrificed reformist ministers and policies in exchange for political support from industrial and economic interest groups as part of the struggle for power (Robinson 2002: 75–81, 110–14). Whilst this enabled him to survive politically, it meant that there was not even a theoretical chance of reversing economic decline.

Although the Russian economy did not collapse to the same extent as some others in the region, its decline damaged recovery in the rest of the post-Soviet space because it meant that trade in the area collapsed (see below). Russia continued to subsidize deliveries of fuel and other goods to other newly independent states for political reasons, but this only served to stabilize many of them in their economic decline. In terms of their strategic responses to Soviet collapse most post-Soviet states fell somewhere in between Russia and the minimalist response of the Belarus, Uzbekistan and Turkmenistan grouping since they were unable to reform fully because of their state weakness, but could not resist some changes due to the knock-on effects of change in Russia. A common pattern has been for reform either to be half-hearted in response to Russian and external pressures (Ukraine, Kyrgyzstan, Armenia, Georgia, Moldova) or to be combined with the political elite's profiteering from oil and gas production (Azerbaijan, Kazakhstan). Russia's economy has managed to make some progress since 1998, with growth in GDP, industrial output and investment. However, this growth will be difficult to maintain since it has been based not on structural economic changes but on oil sales (Russia has still been able to make a profit on oil sales even as the price of oil has fallen globally because its production costs are so low) and the fact that the collapse of domestic demand for imported goods provided a short-term boost for Russian producers (Robinson 2002: 124–8). To effect recovery to 1989 GDP levels will require 15 years of growth at 5 per cent a year; it is highly unlikely that Russia will be able to achieve this since the impact of Soviet economic legacies and continuing weak political institutions prevent it from increasing capital productivity and maintaining investment (Popov 2000b). Russian economic recovery is not, therefore, likely to be big enough to effect a general reversal of economic fortunes across the post-Soviet region in the near future.

The consequence of these failures and the region's inability to overcome Soviet legacies has been that patterns of inequality have broadly been replicated in the post-Soviet era. The figures in column 3 of Table 7.1 show the

Table 7.1 *The post-Soviet space: basic data*

	Population, millions, 2001	GDP, US$ billions, 2001	GDP per capita, 1990	GDP per capita, 1999	Share of total GDP, 1999 (%, calculated by PPP per US$)	Industrial production, 1998 (1990 = 100)	Estimated level of real GDP, 1999 (1989 = 100)	State spending, 1992 (% of GDP)	State spending 1998 (% of GDP)
Average of all post-Soviet states			*100*	*100*	*100*	*49*	*54*	*46.7*	*28.8*
Armenia	3.8	2.12	83	82	0.6	46	42	46.7	24.5
Azerbaijan	8.1	5.72	72	84	1.3	29	47	48.4	21.2
Belarus	10.0	11.63	111	132	4.7	82	80	47.8	46.5
Georgia	4.9	3.21	93	88	1.0	16	34	35.7	22.3
Kazakhstan	14.8	22.32	102	179	5.3	49	63	31.8	25.8
Kyrgyzstan	4.9	1.53	50	45	0.8	50	63	39.0	35.8
Moldova	3.6	1.48	80	46	0.5	36	31	49.0	28.6
Russia	144.0	308.94	116	212	68.7	46	57	58.4	39.7
Kajikistan	6.2	1.03	42	30	0.4	35	44	65.7	15.8
Turkmenistan	4.8	5.96	53	65	1.4	61	64	30.3	24.5
Ukraine	49.0	37.59	85	105	11.5	49	36	58.4	24.5
Uzbekistan	25.1	7.47	65	52	3.8	110	94	49.7	34.5

Sources: Calculated and adapted from Statkomitet SNG (2002) *Sodtruzhestvo Nezavisimikh Gosudartsv v 2001 godu. Statisticheskii ezhegodnik* (Moscow: Interstate Statistical Committee of the Commonwealth of Independent States), p. 105; World Bank figures for 2001 GDP (available at http://www.worldbank.org); Dunford, M. (1998) 'Differential Development, Institutions, Modes of Regulation, and Comparative Transitions to Capitalism', in A. Smith and J. Pickles (eds), *Theorising Transition* (London: Routledge), p. 88; European Bank for Reconstruction and Development (2000) *Transition Report* (London: EBRD), pp. 133, 137, 141, 159, 177, 188, 193, 205, 217, 221, 225; Statkomitet SNG (2000), *Sodruzhestvo Nezavisimykh Gosudarstv v 1999 godu. Statisticheskii ezhegodnik* (Moscow: Statkomitet SNG), p. 87; Goskomstat (2000) *Rossiiskii statisticheskii ezhegodnik* (Moscow: Goskomstat Rossii), p. 611; and Statkomitet SNG (2001) 'Main Economic Indicators', available at http://www.cisstat.com.

pattern of inequalities which Soviet developmental practices produced. Above, or close to average, GDP per capita in the Soviet era was broadly associated with two things: possession of a large Slav population and industrialization. Russia had the highest per capita GDP; Belarus, a Slav republic with a large amount of military production, was also above average, as was Kazakhstan, which had a large Slav population in its northern, industrialized districts; Ukraine, although Slav and industrialized, did less well, but was still close to the average. Russia's size no doubt skews the figures somewhat, but the modest proportion of GDP enjoyed by the less-industrialized central Asian economies is still very noticeable, with Tajikistan having under half, and Kyrgyzstan and Turkmenistan only just enjoying half, of the average per capita GDP.

As indicated, these patterns have been broadly maintained in the post-Soviet period. The figures in columns 4 and 5 of Table 7.1 show GDP per capita as a percentage of the post-Soviet space average and the various states' shares of total GDP in the region in 1999. The gap between the richest and the poorest has increased. This is not surprising. Although the USSR did not eradicate differences between its states, it did seek to redistribute some resources in an egalitarian fashion. A higher degree of variation between the post-Soviet states is thus inevitable since they have in effect been thrown back on to their own resources. Hence the richest, largest and most industrialized states – Belarus, Kazakhstan, Russia and Ukraine – still have the highest per capita GDPs and the largest shares of total GDP, whilst the less-industrialized – Kyrgyzstan, Turkmenistan, Tajikistan and Uzbekistan – have the lowest per capita GDPs and small shares of total GDP. Thereafter, it is noticeable that possession of mineral wealth brings some advantages and that conflict has had negative economic effects. Turkmenistan and Azerbaijan have thus improved their relative positions in terms of per capita GDP, thanks to gas and oil reserves, whilst the poorer central Asian states have been joined in poverty by Moldova, thanks to the secession of Transdnestr and the fragmentation of its economy. Moldova's economy contracted by about 70 per cent of GDP between 1989 and 1999. By 2001, about 90 per cent of Moldovans were subsisting on about US$2 a day; much agricultural activity has been reduced to subsistence and barter, and the decline in government expenditure has meant that educational services have declined and skill levels fallen dramatically as a consequence (United Nations Development Programme 2001). The civil war in Tajikistan has caused GDP to decline at a rate that has more than reinforced its position as the poorest of the post-Soviet states. In 2001 civil war, dictatorial rule and economic decline combined with drought to bring it close to mass starvation; only international food aid, and the fact that it received more international attention in the context of the post-September 11 crisis in Afghanistan, prevented a larger humanitarian catastrophe.

We can also see from Table 7.1 that reform choices have had their own effect on the economic performance of the post-Soviet countries. Columns 6 and 7 of the table show the degree of post-Soviet economic slump in terms of the collapse of industrial production and GDP. On average, industrial production in 1998 was running at just under half the level of production in 1990 and GDP was just over half what it had been in 1989. Only Uzbekistan and Belarus seem to have avoided the very worst of post-Soviet economic collapse, with Turkmenistan also doing less badly than most other states. This was not because of their success in reform, but rather because of their avoidance of it. The leaderships of these states control their economies, take money from them and then use it to direct economic affairs and maintain industrial production (Popov 2000a). As can be seen in the last two columns of the table, the fall in government expenditure as a percentage of GDP is much less in Belarus than in any other post-Soviet state. Although there has been a sharper fall in Uzbekistan and Turkmenistan, the fact that GDP has not fallen as greatly in these countries means that they have maintained a higher level of expenditure relative to all the other post-Soviet states except Belarus. This has enabled all three states to avoid the drops in investment and state demand that most other post-Soviet countries have suffered since 1991. For all that this may look positive, it means that there has been negligible effort at overcoming the weaknesses inherent in that economic system (low technological levels, inefficiency, etc) and consequently very little change from that system. Maintaining expenditure on industry has also come at a cost. Uzbekistan, for example, only had a fifth of the unprofitable enterprises that Russia had in 1998 thanks to state demand, but its population has since suffered dramatically falling living standards as domestic and welfare consumption has been squeezed to fund industrial production. The number of hospital beds per capita in Uzbekistan has thus fallen by nearly half since 1999; in 1991 78 per cent of households had refrigerators, 87 per cent televisions and 68 per cent washing machines; by 1999 the percentages possessing these goods were 39, 34 and 34 per cent respectively (Statkomitet SNG 2000: 576, 43).

The collective failure of post-Soviet states to cope with economic transition and the decline of the Russian economy has created one more problem for the region: to a large degree it has ceased to be a trading zone. Table 7.2 shows that prior to independence the bulk of post-Soviet states' trade was carried out with other post-Soviet states. Only Russia, thanks to its sales of energy abroad, traded at any great volume with non-post-Soviet states. Since independence, intra-regional trade

Table 7.2   *Exports and imports in the CIS states*

	Trade with USSR/CIS as a % of total trade				Trade with Russia as a % of CIS trade	
	Exports		Imports		Exports 1999	Imports 1999
	1990	2000	1990	2000		
Armenia	98	25	87	19	59.8	78.8
Azerbaijan	94	13	84	32	39.3	69.7
Belarus	90	60	83	70	89.0	87.8
Georgia	95	43	84	32	41.6	51.4
Kazakhstan	89	27	82	55	75.8	84.7
Kyrgyzstan	98	42	81	53	38.6	42.2
Moldova	96	58	96	33	75.5	54.8
Russia	61	13	58	35		
Tajikistan	87	49	90	83	36.5	18.0
Turkmenistan[a]	95	26	90	47		
Ukraine	83	31	81	58	73.7	82.9
Uzbekistan[a]	91	25	70	28		
CIS average		34		45		

[a] 1998 figures.
Sources: Smith, G. (1999) *The Post-Soviet States: Mapping the Politics of Transition* (London: Arnold), pp. 164–5; Statkomitet SNG (2000) *Sodruzhestvo Nezavisimykh Gosudarstv v 1999 godu. Statisticheskii ezhegodnik* (Moscow: Statkomitet SNG), pp. 70–1; and Statkomitet SNG (2001) 'Main Economic Indicators', available at http://www.cisstat.com.

has fallen markedly for most of the countries, with the sole exception of Belarus, which is dependent on Russian markets for sales of the military goods that make up a large part of its industrial output (Zaprudnik and Urban 1997: 297–8). At face value, this might seem positive since it could in theory mean that new markets were being explored. In fact, what has happened is that the volume of trade within the post-Soviet space has shrunk and has not been replaced with trade with non-post-Soviet states (Smith 1999: 160).

However, this does not mean that states in the region are less dependent upon one another, and hence that the balance of intra-regional economic power has changed. Where trade is in vital goods, dependency can still be great, even if the volume of trade is declining. This is the case for much trade between Russia and the other post-Soviet states. Energy exports consistently make up 40–50 per cent of Russian exports to the post-Soviet space (Goskomstat 2000: 582, 587). The lack of change in these figures over time indicates that the energy dependency of most post-Soviet states on Russia has not ended (Dawisha and Parrott 1994: 175; D'Anieri 1999). This dependency is compounded by the general economic weakness of post-Soviet states, many of which have no option but to import subsidized energy from Russia because they simply cannot afford to buy it at global prices. They also need subsidized energy to generate revenue for themselves. By February 2000 Ukraine owed Russia some US$3.5 billion in trade debt, with most of this outstanding amount being owed for gas imports. This unpaid fuel bill is a major factor that enables Ukraine to continue trading with the rest of the world, for, if fuel costs were paid, many Ukrainian exports would become uneconomic and unsaleable (Zon 2000: 113, 117). Although the Ukrainian state is not efficient at taxing trade, it does raise revenue from exports, particularly through licences and the arms trade. To an extent, then, Ukraine's ability to maintain even reduced government expenditure results from Russian support. The decline in intra-regional trade is also not the same as a decline in trade between Russia and the other post-Soviet states. As Table 7.2 also shows, Russia is by far the largest trading partner for most post-Soviet states; trade between post-Soviet states excluding Russia has collapsed as transport infra-structures have decayed, states have raised tariffs on goods crossing their territories and recession has caused contraction of demand. The economic exchange that exists within the region is thus largely negative in source and implication. It is not the result of states facing common economic problems and deciding to pool resources and sovereignty to resolve their problems; intra-regional economic integration and cooperation is merely residual, a hangover from the Soviet era and old connections to Russia as the largest economy in the region.

The intra-regional politics of development in the post-Soviet space

The post-Soviet states had the means to cooperate at the end of the USSR. Not only did they share the various problems of post-communist reconstruction, but they also had many characteristics in common that might have supported dealing with these problems collectively – a shared language in Russian, the main language of administration in the USSR; economic ties between enterprises in what had been a single economic space; a common currency, the rouble; overlapping populations and cultures, with some 25 million Russians living in the newly independent states and members of ethnic groups from the new states in the Russian Federation; near identical structures in areas such as social services and local government; and shared standards in such matters as educational provision, legal rules and so on. Moreover, as we have seen, the newly independent states needed each another economically because all were still linked by the legacies of Soviet developmental practices.

These factors did not lead to cooperation because a collective strategy was not deemed to be in the interests of new ruling elites in many of the new post-Soviet states. They feared, in a nutshell, that cooperation would degenerate into dominance. It was thought that Russia's size and power would mean that it would be able to transfer influence from one policy area to another; to legitimate its policies through the processes of cooperation to the detriment of smaller states; and to make it difficult for other states to censure it if it broke cooperative agreements (D'Anieri 1999: 123). In short, there was thus a great deal of anxiety among post-Soviet states that regional cooperation would just become a vehicle for the transfer of policies and priorities from Russia, with the prospect of ruling elites being forced to pursue objectives contrary to their self-interest. This problem was compounded for most of the post-Soviet states because they did not have in their own right strong traditions of statehood and sovereignty with which to bolster elite rule at the national level. Few post-Soviet states had experienced independent statehood in the modern era. Ukraine, Belarus, Moldova and the Caucasian states had been part of the Tsarist empire since the eighteenth and early nineteenth centuries and had only enjoyed brief, and politically unstable, periods of independence during the revolutionary upheavals after 1917. The territories that comprise the central Asian states were only defined in the 1930s by the Soviet government as a part of administrative reform of the USSR as a 'federal' state. This meant that the definition of state territories in central Asia was often arbitrary, rendering them an uneasy patchwork of ethnic groups. Independence and sovereignty were in effect forced on the central Asian states by the collapse of the USSR and were decidedly not the result of struggles by national liberation movements (Menon and Spruyt 1998).

The uncertain statehood of the post-Soviet states was a problem for Russia too. It had to come to terms with dealing with notionally independent nation-states, rather than colonial subjects or 'backward' subject peoples of the USSR. The Russian government formed in October 1991 was interested in radical economic reform and cooperation with the advanced post-industrial states of the West. It was much less concerned about forging forms of cooperation that might hold it back from pursuing these objectives, or establishing structures that would tie its hands in policy matters and link the fate of reforms in Russia with the performance of weak states and unstable, and often unreformed, regimes in the rest of the post-Soviet sphere. However, Russia alone had a strategic interest in the region as a whole; the other post-Soviet states had little in common strategically except their relationship to Russia. The Tsarist empire, and later the USSR, had been created to ensure the security and power of Russian leaders as they expanded the territory they controlled; they thus incorporated areas like the Caucasus and central Asia to deny these territories to great power rivals and establish their hold over the various populations. As the 'federal' Soviet state collapsed, the Caucasus, central Asia, Ukraine, Belarus and Moldova lost any common security concerns that they had as a part of the Soviet bloc. Only Russia, fearing destabilization along its borders, had a general interest in regional security. To be sure, some of the other post-Soviet states had common concerns, such as central Asian fears of destabilization by radical Islam imported from Iran or Afghanistan; but the only genuinely universal security concern in the region was about Russian hegemony. Russia was consequently in an ambiguous position at the onset of independence, increasingly driven to press its security agenda, but desirous of making its own way economically and globally. The result was that it could not win. Russian action to preserve regional security – as defined in Moscow – confirmed fears elsewhere of its imperial agenda and lessened the chances of cooperation in other policy areas; failure to cooperate generally in the region meant that Russia feared it was losing influence and needed to build up relations with the post-Soviet states to exercise some control over them. This basic contradiction in Russian policy has then been further complicated by inconsistency in policy-making in Moscow towards the post-Soviet space. The great differences in the area mean that Russia cannot influence the region using any one policy tool; different agencies of the Russian government inevitably pursue contradictory policies and policy has frequently become entangled in institutional and personal political struggles (Bukkvoll 2001).

The result of these attitudes, fears and ambiguities has been that patterns of cooperation have been uneven, involving different states in different issues; have been built up bilaterally as much as multilaterally; and have led to subregional cooperation as much as regional coordination. The fact that there is no common security interest in the region has also meant that post-Soviet states have been engaged in building relations and cooperative institutions with their other neighbours. In general, however, this dispersal of effort and the unevenness of the results have meant that the chief vehicle established at the demise of the USSR for managing intra-regional cooperation, namely, the CIS, has failed in even this relatively limited task, let alone serving as the basis for substantive regional integration. The CIS was established in December 1991 as a compromise; it was not founded with goodwill and a strong sense of common purpose and it has struggled ever since to overcome the circumstances of its birth. Its creation is best understood as a necessary accident, an event that had to happen to sort out the mess created by the collapse of the USSR and permit the Soviet successor states to disengage from one another. It was certainly not uniformly desired by its participants.

The CIS was in fact initially formed by an agreement between Russia, Ukraine and Belarus, but was then immediately enlarged to include all of the other post-Soviet states, except the Baltic states and Georgia, which joined in 1993. All had very different reasons for joining. Neither Russia, nor the Ukraine, wanted to continue as a part of the USSR, but needed a forum for discussion so that they could dissolve the Soviet Union and assuage sections of their society that were opposed to full independence. Belarus needed some means of cooperation with its two largest neighbours. The central Asian states, Moldova, Azerbaijan and Armenia, with their lack of historical statehood and poorly defined territoriality, feared economic loss and strategic isolation. They felt especially vulnerable to influence from China, Turkey and Iran, as well as destabilization from Afghanistan, particularly if Russia concentrated on its relations with the West, Ukraine and Belarus. Moldova was facing secession threats from Transdnestr and the Gagauz; Armenia and Azerbaijan were in conflict over Nagorno-Karabakh; and the central Asian states were worried about the legitimacy of their mutual borders and concerned that there might be communal violence on the scale that had occurred in Uzbekistan in the Ferghana valley in 1989–90.

These different concerns of the states that were being drawn towards the CIS meant that there was no 'CIS' interest underwriting the new organization that could have informed its institutionalization. Nor did many of its members have the capacity as states to make the new institution work. The weak political systems of all of the CIS states made it difficult for them to implement domestically, let alone internationally, policies that were decided through the CIS. As a result, in the first three years of its existence, under half of the documents adopted at CIS meetings were ratified by national parliaments (Brzezinski and Sullivan 1997: 718). Moldova and Azerbaijan did not become proper members of the CIS until after 1993, when, as we have already seen, Georgia was also forced to join by Russia, very much against its will as a condition of Russian help in resolving the civil and ethnic wars that were destroying Georgia as a state. All this meant that the CIS developed haphazardly as an institution. The initial organization formed by Ukraine, Russia and Belarus was minimal. Only one supranational CIS institution was established, a united military command. Working procedures were left vague and states were allowed to opt out of policies as they wished. There was thus no institutional need to develop consensus on any issue, let alone make commitments to implement common policies. Subsequently, the development of the CIS has been as an intergovernmental discussion body, dominated by summit meetings between heads of state or government, or by meetings of ministers in committees. The record on reaching agreements in these meetings is varied. Very often, members have not even turned up for meetings, or have sent officials rather than executive members of government: no representatives from Turkmenistan or Moldova attended the January 1997 Council of CIS Defence Ministers, for example. A modest attempt was made to develop the CIS as a supranational body with the signing of the 'Charter of the CIS' in 1993. However, none of the bodies created by the Charter have developed any real coordinating or monitoring role and the Charter itself has still not been ratified by Ukraine or Tajikistan.

With no institutional support, intra-regional cooperation could not have been expected to move forward smoothly or evenly. Although they had agreed to maintain unified military structures in December 1991, the post-Soviet states rapidly constructed national armed forces. In May 1992 Russia, Armenia, Uzbekistan, Kazakhstan, Kyrgyzstan and Tajikistan were the only states to sign the CIS Treaty on Collective Security. Azerbaijan and Moldova did not sign because of domestic political opposition and Ukraine had no intention of being bound in a security agreement with Russia. Ukraine, Turkmenistan, Azerbaijan and Belarus also refused to sign a CIS peacekeeping agreement in 1992. With no general agreement in place on peacekeeping, and given that Russia inherited the bulk of the USSR's effective combat forces and felt compelled to protect ethnic Russians in the former Soviet space, it has been the Russian army, rather than CIS forces, which has been involved in the Transdnestrian conflict in Moldova, the border clashes and political chaos of the Tajik civil war, and the regional wars in Georgia (Johnson and Archer 1996). An effort at reviving military cooperation was made in 1995 when CIS leaders approved a so-called 'Collective Security Concept'. However, this explicitly ruled out involvement in conflicts in, or between, CIS states and, in the absence of a commonly agreed external security threat, failed to secure the agreement of Ukraine, Moldova, Turkmenistan and Azerbaijan (Sakwa and Webber 1999: 384).

The failure of military cooperation and Russian involvement in peacekeeping in the CIS did, however, help to change Russian foreign policy quite quickly after 1991. The 1993 'Russian Foreign Policy Concept' (an attempt by the government to bring some order to the conduct of foreign relations by laying out the aims and principles of Russian foreign affairs) made it clear that Russia saw itself as having a unique role in the CIS for historical and cultural reasons (Aron 1994: 29). This view of the post-Soviet space as an area of Russian strategic interest has been upheld in subsequent elaborations of Russian foreign policy and security strategy. Russia has pressed the United Nations to recognize its unique role as a peacekeeper in the former Soviet Union. Attempts to internationalize peacekeeping in the CIS, such as the appeal by Georgian president Eduard Shevardnadze in January 1998 for an international peacekeeping effort to be established in Abkhazia, have been rejected and blocked by Russia (Robinson 1999b: 25–6). By and large, therefore, security issues have not been a matter for regional cooperation, but have been dealt with bilaterally or at a subregional level involving outside partners. Russia has signed agreements with Belarus, for example, which granted Russia the use of military bases and the right to station troops in Belarus and effectively made Russia responsible for Belarusian security. Subregional cooperation in military matters has also developed in central Asia. Joint exercises have been held in Kazakhstan, Uzbekistan and Kyrgyzstan within the NATO Partnership for Peace (PfP) framework and there have been moves to cooperate against drugs trafficking from Afghanistan (Vassiliev 2001: 25; Gleason 2001: 1089).

Economic policy coordination has suffered much the same fate. Throughout its brief history member states have called on the CIS to coordinate economic policy and promote economic integration. Nevertheless, reality has been less edifying than rhetoric. From 1992 onwards Russia and the other post-Soviet states ran very different fiscal policies. Russia attempted to control its spending to stabilize the rouble and reduce inflation, whilst other states tried to maintain spending or only moved slowly to control it. The result, in a common currency zone, was alternating inflationary pressures and currency shortages throughout the post-Soviet space. Efforts were made to coordinate fiscal policies, but these fell short of the creation of a CIS Interstate Bank, Russia's favoured solution to the coordination problem. Ukraine did not want to participate in such a bank because Russia's size would have enabled it to dominate and overrule national central banks (voting would have been by each member state's capitalization). In June 1993 Russia recalled all pre-1993 roubles from circulation and refused to issue more credits to CIS states. The aim was to force those that had not already introduced their own currency to coordinate their monetary policy with Russia. Belarus, Kazakhstan, Armenia, Uzbekistan and Tajikistan subsequently reached an agreement with Russia in September 1993 on a new rouble zone with coordinated monetary, customs and banking policies. However, the demands made by Russia before it would issue new roubles were excessive and in fact accelerated the adoption of national currencies. Only Tajikistan, which had collapsed into anarchy and was being propped up by the Russian military, has remained in the rouble zone.

Other tentative CIS proposals for further policy coordination and integration also stalled (Sakwa and Webber 1999: 386–90). A Treaty on Economic Union in 1993 between Ukraine, Russia and Belarus on economic integration pulled the other states into talks, but Ukraine did not join the Economic Union as a full member. An Interstate Economic Council (IEC) was established to coordinate economic policy in December 1993. The IEC was reformed a year later, but Ukraine and several other states insisted that it could not overrule national legislation, fearing – correctly – that it would have been dominated by Russia. Not surprisingly, the IEC did not develop into a motor for economic integration or coordination; it had no executive powers and no means of ensuring the adoption of common policies. Rhetorically, economic integration has remained an aspiration of the CIS. The 1997 'Concept for Integrated Economic Development' (approved by eight out of the twelve CIS states) even set 2005 as a target date for recreating a common economic space, but there has as yet been no noticeable progress on this issue. In the meantime, and as there has been no improvement in economic integration, bilateral and subregional agreements have tended to come into being. Belarus reached a bilateral agreement with Russia on Belarusian-Russian Monetary Union in 1994, which in theory gave the Russian Central Bank control over currency in Belarus (in practice Russia has been unwilling to take responsibility for the Belarusian economy). Kazakhstan, Russia and Belarus also formed a Customs Union in 1995 to promote free trade after the IEC failed to produce a CIS agreement (Kyrgyzstan and Tajikistan joined later). In 1993 Kazakhstan, Kyrgyzstan and Uzbekistan created a Central Asian Union and in 1994 a Central Asian Bank for Cooperation and Development, although the impact of these initiatives has so far been very modest (Robinson 1999b: 24, 26; Gleason 2001: 1086).

In sum, the CIS has thus not been an effective vehicle for cooperation in the post-Soviet space. Since there has been little institutionalized multilateral cooperation, Russian hegemony has been expressed through its continued domination over the weakest of the post-Soviet states – Georgia, Moldova and Tajikistan – where civil war and ethnic strife have enabled it to use its military might to effect. Relations with other states, most notably with Ukraine, have relied on economic pressure to get some agreement on issues such as the division of military forces, but have otherwise not led to effective cooperation. However, although the CIS has unquestionably not been a success, we have to ask whether any regional organization could plausibly have helped to resolve the region's many problems. Various subregional organizations, in addition to the Kazakhstan–Russia–Belarus Customs Union and the Central Asian Union mentioned above, have been formed in and around the post-Soviet space: the Community of Sovereign States was formed by treaties in 1996 and 1998 between Russia and Belarus; Georgia, Ukraine, Uzbekistan, Azerbaijan and Moldova formed an interstate council (GUUAM) in 1996–97; and Russia, Belarus, Kazakhstan, Kyrgyzstan and Tajikistan formed the Eurasian Economic Community in June 2000. CIS states have also been active in groupings that have set up links to their neighbours, like the Shanghai Forum (which links Russia, Kazakhstan, Kyrgyzstan and Tajikistan with China), Black Sea Economic Cooperation (Russia, Ukraine, Georgia, Armenia, Azerbaijan, Moldova, Turkey, Romania, Bulgaria, Albania and Greece) and BLACKSEAFOR (an agreement between Russia, Georgia, Ukraine, Turkey, Romania and Bulgaria on naval cooperation). These bodies have been successful in that they have initiated links between governments with little record of international dealings and have provided mutual recognition of borders. But their long-term contribution to promoting development strategy or collective problem solving is less certain, although some analysts believe that they have the potential to move beyond discussion to action as recognition of the linkages between problem areas grows (Gleason 2001: 1092). The fact that so many sub-CIS and extra-CIS regional associations have been created also shows that, in the future, the natural focus of states in the post-Soviet space may well be towards other countries and regions such as the Middle East, or Asia, rather than to each other and the post-Soviet space. However, for such a realignment to happen, CIS states need the wider world to be interested in them, so that the power of Russia in the region is moderated. For most of the period since 1991 this interest has been very small, with external attention being directed, overwhelmingly, towards Russia.

The extra-regional politics of development in the post-Soviet space

Despite the involvement of CIS states in regional associations with their neighbours, relations between the rest of the world and the post-Soviet space have been influenced above all other factors by Russia's efforts to find a new role for itself in international politics and its fears that the elaboration of relations between post-Soviet countries and the international community will diminish its great power status in the region. Together, these considerations have meant that the impact of the rest of the world on the region and, vice versa, its impact on the world, has been slight. For most of the period since independence in 1991, the world has either ignored the region, or adopted policies towards it that have been designed essentially to influence Russian behaviour. The reality is that Russia is still seen as the fundamental security problem in the region by most states in the world. As a result, the rest of the post-Soviet space has suffered vicariously from the inability of Russia and the West to construct an effective new architecture within which to meet post-Cold War challenges.

The region's problems in integrating into the wider community of states and taking part more specifically in the global politics of develop-' ment are thus predominantly Russian problems. At independence, Russia was very keen to cooperate with the West, and some progress was made on nuclear proliferation and disarmament and on Russian membership of the IMF and World Bank. However, cooperation between Russia and the rest of the world, and with it the fuller integration of the whole region into global politics, did not last. The West was happy for Russia to join international institutions, but it did not go out of its way to facilitate Russia's entry into them, and even less to take account of its special circumstances and preferences. The IMF and the World Bank followed their customary practices and charters so that Russia had to fit in with criteria that had been designed for states with some form of market economy, rather than for those with a socio-political system in extreme crisis (Rutland 1999). Russian efforts to join the WTO (and its predecessor, the GATT) have been delayed, leading some Russian officials to believe that their country is being set a higher hurdle for membership than other states, thereby causing it to miss out on the benefits that might accrue from a lowering of trade barriers (Stamps 2001). In the area of security, the expansion of NATO and differences over the conflict in Yugoslavia led to a growing rift between Russia, the US and Europe over the course of the 1990s. Coupled with an obvious Russian desire, already discussed, to protect its interests in the post-Soviet space from the mid-1990s onwards, these problems led to a shift in Russian foreign policy from being determinedly pro-Western to an 'assertive realism', which looked to protect Russian interests by building relations with powers other than the US (Shearman and Sussex 2001: 160). This change of foreign policy orientation did not bring any great benefits to Russia, but rather betokened a simple loss of direction. Russia still tries to pursue closer relations with the West, but at the same time seeks to prove its autonomy by making alliances elsewhere. In the process, Moscow does not seem to make much headway anywhere.

Problems with Russia and the West's lack of security concerns in the region have in turn meant that the engagement of the countries of the post-Soviet space with the wider world has been uneven. Russia is not, however, solely to blame for the low intensity of these relations. Domestic factors have hindered the process in respect of some post-Soviet

Table 7.3   *Share of world trade (%)*

	Exports		Imports	
	1992	*1999*	*1992*	*1999*
Armenia				0.1
Azerbaijan	0.02	0.02	0.01	0.02
Belarus	0.03	0.1	0.02	0.1
Georgia			0.01	0.01
Kazakhstan	0.04	0.1	0.1	0.1
Kyrgyzstan		0.01		0.01
Moldova		0.01	0.01	0.01
Russia	1.5	1.3	1.1	0.5
Tajikistan		0.01		0.01
Turkmenistan[a]	0.02	0.01		0.02
Ukraine	0.1	0.2	0.1	0.2
Uzbekistan[a]	0.02	0.1	0.02	0.1
US	12.2	12.7	14.7	18.7
China	2.3	3.6	2.1	2.9
Hungary	0.3	0.5	0.3	0.5

[a] 1998 figures.

Sources: Compiled from Goskomstat (2000) *Rossiiskii statisticheskii ezhegodnik* (Moscow: Goskomstat Rossii); and Statkomitet SNG (2001) 'Main Economic Indicators' at http://www.cisstat.com

states: for example, Belarus's human rights record has soured its relations with the European Union. Soviet legacies of economic backwardness and negative value-added production, poor reform records, high corruption and low political recognition of legal norms and property rights have inevitably weakened the forging of economic relations with the rest of the world. Table 7.3 shows that the post-Soviet states' share of world trade was low at independence in 1992 and has barely improved since; indeed, Russia's share of world exports actually declined between 1992 and 1999. Other post-communist states like Hungary and emerging economies like China have performed better in the global economy than the CIS states, whilst, to state the obvious, Russia's place in the global economy is dwarfed by the US. Few post-Soviet states have been able to run trade surpluses: in 1998, the last year for which there is complete data, only Russia, Uzbekistan and Kazakhstan did so (Robinson 1999a: 546; Statkomitet SNG 2001) and, of those countries, only Russia, thanks to its energy exports, has consistently been able to do so. However, Russia's trade surplus has not had a great effect on its overall economic health. Export revenue has largely disappeared as capital flight continues to run at an estimated US$11–20 billion a year and was dwarfed by the build-up of government debt in the mid-1990s when the Russian state relied on the sale of treasury bonds for deficit financing, a measure that led to the collapse of the rouble in 1998 (Loungani and Mauro 2001). Similar patterns of capital flight have been observed for states such as Ukraine (Zon 2000: 11, 115). Elsewhere, the sale of energy has been used to support dictatorial rule by funding patronage (Azerbaijan) or neo-Soviet personality cults (Turkmenistan).

In general, then, what advantages post-Soviet states do have in trade have not been passed on to their populations. The isolation of the Soviet economy and the poor quality of the goods that it produced has meant, even now, that investing in the region has not been an attractive proposition. Inflows of foreign direct investment to post-Soviet states grew only very slowly in the 1990s and were much lower than to eastern Europe. On average, cumulative FDI inflows per capita between 1989–99 were US$636 in eastern Europe; in the post-Soviet space they stood at US$146. The post-Soviet states that have received larger amounts of FDI have done so because of their oil and gas deposits. Hence, Azerbaijan and Kazakhstan have received relatively large amounts of FDI per capita (over US$400), and Turkmenistan has done better than the more industrialized Ukraine because of its gas fields (US$159 to US$55) (European Bank for Reconstruction and Development (EBRD) 2000: 74). Similarly, areas with oil and gas deposits in Russia have done far better than parts of the country where manufacturing or agriculture dominates economic activity, although overall FDI inflows into Russia remain small (US$71 per capita) (Robinson 1999a: 543–4). Consequently, investment in the post-Soviet states has been 'enclave' investment, limited to a few sectors and areas, and unable to produce a general change transformation in national economic fortunes (Kuznetsov 1994: 112–14). Debt, rather than trade and investment, has been the main growth area in international economic relations. As domestic economies have shrunk, the foreign debts of post-Soviet states have grown. On average, external debt as a percentage of GDP and relative to export earnings has doubled in the post-Soviet states since 1995 (the exception being Belarus) (EBRD 2000).

What longer-term influence on development strategy and prospects the low levels of effective political and economic international reintegration of the post-Soviet space will have is difficult to assess. The peripheral status of the region as a whole leaves a gap that Russia must fill: Russia's security concerns, economic ties and large diaspora mean that it must maintain, and indeed conceivably increase, its role and power over the sphere. For some, this implies 'reimperialization': 'compared to the United States...Russia may be a third world state with nuclear arms, but compared to its neighbours, Russia is still a military superpower and an economic giant' (Motyl 2001: 98, 113). For this to happen, however, Russia will have to have the will and power to act as an imperial hub. Although Russia's economy has bucked global trends over the last few years and grown, it is still far from being rich enough to project its power across the region. Moreover, growing wealth may pull Russia away from the rest of the region. Changes in global politics and economics have impacted on post-Soviet states very differently and even the region's common Soviet legacy creates tensions as the perpetuation of inequalities in the region shows. A common future – imperial or otherwise – is far from certain; centrifugal forces in the area helped to drive the USSR apart and cannot be discounted in the future. Even a common Russian interest in the area cannot be safely predicted. Change in Russia is not always national; much activity and linkage with the outside world, as enclave investment shows, has taken place at local level, whilst political and economic transformations are also highly differentiated by internal region. Although the current president, Vladimir Putin, has increased central power over Russia's internal regions since his election, great political differences and varying economic prospects exist between them, whether they be gateway regions like St Petersburg, Moscow or Primorskii Krai (on the Pacific coast), energy-producing regions like Tyumen, modernizing industrial regions like Nizhny Novgorod, or impoverished, unreformed 'rust-belt' regions like Ulyanovsk. The impact of such differences has not so far been decisive on politics and economics in the post-Soviet space, or on Russia's international outlook, but this may alter. Economic power and political influence has moved between regions in other states in the past, reformulating their political and security outlooks, and this may yet occur in Russia if global connections transform its regional elites' inevitably varying perceptions of national interest. Finally, we should not overlook similar trends elsewhere in the post-Soviet space which may also be centrifugal in effect. Energy wealth may yet lead to change in parts of central Asia and the Caucasus, where a generational shift in elites will also impact on their future development as leaders inherited from the USSR die off. If prosperity moves east with EU enlargement, benefits may accrue to Ukraine, Belarus and Moldova as the new borderlands of the EU. Just as a common future for the states of the region was not guaranteed by their membership of the USSR, so a common future because of their ties to Russia and dependence on Russian policy is not a given for all times.

Conclusion

The states of the post-Soviet space have so far not been very effective in coping with the multiple problems that Soviet collapse placed before them. Elites have diverted resources to sustain their political power, avoided reform for similar reasons, impoverished their populations and presided over what is probably the greatest economic depression in modern history. The post-Soviet states have not been able to draw resources from the global economy or the international community to ameliorate their economic decline or more widely to effect any collective solutions to economic problems or issues such as security, the resolution of which might, in time, do much to facilitate economic growth and regional cooperation. The post-Soviet states have remained largely isolated from the wider world and focused on their unsatisfactory mutual relations. The inequalities that the region inherited from the USSR have endured and so has dependency on Russian energy and subsidy. What connections have been made to the global order have so far not led to widespread systemic change, but have enriched a small elite or generated revenues for a few areas. In general, this means that the post-Soviet space comprises a collection of weak states; they are economically impoverished, often lack political legitimacy, and have little capacity to pursue domestic change or international association. Arguably, many of them actually have less capacity than they did at their moment of independence, which was only a little more than a decade ago.

The frailties of the countries of the post-Soviet space have, however, left them vulnerable to Russian influence. In turn, Russia's inability to escape the full depths of Soviet economic decline and the full extent of the Soviet structural grip has meant that it only acts as a weak hegemon in the region, influencing the constituent states through military power and their poverty-driven dependence on it for energy subsidies. In many ways, Russian influence in the region could be said to be the result of a global lack of interest in many post-Soviet states as much as because of its strength. Changes that might be wrought by states from outside the region have yet to transform this part of the world by helping to build up state capacity; equally, the fact that they might soon begin to have a substantial influence on some of the countries shows that the ties that bind together the many weak regional states may easily be loosened. If, for whatever reason, this happens, the differences between states in the region will be reinforced. Those that receive the aid necessary to build capacity or make the connections to extra-regional powers will move forward, although no doubt in a neoliberal direction, and the rest will continue their seemingly inexorable decline.

Further reading

Bremmer, I. and Taras, R. (eds) (1997) *New States, New Politics: Building the Post-Soviet Nations* (Cambridge: Cambridge University Press).

Cummings, S.N. (ed.) (2002) *Power and Change in Central Asia* (London: Routledge).

Hellman, J.S. (1998) 'Winner Takes All: The Politics of Partial Transition', *World Politics*, vol. 50, no. 2, pp. 203–34.

Robinson, N. (2001) *Russia: A State of Uncertainty* (London: Routledge).

Sakwa, R. and Webber, M. (1999) 'The Commonwealth of Independent States, 1991–1998: Stagnation and Survival', *Europe-Asia Studies*, vol. 51, no. 3, pp. 379–415.

Smith, G. (1999) *The Post-Soviet States: Mapping the Politics of Transition* (London: Arnold).

Chapter 8

The Middle East

SIMON BROMLEY

Identifying the Middle East as a coherent region is a difficult and, perhaps, somewhat artificial exercise. Elie Kedourie (1992: 1) says that: 'Whether it is defined in geographical or cultural terms, and whatever its exact boundaries are held to be, there can be no disputing the fact that the Middle East is predominantly Muslim'. This is true, except that most of the world's Muslims live not in the Middle East (however defined) but in South and Southeast Asia. Moreover, as Bernard Lewis (1998: 133) has pointed out, 'unlike India, China or Europe, the Middle East has no collective identity. The pattern, from the earliest times to the present day, has been one of diversity – in religion, in language, in culture, and above all in self-perception.' This may be an overstatement, but it does capture an important truth. Muslims have shared and contested the Middle East with Jews and Christians (to speak only of the major monotheisms); Arabs have coexisted with Persians, Turks, Kurds and Berbers (among others); and social identities have ranged from the religious, to the linguistic and ethnic, to the (national) territorial, to the secular political.

Perhaps more importantly, ever since the extension of the European states-system to the region and the development of industrial capitalism in north-west Europe, the identification of a group of countries as constituting the Middle East has been one made by powers *outside* the region; it has not, for the most part, been a term of identification used within it. In the days of their empire the British referred to the 'Near East' as those countries that were strategically important in protecting its economic and military links to India and thence to the Far East – what are, nowadays, Turkey, Iran, Egypt, Jordan, Palestine and Israel, Iraq, Lebanon, Syria, Saudi Arabia, Yemen and the Gulf States. In Arabic, the term Mashrek refers to the countries of the Arab East – that is, the British 'Near East' minus its two non-Arab but Islamic states, Turkey and Iran, and minus the Jewish state established in 1948, Israel; and the term Maghreb refers to the Arab states of north Africa, namely Libya, Tunisia, Morocco, Algeria and Mauritania. In the present era the dominant outside power in the region, the United States, defines the

Middle East as part of southwest Asia for the purposes of military planning, a region spreading from the Arab East through Iran to Afghanistan, Pakistan and the largely Muslim successor states of the former Soviet Union in central Asia. In its data tables the World Bank treats as an entity countries in the Middle East and North Africa (MENA), but not including Turkey, whereas the UNDP groups *all* Arab countries together, that is, the Mashrek and the Maghreb, as well as Comoros, Djibouti, Somalia and the Sudan.

Developmentally speaking, Israel is set apart from the rest of the region, except to the extent that its conflicts with the Palestinians and the wider Arab world impact on both sides of that antagonism. Turkey and Iran, by contrast, share many development issues with the core Arab states, and the fortunes of the latter and Iran (as well as some of the Maghreb countries, such as Algeria and Libya) have been strongly conditioned by oil-based development. Politically and economically, the core regional interactions are among these states, and not with the wider west Asian or African Arab countries. This chapter will thus concentrate mainly on what the British used to call the 'Near East', although attention will occasionally be paid to the Maghreb as well. It will not, however, consider the political economy of development in Israel, except where this impacts on the surrounding Arab world.

Country development strategies in the Middle East

The problems of development in the contemporary Middle East are far-reaching, deeply entrenched, serious and urgent. The responses of states within the region, both individually and collectively, to the challenges posed by the end of the Cold War, the selective and uneven liberalization of the world economy over the last several decades and the new emphasis placed on human and sustainable development have generally been limited, falling far short of what is needed to generate a prosperous and secure future for their populations. Table 8.1 presents some basic statistics about the countries of the region at the end of the millennium. As is revealed, the story is in many respects one of failure. The result is that the rest of the world often sees the Middle East as a source of problems – a region of conflicts with the West, as well as a region in conflict – and thus frames strategies towards it in military and geopolitical, rather than developmental, terms. While this perception is not in itself inaccurate, it is profoundly misleading not to situate these problems in a developmental context. What is more, this very context is itself fundamentally shaped by the region's place in the international system and the role of external forces in shaping that context (Hinnebusch and Ehteshami 2002).

Table 8.1   *The Middle East: basic data*

Country	Population (millions)	GDP (billion US$)	GDP per capita (PPP US$)
Algeria	28.9	47.3	4,792
Bahrain	0.6	5.3	13,111
Comoros	0.7	0.2	1,398
Djibouti	0.6	0.5	1,266
Egypt	60.7	82.7	3,041
Iraq	21.8	–	3,197
Iran	63.7	101.6	1,650*
Jordan	4.8	7.4	3,347
Kuwait	2.3	25.2	25,314
Lebanon	3.4	17.2	4,326
Libya	5.2	–	6,697
Mauritania	2.5	1.0	1,563
Morocco	28.8	35.3	3,305
Oman	2.3	15.0	9,960
Qatar	0.5	9.2	20,987
Saudi Arabia	20.7	128.9	10,158
Sudan	29.5	10.4	1,394
Syria	15.6	17.4	2,892
Tunisia	9.3	20.0	5,404
Turkey	66.2	147.7	2,230*
United Arab Emirates	2.8	47.2	17,719
Yemen	17.1	4.3	719

– Data not available; * Current US$.
Source: Compiled from World Bank 'Country Profiles' accessed online at http://www.worldbank.org; and UNDP, *Arab Human Development Report* (New York NY: United Nations, 2000). All data are for the year 2000.

Models of development

Strategies of development in the states of the Middle East have reflected patterns of social structure inherited at independence, the role of international factors and the resources available to the state, especially oil. On this basis, it is possible, broadly speaking, to identify three models of development (Gerber 1987; Bromley 1994 and 1997).

There are, first, the revolutionary nationalist, socially modernizing and politically authoritarian regimes of Egypt, Iraq and Syria, which followed, in different circumstances, the import-substituting industrialization originally pursued by Turkey (and to a lesser extent Iran) in the years between the First and Second World Wars. These regimes all pursued state-led, national and protectionist models of development, albeit with important variations within the category. Different social structures and different relations to external powers characterized the Arab states (Egypt, Iraq and Syria), on the one hand, and Turkey and Iran, on the other. In the Arab states, urban-based landowners had large holdings alongside a dependent peasantry, while in Turkey and Iran land ownership was more dispersed and fragmented. Furthermore, the Arab states experienced a greater degree of European colonial control and influence, with effective independence coming later after 1945. One result of this different social structure and history was that Turkey and Iran underwent essentially nationalist coups directed against weakened imperial states and religious establishments, whilst the Arab states experienced military-led revolutions from above directed against domestic landed classes and foreign influence. It was also the case that some of these states – notably, Iraq and Iran – became major oil producers, especially after the 1960s and 1970s, while Turkey, Egypt and Syria did not. The development of the oil sector meant that the state could rely on externally generated rents to finance its own activities and accumulate foreign exchange for the national economy. As we shall see, this *rentier* model of development had a range of wider implications for the state and society as a whole (Davis 1991).

Second, there are the smaller countries, such as Jordan and Lebanon, which lacked either large-scale land ownership or oil wealth, where the state has played a more limited role in development, neither expropriating a land-owning class, nor controlling access to oil revenues. A more pluralistic mobilization of resources and politics has generally been the result. Although neither state has established proper democratic rule on a stable basis, both have some experience of partial democracy, Jordan through a monarchical system and Lebanon by means of 'consociationalism'.

Third, there are the pure *rentier* cases of Saudi Arabia and the Gulf States, which lacked landed classes, or indeed any significant productive socio-economic forces, prior to the formation of the modern state and grew economically almost solely on the basis of oil rents and more or less direct external support. The limited social basis of these regimes and the fact that the state appropriates virtually all its resources from external sources has meant that there has been very little scope for the emergence of independent organization in either the economic or the political sphere. Ruling tribes have been turned into monarchies and authoritarian monarchical rule is the norm (Luciani 1990).

Historically, Turkey was the first state in the region to undertake an active, national, state-led model of development (Keyder 1987). But it did so in a generally supportive international context. In the interwar years it received diplomatic support from Britain as a barrier to Soviet influence, whilst the state-led development that began in the 1930s coincided with a more general drift towards economic autarchy. Again, during the Cold War, Turkey benefited from economic and military assistance from the US and its ISI project was able to take advantage of the 'long boom' of the world economy during the 1950s–70s. By contrast, both the Egyptian (1956) and Iraqi (1958) revolutions were anti-imperialist in orientation and were defined against the interests of the dominant imperialist powers in the region, the UK and the US (Aulas 1988; Farouk-Sluglett and Sluglett 1990). Both countries rejected strategic alliances with the West, maintained hostile relations with Israel, courted the USSR and attempted to play an independent role in the regional politics of the Arab world. Syria followed a similar path in many respects. Egypt was able to gain international assistance from both sides in the Cold War, but was economically disadvantaged by the events of 1956 – the nationalization of the Suez Canal and the subsequent Anglo-French and Israeli military operations against Egypt – and suffered a major political setback with the 1967 Arab–Israeli war and the subsequent ascendancy of the conservative oil states in the Gulf and Saudi Arabia (Amin 1978). Its hesitant economic liberalization – the *infitah* (opening) – was undertaken before its import-substitution strategy had produced any genuine industrial deepening and it has thus far been unable to replicate Turkey's limited successes in this area (Waterbury 1993). However, Egypt's turn to the West after 1973 did help it to become a major recipient of US aid. On the other hand, Iraq's formative years – those of the rise of the Ba'ath after 1968 – coincided with rapidly rising oil prices. These added significantly to the resources available to the state and enabled the regime both to consolidate its repressive apparatus and become a major distributor of economic and social largesse. After the early 1970s Iraq (like Syria also) allied itself with the Soviet Union.

After the initial consolidation of Ibn Saud's rule (in the late 1920s and early 1930s) with British backing, the external environment of Saudi development was determined by a pattern of integration into the world market through a single commodity, oil, and by an increasingly strong strategic alliance with the United States (Salame 1989). Although not without tensions, this relationship was founded on common interests based on an exchange of oil for security, especially after 1967 and the political and military defeat of radical nationalist forces in the Arab world. In Iran, after a coup in 1953, nationalist and communist forces were placed on the defensive and the power of the Shah increased as a result of rising oil revenues and the economic, military and security assistance of the US. This meant, in marked contrast to the Egyptian and Iraqi cases, that the programme of land reform and state-led industrialization in Iran was pro- rather than anti-imperialist. Iran thus became, alongside Israel, the major US ally in the region – a partnership maintained until the drama of the clerical revolution of 1979 (Halliday 1979).

The size and influence of oil and strategic rents has differed widely across the states of the Middle East. Saudi Arabia and the Gulf states (Oman, Kuwait, Qatar, Bahrain and the United Arab Emirates) lie at one end of the spectrum, with huge reserves and levels of production in comparison to their populations and the non-oil sectors of their economies. These are unambiguously *rentier* economies and *rentier* states, with oil incomes accounting for some 65–75 per cent of GNP and oil (as well as oil-financed overseas investments) providing virtually all of the state's revenues. At the other end of the spectrum Turkey has no oil, but nevertheless gains some rents from transit fees. In addition, it received significant strategic rents in the form of US aid because of its role in the Cold War and benefited from the post-1945 boom in western Europe via workers' remittances, mainly from (West) Germany. Egypt also had no petroleum production until the 1980s: oil and gas now provide major sources of foreign exchange, but this does not make Egypt a *rentier* economy or state. However, high levels of US assistance after 1973, aid from the Arab oil states, transit fees, earnings from the Suez Canal, tourism and workers' remittances have all made Egypt highly dependent on external sources of income for foreign exchange.

Iran, Iraq and Algeria are intermediate and more complex cases. According to Karshenas (1990), the share of oil revenues in total government income in Iran was about 50 per cent during 1963–67, rising to over 75 per cent during 1973–77. In the latter period oil income accounted for approximately 30 per cent of GNP and between 80–90 per cent of foreign exchange earnings. Thus, while it is accurate to refer to the existence of a *rentier* state in Iran during the 1970s, this is not an accurate characterization of the Iranian economy as a whole. In Iraq oil accounted for about 30 per cent of GNP prior to the 1973–74 price rises, the figure rising to over 60 per cent by the mid-1970s; oil income already provided more than half of total state revenues in the mid-1960s. By the late 1970s virtually all of Iraq's foreign exchange was earned by oil exports. This was also the case in Algeria (if one includes exports of natural gas).

In sum, where they existed, breaking the power of the notables – the landed classes allied to the Western imperial powers – was a precondition for launching encompassing strategies of national development after independence. The absence of such a class in Turkey meant that state-led industrialization faced no such obstacles. In Egypt, Iraq and Iran, by contrast, 'land reform was the handmaiden of state-led industrialization strategies' (Richards and Waterbury 1990: 151). Though unavowed as such, the Turkish model was the basic paradigm for these states. In the process, reformers expropriated their political enemies: new professional middle-class and military groups displaced the old order grounded in external control over the economy and foreign policy. In marked contrast, in the oil-rich states of Saudi Arabia and the Gulf, oil provided the basis for a rather different path of socio-economic transformation, dependent on the West not just for the import of capital goods but for skilled labour power and security as well.

Conservatives and radicals, monarchies and republics?

Against this background, some analysts have distinguished between 'conservative' and 'radical' regimes based on the model of state-led development adopted (Richards and Waterbury 1990). In the conservative, state-capitalist variant, the state seeks to mobilize resources and provide the infrastructure for capitalist development while transferring its own surpluses to the private sector – the cases of Turkey since 1950, Iran between 1963–79, Egypt since 1973, Saudi Arabia in the 1980s and 1990s. In the radical variant the state retains the surpluses on its own operations, captures a large share of those in the remaining private sector and then attempts to secure for itself more or less complete control over resource mobilization, if not over all property – Turkey hesitantly in the 1930s, Egypt nominally after 1961 and Iraq after 1963. It is worth noting that oil states are to be found in both camps and that the main impetus behind the radical model appears to have been more the degree of difficulty, and hence the level of social conflict, involved in consolidating state power than the ideological orientation of or resources available to the regime. In other words, the radical strategy has been very largely a response to weak and contested political legitimacy. Where the process of establishing the legitimacy of the state and the regime was protracted or violent, then the state tended to assume a greater presence throughout society, including in the economy.

Another distinction that has often been drawn concerns the political form of the regime (Ayubi 1995). On the one side, there are the monarchies, such as Jordan, Saudi Arabia, the Gulf states and Morocco; on the other, the nominally republican systems of Syria, Egypt, Iraq and the like. Turkey is a restricted democracy (its scope limited by a military-dominated national security council) and Iran a clerical dictatorship with significant elements of popular participation. But, in practice, these distinctions count for less than might appear, and one certainly cannot conclude that the republican regimes are in some sense more successful economically than the monarchies, whatever their ideological proclamations to the contrary. The reality is that across the region – Turkey and Iran aside – sectarian, tribal and family patrimonialism has 'blurred the distinction between monarchies and republics' (Hinnebusch 2002: 12).

Contemporary issues

Across the Middle East as a whole, socio-economic progress was impressive in the 1960s and 1970s, falling off thereafter as the quick returns to domestic capital accumulation diminished and the global economic slowdown, whose effects were delayed and cushioned by oil rents, belatedly made an impact from the mid-1980s onwards (El-Ghonemy 1998; Owen and Pamuk 1998). Although the early 1980s did see higher growth based on oil rents, by the decade's end war, falling real oil prices, rising debts and internal difficulties of public-sector performance had restricted the opportunities for growth. Outside the oil sector, the overall performance was not good: the region was characterized by rising food imports as agricultural output failed to keep pace with population growth; a modest manufacturing sector accounting for a mere 15 per cent of GNP; and a small and declining share of world exports and foreign investment (Issawi 1982). Since then the challenges facing development strategists in the contemporary Middle East can be said to fall into three main areas: a generally deteriorating economic performance in the context of the underdevelopment of the region's human resources; the serious and worsening problems of environmental sustainability; and the continuing problems of statehood, political legitimacy and conflict.

Economic performance

The recent economic record of the Middle East is unquestionably a cause for serious concern (Owen and Pamuk 1998). Considering the Arab countries of the region first, their combined GDP is less than that of Spain and the value of their non-oil exports similar to Finland. Growth rates have varied over time and in relation to oil prices, but, translated into real per capita incomes, they imply an annual improvement of just 0.5 per cent over the last 25 years or so. The richest Arab countries, the Gulf states and Saudi Arabia, actually witnessed a *decline* of GDP per capita of 1.8 per cent per year over the last quarter of a century. Low-income Arab countries (Yemen, Algeria and Djibouti) had a marginally negative rate of growth over the same period (−0.1 per cent). In other words, only the middle-income Arab countries – Egypt, Jordan, Morocco, Oman, Sudan, Syria and Tunisia – experienced a positive growth rate of per capita GDP (0.9 per cent). Inevitably, therefore, Arab countries have been falling further behind the advanced, post-industrial world. In 1975 the real per capita GDP of the Arab world was around a fifth of that of the OECD grouping; by 2000 it was only a seventh. As the Arab Human Development Report (UNDP 2002: 88–9) noted, 'only Egypt and to a lesser degree Jordan and Tunisia had a tendency towards convergence with OECD countries. All other countries, without exception, moved in the opposite direction.'

What underlies this poor economic performance is an inefficient economic system. Perhaps surprisingly, the investment effort in the Arab world has been substantial, with gross fixed-capital formation as a proportion of GDP averaging around one-quarter over the last quarter of a century. Yet, with the partial exceptions of Egypt, Jordan, Oman and Syria, the efficiency of investment has been limited. Much of the private-sector investment in the labour-surplus economies was financed by workers' remittances from the oil-rich states and went into non-tradeable sectors, especially housing (Page 1998). This has had the effect of limiting the growth of income inequality in the region, but it has done little to advance the long-run productive potential of the economies in the labour-exporting countries. Productivity performance, whether measured in relation to capital, labour or total factor productivity, has been very poor.

The World Development Report (World Bank 1998–99) showed that the levels of labour productivity in the oil-rich Arab states were about a half of that in Argentina and South Korea; in Egypt, Syria and Tunisia it was less than a sixth of that in the comparator countries; and in the oil-poor countries – Djibouti, Jordan, Lebanon, Mauritania, Morocco, Somalia, Sudan and Yemen – it was less than a tenth. Similarly, the United Nations Industrial Development Organization (1992–93) found that levels of labour productivity in Arab industry fell from around a third of those in the US in 1970 to less than a fifth in 1990, despite massive investments in infrastructure, capital accumulation and human capital. Indeed, the returns to investment in the latter have been particularly disappointing. There are still over 60 million adults who are illiterate in the Arab Middle East, the majority of whom are women, despite higher than average spending on education in relation to other similar parts of the world. Inevitably, too, there are serious concerns about the quality of much of that education.

The overall consequences have been severe. For the MENA region as a whole, the World Bank (1995) estimates that total factor productivity showed a steady annual decline (-0.2 per cent per year) from 1960 to 1990. Perhaps not surprisingly, the Arab Middle East receives a mere 0.7 per cent of the net flows of global foreign direct investment and over half of that goes to just one country – Egypt. Over the last decade 'exports from the region (over 70 per cent of which are accounted for by oil and oil-related products) grew at 1.5 per cent per year, far below the global rate of six per cent. Manufacturing exports have remained stagnant and private-capital flows have lagged behind those of other regions' (United Nations Development Programme 2002: 4).

As regards the major non-Arab countries of the region, Turkey and Iran, the picture is again one of interesting contrast. Recent economic performance in Iran has been relatively good: foreign indebtedness is limited and debt–service ratios are small; growth has been limited, but has more or less matched the increase in labour-force participation; and an ambitious but gradual programme of reform to liberalize much of the state-controlled and nationally protected economy is underway, with World Bank support. To be sure, Iran's performance remains closely tied to movements in the international prices of oil and gas, but the current Five-Year Plan (2000–05) is based on conservative estimates and macroeconomic management has to date been prudent. Turkey, by contrast, continues to struggle with a considerable foreign debt burden, as well as high and unstable levels of inflation, and has yet to put its public finances on a sustainable footing, notwithstanding over 20 years (on and off) of IMF-sponsored reform. Following a renewed economic crisis (2000–01) it embraced a more far-reaching programme of adjustment, but whether this will, at last, generate more stable economic management remains to be seen.

Sustainable development

Problems of economic failure, poor human resources and environmental stress interact in damaging ways. While Turkey and Iran are not free of environmental problems, by far the most serious issues arise in the semi-arid, yet oil-rich, Arab Middle East. For the MENA region, for example, the World Bank has identified four major problems of sustainable development: urban air pollution from heavy industry and vehicle emissions; access to safe drinking water and sanitation, especially in rural areas; a declining per capita availability of fresh water; and land, pasturage and forest degradation. They are estimated to cost nearly US$15 billion per annum, or 3 per cent of GDP, in impaired health, premature deaths, disappearing natural resources and tourism losses. Hamid Mohtadi (1998: 262, 274) argues that the roots of many of these difficulties can be traced to the inheritance of a semi-arid ecology and the abundance of oil and gas deposits. He suggests that this has produced a distinct pattern of environmental degradation:

> Oil has allowed the countries in the region to pursue inward-oriented policies that protect the industrial sector at the expense of natural

resources and the environment; it also has supported massive energy subsidies, causing an overreliance on highly polluting fossil fuels ... The empirical results suggest a sequential and triangular chain of causation in which oil and raw material exports are significantly associated with excessive energy consumption; such exports are also significantly associated with economic inwardness, and economic inwardness is associated with greater energy use.

More specifically, Mohtadi identifies a number of routes by which this combination of oil and aridity has fed through into environmentally unsustainable models of development. The relatively easy access to foreign exchange from oil rents has enabled states to act in a highly protectionist manner, producing a pattern of heavy and capital-intensive industrialization. Together with low energy costs deriving from fossil-fuel subsidies, this has resulted in excessive and inefficient energy use in industry. Not only are fossil-fuel resources being rapidly depleted, but the overuse of energy contributes to the poor quality of air and water. In urban areas, 60 million people in the MENA region are exposed to air pollution levels significantly in excess of World Health Organization guidelines; and, mainly in rural areas, 45 million lack safe water. Heavy industry and high-sulphur fuel oil are major sources of air pollution, whilst industrial discharges and (subsidized) agricultural chemical runoffs are the major contributors to water pollution.

Sharing limited water resources between states and allocating scarce resources between different activities within states are major developmental challenges for the future in the Middle East. The 'water question' looms large in Egypt, Turkey, Syria, Iraq, Israel and Palestine and elsewhere in north Africa, whilst the role of water as an underlying source of conflict in relation to Israel's relations with Palestine, on the one side, and Syria, Lebanon and Jordan, on the other, is well-known. Proposals to dam rivers and alter flows in south-east Turkey are also a source of potential conflict with Syria and Iraq. Egypt shares the north-eastern African acquifer with Libya, Chad and Sudan, but receives the vast majority of its water from the Nile. Whereas the mutual control of reciprocal externalities is at least in principle feasible, the Nile is unique as a river basin in that most of the consumption is accounted for by two downstream states, Egypt (66 per cent of water use) and Sudan (22 per cent), which contribute nothing to its flow, most of which (86 per cent) originates in Ethiopia (Rogers 1997). Given the use of the highly contested notion of 'prior appropriations' by successive Egyptian governments to legitimize their claims to Nile water, and Egypt's regular reminders to its co-riparians of its military power, the scope for future conflict in this sphere should not be overlooked. Water use is also problematic: although the vast majority of water consumption in the economy is accounted for by agriculture, where it is often provided free or at great subsidy to farmers, the value added per unit of water use is considerably greater in industry. Within the rural/agricultural sector, the economic allocation of water resources involves a fundamental break with past agricultural practices and priorities. In Egypt, for example, as in many other countries in the region, agricultural water has been managed as a common property resource. The recent introduction of clearer private property rights in land and water cost-recovery systems thus threatens to disenfranchise the rural poor from their already limited environmental assets in a dramatic way.

Political legitimacy

Disappointing though the economic performance of the region has been, it is arguably politics rather than economics that explains this state of affairs. For it can be argued that the single biggest constraint upon any strategy of development in the Middle East remains the difficulty of establishing durable forms of political authority that are capable of commanding the mass loyalties of their populations and pursuing encompassing strategies of social and economic transformation (Bromley 1994 and 1997). There is presently not a single state in the region that can be said to enjoy a settled legitimacy among its population, let alone the capacity to secure guarantees of individual civil and political rights and democratic means of effecting a change in government.

There are at least three dimensions of this situation to unpack. In the first place, the task of state formation, of constructing states that can make an effective claim to sovereign authority over their territories and establish the recognition of that claim by other, similarly constituted, states, has been a difficult and protracted process in the Middle East. Since independence, the states of the region have struggled not only to impose domestic authority, but also to manage peaceful and cooperative relations with one another. While the levels of military control of domestic politics and of inter-state conflict were not substantially higher in the Middle East than in many other regions during the 1950s–70s, thereafter the fortunes of the region have steadily diverged from the limited trend towards greater civilian control of the state and the initiation of democratic politics (Picard 1990; Tilly 1991). As oil revenues rose during the 1970s and 1980s, the share of military expenditure in GDP in the Middle East was very nearly twice that of the next most militarized region (the Warsaw Pact countries) and over three times the world average. Across the region the exigencies of rapidly consolidating state power in a threatening inter-state environment, fostering industrialization from a subordinate position in the international division of labour and forging a social basis for the new, post-independence regimes all conspired to augment the power of the military within the state. The activities of outside powers, especially the US and to some degree the USSR, served only to facilitate this. It is important, too, to note that the process cannot be attributed solely or even primarily to the Arab–Israeli conflict. The biggest military spenders – Iran, Saudi Arabia and Iraq – have been those countries with the most access to oil rents, not the so-called frontline states in that conflict, namely, Egypt, Jordan and Syria. Moreover, the largest conflicts experienced in the region, whether measured in human or economic terms, have been those between Iraq and Iran (1980–88) and those arising from intra-Arab and Arab–Western rivalries, specifically the Iraq–Kuwait–US war of 1990–91. In sum, then, the crippling weight of the military in the political economy of the region has been a massive drain on prospects of economic and social progress (Sayigh 1992).

Second, even where the sovereign authority of the state has been established and is reasonably secure, political regimes in the Middle East have displayed strong elements of what Linz and Stepan (1996) have called 'sultanism'. In such a system:

> The private and public are fused, there is a strong tendency toward familial power and dynastic succession, there is no distinction between a state career and personal service to the ruler, and, most of all, the ruler acts only according to his own unchecked discretion, with no larger, impersonal goals (Linz and Stepan 1996: 52).

To be sure, sultanism has been combined with more conventional forms of authoritarianism and, in a few cases, with elements of democracy. Nevertheless, it is an important feature of politics in the Middle East and has proved to be a significant obstacle to both political change and socio-economic improvement. Such regimes have been vulnerable to the idiosyncracies of rulers and their cliques, often beholden to narrow factional interests, and generally unresponsive to broad national interests in development. What is equally striking has been the limited movement away from sultanism and authoritarianism towards democracy – Turkey excepted. Huntington's (1991) 'Third Wave of democratization' has had very little impact on the Middle East (Bromley 1997). Turkey is admittedly something of an exception to this generalization. Since the military coup of 1980 it has held regular elections, although certain parties and politicians have been banned from participation and the military retains an effective veto over the political process, helping to bring down a democratically elected government in 1997. However, Turkey's desire for European Union membership (alongside internal struggles for human rights and democratic reforms) has improved the prospects for democratic government. There have also been some interesting movements towards reform in Iran as well. A young and increasingly articulate population coexists with an elderly (male) clerical oligarchy and the political system is now divided between an elected component and a self-perpetuating religious elite, with the latter currently controlling the key aspects of state power (Hooglund 1992).

Third, the harsh truth is that the states of the region have displayed only limited interest in forging serious developmental strategies. Notwithstanding impressive contributions to physical and social infrastructure and, in some cases, significant resource mobilization for capital accumulation, no Middle Eastern country has approximated the developmental achievements of east Asia (Issawi 1995). Turkey, Egypt and Iran all have significant achievements to their credit in specific sectors and in some periods of their recent history, but not even these countries begin to compare with the likes of South Korea and Taiwan, or even Malaysia and Thailand.

The explanation of these problems of state formation, and of arbitrary and unresponsive regimes, remains the subject of sharp disagreement among analysts of Middle Eastern politics and political economy. A recent report from the Arab Fund for Economic and Social Development argued that 'the region is hampered by three key deficits that can be considered defining features: the freedom deficit; the women's empowerment deficit; [and] the human capabilities/knowledge deficit relative to income' (United Nations Development Programme 2002: 27). There is widespread agreement that encompassing models of development committed to a degree of social inclusiveness and geared to systematic and credible economic reform and a determined attempt to nurture human resources and the conditions for sustainable livelihoods have generally been absent. As we have seen, Turkey and Iran fare better in some respects, but neither is a secure, stable democracy and both face considerable challenges in building up the capabilities of their peoples. There is, then, considerable accord about the extent to which development efforts in the Middle East fall short of the challenges facing the region; there is far less agreement about the causes of, and hence the solutions to, these problems.

The intra-regional politics of development in the Middle East

The most common candidate to capture the regional identity of the Middle East is, of course, Islam. Even if one limits the region to its Arab states (see below), the cultural core of Arabic civilization apart from the language is still Islam. Prior to the Renaissance, the Reformation and the scientific and technological revolution of the seventeenth century in Europe, Islamic civilization had some claim to be, as Lewis (2002: 159) puts it, 'the greatest, most advanced, and most open civilization in human history'. How, then, can we account for what he calls its 'eclipse'? Why has it apparently had such great difficulty accommodating to the demands of a modern world made global by the power and example of the West?

Written by Arab and Muslim scholars, the Report of the Arab Fund for Economic and Social Development quoted previously argues that the root cause of the region's relative lack of developmental achievement has been a multifaceted denial of freedom and a failure to address the individual and collective prerequisites of the resources and opportunities needed to expand human capabilities. Drawing on the work of Amartya Sen (1999), it asserts that freedoms are not only important in their own right but also because of their instrumental value in laying the basis for development. Lewis (2002: 159) similarly concludes his discussion of *What Went Wrong?* by saying:

> It is precisely the lack of freedom – freedom of the mind from constraint and indoctrination, to question and inquire and speak; freedom of the economy from corrupt and pervasive mismanagement; freedom of women from male oppression; freedom of citizens from tyranny – that underlies so many of the troubles of the Muslim world.

Where the authors of the Report and historians such as Kedourie and Lewis part company is in their assessment of the causes of this pervasive lack of freedom, since for the latter it is the very force which unites the Middle East and once made it such a great civilization that now accounts for its misfortunes. To invert a well-known slogan of Islamist political groupings ('Islam is the way'), Islam has become the problem.

Lewis argues that Islam has failed to follow the path of secularization pioneered in the West. This involved two transformations: first, faith became a matter of private, not public, belief, such that public identity became predominantly national, not religious; and, second, the source of political authority and the basis of sovereignty was transferred from God to the people. 'Both of these ideas were alien to Islam, but in the course of the nineteenth century they became more familiar, and in the twentieth they became dominant among the Westernized intelligentsia who, for a while, ruled many if not most Muslim states' (Lewis 2002: 106). Secularism in the Middle East has thus meant not a separation of religion and the state and a consequent privatization of religious belief, but rather an attempt by modernizing states to control the political expression of religion. On this account, the political problems of the region stem predominantly from the difficulty of establishing the national state as the primary focus of political loyalty and identity in competition with Islam. In Kedourie's (1992: 346) words, modern politics has thus been a 'tormented endeavour to discard the old ways'.

Why has Islam presented such an obstacle to the construction of secular, popular forms of national loyalty and identity? The answer, again according to Lewis (2003), is that, unlike Christianity, it represents a *fusion* of religious and political authority, providing the basis for an extensive politico-legal order as well as a moral code. He illustrates this as follows: Christianity teaches its followers what is right and wrong, good and evil, but the Qur'an enjoins believers to '*command* good and *forbid* evil' (my emphasis). That is to say, there is no equivalent in Islam to Christ's teaching to 'render unto Caesar what is Caesar's'. What is more:

> Islam is not so much a matter of orthodoxy as of orthopraxy ... What Islam has generally asked of its believers is not textual accuracy in belief, but loyalty to the community and its constituted leader ... [Islam establishes a] boundary – not between orthodoxy and heterodoxy, which is relatively unimportant, but between Islam and apostasy ... and apostasy, according to all schools of Muslim jurisprudence, is a capital offence (Lewis 1998: 126).

Others have argued that what a given religion amounts to, politically speaking, is socially contingent on the contexts in which it operates and the interests that it expresses; and that, while the lexicon and idiom of politics in the Middle East is indeed often 'Islamic', its practice can still be understood in essentially secular terms (Zubaida 1989 and 2003). On this account, it is the context of authoritarian politics – explicable by reference to the presence of *rentier* states, arbitrary colonial state formation, inter-state conflict and the like – which produces authoritarian (and patriarchal) interpretations of Islam. In either case, secular political power, which derives its authority from a nationally defined people and is oriented towards regulating a complex modern society based on open inquiry and high levels of personal freedom, is a standing challenge to the currently dominant interpretations of Islam and, in particular, to the demand for rule according to Islamic law, the *shari'a*.

In Iran, the secular project was pursued so vehemently under the Shah that it provoked an event unique in modern history, a social revolution carried out under the leadership of religious forces, resulting in the construction of a hybrid revolutionary and theocratic regime. In Turkey, the paradigm example of secularism in the Middle East, there has also been a gradual reassertion of the force of Islam in public life, notwithstanding the role of the armed forces as the self-appointed guardians of a secular constitution. In Algeria, religious–political opposition to the nominally secular and socialist regime that gained independence from France has resulted in a violent civil war. In Saudi Arabia, the monarchical regime of the House of Saud has relied on religious support to legitimate its rule, but now faces religiously inspired challenges to its legitimacy. In Syria and Egypt, secular regimes backed by the armed forces remain in power, but confront considerable, if varying, degrees of domestic opposition. Until the second US-led war against it in 2003, Iraq was also a secular, military regime. Viewing these and similar trends, authors such as Lewis and Kedourie judge that the project of state secularism has failed.

The result of that failure, they argue, is a general spread of pan-Islamic challenges to the authority of particular states and regimes. Analysis of the significance of this is complicated by the fact that many regimes have used state-controlled religion as an ideological weapon, especially against the secular left, namely, communists and liberals. The result, as Lewis (1998: 143) points out, is that there are two sorts of pan-Islamic politics:

> One is political in inspiration, sometimes diplomatic in method, and usually conservative in policy. The other is popular, usually radical, often subversive. Both at times enjoy governmental support, the one by patriarchal, the other by revolutionary regimes. Both also receive significant financial support from private individuals, mainly in Arabia and the Gulf, who combine new wealth with old aspirations. There is of course no clear differentiation, since governments try to exploit popular movements elsewhere, while popular movements seek to influence or even control government.

The point is that, if the fusion of religion and politics, of faith and power, in Islam is correctly interpreted as being fundamentally inimical to the forms of modern freedom that are essential to the pursuit of development, then any unity founded on Islamic principles is unlikely to offer the region much hope. In any case, such pan-Islamic unity as exists has, thus far, been primarily informal and lacking in institutionalization.

In reality, the modern history of regional cooperation for development in the Middle East – and it must be said that it too has been extremely limited – has been pan-Arab, not pan-Islamic. Among the Arab countries a common language and culture forms the basis for integration, at least at the level of the movement of people and ideas. Moreover, pan-Arabism has played an important ideological role both within particular Arab countries and as an ideology of inter-state manoeuvre (Korany and Dessouki 1991). But it is a mistake to posit an Arab identity in opposition to other national forms of identification. Arab nationalist movements have in fact been weakest in those places with the most homogeneous Arab populations (Egypt and Saudi Arabia) and strongest among minorities in the ethnically and religiously most heterogeneous states (Syria and Iraq).

Nevertheless, there exist a number of pan-Arab organizations, some examples of which are set out in Table 8.2. The forerunner was the Arab League, which was founded in 1945 in the days when pan-Arab aspirations were real competitors to the weakly articulated national loyalties of the newly emerging states. The Arab League has a Council and General Secretariat and a Council of Joint Arab Defence, as well as an Economic and Social Council. These councils meet to coordinate policies; to propose common projects; to reach unified Arab positions in international negotiations (for example, on conventions on the environment and human rights); and to discuss candidates for Arab representation within important international institutions such as the Security Council and other UN organizations. There are also a number of smaller groupings of Arab states, such as the Gulf Cooperation Council (founded 1981), comprising the Gulf states and Saudi Arabia, and the Arab Maghreb Union (1989). There are also the Arab regional funds – the Arab Fund for Social and Economic Development (1967) and the Arab Monetary Fund (1976); the national funds – the Kuwait Fund for Arab Economic Development (1961), the Abu Dhabi Fund for Development (1971) and the Saudi Development Fund (1974); and the international funds – the Islamic Development Bank (1975, over 70 per cent of whose funds come from Arab countries) and the OPEC Development Fund (1976, which gets some two-thirds of its resources from Arab oil producers).

Yet all of this has produced very little, if any, change on the ground in terms of economic integration and political unity. Inter-Arab trade accounts for 7–10 per cent of total Arab trade, a figure which has not changed since the 1950s. Foreign investment originating in Arab countries goes overwhelmingly to the high-income, post-industrial countries. Politically, Arab states have failed to take unified positions on matters of international concern, even on the Arab–Israeli conflict. As the Report of the Arab Fund for Economic and Social Development lamented, 'Arab countries continue to face the outside world and the challenges posed by the region itself, individually and alone' (United Nations Development Programme 2002: 121).

Table 8.2 *Main regional organizations in the Middle East*

Organization	Membership	Purpose
Arab League	Arab states	Originally founded in 1945 to promote pan-Arab unity but increasingly recognized, and constrained by, the national sovereignty of independent Arab states. Since 1973 it has held summits of Arab heads of state but is increasingly regarded as lacking in political authority.
Gulf Cooperation Council	Bahrain, Kuwait, Oman, Qatar, Saudi Arabia and the United Arab Emirates	Founded in 1981, in response to the events of the Iranian Revolution (1979) and the outbreak of the Iran–Iraq war (1980–88), to bring about economic and security cooperation among the Gulf states under Saudi Arabian leadership.
Euro-Mediterranean Partnership Initiative	The EU 15 + Algeria, Cyprus, Egypt, Israel, Jordan, Lebanon, Malta, Morocco, Syria, Tunisia, Turkey and the Palestinian territories	Established in 1995, in the wake of the Madrid Israeli–Palestinian agreements and the Oslo Accords. Strictly speaking not a 'regional' organization, but relevant to the political order of the region. Aimed at promoting economic and political cooperation, regional security and cultural and educational links. Its core is an ambitious project for a free trade agreement, alongside European attempts to promote human rights and better governance.

Taking a somewhat wider focus and including Turkey and Iran fully within the definition of the region does not improve the picture. Iran and Turkey are not members of any of the Arab regional organizations (though Turkey is part of the Euro-Mediterranean Partnership) and

Turkey is, in fact, more closely linked to the West than to the rest of the Middle East. It is a longstanding and important member of both NATO and the OECD. Despite possessing significant elements of a common Islamic culture, Iran is divided from the Arab world by language, by doctrinal differences within Islam – the majority of Iranian Muslims are Shi'a whereas the majority in the Arab world are Sunni – and, above all, by geopolitical differences over the strategic management of the Gulf and the implications of the rise to power of a revolutionary Islamic regime in Tehran since 1979. Moreover, both Turkey and Iran see their futures as much in relation to future trends in central Asia as in connection with the Middle East.

In short, whether understood as the centre of the Islamic world, as Arab, or as an externally defined region of interacting states, the Middle East is not well-integrated regionally, either economically or politically. Whereas the pressure of globalization is producing elements of effective political regionalism in many parts of the world, this is emphatically not the case in the Middle East.

The extra-regional politics of development in the Middle East

Considered as a region, the Middle East (however defined) does not act with one voice in the international development agenda, though individual countries play a role on particular issues. The most important way in which the region impacts on this agenda is through the political economy of oil. The Middle East is home to around 65–70 per cent of the world's oil reserves and thus constitutes a vital interest for both the post-industrial countries of the OECD and rapidly industrializing countries such as China and India. Middle Eastern states form the core of the Organization of Petroleum Exporting Countries and seek to use the body to control levels of oil output in relation to market demand in order to maximize their long-run revenues. On occasion (in 1973–74 and again in the late 1970s), OPEC has been in conflict with the major oil-importing countries over the price and security of supplies of oil. Many oil-producing countries in the region are also reluctant to open their oil sectors fully to Western companies and competitive pressures. Most states regard the control established after the nationalization of Western companies in the 1970s as a form of economic sovereignty to be safeguarded.

The dominance of oil in the region's political economy affects not only the oil-producing states. This is so for two reasons. First, to a limited but still significant extent, the rents of the oil states have been recycled to the non-oil Arab states via the remittances of migrant workers, transit fees for pipelines and shipments, and aid. Second, because of oil, the region has assumed a wider geopolitical significance in international politics and has thus long been the recipient of very large location, or strategic, rents in the form of aid and military assistance. Hazem Beblawi (1990: 98) concluded accordingly that:

> The oil phenomenon has cut across the whole of the Arab world, oil rich and oil poor. Arab oil states have played a major role in propagating a new pattern of behaviour, i.e. the rentier pattern...The impact of oil has been so pre-eminent that it is not unrealistic to refer to the present era of Arab history as the oil era, where the oil disease has contaminated all of the Arab world.

Similar arguments were advanced in relation to Pahlavi Iran during the 1960s and 1970s and apply equally to the revolutionary regime since 1979.

In addition to its sustenance of *rentier* economies and states, the presence of oil in the Middle East has had two further effects. It has attracted the interests of outside powers and the associated provision of support for friendly regimes. The regional role of the US in particular has served to contain or frustrate radical movements in the region that might have threatened the West's access to oil on favourable terms. Defence of the *status quo*, in which the distribution of oil reserves in relation to population (particularly marked in Saudi Arabia and the Gulf states) favours the West, has been the main aim of US foreign policy in the region. At the same time, the threat to these arrangements posed by radical nationalist forces (Nasser's Egypt in the 1950s and 1960s, Saddam's Iraq until 2003 and Khomeini's Iran in the 1980s and 1990s) has resulted in equally solid support for Israel. In turn, the continued reproduction of the Arab–Israeli conflict and the availability of *rentier* incomes have conspired to make the Middle East the most armed region of the world and, as we have seen, have thereby bolstered the presence of military and authoritarian forces in the region's polities. Whether the second US-led war against Iraq proves to be a turning point or simply another phase in this vicious cycle remains to be seen.

One consequence of the importance of oil in the region's economy has been a lack of enthusiasm for aspects of the global environmental agenda, especially the reduction of carbon dioxide emissions to abate global warming. While some countries in the region are likely to be among the worst affected by rising sea levels – for example, the Egyptian delta – others such as Saudi Arabia have a direct interest in continued oil consumption at high and increasing levels. For example, in the negotiations surrounding the first and second reports of the International Panel on Climate Change, Saudi Arabia, supported by Kuwait and in alliance with a coalition of major oil companies, actively campaigned to have the scientific drafting of the reports watered down, with some considerable success. Mohamed Al-Sabban, an oil ministry official and leader of the Saudi delegation in these negotiations, later told *Nature* that 'Saudi Arabia's oil income amounts to 96 per cent of our total exports. Until there is clearer evidence of human involvement in climate change, we will not agree to what amounts to a tax on oil' (quoted in Leggett 2000). The OPEC countries were not in the end able to prevent the signing of the Kyoto Protocol on climate change in 1997, but they have lobbied effectively in the aftermath of the agreement to soften many of the tougher aspects of the proposed regime (Grubb with Vrolijk and Brack 1999).

Another aspect of the oil economy is the relatively marginal role played by the region in other forms of international trade. Significantly, while all the countries in the region are members of the IMF and the World Bank, and many have extensive programmes with these institutions, especially with the Bank, far fewer are members of the WTO. At present there are only Djibouti, Egypt, Jordan, Kuwait, Morocco, Oman, Qatar, Tunisia, Turkey and the United Arab Emirates (although Algeria, Lebanon, Saudi Arabia, Sudan and Yemen have expressed an intention to join). Of the member states only Egypt has taken an active role in the various coalitions of non-OECD countries that formed in the run-up to the Doha ministerial, which was, of course, held in Qatar.

Oil aside, the most extensive linkages of the regional to wider global agendas have been effected by means of Turkey's longstanding commercial agreements, including a customs union, with the EU and the EU's own Euro-Mediterranean Partnership Initiative. Turkey aims for membership of the EU and, although the formal position is that this remains a long-run possibility, there is considerable doubt within the Union – openly expressed in Greece, Germany, France and Italy – that Turkey could ever qualify for accession. Even if it did meet the objective criteria for membership, many still doubt that it could actually join, partly because its size would imply a considerable shift of power within the governance of the EU and partly on the grounds that, culturally speaking, Turkey is not a European country. For its part, the US has consistently maintained that Turkey should become a member of the EU in order to bind it firmly into the Western political and economic camp. It views Turkey's role in central Asia after the Cold War as an important balance to Iranian and Russian influence.

At the same time, the European Union has pursued an ambitious regional cooperation programme – centred on the creation of a free trade area between the EU and the Mediterranean countries running from Morocco to Turkey – since the EU–Med summit in Barcelona in 1995. It embraces 12 Mediterranean countries: Algeria, Cyprus, Egypt, Israel, Jordan, Lebanon, Malta, Morocco, Syria, Tunisia, Turkey and the Palestinian territories. The agenda extends beyond economic relations and includes measures to enhance regional security and strengthen cultural and educational ties. The core, however, is the drive for freer trade and investment links: this requires the EU to negotiate separate accession agreements with the 12 Mediterranean states and for the latter to negotiate similar arrangements with one another. In 2001, for example, the EU signed a Partnership Agreement aimed at freeing trade (with significant exceptions in the agricultural sector) with Egypt, which in turn had concluded agreements with Lebanon, Syria, Morocco, Tunisia, Libya, Iraq and Jordan. While the original grand scheme of an EU–Mediterranean free trade area is unlikely to be realized in the near future, the project has served to institutionalize a degree of cooperation on trade and aspects of development strategy, including the holding of biennial summits to monitor progress.

The United States has voiced its concerns that the EU–Mediterranean initiative should not operate at the expense of other countries, and in 1999 formally served notice that it would not relinquish commercial opportunities to the EU or others. Given that the EU aims to make its agreements WTO/GATT compatible, this is unlikely to involve significant conflict (except perhaps over agriculture) as both the EU and the US are pushing for freer trade and investment in the region. Indeed, immediately after the war against Iraq in 2003, President George W. Bush announced a proposal for a free-trade agreement between the Middle East and the United States and committed his administration to assisting the states of the region in their proclaimed wish to join the WTO. That said, the politics underpinning these various plans is immeasurably complicated by the wider Middle East 'Peace Process', in which the US, Russia and the UN also have roles to play, along with the EU.

As we have seen, then, the countries of the Middle East have responded to global development agendas largely independently, not on the basis of coordinated regional initiatives. The limited regional coordination that has taken place has largely been imposed by external actors, such as the EU through its Mediterranean initiative, or by the need to respond to global initiatives to control global warming, which prompted OPEC into action. More encompassing organizations or policies of regional economic and political cooperation have not yet taken root in the Middle East, thereby limiting its bargaining power in international development diplomacy.

Conclusion

As noted at the outset, the Middle East is in many respects an artificial region. It lacks a clear cultural or political identity, and the levels of economic integration within it are very low. Every country in the region relates much more to the world outside than it does to its neighbours. The region has been unable to organize its affairs and define its voice in terms of a single, or even a dominant, inter-governmental organization. There are, at root, two reasons for this. First, the countries of the region and the regimes that preside over them have, by reason of colonial history and the particular political consequences of oil-based development, had great difficulty in establishing legitimacy. Rule has been authoritarian, often capricious and, above all, ineffective in securing broad based socio-economic progress. Inter-state rivalries and conflicts, which distort all developmental priorities, are, to a very considerable extent, a function of these underlying domestic insecurities. Second, mainly because of oil and partly because of Israel, the region has long attracted the attention and intervention of the major powers, above all the United States. For complex (and sometimes unintended) reasons, Western strategy has contributed substantially over many years to reinforcing authoritarian rule and exacerbating levels of militarization.

Taken together, domestic insecurities and external intervention, the problems of state formation and regime legitimacy, and the distortions induced by the oil-based political and military aggrandisement of the state have produced regional rivalries rather than integration. The Middle Eastern strategy of the Bush administration, as it has gradually unfolded since the events of 11 September 2001, can be read as a bold attempt to break decisively with these inherited patterns. Whether that is what the US actually has in mind for the region – and it now enjoys a degree of influence unparalleled since the days of European colonial control – remains to be seen. In the light of Middle Eastern history one might reasonably be sceptical of the prospects for success of *any* project to reorder the region from the outside. Against such a cautionary, concluding note, the grounds for optimism, although slim, are not non-existent: first, and most important, many people in the region, including many elites, recognize that the old order is no longer sustainable; and, second, the US would face a massive loss of global credibility were it to leave the region worse off than it found it prior to its military intervention in Iraq.

Further reading

Bromley, S. (1994) *Rethinking Middle East Politics* (Cambridge: Polity Press).
Hinnebusch, R. and Ehteshami, A. (eds) (2002) *The Foreign Policies of Middle East States* (Boulder CO: Lynne Rienner).
Issawi, C. (1995) *The Middle East Economy* (Princeton NY: Markus Wiener).
Lewis, B. (2003) *The Crisis of Islam* (London: Weidenfeld & Nicolson).
Sahfik, N. (ed.) (1998) *Prospects for Middle Eastern and North African Economies* (London: Palgrave Macmillan).

Chapter 9

Sub-Saharan Africa

GRAHAM HARRISON

The politics of development in Sub-Saharan Africa (SSA) does not centre straightforwardly on the actions of states. In the context of this book SSA is therefore somewhat different, not necessarily uniquely so, but to a degree that merits emphasis at the outset. In SSA, constructions of formal political authority are fragile; much of the state's power derives from its ability to work *outside* constitutions, international agreements and formal economic plans. The state's fragility is also reflected by (and reproduced in) the ability of groups within African societies selectively to adhere to and evade state authority. This key feature – the elision of the formal–informal social boundary – constitutes the particular African context for the discussion that follows. The region is also beset by problems of poverty and insecurity which are arguably of a different order to those of other regions within the global political economy. A central cause and effect of these extreme levels of poverty is a high incidence of insecurity, manifest in various forms of civil conflict. As a result, the politics of development in SSA has often been elaborated as a kind of crisis management rather than as a formative process.

It is also the case that SSA is unusually complex and diverse. It comprises no less than 47 states; west Africa alone is generally taken as a subregion of 16 states. The region is manifestly traversed by a great deal of social and political diversity. So, why speak of Sub-Saharan Africa? Is there meaningful generalization to be made? Or is Sub-Saharan Africa less a concrete social entity and more a product of Western imaginations? These questions have been dealt with in detail elsewhere (Appaiah 1992; Mudimbe 1998; Young 1999). Here we will do no more than briefly identify those fundamental features that allow us to employ the notion of SSA as a meaningful region of the global political economy:

- Late and brief colonization. It was only in the last decade of the nineteenth century that Africa was 'effectively' colonized by Europe. Within 70 years, colonial powers were by and large decolonizing. During the colonial interlude, colonial powers imposed substantive similarities on African social landscapes: authoritarian colonial states, national economies based by and large on the extraction of primary commodities, small Europeanized elites, and centralized chieftaincies to rule the rural population on behalf of the colonial government (Mamdani 1996).

- An international division of labour. During and after colonialism, African economies were restructured as primary commodity producers, serving the expanding industrial economies of Europe. Coffee, cotton, cocoa, copper, sugar and tea were the main export commodities. Today, many African economies remain dependent on one or two primary exports for 80 per cent or more of their formal export revenue. In the 1990s over two-thirds of SSA countries were dependent on a single primary commodity export for over 50 per cent of their export earnings (Barratt-Brown and Tiffen 1992; Van de Walle 2000: 265).

In these two fundamental respects, SSA's social uniformity was externally imposed. Indeed it is not difficult to portray African societies as victims of externally driven processes. Yet one should not allow these societies to be represented as passive victims (Harrison 2002). In fact, a key and enduring feature of SSA's interactions with the global political economy has been an ability to engage with powerful external forces (Bayart 2000). This engagement has produced a small number of 'winners' and a persistent majority of 'losers' – either exploited or marginalized by the forces of global capitalism and their constitution in particular places and times. This requires that we note a key 'internal' feature of SSA which is particularly relevant to our understanding of SSA's regional politics of development.

- SSA encompasses a variety of peasant societies. SSA is the most agrarian region of the world, followed closely by South Asia. Although the social patterns of peasant production are constantly changing (Bryceson *et al.* 2000), formally about 70 per cent of the population live in rural areas (World Bank 2000: 320). Behind this figure – which should be taken as only the broadest of indicators – work more complex social relations. First, many urban residents farm or migrate to and from a village of origin where they still have land. Second, the lineage relations that by and large define entitlements to land in peasant societies have been reconstructed in urban areas, defining the social geography of neighbourhoods and providing the 'raw material' for elite strategies of patronage along politicized ethnic lines.

In a nutshell, then, what can and do we mean when we speak of SSA as a single entity? We are referring to a region of the world where peasant society has adapted and survived to an exceptional extent, engaging (often on extremely unequal terms) with a late, brief and violent colonial period which tied the economy into a particular role within the global political economy. One might argue that some of these features can be found elsewhere, but perhaps not in such a concentrated and integrated fashion as in the 47 states of this region.

Country development strategies in Sub-Saharan Africa

We turn now to consider how the distinctive nature of the post-colonial order in Sub-Saharan Africa has affected the national politics of development in the region. There is no watertight way to deal with this question in a single chapter. Table 9.1 presents basic data for all of the many countries of SSA. Yet a method of analysis which sought to encompass every state would be excessively shallow in tone and unnecessarily descriptive in narrative; equally, deeper analysis would push one to recognize the particularities of each country at the expense of identifying common patterns of development. Here we will elaborate a rough 'developmental typology', based on a selection of SSA states which define cardinal trajectories of public action and socio-economic change within the region. The purpose of this typology is less definitive than illustrative: some of the features expounded within one category will be present within states located in another category, and some states will be left out altogether. But the typology will provide a sense of the patterns of stratification, both between and within countries, and will highlight some of the key issues in SSA's development politics. A summary of this typology is given in Table 9.2.

Peasant states

As already suggested, most SSA countries are constituted by a large majority of peasant producers. However, for a smaller subset peasant production is especially important. Taking rates of urbanization as a rough proxy, we can identify the following states as 'peasant states': Burundi, Malawi, Burkina Faso, Uganda and Niger. Each of these has over 90 per cent of its labour force dedicated to agriculture (World Bank 1997: table 4). One might add Ghana and Tanzania to this category, the latter with 75 per cent rural population and 45 per cent of its value-added as a percentage of GDP deriving from peasant agriculture (World Bank 2002: table 3). All of these states (with the exception of Burkina Faso where large remittances from Burkinabé migrants skew the sectoral distribution in favour of the catch-all category of services) register above 40 per cent of their value-added as a percentage of GDP from agriculture, against an average of 23 per cent for low-income countries (a World Bank category which contains almost all SSA states).

Table 9.1   *Sub-Saharan Africa: basic data*

Country	Population (millions)	GNI[1] (PPP) (US$ billions)	GNI (per capita) (US$)	Value added % GDP (ag./ind./services)[2,3]
Angola	13.5	21	1,550	8/67/25[4]
Benin	6.4	7	1,030	38/15/47
Botswana	1.6	14	8,810	4/44/52
Burkina Faso	11.6	12	1,020	35/17/47
Burundi	6.9	4	590	50/19/31
Cameroon	15.2	25	1,670	46/21/33
Cape Verde	0.454	2.211	4,870	#
Central African Republic	3.8	4	1,180	55/21/25
Chad	7.9	7	930	39/14/48
Comoros	0.572	0.922	1,610	#
Congo, Dem. Rep.	52.4	–	–	–
Congo, Rep.	3.1	2	580	6/67/26
Côte d'Ivoire	16.4	24	1,470	24/22/54
Equatorial Guinea	0.469	2.644	5,640	#
Eritrea	4.2	4	970	17/29/54
Ethiopia	65.8	47	710	52/11/37
Gabon	1.261	6.890	5,460	#
Gambia, The	1.341	2.319	1,730	#

continued overleaf

Table 9.1 *Continued*

Country	Population (millions)	GNI[1] (PPP) (US$ billions)	GNI (per capita) (US$)	Value added % GDP (ag./ind./services)[2,3]
Ghana	19.7	39	1,980	36/25/39
Guinea	7.6	15	1,980	25/38/37
Guinea-Bissau	1.226	0.872	710	#
Kenya	30.7	31	1,020	21/19/60
Lesotho	2.1	6	2,670	20/46/34
Liberia	3.216	–	–	#
Madagascar	16	14	870	#
Malawi	10.5	7	620	8/50/42
Mali	11.1	9	810	38/26/36
Mauritania	2.8	5	1,680	21/29/50
Mauritius	1.198	12.468	10,410	#
Mozambique	18.1	18	1,000	22/26/52
Namibia	1.8	12	6,700	11/28/61
Niger	11.2	9	770	38/18/44
Nigeria	129.9	108	830	30/46/25
Rwanda	8.7	9	1,000	44/22/34
São Tomé and Principe	0.151	–	–	#
Senegal	9.8	15	1,560	18/27/55
Seychelles	0.082	–	–	#
Sierra Leone	5.1	2	480	49/31/21
Somalia	–	–	–	–
South Africa	43.2	411	9,510	3/31/66

Sudan	31.687	51.135	1,610	–
Swaziland	1.068	5.006	4,690	#
Tanzania	34.5	19	540	45/16/39
Togo	4.7	7	1,420	39/21/40
Uganda	22.8	29	1,250	42/19/38
Zambia	10.3	8	790	22/26/52
Zimbabwe	12.8	30	2,340	18/24/58

Notes: Health warning: all World Bank figures should be treated as estimates. The large amount of informal economic activity, described in the chapter, and the weakness of many states (which collect statistical data) cast serious doubts on the accuracy of the data. These figures should be treated as indicative of general social features and not as specific quantifications.

All figures unless indicated are for 2000.

– Figures unavailable; # Countries excluded by the World Bank because of sparse data or populations less than 1.5 million; [1] From 2002, gross national income replaced gross national product in line with the 1992 System of National Accounts; [2] Figures for 2001; [3] Note that low figures for agriculture do not relate to numbers who labour in agriculture or levels of production. Thus, an economy based in widespread low-productivity agriculture can generate a low value added index; [4] The figure for industry includes oil production for all countries.

Source: Compiled from World Bank (2000) *African Development Indicators* (Washington DC: World Bank); World Bank (2003) *World Development Report 2003* (Oxford: Oxford University Press), tables 1, 1a and 3; and World Bank Development Indicators, available at http://devdata.worldbank.org/data-query/

Table 9.2 A developmental typology of Sub-Saharan Africa

Type	Development issues	Examples	Political issues
Peasant state	Peasant engagement with national/global markets	Tanzania, Malawi, Burkina Faso, Burundi	The top-down nature of state–peasant relations
Settler state	Inequality and dualism between types of rural regions	Kenya, Zimbabwe, Namibia	The redistribution of land?
Industrializing state	Modernization and economic nationalism	Ghana, Côte d'Ivoire, South Africa, Mauritius	The failure of government industrial policy and 'overstretched' states
Mineral state	High export revenues and ineffective public action	Angola, Nigeria, Zambia, Botswana	*Rentier* states, corruption and the struggle for resource control

Conflict state	Provision of humanitarian relief and its relationship with rehabilitation	Sierra Leone, Liberia, Somalia	Effective conflict resolution?
Entrepôt state	Inequalities between the coast and the hinterland	Mozambique, Guinea-Bissau	Creole elites and relations with peasant societies inland
Micro state	Dependence on global economy	Cape Verde, Equatorial Guinea, Swaziland	Extreme vulnerability of states

Sources: Compiled from World Bank (2000) *African Development Indicators* (Washington DC: World Bank); World Bank (2003) *World Development Report 2003* (Oxford: Oxford University Press), Tables 1, 1a and 3; and World Bank Development Indicators database, 2003, retrieved from http://devdata.worldbank.org/data-query/

How has this affected the nature of development in these states? It has placed certain issues high on the agenda for state action: agricultural pricing policy, extension services to farmers, the politics of urban bias and the introduction of cash crops. The latter issue has been at the forefront of development planning for peasant societies and one can identify key peasant cash crops as central to the economies of these states: for example, coffee (the bushes of which are grown by farmers in Burundi and in parts of Uganda), cotton (key to parts of Uganda and Burkina Faso) and cocoa in various countries, especially Ghana. The poor terms of trade for peasant cash crops have restricted the extent to which peasant societies have gained from their participation in commodity markets. Furthermore, until recently these markets tended to be monopolized or regulated by oppressive states, often keen to extract surplus from peasant farmers through the control of exchange prices. The poor rural infrastructure left by colonial regimes has also left many areas of these countries remote from markets, whether controlled by state marketing boards or private merchants, especially in the more geographically expansive states such as Tanzania and Burkina Faso. Here, poverty and the politics of national regional inequality interact to present serious problems for states.

Nevertheless, and in anticipation of categorizations to come, peasant states appear to have maintained relative stability. Boone's careful dissection of the notion of collapsed states leads her to identify what we have called peasant states as a category of relatively successful state projects:

> It seems that state formation has been more successful – that is, it has produced stronger and better institutionalised means of political and economic integration – in the Africa of peasant commodity production that it has been in the extractive and plantation enclaves (Boone 1998: 131).

This is a result of a simple fact: because peasant production matters economically, states have had to engage with their own societies in order to reproduce themselves fiscally. This engagement – for all its urban bias, elitism and other exploitative features – has involved a moment of state institutionalization and public regulation, a point which is thrown into sharp relief in comparison with the mineral states discussed later.

Settler states

By comparison with peasant states, settler states have large agricultural sectors and peasantries, but also inherit a particular legacy from the colonial period. In Kenya, Zimbabwe, Namibia (and relatedly Mozambique and Angola which appear elsewhere in the typology) prime areas for farming were commandeered by the colonial state for

European commercial farmers. During the colonial period the eastern highlands of Zimbabwe or the 'white' highlands of Kenya were the preserve of a European settler class. This introduced a dualism to rural areas which was far less prominent in the peasant states noted above: between well-served, environmentally propitious and racially-defined areas, on the one hand, and peasant 'hinterlands', on the other. Thus the main developmental issue facing these post-colonial states was how to react to the dualism bequeathed by settler colonialism. Kenya, for example, took a reformist approach, implementing a 'million acre scheme' (Leo 1984) to allocate land to a group of 'progressive' farmers. But the distribution of this land also became tied up with clientelist politics in Kenya and elsewhere; land became a political resource. This has clearly been the case in Zimbabwe, where redistribution has – until recently – been cautious and beset by scandals, since it has been discovered that land has been hived off to party-state cronies. Since the early 1990s, the government of Robert Mugabe has used compulsory land redistribution to reward those tied to the ruling party's clientelist networks and thereby evoke a racial-populist politics to shore up state power in the countryside.

As regards development strategy, the existence of commoditized rural areas has presented states with difficult policy choices. It is clear that all countries in this category have been keen to ensure that these areas continue to produce tradeable commodities for international markets: tobacco, beef, garden crops (salads, etc.) and, most recently, cut flowers. The value of these large-scale commercial farming areas has been bolstered by a common sense assumption that this form of agriculture is more efficient and productive than 'traditional' peasant agriculture, even if this contrast is very misleading (Bush and Cliffe 1984). However, the control of these areas has long been intensely political, underpinned by racial divisions and shifting patterns of clientelism. The significance of control of developed agrarian areas is only heightened by the fact that these areas are coterminous with extremely poor peasant societies, many of which were historically dispossessed of the land now owned by settlers' sons or party-state elites. As such, and in distinction to the peasant societies discussed above, the politics of development in settler states has been more keenly focused around issues of rural inequality. For all that, as a group, the settler states have managed a relatively high level of economic growth based on agricultural commodity exports, the emergence of a rural working class and the creation of a national market.

Industrializing states

We come here to a most tentative category. Strictly speaking, South Africa and Mauritius are the only states in SSA which might properly be called industrializing. Nevertheless, this section serves to acknowledge that many African states have undergone an industrialization process, albeit one that has generally been erratic and halting. In addition to the countries noted above, the following have over 10 per cent of their labour force employed in manufacturing: Togo, Ghana, Côte d'Ivoire, Congo, Lesotho and Botswana (World Bank 1997: table 4). More strictly, a subset of Botswana, Congo, Lesotho and South Africa have economies in which over 25 per cent of value-added derives from manufacture (World Bank 2001a: table 3). However, this latter achievement is as much a reflection of the overall size of the economies of these states as it is of the significance of their industrial sectors. Thus it does not seem unreasonable to keep larger economies such as Ghana and Côte d'Ivoire in this section, especially bearing in mind the relatively concerted state action that has underpinned industrialization in these two cases. Indeed, it has been said that:

> For a sub Saharan African country of its size, Ghana has a broad and diverse industrial base covering aluminium smelting, saw mills, timber and agricultural processing plants, brewing, cement manufacture, oil refining, textiles, electronics, pharmacy, mining, and many others (EIU 1998–99: 24).

Processes of industrialization in SSA may not have generated an easily recognizable category of 'industrial states', but they have raised two key issues, as follows.

The first is that specific case histories of industrialization reveal a common theme, namely, that industrialization in Africa has been propelled by the state itself. A suspicion of foreign capital, a weak bourgeoisie and the dominant ideology of development economics at the time combined to produce a model of an African industrial – perhaps developmental – state in the 1960s and 1970s. SSA's industrialization had commenced in the late colonial period (1950s), but only became codified (and 'ideologized') in the post-colonial period as import-substitution industrialization. The principal components of ISI in SSA were: control of international trade through tariffs and quotas, investment in large-scale infrastructure, and an attempt to integrate the development of natural resources with industrial development and the growth of a domestic urban market. This strategy only 'worked' in South Africa, but it did leave Ghana and Côte d'Ivoire with relatively healthy growth prospects in the early post-colonial period. The general faith of economists of the time was that industrialization was a prerequisite for development, and Ghana's large-scale investments in hydro-electric power, the presence of some transnational corporations in the country and the assertive economic nationalism of Kwame Nkrumah during the early 1960s led many, albeit wrongly, to look to Ghana as a model for Africa's prospects. Whilst Ghana's ISI strategy collapsed ignominiously under its own authoritarianism and statism, Côte d'Ivoire maintained its industrialization in close cooperation with France, making it the main industrializing economy of west Africa after Nigeria. Generally speaking, within the rest of SSA economic protectionism, excessive state regulation and the tenacity of small urban elites undermined the ISI project, much indeed as it did in other parts of the world in the 1970s.

The second issue worthy of comment pertains to industrialization and regional inequality. It needs to be acknowledged that South Africa's industrialization was fired by a racially constituted and extremely authoritarian state which ensured that extremely cheap and oppressed black labour would facilitate the growth of a significant mineral industrial complex (Fine and Rustomjee 1996). South Africa's relative industrial prominence raises a special set of issues about its relations with the rest of SSA. The racialized regime of labour in South Africa was not only a national one, but also a regional one, based on closely regimented systems of migration from the rural areas of neighbouring states to the mines and plantations of Johannesburg and the Cape. Initiated in the 1900s, this system involved over 100,000 men per year during the 1950s, causing women to experience extra labour and insecurity in the 'home' villages (Van Onselen 1976; First 1983).

Mineral states

Nigeria, Angola, Botswana and Zambia all depend on a single mineral for the vast majority of their export revenue. In all but the last case (copper's value having fallen constantly since the Vietnam war) this has provided states with lucrative sources of revenue, principally from oil and diamonds. As a result, the development prospects of these states have often been considered to be good: relatively large revenues of hard currency allow states to invest large amounts of money in infrastructure, social services and industry. However, such happy outcomes have not been realized in any of these cases, chiefly because the political economy of high value minerals has generally proved to be one of inequality and conflict (Ross 1999). Control of minerals becomes not a base for development but an end in itself for governing elites, creating *rentier* states concerned with deriving revenues from mineral exports and little else. The contradiction could be seen vividly in Nigeria in the mid-1970s (Forrest 1995) when the country's ports were jammed with ships carrying cement – not a symbol of Nigeria's developmental drive to construct new houses, schools and industrial plant as much as a manifestation of the desire of well-connected individuals to 'skim off' a percentage of the cement contract to feather their own nests. At the extreme of this argument, Angola can be said to have been cursed by oil and diamonds. From the late 1970s until 2002 (when rebel leader Jonas Savimbi was killed in combat) Angola was subjected to a civil war that was fuelled by government-controlled oil and rebel-controlled diamonds (Hodges 2001). An estimated 100,000 civilians died during the conflict. On the other hand, Botswana's development trajectory has been far more healthy. Diamond wealth has coexisted with a reasonably unified and politically stable rural population to produce GNP growth rates of between 5 and 10 per cent per year for all of its post-colonial history. Even so, problems with dependence on diamonds persist (Love 1994). For Zambia, because copper is not a high-value mineral, the developmental questions faced by the government have been of a different order. After independence a strong case was made for nationalization, but once the Anglo-American corporation had been removed from the direct production process Zambia had to reconcile itself to the extreme volatility and secular decline of copper prices, making development planning very difficult when about 90 per cent of the country's export revenue comes from this source.

The key challenge that each of these states has had to face (with drastically varying levels of success) is the strategic importance of high-value minerals. They are concentrated in small areas, attract high levels of interest from domestic and international capital, and constitute a source of unimaginable riches (Sani Abacha of Nigeria managed to salt away an estimated US$3 billion during his relatively brief period as president of Nigeria). As we have seen, the possession of high-value minerals is as likely to create conflict and state collapse as it is growth and social progress. Mick Moore's conceptualization of 'bad governance' nicely encapsulates the political contradictions of mineral states: entranced by the factionalized control of rents from fixed-location high value resources, mineral states make minimal effort to tax or otherwise engage with their citizenries more generally. It is this low level of 'fiscal effort' which alienates the state from its population (Moore 2001) and epitomizes bad governance (Malaquias 2001).

Conflict states

Leading on from the latter category, we must take note of a group of states that have been subjected to periods of protracted civil conflict. These are often mineral states that have found the struggle for control of minerals too fractious to maintain the basic presence of a state and the rule of law throughout national territory. Sierra Leone and the Democratic Republic of Congo (DRC) (former Zaïre) are key exemplars.

Other cases that fit this category are Liberia, Somalia and Angola (Le Billon 2001). States such as Mozambique (1977–92) and Rwanda (1994) also experienced terrible civil wars, but with very specific origins (South African destabilization and the complex origins of genocide respectively). The point is that civil conflict renders the state ineffective as a developmental institution. Notions of collapsed states (Zartman 1995) imply also the collapse of the development project in general terms. Almost all developmental thinking is based on assumptions about the nature of state agency or the regulation of economic activity. Civil conflict throws all of this into uncertainty. Revenues from minerals are mainly employed to maintain fighting forces and create personal fortunes; their extraction and trade is infused with compulsion and violence; conflicts inevitably destroy schools, homes and human beings (Simon 2001). Conflict states symbolize the collapse of development *tout court*: it is not a question of how a rate of GNP per capita has been changing, it is rather that these measures have ceased to exist or have become meaningless. Future development agendas will be based on how the relationship between humanitarian relief, conflict resolution and reconstruction is organized. In these circumstances, states are so weak that this agenda rests mainly within the purview of external agencies.

Entrepôt states

An important aspect of the legacy of colonialism was geographic: some states were divided between coastal cities and ports and rural hinterlands. This general trend can be seen along the Indian Ocean and Atlantic coast, most notably in Mozambique, Sierra Leone and Liberia (in fact this division between littoral and hinterland is important to understanding the conflicts in these states), as well as Guinea-Bissau. These are best described as *entrepôt* states because the key developmental issue raised is the tension between the nature of their integration with the world economy and the nature of their integration with their own societies. These states also evoke a more general question, to be returned to later, about the way states' integration with the global political economy has 'extroverted' development in SSA.

In Liberia, Sierra Leone and other states along the Atlantic coast, the socio-historical basis for this geographical division was the rise of Creole elites on the coast, a product of the slave trade which either created powerful trading classes intermixed with merchants and colonial classes or 'recaptives', that is, those who returned to Africa having been freed from slavery (Davidson 1992). Educated, Christian and in many ways Westernized, these elites saw their co-nationals in 'the bush' as backward and essentially part of the 'problem'. These social origins only served to sharpen the generally elitist nature of all models of development in SSA, wherein development was envisaged at its core as a project to be enforced on the masses through state power in the interests of modernization. In the case of Mozambique, covering the whole of the Indian Ocean coast for southern Africa, the governing elite since independence has not only had to reconcile itself with the country's peasant hinterland, but with its mutual dependence on neighbouring states, upon which its own economic prospects rested. In turn these states relied on Mozambique's transport network and ports as the easiest means to export goods. This highlights another important fact of geography, namely, SSA's high number of land-locked states. In these countries ensuring the terms of evacuation of exports to the high seas has been the source of much politicking and, occasionally, war-making.

It is also the case that *entrepôt* states are products of state action as well as geography. Benin, Togo and the Gambia are small coastal states, but their governments have maintained very liberal trade regimes, rendering their economies as points of entry and exit for a diverse range of products (crops and consumer goods) as traders attempt to evade the tariffs and import–export procedures of neighbouring states.

Micro states

Examples of micro states include Cape Verde, Equatorial Guinea, the Gambia, São Tomé e Principe, Swaziland and Lesotho. At the extremes, São Tomé e Principe musters a total GNP of about US$47 million per year. As with micro states more generally, the main development question has been: how to define a strategy with practically no autonomy from the global political economy and such a small population base? In fact, most of these states have remained reasonably stable and have GNP per capita levels which are not distinctly lower than other parts of the continent – Cape Verde in fact does quite well. Swaziland and Lesotho's economies are relatively large within the terms of the grouping, but they still remain small states, engulfed by South Africa and extremely dependent on their political and economic relations with the latter.

Summary

The categorization just elaborated, selective and contestable as it is, nevertheless serves to illustrate the diversity of nationally based development trajectories in SSA. It also serves to reveal inter-state relations and the main themes that have emerged in SSA's post-colonial development plans and projects. The general image is not a positive one: the challenges faced by African states have proved, on the whole, to be insurmountable, largely as a result of two key factors: the venality and authoritarianism of ruling elites and the vulnerability and marginality of African economies to global market forces. We can now pursue the political implications of this record by looking at attempts to construct a regional project in SSA.

The intra-regional politics of development in Sub-Saharan Africa

Mahmood Mamdani (1995: 17) has written that, although Africa 'is not homogeneous', it is still 'a unity'. This unity has been the basis for a long line of political projects and images of regional/continental identity, which run from the first Pan African Congress, held in Manchester in the UK in 1945, to the present-day formation of an African Union (AU). Within this long history one can discern two key tenets which have, in various formulations, given African unity its conviction: first, that there is strength in numbers, reflecting the belief that small, vulnerable African states will find that they are more effectively represented collectively within the various multilateral institutions of the global political economy; and, second, that economic integration will create economies of scale and scope that will promote a general process of economic growth. Although the latter logic underpins almost all regionalisms, both core and peripheral, the main component of the economic argument in SSA derives from the fact that most national economies in Africa have such small domestic markets. These two theses provide a critical avenue into the region's constitution within the broader global system and it is our task in this section to identify how this constitution has posed particular issues concerning the region's strategy of development. Regional development organizations are listed in Table 9.3.

The Organization of African Unity (OAU) was created in 1963, on the cusp of the wave of independence. In the heady and politicized intellectual climate of the time African writers hoped that the OAU would develop into a substantive regional bloc, for the more radical 'Casablanca Group' (closely aligned with Nkrumah's ideas) leading to a full-blown political union which would radically reconfigure the political geography of the nation-states left behind by the colonial powers. In fact, the OAU failed either to unite the continent or articulate a collective development agenda *vis-à-vis* the rest of the world, and its commitment to regional integration made no discernible progress. The organization was based on profoundly realist premises (Clapham 1996: 110–11): state sovereignty, annual summits of heads of state and an

Table 9.3 *Main regional organizations in Sub-Saharan Africa*

Organization	Duration	Member states	Notes
AU	2001–	SSA	Formed at final OAU meeting with stronger executive powers.
EAC	1967–77; 1999–	Tanzania, Uganda, Kenya	Collapsed because of inter-state rivalries, but recently revived in very different circumstances to promote market integration.
ECOWAS	1975–	16 west African states	Set up to promote trade, cooperation and self-reliance in west Africa.
OAU	1963–2001	SSA	Created in Addis Ababa, committing states to defend sovereignty, eradicate colonialism, promote cooperation between states and promote international cooperation within UN structures.
SADC	1980/1992–	12 southern African states	SADCC (SA Development Coordination Conference) changed to SADC in 1992, preparing for South Africa's membership and a shift from anti-*apartheid* activities to development cooperation.
UEMOA	1994–	8 west African states	Sahelian union based in a common currency: the Central African Franc.
UNECA	1958–	SSA	Regional organization of the UN, charged to promote regional economic integration and international cooperation.

indifference to the suffering of large groups in the name of the preservation of the colonially designed boundaries of the Treaty of Berlin (1884–85). The two most drastic examples of the latter were the OAU's support for the Nigerian government during the Biafran war of secession (1967–70) and its failure to recognize Eritrea's 30-year struggle for independence (1961–91) (Schraeder 2000: 301). This effectively meant that the OAU sanctioned the use of famine as a weapon of war (Nigeria and Eritrea) and the routine indiscriminate strafing of towns and villages by MiG bombers (Eritrea). For ordinary people, the OAU only became relevant when their country hosted the annual summit, and then the main bone of contention was how many millions were spent in prestige projects to impress visiting dictators and dignitaries.

In fact, African concerns with the region's development were more effectively projected through the Non-Aligned Movement and the Group of Seventy-seven (Harris 1986). Leaders, such as Tanzania's Julius Nyerere, actively called for a New International Economic Order (NIEO), but, even here, the impact of African developmental advocacy was negligible. Some African states have also actively contributed to producer associations: for example, in the case of mineral states OPEC and CIPEC (Intergovernmental Council of Copper Exporting Countries) and for peasant states (coffee is by and large a peasant crop) the International Coffee Organization. Only OPEC has met with any tangible success in its aims, and not generally because of African involvement.

In the early 1980s another current in regional developmental thinking emerged from within the OAU, supported by the UN Economic Commission for Africa (UNECA). The key document here was the *Lagos Plan of Action for Economic Development in Africa 1980–2000* (LPA). The LPA boldly set out plans for an African Economic Community and Common Market, designed to lead to 'self-reliance and self-sustaining development'. In addition to familiar arguments about the economies of economic regionalism, the specific strategy had three noteworthy points. First, a cardinal aim of the LPA was to 'integrate' national economies around an equitable articulation of industrial and peasant production. This has been an enduring theme in the development discourse of peasant states where urban bias arguments have highlighted the systematic marginalization of peasant in favour of industrial sectors. Second, economic integration was to be built on subregional blocs (Johnson 1991: 2). Third, the agent of integration was to be the national state itself. Having noted that African states have never enjoyed uncontested political power or institutional robustness, one must wonder if states were, or are, the most appropriate institutions for region-building. Effectively, the OAU worked more to strengthen formal states in Africa than pave the way to their integration in the pursuit of development or changed relations with the rest of the world (Clapham 1996: 111). Nwokedi gives a damning summary:

> What the Lagos Plan embodies is a profession of intent not a commitment to the basic needs of the rural population. The world view of a greater number of African leaders is conditioned by their class interests and so long as these interests are under no immediate threats, they will continue to pay lip service to the fundamental question of development. This is precisely why the Lagos Plan feigns a homogeneity of interests between, on the one hand, the various bourgeoisies and their foreign mentors and, on the other, between the former and the rest of the population (Cited in Cummings 1992: 33).

Nevertheless, the grand aspiration continues. In 2001 the OAU became the African Union (*Africa Confidential* 13 July 2001). The developmental norms embedded in this latest model have shifted significantly from the confident autarky of the post-colonial period and the slightly more self-reflective LPA. Both within the AU, and with regard to other subregional groupings, development is now closely associated with economic integration through market liberalization. Planned and statist integration (always mainly rhetorical in any case) has been fully replaced by a virile faith in market forces (Gibb 1998; Mistry 2000). The AU's principal mission is to prepare the formation of an African Economic Community, supported by the New Partnership for Africa's Development (NEPAD) and based on free-market integration in the context of globalization.

The point about subregional groupings needs further elaboration. A more substantive integration can be found in SSA's *sub*regions. This is essentially because integration has taken place upon the basis of existing political economy: in west, east and southern Africa (and these are just the most prominent examples), subregional political organizations have been constructed on subregional networks of trade, migration and common colonial experience. In east Africa, the East African Community (EAC) was abolished in 1977, a result principally of the emerging ideological rivalries of the three member-states, tensions over the allocation of compensation funds, and the predominance of Kenya. It was recently resurrected and led to the creation of the East African Association in 2001. In west Africa, the Economic Community of West African States (ECOWAS), created in 1975, remains in existence, most notably as the organization within which the regional peacekeeping force ECOMOG (ECOWAS Monitoring Group) was created. In southern Africa, the Southern African Development Community (SADC), based on opposition in the region to *apartheid*, is currently attempting to transform itself with the accession of South Africa in 1994 and is reorienting its development ideology away from European aid and regional planning towards regional market integration.

Nevertheless, a broad summary of subregionalism in SSA would necessarily have to recognize that, as with continent-wide projects, little progress has been made in terms of the integration and coordination of development projects, despite the fact that all subregional agreements were based on developmental aims. Perhaps a clearer distinguishing feature of subregional endeavour has been the concern with security (Gambari 1996). ECOMOG's operations in Liberia and Sierra Leone have had a profound impact on the conflicts in each country – for better or worse. With respect to the SADC, especially since South Africa's accession, concerns with drugs trafficking, migration and the trade in small arms have become a priority. Furthermore, region-building has not led to a convincing increase in self-reliance: the SADC still relies on foreign sources for 85 per cent of its finances; the north-east African regional association – the Inter-Governmental Agreement on Development (IGAD) – holds its technical meetings in the country that chairs the organization's foreign forum; and the Economic and Monetary Unions of West African States (UEMOA), the 'French west African' regional association, remains historically embedded in French patronage and power (Mshomba 2000: 188, 195–6). External dominance of the development agenda (to be dealt with below) has ensured that subregionalism remains weak and tied to neoliberal concerns about external orientation in trade, as most clearly seen in the case of the SADC throughout the 1990s (Tsie 1996; Weeks 1996).

The failure of all these attempts to forge a regional politics of development, based on state integration, coordination and the articulation of a common voice on the international scene, relates directly to the underlying themes of this chapter, namely, the weakness of states and the pervasive social practice of straddling between the formal and informal (Bayart 1993: 269). An acute metaphor employed by one researcher to encapsulate the nature of African state politics distinguished between the politics of the air conditioner and the politics of the veranda (Reno 1995). African statesmen and women, when addressing the UN or negotiating with a World Bank mission and the droves of other visiting modern Western missionaries, perform the politics of the air conditioner: a discursive realm of Weberian rational instrumentalism. Concurrently, though, they employ the resources gathered from the air-conditioned room and distribute them on the veranda according to the logic of clientelism, security concerns and strategies of nest-feathering. The argument is that African states work in *both* spheres, producing what Reno calls 'shadow states' in which ruling elites make laws and participate in their violation with the unifying aim of accumulating wealth and resources for their own social group. It is hardly surprising that states that function, even if only partially, according to this logic should not succeed in prosecuting any form of developmental regionalism. More profoundly, it needs to be recognized that African states simply do not operate as agents of development: they are weak states and what strength they do have derives from their capacity to capture or regulate illicit trade, rents from trade and aid from external sources (Moore 2001). Accordingly, we must pay attention to less well-known forms of social and political activity which condition the state and define SSA in more profound ways than the summitry and rhetoric of those who drive a Mercedes Benz. A brief sketch will provide at least an overview.

A testament to the substantive weakness of African states is the porosity of their borders and the massive movement of people across national frontiers with no recourse to immigration authorities. The most extreme example is provided by refugee movements, for example Mozambicans moving into southern Malawi during the 1980s. In a more mundane sense, traders and workers cross borders in their thousands: from southern Africa to South Africa, from Burkina Faso to Côte d'Ivoire, from Ghana to Nigeria, from southern DRC to the diamond fields of Angola, and so on. These patterns of migration often delineate a conduit of illicit trade. Immigration officials are either avoided, or bribed, depending on the bulk of the trade, its value and the durability of established population movements. For pastoralists in the semi-arid and arid areas of east Africa, borders are not so much evaded as ignored. Informal trade is often based on differentials in tariffs, price subsidies and other controls between states. Border officials are routinely and easily bribed (most public servants would not survive on their official salary). MacGaffey (1991: 18–19) gives a striking account of a highly developed 'shadow' commerce in (then) Zaïre where between 1975 and 1979 up to 60 per cent of coffee production was in some way illegally exported and in 1979 alone US$59 million of diamonds were smuggled out of the country. Again, in relation to the previous point, regional trade patterns are often interlinked with contested military control. During the post-Cold War period, in conflict states such as the DRC, Sierra Leone and Angola, illicit trade in precious stones has taken place within territories controlled by local warlords, often under extremely brutal conditions. The revenues from the stones subsequently fuelled civil war and the massive suffering of ordinary people – a terrible state of affairs captured by the awful phrase 'gemocide'. More formatively, the organizations of civil society have begun to build up functional regional networks with increasing confidence. Odén (2000: 242) notes that in southern Africa 'countries [have] also generated a number of intra-regional networks in civil society, such as among [*sic*] national professional associations, churches, media and in the field of culture and sports'. Söderbaum (2001: 74) refers to similar processes in west Africa, dubbing them 'bottom-up regionalization'. Such networks have lately attempted to address issues such as HIV/AIDS, economic justice, human rights and regional research and education.

We have seen, then, that in SSA regionalism as a project, effected through design and execution by public bodies (Gamble and Payne 1996), has been a failure. The politics of post-colonial elites has rendered the phenomenon an occasional means to promote their own grandeur. Subregionalism has suffered from similar problems, as well as a dependence on external finance. Where states have acted regionally, this has often been prompted by military, rather than developmental, strategy. Yet, interwoven within these partial projects has been a diverse set of informal processes of regionalization, often centred on illicit economic activity and generated generally, although no longer exclusively, within the broader context of contested security.

The extra-regional politics of development in Sub-Saharan Africa

We have seen that SSA's politics of development raises issues of security, state capacity and informal/illicit social change to a far greater degree perhaps than in most other regions. These concerns have not been centrally addressed within development studies which, in one form or another, makes assumptions about agency and capacity that are problematic for this region (Cowen and Shenton 1998). But we should perhaps not draw too stark an image of African exceptionalism when it comes to a consideration of SSA's engagement with the global politics of development. In fact, in the messy terrain of 'globalization studies', one argument that is widely made is that it is *precisely* these social processes that give globalization its novelty, namely, a bypassing of the state, a growth in global forms of corruption and the emergence of new global security issues. Sub-Saharan Africa has suffered a modern history in which it has been forced to play the role of a region 'catching up', to act as a kind of global 'policy-taker', whether it be statist modernization derived from Latin America and the 'socialist' bloc or the contemporary neoliberalism of the IFIs. Maybe globalization studies should move to debunk this inaccurate and imperialist epistemology and recognize – for better or worse – that, in some respects, SSA is an innovative actor in much of what passes as novel within globalization.

Let us explore the features of SSA's 'informal' globalization. As nation-states in the periphery have weakened, some transnational corporations have had to acquire more 'savvy' in respect to issues of security. Strikingly, some transnationals have invested in areas outside the formal control of states. Hardwoods were widely exported from 'Greater Liberia', the fiefdom until very recently of warlord Charles Taylor (Reno 1995), whilst Swedish and Japanese companies also invested in iron-ore mining and rubber plantations respectively under his aegis (Clapham 1996: 255). Italian companies have made their own security arrangements to produce and export bananas in Somalia, despite the fact that 'Somalia' has not had a national state since 1991 (*ROAPE* 1995: 274–5). These and other examples tell us as much about the corruption and shadow aspects of *Western* states as they do about the instability of African states – witness, too, the recent arms-for-oil scandal (hardly surprising to Africanists who have been following international crony politics for a generation) concerning the French and Angolan governments and oil companies (*Africa Confidential* 9 February 2001). Likewise, when Laurent Kabila took power in the DRC in 1997, he had already received millions of dollars in payments from Western transnationals in search of new concessions. It is important to bear in mind that corruption is a transaction and that many transnationals purposefully employ bribes to gain favours (Moody-Stuart 1997), special security arrangements or cheap property being sold off by state elites under pressure from the World Bank and IMF.

As with investment, so with security. Conflict and security are not just the preserves of states and warlords. Private companies have also become involved in the provision of security. The best-known examples are the operations of Executive Outcomes in Angola (Harding 1997; Howe 1998) and Sandline International in Sierra Leone (*Africa Confidential* 6 March 1998). In both cases contracts were related to access to high-value minerals, often via opaque networks forged between different companies. In Angola Executive Outcomes trained the Angolan Army; in Sierra Leone Sandline's involvement is not entirely clear, although infamously it broke the UN arms embargo after the Kabbah regime had been ousted in a coup in 1997 (Polidano 2001).

As with security, so with diplomacy. It is notable that African states have pursued their international agendas as much through informal means as through the 'proper channels' of diplomacy, the UN General Assembly and multilateral organizations. The oldest example of this is the relationship between French and African presidents, historically based on close personal ties and the exchange of patronage. More recently, African states have employed US lawyers and funded pressure groups to lobby 'their' issues where it matters most: in Washington DC. States with oil concessions have been the most assiduous. Nigeria has paid Goodworks International US$1.5 million to ameliorate Nigeria's negative image in the US since the period of Abacha's rule (1993–98). SSA's ultimate 'pariah state', Sudan, has been trying similarly to reverse its negative image through professional lobbying (*Africa Confidential* 18 May 2001). Since the US declaration of the 'war on terrorism' the Sudanese government has attempted to align itself with US security concerns, although domestic pressure groups and oil politics have produced a complex terrain of lobbying and counter-lobbying around security and human-rights issues. African states also pursue foreign policy objectives through transnational firms with substantial (potential) interests in enclave investments, especially in highly insecure states (Reno 2000). A related point here touches upon the politics of African diasporas and the Afro-American community in the US. Both of these groups have created networks of international political influence and opinion-making. Two examples must suffice: the pressure from Afro-American organizations to impose sanctions on South Africa during the 1960s, and the centrality of the Eritrean diaspora in supporting the Eritrean People's Liberation Front in a war which ran from the early 1960s to the early 1990s and, uniquely during the Cold War, generated no external backing from either superpower.

More formally, SSA's development history narrates the 1980s as the 'lost decade'. Whilst most regions of the world experienced growth, albeit not at levels that matched the 'golden age' of the 1960s, SSA experienced a general economic decline during this decade. From 1982 to 1992 annual GDP per capita growth rates were: −1.2 per cent for Africa, +2.9 per cent for South Asia and +6.4 per cent for east Asia (Callaghy 2000: 45). Although the 1990s ushered in some partial successes, a general picture of economic crisis and instability remains – along with extremely high levels of debt in relation to the size of national economies. Thirty-one of the world's Highly Indebted Poor Countries, as defined by the World Bank and the IMF, are found in SSA.

The extent and the pervasiveness of poverty in SSA powerfully conditions African states' relations with the rest of the world. They are structurally positioned as subordinates: dependent on aid, highly indebted and impoverished. Poverty also frames the development issues that international actors bring to bear on the region, not merely in the basic empirical sense that states with small vulnerable economies have little international sway, but just as importantly in the way it establishes the nature of the discourse relating to SSA. The economic crises of the 1980s created a conjuncture within which African states effectively lost their agency as developmental actors. This is most clearly illustrated by the way the World Bank moved from a faith in government-led development planning to espousal of the 'roll back' of the state as a precondition for economic recovery (World Bank 1981). Along with other agencies, it pressured African states to weaken or abolish a wide range of mechanisms to control the economy. Humanitarian crises also brought about a truly spectacular influx of international development agencies into SSA: private NGOs, UN agencies and religious charitable organizations. Indeed, some NGOs have established development projects which have *replaced* the state in certain parts of some countries, making international agencies responsible for basic food provision and even health and education. Duffield (1993: 140) draws the conclusion that basic social provision has been partially internationalized:

> In Africa, northern intervention has encouraged the emergence of a neoliberal, two-tier system of public welfare. From the end of the 1970s, World Bank/IMF structural adjustment programmes have been attempting, with highly debateable consequences, to stimulate market reform and encourage producers. For those people unable to benefit from these measures a welfare 'safety net' has emerged ... largely as a result of NGO activity.

As the 1980s progressed, it became clear that SSA's development rested in the hands of the World Bank and IMF. Indebted countries had to negotiate relief and rescheduling with these two institutions and in the process had to implement structural adjustment programmes (SAPs), often designed by Bank/IMF economists and – *mutatis mutandis* – all adhering to the same neoliberal nostrums. Development became synonymous with structural adjustment. Alternatives were made unthinkable by reference to conditionality: debt rescheduling became dependent on the implementation of SAPs, which thus became the principal way of evaluating a country's development. Good 'adjusters', or so it was argued, would be good developers; bad 'adjusters' would fail to develop (World Bank 1989; Schatz 1994). The debt crisis and the precipitous rise in the power of the Bank and the Fund thus put development in a straitjacket, confined to the specifications of adjustment and liberalization. Notwithstanding more recent innovations concerning 'partnership', 'participation', 'civil society' and so on, African states remain heavily indebted and dependent on the two leading IFIs. Similarly, faith in the market remains sacrosanct, despite the emergence of the so-called 'post-Washington consensus' which has claimed to move away from the market fundamentalism of its predecessor (Fine, Lapavitsas and Pincus 2001).

In short, SSA's particularly poor economic performance over the last two decades has substantially reduced its participation in the global politics of development to relations with the World Bank and IMF and other external agencies. As always, this is not to say that Africans have no agency. The 'shadow state' has proved able to 'play' the game of structural adjustment to some extent, selecting aspects of the SAP bible to implement, subverting or ignoring others, and yet maintaining the flow of money from Washington (Mosley *et al.* 1991; Hibou 1999). Privatization – a key component of SAP – has, for example, often meant putting state companies under the control of politicians-turned-entrepreneurs via tenders that have been far from transparent. Some countries that have experienced economic growth (Uganda and Ghana for example) have also lately gained influence *vis-à-vis* the World Bank and IMF by presenting themselves as 'showcases' which purport to prove that SAP works (Harrison 2001).

A great deal has been written about the impact of neoliberalism more generally and so we will limit ourselves here to a brief discussion of the way that its ideology and practice have affected SSA's political relations with the global political economy. Most importantly, there is the dilemma of what Mkandawire (1999) calls 'two constituencies'. From the moment when structural adjustment and conditionality enmeshed the continent in the early 1980s, African governments have had to deal with both donors and creditors *and* domestic populations – external and internal constituencies respectively. In the 1980s orthodox thinking suggested that adjusting states should adopt an authoritarian stance with domestic constituencies, administering a necessary 'shock' of liberalization with a view to reinvigorating the free market in its wake. 'IMF riots' throughout the latter part of the decade both challenged the applicability of SAPs and destabilized the governments implementing them. A new rhetoric and practice of 'good governance' emerged in the 1990s in an endeavour to square the circle of the 'two-constituencies' dilemma. It has been variously defined and serves as a kind of catch-all for different but related ideals and reforms: *inter alia*, institutional capacity building, anti-corruption reform, training, less military expenditure, civic participation in policy making, transparency in state processes and for the major bilaterals a commitment (at least rhetorically) to multi-party democracy. Given the many issues that governance raises, we should note how, as a discourse, it radically expands the scope of action for external agencies in African polities. Not only must African states adopt certain policies, they must implement them in a certain way. External agencies not only influence key ministries, they shape the scope and nature of the state itself, encourage societal pressures on the state, fund the placing of huge numbers of expatriates at the highest levels of government and embed themselves in the routine processes of policy-making, monitoring and evaluation. In other words, Western agencies have a purchase over African politics unprecedented during the post-colonial period.

No-one could deny that SSA's engagement with the West during the SAP period has been problematic. Even those with huge interests in demonstrating the success of SAPs and with massive resources to mobilize to generate research in this vein have been defensive, evasive and generally underconfident in their portrait of SSA's development under this regime. In the space provided by this shaky performance, have alternative strategies of development emerged, and how strongly have they been articulated at the international level? Various initiatives are worth examining. The first came in 1989 when the UN Economic Commission for Africa once again tried to articulate an Africanist alternative, having seen the LPA fall into abeyance. The *Alternative African Framework* was, however, more effective in criticizing SAPs than it was presenting a convincing alternative (Browne 1992). In this respect UNECA can be said to have contributed to the World Bank's introduction of 'social components' to SAPs, but not to the articulation of an alternative programme. By the late 1990s writers had begun to popularize the notion of an African renaissance (Vale and Maseko 1998). This was not actually a developmental programme based on an alternative to SAP, but it did emphasize a shift in focus, away from the issues of debt, loans and reform towards economic growth and international investment. This discourse was buoyed up briefly by a patchy economic upturn in 1997–98 (Callaghy 2000: 60) and was reflected in the US 'Africa Initiative', announced by President Bill Clinton in 1996 and producing the Africa Crisis Response Initiative in 1997 and the Africa Growth and Opportunity Act (AGOA) in 2000. The former defined a series of training projects to allow selected militaries in the region to carry out more effective peacekeeping and humanitarian operations and the latter opened US markets to certain African exports. Once again, development and security are seen as closely interrelated. To the extent that the notion of an African Renaissance is based on a faith in neoliberalism and an anticipated influx of foreign investment (which is clearly the hope of its African supporters, notably the South African president Thabo Mbeki), then it is necessary to note that external investment in SSA remains sluggish at best and disinvesting at worst. The strongest initiative that fits the new rubric is NEPAD. This is an agreement between African governments to attain enhanced development outcomes, based on enhanced cooperation with the West. In 2002 the leaders of the G7 advanced post-industrial states supported NEPAD by announcing the Africa Action Plan which details increased aid for reforming states and improved 'partnership' between African and G7 states. All of these initiatives are based on a hope that market-friendly reform will bring in new resources and that 'partnership' can resolve the massive material inequalities between African and Western states

(Loxley 2003). The AGOA in turn serves as the template for the Millennium Challenge Account (2003–), President George W. Bush's main development initiative for Africa, signifying a certain continuity in US Africa policy.

A more radical set of alternatives resides in African societies as actors engaging in global discussions about development. African NGOs, acting with or through international pressure groups and non-governmental organizations, have articulated a set of positions concerning the environment, security and, most prominently, debt write-off. Jubilee 2000 was a truly international network of affiliated organizations which made a real impact on the scope and nature of debt relief as G7 finance ministers at last focused on this issue at the end of the 1990s. For its part, the Movement for the Survival of the Ogoni People (MOSOP), and its networking through Greenpeace and various UN fora, put real pressure on Shell-BP in Nigeria and on the Commonwealth concerning Nigeria's membership; environmental groups in South Africa have also protested internationally against environmental 'dumping' in SSA. In South Africa, too, unions have cooperated and lobbied at the international level against firms that have polluted rivers after the process of privatization. Of course, familiar questions concerning the extent of Western dominance (albeit clothed in more progressive garb than the IFIs) remain, but the differences in notions of development between the two general models remain substantive and, for those concerned with the impact of neoliberalism in SSA, debt and environmental networks remain a preferable point of departure.

In summary, globalization has narrowed the development agenda in SSA in one profound way: the extensive involvement of external institutions, in conjunction with the region's persistent economic marginality, has encased debate and policy in neoliberal doctrine. SSA's poverty produces a global vulnerability with political as well as economic effects; but SSA's engagement with global forces is too complex to be contained within the realms of state relations and official economic flows. Cooper (2000: 212) provides a useful summary:

> International finance institutions that tell African leaders that development will follow if they open up their economies will not get to the bottom of the continent's problems unless they address how specific structures within African societies, within or across borders, provide opportunities and constraints for production and exchange, and how specific mechanisms in external commodity markets provide opportunities and blockages for African products. State institutions, oligarchies, warlords, regional mafias, commercial diasporas, oligopolistic foreign corporations, and varied networks shape the nature of capitalism and its highly uneven effects.

There is a great deal to unpack in this reflection, but it strongly suggests that we must ground any such analysis in an acknowledgement of the institutionally differentiated and complex nature of SSA's engagement with globalization, a point we have been at pains to stress throughout this section.

Conclusion

We can usefully conclude by elaborating a number of defining features of the politics of development in Sub-Saharan Africa:

- Development in the context of weak or unstable states. States have failed to articulate a common development discourse at the global level, a result of their historically constituted weakness and the orientation of ruling elites towards their own means of accumulating power and wealth.
- Development traversing the formal–informal divide. Attempts to create regional and subregional models of development have been interwoven with social dynamics which undermine official state fiat. Much of the activity here can be seen as illustrative of a rather brutal regionalism, defined by illicit trade and conflict.
- Development in the context of economic crisis and extreme poverty. Poverty establishes powerful relations of inequality at the global level. It allows Western agencies to indulge in the most patronizing and intrusive statements and actions through the moral field of humanitarianism and reconstructed notions of modernization within which development is essentially reduced to a process whereby SSA becomes more akin to the West.
- Development and high levels of insecurity. Conflict and development are inextricably linked in SSA. Military conflict not only leads to civilian victims; it creates waves of migration, mines fields, destroys schools and leads to the plunder of high-value resources, which have proven to be more of a curse than a blessing to those countries endowed with them.

Under the influence of these features, SSA has maintained both centrality and marginality within the global political economy. No other region has been so thoroughly pervaded by external agencies; yet the economies of the region command minimal percentages of global trade and investment.

It has also become apparent that many of the basic assumptions of almost all development theory are rendered problematic in the African context. Such thinking generally begins by assuming the presence of a minimally stable and purposeful state and the existence of a national economy which, however open it might be, is open precisely because it has boundaries that can be modified as part of a purposeful strategy. For much of SSA, states are more complex and contradictory constructions, far more difficult to map and conceptualize. National economies exist, but so do war economies, trafficking networks and webs of migration that threaten to construct a different kind of (sub)regionalism to that defined by formal agencies.

Finally, it is an inescapable fact that SSA has failed to make a positive impact on development politics at the global level. There is no model of the developmental state as forged in Northeast and Southeast Asia, or of ISI as outlined by the UN Economic Commission for Latin America. There are no institutions of economic regionalism with the robustness of ASEAN or MERCOSUR. SSA remains in the thrall of an unstable and occasionally floundering neoliberalism, in the last instance underwritten by the World Bank and the IMF. Ways out of this impasse will only derive from changes in the relations between African states and their peasant societies. In the words of Vale and Maseko (1998: 281), 'the majority of Africans consider themselves marginalized from the affairs of the continent and the world. Unless this is changed, there will be no renewal.' For renewal, read development. Africa as a region is yet to establish an approach to development that derives from its regional features; instead it has been subjected to a sequence of models and frameworks that have been imposed from outside, although these impositions have always been mediated by local social groups. In such circumstances it would be foolhardy and preemptory to speculate on what an 'African developmental model' might look like.

Further reading

Clapham, C. (1996) *Africa and the International System: The Politics of State Survival* (Cambridge: Cambridge University Press).

Harbeson, J. and Rothchild, D. (eds) (2000) *Africa in World Politics: Globalization and the Changing State*, 3rd edn (Boulder CO: Westview Press).

Harrison, G. (2002) *Issues in the Contemporary Politics of Sub-Saharan Africa* (London: Palgrave Macmillan).

Sandbrook, R. (2000) *Closing the Circle: Democratisation and Development in Africa* (London: Zed).

Chapter 10

Concluding Thoughts and Next Steps

ANTHONY PAYNE

We do not seek in this last chapter to assess or sum up all of the many, many arguments about the politics of development in different parts of the world advanced by the various authors of the preceding eight chapters. They have painted rich and subtle portraits of the development strategies and options, the development successes and failures, of regions of the world about which they know a lot. In every case they have presented a mass of fascinating material in commendably concise fashion and established beyond doubt the extraordinary complexity of the politics of a world with so many countries, each with its own specific history of development. It would be pretentious and glib to try to draw out from these analyses some kind of overview of the contemporary world of development and, as indicated, no attempt will be made to do that here. What we can usefully do by way of conclusion is reiterate the core elements of the approach to the study of development deployed in this book and set out the next steps that need to be taken to refine and deepen the nature of the analysis it can provide.

The central organizing insight with which we began was that the study of development would benefit from being rethought within the framework of international political economy. The case for grounding a new approach to development inside the field of IPE was that this sub-discipline of the academy necessarily constituted a much broader and wide-ranging intellectual environment than development studies had become. It came into being in order to understand the substantial reconfiguration of the economics and politics of the post-1945 world order which began to take shape in the early 1970s and has always been willing to grapple with the big questions raised by that process, such as the changing role of states, the apparent new significance of regions and, of course, the proclaimed trend towards globalization and global governance. Given its propensity to make bold claims about the state of the world, it was always striking that development was not generally prioritized as an issue or a problem within IPE. This was actually a revealing and worrying omission, indicative both of IPE's preoccupation with the core, post-industrial political economies of the world and its attendant presumption that development could safely be left to development studies.

This book derives from the belief that this academic division of labour is confining and thoroughly unsatisfactory. To reiterate for a moment, we argued in the introduction to this book that what was required was in effect a marriage between development studies and international political economy. The four main features of a new approach forged within this framework were identified as follows:

- a rejection of a special category of countries deemed to be in need of development, and a recasting of the whole question of development on a universalist basis;
- a focus upon development strategy, principally as still pursued by a national economy, society and/or polity;
- a recognition that such strategy for all countries necessarily involves the interaction, and appropriate meshing, of internal and external elements; and
- a recognition of the many variations of time, place and history in development predicaments.

On this basis, then, we redefined development for the contemporary era as the collective building by the constituent social and political actors of a country (or at least in the first instance a country) of a viable, functioning political economy, grounded in at least a measure of congruence between its core domestic characteristics and attributes and its location within a globalizing world order and capable on that basis of advancing the well-being of those living within its confines. The salient point underpinning this definition was that *all* countries in the world were seen as having to pursue development. It no longer made sense to think of it as something that only 'developing countries' needed to worry about. By the same token, the so-called 'developed countries' could not be thought somehow to have completed their development, for they too manifestly still had to engage with the world order and chart domestic strategies for so doing. In short, the argument was that development was an issue for everybody.

All of the authors of the various regional chapters have worked with this definition. Some of them, principally those writing about the Americas, Europe and Northeast Asia, have therefore had to embrace within their analyses discussion of countries conventionally considered to lie outside the ambit of development studies – countries, if you like, which have not been supposed to be in need of development strategies – namely, the US and Canada, the western European countries and

Japan. They have convincingly demonstrated the nonsense (literally defined) of this exclusion by showing how all of these countries, just like other notionally 'developing countries', can be located within the trade, production, finance and security structures of the world order and are required to think through and seek to implement policies designed to adjust their current positioning in these structures in appropriate and desirable ways. At the same time, the authors of other chapters, which focus on conventionally understood 'developing areas', namely those on Southeast Asia, South Asia, the Middle East and Sub-Saharan Africa, have not been able to describe and analyse their groups of countries as if they all possess in broad terms much the same endowment of resources, a common history and a similar strategic location in the world order. Instead, what comes through time and again in their accounts is the sheer variety of development predicaments and strategies they encounter, even in regions, such as these, which have always been the classic terrain of development studies and supposedly share so much. Finally, the authors of the chapters on Europe and the post-Soviet space have had to address the countries of the former communist world. They do deploy the notion of 'transition' as a way of encapsulating the shift of these parts of the world from communism to some form of capitalism, but they find that they cannot take this concept too far. At the end of the day these various countries have also to be seen as part of the same pot, for the most part trying to find coherent development strategies to move them from their particular historical bases to preferred positions in the global order.

In other words, we have genuinely found the approach to the study of development deployed here to be liberating. It has broken down categories and barriers and that is nearly always beneficial in academic enquiry. The marriage, it could perhaps be said, looks at the moment as if it is working rather nicely. The only 'problem' is that, necessarily, there often has to be something of a pause between recognition of the necessity of moving on from old ways of thinking and successful completion of the task of constructing new ones. This creates anxieties. Shorn of familiar categories of analysis – of camps, for example, within which we can place countries, however crudely – it can seem as if all that is left is complexity, which then quickly degenerates into confusion and mess. The best response one can make to such fears is to insist that, with more time and more work, it will be possible to describe the pattern of this new world of development with greater precision, perhaps to discern within it a shape we cannot currently see. We have certainly tried in this book to construct a platform from which to go about this task and indeed to put in place some pointers to what we must do next to bring about this outcome. To establish what these might be, we need to return to the three questions about the new politics of development which were placed before each of our authors. In doing this we can identify the research themes that must now be addressed if we are to build on the emergent analyses contained in this book.

The first question asked, straightforwardly and factually, what were the main development strategies currently being pursued by the component countries of the region in question. The only answer that can be given in respect of all the countries in all of the regions considered is that contemporary country development strategies are extraordinarily diverse in character. It is not quite that one has to retreat into saying that there are 190 nation-states in the world and therefore there are 190 different national development strategies. But, at the other extreme, it is laughable to suppose, as to all intents and purposes the 'models of capitalism' debate once did, that there were only really two or perhaps three such models worthy of either attention or emulation. There are better ways to advance this debate. It may be true that one can distinguish between Anglo-American free market and western European social market brands and note further that the former has been on the attack for the past couple of decades, responsible for laying down the classic neoliberal template of our times, and that the latter correspondingly has been pushed more and more onto the defensive in the face of the same neoliberal trends. But, as the various chapters in this book reveal, the fact is that most national models these days are variant forms of neoliberalism, at least in the sense that even would-be alternative, historically nationalist or statist strategies have had to make their compromises with the new global market. But such is the actual number of broadly neoliberal strategies being pursued around the world that, of itself, this generalization does not carry much impact. Immediately, we need to know, for example, whether neoliberal tenets have been embraced enthusiastically, with the zeal, as it were, of the convert, or whether they have been taken on board reluctantly and hesitantly *faute de mieux*, or whether they have been adopted in some manner that is not quite either of these modes. We need similarly to explore all the variations of neoliberal practice, which shift according to geographic location, nature of the resource base, character and capacity of the state, social structure, cultural context and historical path-dependency in general. We need to assess the extent and intensity of external influence, which again changes with time and place. All of this, and much more, is required to begin to make sense of the subtle differences that exist even between those many, many countries that are seeking to follow, broadly defined, a 'model of capitalism'.

Two other points can be made about the diversity of country development strategies. First, it should not be forgotten that state-socialist models of development, or aspects of them, have not yet been completely obliterated from the world. A few countries of this type, such as Cuba and North Korea, grind on, albeit with their socialism fraying somewhat around the edges. Others remain nominally communist, even though, like the People's Republic of China, Vietnam and Laos, they may lately have been drawn more extensively into the global market order. Others in the post-Soviet space have only half-heartedly, or hardly at all, confronted the structural constraints on development still imposed by their former membership of a state-socialist system. Second, it is also the case that some countries, several of them in Sub-Saharan Africa, have weak, malfunctioning or virtually non-existent state apparatuses and, as a result, cannot really be said to have assembled a set of policies of any type which seriously merits being described as a development strategy. Some countries, such as Sierra Leone and the Democratic Republic of the Congo, have been riven by civil war or its aftermath and have struggled to establish order, let alone movement in any economic or social direction. In development terms, they have festered. Others are ruled by military or family dictatorships and pursue only gains for the ruling group. This, too, excludes them from consideration as genuine examples of national development strategy.

Unavoidably, the organ of the state remains at the centre of this whole area of research. For what other body can take responsibility for charting policy for a nation as a whole? Where states do not work properly, then it is the case that other non-state actors endeavour over time to fill some of the gaps left by their absence or weakness. But the national development project suffers as a consequence. Where they are brutal or corrupt, they stand as major obstacles to national economic growth and collective social progress. Where they do work, it is important to recognize that they operate in different ways and that there is no single model that deserves to be held up and advertised as exemplar, whether it be the 'limited state' favoured by liberals or the 'interventionist state' admired by social democrats and other believers in state leadership. It is the diversity of forms of state and their relations with the societies they seek to govern that ultimately lies at the core of the diversity of country development strategies.

The second question posed to the chapter authors asked them to explore the ways in which intra-regional politics affected these national development strategies. All treated this question as having two dimensions, which inevitably intertwine: the impact of specific inter-state regionalist projects, on the one hand, and the role played by looser social processes of regionalization, on the other. Formal regionalist organizations exist everywhere, often in bewildering numbers in some regions and in overlapping fashion in respect of membership. But, that said, only one merits consideration as an effective means of developmental regionalism, if by this notion one means a regionalist project which supports and sustains the national development strategies of its member states in fundamental ways, wherein perhaps national strategy cannot even be imagined, let alone effectively implemented, outside of the regional context. That case is of course the EU. It may still be premature to think of the EU as being fully possessed of a common and collective development strategy (which would require us to step beyond the current vision of countries as the only agents capable of pursuing development strategy), but, as EMU proceeds, that stage in its evolution may be reached, which would render existing, rather unsatisfactory, statist modes of explanation of this 'in-between', conceivably entirely novel, organization at last appropriate. For the moment, it is clear that an 'EU model' of development is close to being hegemonic within the European region. By comparison, NAFTA and the prospective FTAA are quite different. Although the USA turned to regionalism at the end of the 1980s as a response to its sense of a fading global hegemony (notwithstanding the ending of the Cold War) and can therefore be said to view NAFTA and the FTAA as major planks of its post-Cold War development strategy, its continuing, powerful, regional hegemony within and across the whole of the Americas means that NAFTA remains predominantly its tool and makes the FTAA process at heart a reflection of its ideological dominance. The other subregionalisms of the Americas, even a prospective joint Southern Cone–Andean platform dreamed about by Brazil, can only really hope to use the negotiations to mitigate as best they can the unilateral demonstration of US regional hegemony.

For the rest, there is more evidence of effective developmental regionalization than developmental regionalism. As is shown in the various preceding chapters, some regional organizations are notoriously weak, such as the Arab League, which has existed since 1945 without bringing about much economic integration or political unity amongst Arab states, and SAARC, which has been reduced almost to impotence by the ongoing tension between India and Pakistan about Kashmir and other security concerns. As for the poor CIS, its creation has been portrayed as a necessary accident, a contrivance that had to happen to sort out the chaos caused by the collapse of the USSR. It survives, but articulates no collective developmental interest across the post-Soviet space. Within other regions MERCOSUR has been launched and relaunched; ASEAN has grown to ASEAN + 3; and a new African Union has been proclaimed. What perhaps makes these last three examples a little different, and gives ground for some optimism from the perspective of development, is that, according to our authors, wide-ranging and informal processes of regional interdependence do seem to be giving sustenance to the national development strategies of countries within these regions. For example, within the Americas an embryonic 'Southern Cone model of regional capitalist development' has been discerned, grounded in something deeper than the mechanics of MERCOSUR alone. Within Northeast and Southeast Asia the significance of the presence of complex informal production and business networks, many of them cohering around Japan as the 'headquarters economy', has long been acknowledged and is reiterated again here. Even within Sub-Saharan Africa it is now suggested that forms of 'bottom-up rationalization' have come into existence, often centred on illicit economic activity and generated generally, although no longer exclusively, within the broader context of contested security.

The lesson is that in exploring the intra-regional politics of development around the world one has to embrace the informal as much as the formal, regionalization as much as regionalism. The former can undoubtedly support country development strategies, although it should be recognized that this type of unpublicized region-building is still very much at its formative stage in most regions of the world, and indeed more or less non-existent still in some. Yet it will grow, because globalization as a process also facilitates regionalization as a process. It is not so clear at all that effective regionalist organizations can be constructed where they do not presently exist. As many of the chapters testify, serious political obstacles (of different sorts in different regions) stand in the way. This is a major inhibition on the pursuit of development of whatever form. For, as the EU shows, regionalism can become a powerful mechanism for harnessing and pushing forward national strategies. There *is* strength in numbers. For the moment, though, that is a truth honoured more in rhetoric than substance. The prevailing feature of the intra-regional politics of development in the contemporary world order is immaturity.

The third and last question posed asked how the various national (and regional) strategies of development described and analysed were carried forward into the extra-regional politics of development and thus in effect took the discussion to the global level. The range of answers offered here combine to present a picture of striking (and unacceptable) inequality in respect of the impact which different states have on global forums and the outcome of global negotiations. Lack of impact can also lead to lack of involvement, which only adds to the lack of impact. It is important, too, at this level of analysis of the politics of development to note, and give due weight to, the role of a number of multilateral organizations, in particular the leading international financial institutions, the IMF and the World Bank. They are both bodies created by states and structured around state participation, but over time they have hardened their own institutional personalities and become quasi-autonomous actors in the global politics of development in ways that transcend to some degree their statist origins. The prospect of a global governance, as well as a global politics, of development is thereby opened up.

In this domain, at least, the US is not like any other country in the world: it is unquestionably a special case. Throughout the post-1945 period a fundamental aspect of its own development strategy has been the promotion of a multilateralism that it can control. It has been pivotal to the design and establishment of all of the multilateral bodies that currently exist and, unsurprisingly, has emerged as the dominant actor within these organizations, either by virtue of the possession of veto powers on key decisions or by means of sheer negotiating clout. In similar fashion, within international negotiations, such as those pertaining to global trade or global climate change, the US is the one country which can make or break deals. As and when it chooses to opt out, as in the Kyoto Protocol, it may not have been able to prevent other states signing the document, but it has substantially reduced the chances of the policy being effective. The EU states, Japan and Canada also play major roles in these global matters alongside the US. In consequence, the G7, the forum within which they meet annually, comes closest to being the ruling council of the globe, especially in respect of matters of finance. But even within this grouping there is significant inequality. Canada is the least significant player; Japan has long 'led from behind', to quote the phrase of one observer cited earlier, and is only lately beginning to take on a more normal proactive role, and then mainly in forums where decision-making processes are opaque and its role is not overt and controversial; and the EU sometimes operates as a bloc, sometimes not, and sometimes works closely with the US and sometimes opposes it. Its degree of influence on events varies accordingly.

As for the rest of the world, a few countries emerge as players of note – Brazil, China, India, South Africa, Egypt, Pakistan, Bangladesh, Malaysia, to name the most obvious. But their activism is partial and uneven across the different arenas of global negotiation and only fitfully harnessed to the interests of the non-G7 states as a whole. There do exist collective groupings, such as the Group of 77 within the UN system and the Non-Aligned Movement more generally, which seek to mount a 'Southern' response to perceived 'Northern' interests and it is the case in the environmental arena and, to a limited extent, in the trade arena that 'developing countries' constitute an identifiable category and carry some weight, at least emotionally, in the relevant diplomacy. But, for the most part, what becomes apparent from the analyses of the chapters is the many fissures which exist not only across the non-G7 world but also within specific regions, and even subregions, when it comes to taking up positions on the global stage. The reality is that there are such large disparities between countries in their weight and position in global politics, as well as in their roles and overall strategies, that the bargaining positions that do emerge are kaleidoscopic in their complexity and fluidity.

One sphere where a pattern can be detected relates back to the global governance of development. Many, many countries are forced into relations of subservience with the IFIs. The IMF and the World Bank are the joint repositories of the doctrines of structural adjustment, 'good governance' and social capital and have imposed the policies associated with these tenets upon multiple supposed beneficiaries in Sub-Saharan Africa, the Americas and Asia. They generally come as a package and are not 'adjusted' to suit the specific social and political settings into which they are inserted. Recipient countries have been completely unable to wield any collective pressure on the IFIs to vary or soften or indeed change completely their approach to these matters. In fact, there is no political forum available within which they can even try to do this. The Fund and the Bank are not like the UN and the WTO where there is at least a diplomatic game to be played in an openly inter-state framework. Rather, they are institutions of governance where the power of any particular poor state is limited to the tiny percentage of the votes allocated to it on the executive council. At the same time, because they are mechanisms of global governance, the staff of the IFIs, especially the most senior staff at managing director level and just below, come close to acting as guardians not of any state interest but of that of the global order as a whole. To this degree, they escape the complete control of even the US and the other leading G7 states.

To sum up, then, we can see that the preliminary findings of this first regional exploration of the 'politics of the political economy of development' (built, as already stated many times, by seeking to draw on the best of development studies and IPE) point strongly to the need to pursue much further a number of major research themes. One would address the diversity of country strategies of development and involve a wide-ranging, comparative, cross-regional survey of development models, building on but also seeking to go well-beyond the old 'models of capitalism' and 'models of development' literatures. A second would investigate the immaturity of the intra-regional politics of development and again would draw on the existing 'new-regions' literature but focus its enquiry centrally upon the potential impact of regionalism and regionalization on development. A third would probe more fully the inequalities which sit at the heart of the global politics of development and attempt to map that continuing strand of international relations which even at the beginning of the twenty-first century still seems to pitch the interests of rich countries against those of poor countries. There are no doubt other questions too which emerge, but there is more than enough to do for the moment within this agenda. The preparation of good books on each of these three themes would be a valuable start and should be the next steps that we try to take.

Bibliography

Abelin, A. (1996) *Long-term Economic Growth Strategy*, Working Paper no. 47, Economic Planning Agency, Tokyo.

Acharya, A. (2001) *Constructing a Security Community in Southeast Asia: ASEAN and the Problem of Regional Order* (London: Routledge).

Akamatsu, K. (1962) 'A Historical Pattern of Economic Growth in Developing Countries', *The Developing Economies*, no. 1, March–August, pp. 3–25.

Alatas, A. (2001) ' "ASEAN Plus Three" Equals Peace Plus Prosperity', *Trends in Southeast Asia* no. 2, January (Singapore: Institute for South East Asian Studies).

Ali, I.A. (2001) 'Business and Power in Pakistan', in A.M. Weiss and S.Z. Gilani (eds), *Power and Civil Society in Pakistan* (Oxford: Oxford University Press), pp. 93–122.

Allen, D. (2000) 'Cohesion and the Structural Funds: Transfers and Trade-Offs', in H. Wallace and W. Wallace (eds), *Policy-Making in the European Union*, 4th edn (Oxford: Oxford University Press), pp. 243–65.

Allen, T. (2001) 'The Candidate Countries' Trade with the EU in 2000', *Eurostat, Statistics in Focus*, External Trade, Theme 6–8/2001, available at http://www.eu-datashop.de/download/EN/sta-kurz/thema6/no 01 08.pdf

Altbach, E. (1998) 'Weathering the Storm? Japan's Production Networks in Asia and the Regional Crisis', *Japan Economic Institute Report*, no. 35, Tokyo.

Amin, S. (1978) *The Arab Nation* (London: Zed).

Amirahmadi, H. and Wu, W. (1995) 'Export Processing Zones in Asia', *Asian Survey*, vol. 35, no. 9, pp. 828–49.

Amoore, L., Dodgson, R., Gills, B.K., Langley, P., Marshall, D. and Watson, I. (1997) 'Overturning "Globalisation": Resisting the Teleological, Reclaiming the "Political" ', *New Political Economy*, vol. 2, no. 1, pp. 179–95.

Amorim, C. (2003) 'A Alca possível', *Folha de São Paulo*, 8 July.

Amsden, A. (1989) *Asia's Next Giant: South Korea and Late Industrialism* (Oxford: Oxford University Press).

Anonymous (2000) 'Global Warming: "Clean" Energy Trap', *Economic and Political Weekly*, vol. 35, no. 13, p. 1041.

Appaiah, K.A. (1992) *In My Father's House: Africa in the Philosophy of Culture* (Oxford: Oxford University Press).

Aron, L. (1994) 'The Emergent Priorities of Russian Foreign Policy', in L. Aron and K. Jensen (eds), *The Emergence of Russian Foreign Policy* (Washington DC: United States Institute of Peace Press), pp. 17–34.

Arrighi, G. (2002) 'The African Crisis: World Systemic and Regional Aspects', *New Left Review*, Second Series, no. 15, pp. 5–36.

ASEAN (1998) *Hanoi Plan of Action*, available at: http://www.aseansec.org/menu.asp?action=8&content=8

Åslund, A. (1989) *Gorbachev's Struggle for Economic Reform* (London: Pinter).

Athukorala, P. and Rajapatirana, S. (2000) *Liberalization and Transformation: Sri Lanka in International Perspective* (Delhi: Oxford University Press).

Aulas, M. (1988) 'State and Ideology in Republican Egypt', in F. Halliday and H. Alavi (eds), *State and Ideology in the Middle East and Pakistan* (London: Palgrave Macmillan), pp. 133–66.

Austin, G. and Harris, S. (2001) *Japan and Greater China: Political Economy and Military Power in the Asian Century* (Honolulu: University of Hawaii Press).

Ayubi, N. (1995) *Over-Stating the Arab State* (London: I.B. Tauris).

Baer, W. (1972) 'Import Substitution and Industrialization in Latin America: Experiences and Interpretations', *Latin American Research Review*, vol. 7, no. 1, pp. 95–122.

Bajpai, K. (1998) 'India: Modified Structuralism', in M. Alagappa (ed.), *Asian Security Practice: Material and Ideational Influences* (Stanford CA: Stanford University Press), pp. 157–97.

Balino, T. and Ubide, A. (1999) *The Korean Financial Crisis of 1997 – A Strategy of Financial Sector Reform*, IMF Working Paper, no. WP/99/28, Washington DC.

Bandelj, N. (2003) 'Varieties of Capitalism in Central and Eastern Europe', Department of Sociology, Princeton University, mimeo.

Bankoff, G. (2001) 'Environment, Resources, and Hazards', in P. Heenan and M. Lamontagne (eds), *The Southeast Asia Handbook* (Chicago IL: Fitzroy Dearborn), pp. 179–92.

Barratt-Brown, M. and Tiffen, P. (1992) *Short Changed: Africa and World Trade* (London: Pluto).

Barton, J. (1999) 'The Environmental Agenda', in J. Buxton and N. Phillips (eds), *Developments in Latin American Political Economy: States, Markets and Actors* (Manchester: Manchester University Press), pp. 186–204.

Batt, J. (2002a) 'Introduction: Regions, State and Identity in Central and Eastern Europe', *Regional and Federal Studies*, vol. 12, no. 2, pp. 1–14.

——(2002b) 'Transcarpathia: Peripheral Region at the "Centre of Europe"', *Regional and Federal Studies*, vol. 12, no. 2, pp. 155–77.

Bauer, J.R. and Bell, D.A. (eds) (1999) *The East Asian Challenge for Human Rights* (Cambridge: Cambridge University Press).

Baxter, C., Malik, Y.K., Kennedy, C.H. and Oberst, R.C. (1998) *Government and Politics in South Asia* (Boulder CO: Westview Press).

Bayart, J.F. (1993) *The State in Africa: The Politics of the Belly* (London: Heinemann).

——(2000) 'Africa in the World: A History of Extroversion', *African Affairs* vol. 99, no. 395, pp. 217–69.

Beblawi, H. (1990) 'The Rentier State in the Arab World', in C. Luciani (ed.), *The Arab State* (London: Routledge), pp. 85–98.

Beeson, M. (1998) 'Indonesia, the East Asian Crisis and the Commodification of the Nation-state', *New Political Economy*, vol. 3, no. 3, pp. 357–74.

——(1999) 'Reshaping Regional Institutions: APEC and the IMF in East Asia', *The Pacific Review*, vol. 12, no. 1, pp. 1–24.

Beeson, M. (2000) 'Mahathir and the Markets: Globalisation and the Pursuit of Economic Autonomy in Malaysia', *Pacific Affairs*, vol. 73, no. 3, pp. 335–51.

—— (2001) 'Japan and Southeast Asia: The Lineaments of Quasi-hegemony', in G. Rodan, K. Hewison and R. Robison (eds), *The Political Economy of South-East Asia: An Introduction*, 2nd edn (Melbourne: Oxford University Press), pp. 283–306.

—— (2002) 'The More Things Change ... ? Path Dependency and Convergence in East Asia', in M. Beeson (ed.), *Reconfiguring East Asia: Regional Institutions and Organisations After the Crisis* (London: Curzon Press), pp. 246–56.

—— (2003) 'ASEAN Plus Three and the Rise of Reactionary Regionalism', *Contemporary Southeast Asia*, vol. 25, no. 2, pp. 251–68.

Beeson, M. and Robison, R. (2000) 'Introduction: Interpreting the Crisis', in R. Robison *et al.* (eds), *Politics and Markets in the Wake of the Asian Crisis* (London: Routledge), pp. 3–24.

Berger, M. and Borer, D. (eds) (1997) *The Rise of East Asia: Critical Visions of the Pacific Century* (London: Routledge).

Bernard, M. and Ravenhill, J. (1995) 'Beyond Product Cycles and Flying Geese: Regionalization, Hierarchy, and the Industrialization of East Asia', *World Politics*, vol. 47, no. 2, pp. 171–209.

Betke, D. and Küchler, J. (1987) 'Shortage of Land Resources as a Factor in Development: The Example of the People's Republic of China', in B. Glaeser (ed.), *Learning from China? Development and Environment in Third World Countries* (London: Allen & Unwin), pp. 85–107.

Bockman, J. and Eyal, G. (2002) 'Eastern Europe as a Laboratory for Economic Knowledge: The Transnational Roots of Neoliberalism', *American Journal of Sociology*, vol. 108, no.2, pp. 310–52.

Boniface, D.S. (2002) 'Is There a Democratic Norm in the Americas? An Analysis of the Organization of American States', *Global Governance*, vol. 8, no. 3, pp. 365–81.

Boone, C. (1998). 'Empirical Statehood and Reconfigurations of Political Order', in L. Villalon and P. Huxtable (eds), *The African State at a Critical Conjuncture: Between Disintegration and Reconfiguration* (Boulder CO: Lynne Rienner), pp. 129–41.

Booth, D. (1985) 'Marxism and Development Sociology: Interpreting the Impasse', *World Development*, vol. 13, no. 7, pp. 761–87.

—— (1993) 'Development Research: From Impasse to New Agenda', in F.J. Schuurman (ed.), *Beyond the Impasse: New Directions in Development Theory* (London: Zed), pp. 49–76.

Booth, J. (2002) 'The Transformation of Professional Practices in Postcommunist Poland: Observing the Dynamics of Globalisation', unpublished PhD thesis, Oxford Brookes University.

Borden, W. (1984) *The Pacific Alliance: United States Foreign Economic Policy and Japanese Trade Recovery 1947–1955* (Madison WI: University of Wisconsin Press).

Borràs, S. and Johansen, H. (2001) 'Cohesion in the Political Economy of the European Union', *Cooperation and Conflict*, vol. 36, no. 1, pp. 36–60.

Bowles, P. (2000) 'Regionalism and Development after (?) the Global Financial Crises', *New Political Economy*, vol. 5, no. 3, pp. 433–55.

Bowles, P. and MacLean, B. (1996) 'Understanding Trade Bloc Formation: The Case of the ASEAN Free Trade Area', *Review of International Political Economy*, vol. 3, no. 2, pp. 319–48.

Box, L. and Goodison, P. (1994) 'Coordinate or be Coordinated: Europe–ACP Development Policies from a Maastricht Perspective', in J.L. Rhi-Sausi and M. Dassù (eds), *Coordinating the Development Aid Policies of European Countries* (Rome: Centro Studi di Politica Internazionale).

Bradnock, R.W. and Saunders, P. (2002) 'Rising Waters, Sinking Land? Environmental Change and Development in Bangladesh', in R.W. Bradnock and G. Williams (eds), *South Asia in a Globalising World* (Harlow: Pearson), pp. 51–77.

Brandt Commission, The (1980) *North–South: A Programme for Survival* (The Report of the Independent Commission on International Development Issues under the Chairmanship of Willy Brandt) (London: Pan).

Brass, P.R. (1994) *The Politics of India since Independence* (Cambridge: Cambridge University Press).

Bremmer, I. and Taras, R. (eds) (1997) *New States, New Politics: Building the Post-Soviet Nations* (Cambridge: Cambridge University Press).

Breslin, S. (2003) 'Paradigm Shifts and Time-lags? The Politics of Financial Reform in the People's Republic of China', *Asian Business and Management*, vol. 2, no. 1, pp. 1–24.

Breslin, S. and Higgott, R. (2000) 'Studying Regions: Learning from the Old, Constructing the New', *New Political Economy*, vol. 5, no. 3, pp. 333–52.

Breslin, S. and Hook, G. (eds) (2002) *Microregionalism and World Order* (London: Palgrave Macmillan).

Breslin, S., Higgott, R. and Rosamond, B. (2002) 'Regions in Comparative Perspective', in S. Breslin, C. Hughes, N. Phillips and B. Rosamond (eds), *New Regionalisms in the Global Political Economy: Theories and Cases* (London: Routledge), pp. 1–19.

Bromley, S. (1994) *Rethinking Middle East Politics* (Cambridge: Polity Press).

——(1997) 'Middle East Exceptionalism – Myth or Reality?', in D. Potter *et al.* (eds), *Democratization* (Cambridge: Polity Press), pp. 321–44.

Browne, R. (1992) 'Alternative Policy Frameworks for African Development in the 1990s', in J. Nyang'oro and T. Shaw (eds), *Beyond Structural Adjustment in Africa* (New York NY: Praeger), pp. 71–83.

Bruun, O. and Odgaard, O. (eds) (1997) *Mongolia in Transition* (London: Routledge/Curzon).

Bryceson, D., Kay, C. and Mooij, J. (eds) (2000) *Disappearing Peasantries? Rural Labour in Africa, Asia, and Latin America* (London: Intermediate Technology Publications).

Brzezinski, Z. and Sullivan, P. (eds) (1997) *Russia and the Commonwealth of Independent States* (Armonk NY: M.E. Sharpe).

Bukkvoll, T. (2001) 'Off the Cuff Politics – Explaining Russia's Lack of a Ukraine Strategy', *Europe-Asia Studies*, vol. 53, no. 8, pp. 1141–57.

Bullion, A. (2001) 'Sri Lanka: On the Brink', *The World Today*, vol. 57, no. 10, p. 16.

Burnham, P. (1999) 'The Politics of Economic Management', *New Political Economy*, vol. 4, no. 1, pp. 37–54.

Bush, R. and Cliffe, L. (1984) 'Agrarian Policy in Migrant Labour Societies: Reform or Transformation in Zimbabwe?', *Review of African Political Economy*, vol. 11, no. 29, pp. 77–94.

Bustillo, I. and Ocampo, J.A. (2003) 'Asymmetries and Cooperation in the Free Trade Area of the Americas', paper presented at the seminar 'Confronting the Challenges of Regional Development in Latin America and the Caribbean', Milan, 22 March.

Callaghy, T. (2000) 'Africa and the World Economy: More Caught Between and Rock and a Hard Place', in D. Rothchild and J. Harbeson (eds), *Africa in World Politics: The African State System in Flux* (Boulder CO: Westview Press), pp. 43–83.

Campbell, J.L. (2001) 'Convergence or Divergence? Globalization, Neoliberalism and Fiscal Policy in Postcommunist Europe', in S. Weber (ed.), *Globalization and the European Political Economy* (New York NY: Columbia University Press), pp. 107–39.

Canadian Department of Foreign Affairs and International Trade (2003) *Fourth Annual Report on Canada's State of Trade*, available at http://www.dfait-maeci.gc.ca/eet/trade/sot_2003/SOT_2003-en.asp?#3

Candland, C. (2001) 'Institutional Impediments to Human Development in Pakistan', in A. Shastri and A.J. Wilson (eds), *The Postcolonial States of South Asia: Democracy, Identity, Development and Security* (London: Curzon Press), pp. 264–83.

Cardoso, F.H. and Faletto, E. (1979) *Dependency and Development in Latin America* (translated by M.M. Urquidi) (Berkeley CA: University of California Press).

Case, W. (2001) 'Indonesia', in P. Heenan and M. Lamontagne (eds), *The Southeast Asia Handbook* (Chicago IL: Fitzroy Dearborn), pp. 97–109.

Castañeda, J.G. (2003) 'The Forgotten Relationship', *Foreign Affairs*, May–June, online version, pp. 1–8.

Castells, M. (1996) *The Rise of the Network Society* (Oxford: Basil Blackwell).

Caufield, C. (1996) *Masters of Illusion: The World Bank and the Poverty of Nations* (New York NY: Henry Holt).

Chan, S. (1993) *East Asian Dynamism: Growth, Order, and Security in the Pacific Region* (Boulder CO: Westview).

Chandler, D. (2000) *A History of Cambodia* (Boulder CO: Westview Press).

Chang, G. (2003) *The Coming Collapse of China* (London: Random House).

Chen, E. and Kwan, C.H. (eds) (1997) *Asia's Borderless Economy: The Emergence of Sub-Regional Zones* (London: Allen & Unwin).

Cherian, J. (2001) 'Uneasy Neighbours', *Frontline*, vol. 18, no. 13, available at http://www.frontlineonnet.com/fl1813/18130140.htm

Chia Siow Yue (1998) 'The ASEAN Free Trade Area', *The Pacific Review*, vol. 11, no. 2, pp. 213–32.

Chowdhury, A. and Islam, I. (1993) *The Newly Industrialising Economies of East Asia* (London: Routledge).

Clapham, C. (1996) *Africa and the International System: The Politics of State Survival* (Cambridge: Cambridge University Press).

Cleary, M. and Wong, S.Y. (1994) *Oil, Economic Development and Diversification in Brunei Darussalam* (London: Palgrave Macmillan).

Coates, D. (2000) *Models of Capitalism: Growth and Stagnation in the Modern Era* (Cambridge: Polity Press).

Cohen, S.P. (2001) *India: Emerging Power* (Washington DC: Brookings Institution).

Cooper, F. (2000) 'What is the Concept of Globalization Good for? An African Historian's Perspective', *African Affairs*, vol. 100, no. 399, pp. 198–215.

Cooper, A.F. and Legler, T. (2001) 'The OAS Democratic Solidarity Paradigm: Questions of Collective and National Leadership', *Latin American Politics and Society*, vol. 43, no. 1, pp. 103–26.

Corbridge, S. (1990) 'Post-Marxism and Development Studies: Beyond the Impasse', *World Development*, vol. 18, no. 5, pp. 623–39.

Corbridge, S. and Harriss, J. (2000) *Reinventing India: Liberalization, Hindu Nationalism and Popular Democracy* (Cambridge: Polity Press).

Cotton, J. (1994) 'The State in the Asian NICs', *Asian Perspective*, vol. 18, no. 1, pp. 39–56.

——(1999) 'The "Haze" over Southeast Asia: Challenging the ASEAN Mode of Regional Engagement', *Pacific Affairs*, vol. 72, no. 3, pp. 331–51.

Cowen, N. and Shenton, R. (1998) *Doctrines of Development* (London: Routledge).

Cox, R.W. (1981) 'Social Forces, States and World Orders: Beyond International Relations Theory', *Millennium: Journal of International Studies*, vol. 10, no. 2, pp. 126–55.

——(1983) 'Gramsci, Hegemony and International Relations: An Essay in Method', *Millennium: Journal of International Studies*, vol. 12, no. 2, pp. 162–75.

——(1987) *Production, Power and World Order: Social Forces in the Making of History* (New York NY: Columbia University Press).

Crane, G.T. and Amawi, A. (eds) (1991) *The Theoretical Evolution of International Political Economy: A Reader* (New York NY: Oxford University Press).

Crone, D. (1993) 'Does Hegemony Matter? The Reorganization of the Pacific Political Economy', *World Politics*, vol. 45, no. 4, pp. 501–25.

Cumings, B. (1984) 'The Origins and Development of the Northeast Asian Political Economy: Industrial Sectors, Product Cycles, and Political Consequences', *International Organization*, vol. 38, no. 1, pp. 1–40.

——(1987) 'The Origins and Development of the Northeast Asian Political Economy: Industrial Sectors, Product Cycles, and Political Consequences', in F.C. Deyo (ed.), *The Political Economy of the New East Asian Industrialism* (New York NY: Cornell University Press), pp. 44–83.

Cummings, R. (1992) 'A Historical Perspective on the Lagos Plan of Action', in J. Nyang'oro and T. Shaw (eds), *Beyond Structural Adjustment in Africa* (New York NY: Praeger), pp. 29–49.

D'Anieri, P. (1999) *Economic Interdependence in Ukrainian–Russian Relations* (Albany NY: State University of New York Press).

Davidson, B. (1992) *The Black Man's Burden: The Curse of the Nation-State in Africa* (London: James Currey).

Davis, E. (1991) 'Theorizing Statecraft and Social Change in Arab Oil-Producing Countries', in E. Davis and N. Gavrielides (eds), *Statecraft in the Middle East* (Miami FL: Florida International University Press), pp. 1–35.

Dawisha, K. and Parrott, B. (1994) *Russia and the New States of Eurasia: The Politics of Upheaval* (Cambridge: Cambridge University Press).

——(1997a) *Democratic Changes and Authoritarian Reactions on Russia, Ukraine, Belarus and Moldova* (Cambridge: Cambridge University Press).

——(eds) (1997b) *Conflict, Cleavage and Change in Central Asia and the Caucasus* (Cambridge: Cambridge University Press).

Deans, P. (2000) 'The Capitalist Developmental State in East Asia', in R. Palan and J. Abbott with P. Deans, *State Strategies in the Global Political Economy* (London: Pinter), pp. 78–102.

de Paiva Abreu, M. (2002) 'The Political Economy of Economic Integration in the Americas', paper presented at the IDB/INTAL Conference on 'Economic Integration in the Americas: Prospects and Policy Issues', Punta del Este, 15–16 December.

——(2003) 'Latin American and Caribbean Interests in the WTO', in D. Tussie (ed.), *Trade Negotiations in Latin America: Problems and Prospects* (London: Palgrave Macmillan), pp. 19–31.

Department for International Development (2001) *Working in Partnership with the European Community*, available at http://www.dfid.gov.uk/Pubs/files/ec_isp.pdf

de Rynck, S. and McAleavy, P. (2001) 'The Cohesion Deficit in Structural Fund Policy', *Journal of European Public Policy*, vol. 8, no. 4, pp. 541–57.

Diamantopoulou, A. (2000) 'The European Identity in a Global Economy', speech to the Europe Horizons Conference, Sintra, 18 February, available at http://europa.eu.int/comm/dgs/employment_social/speeches/00021ad.pdf

——(2002) 'European Integration and Governance: Challenges and Opportunities', address to the Institute of European Studies, University of Montreal, 25 April, available at http://europa.eu.int/comm/dgs/employment_social/speeches/250402ad.pdf

Dirlik, A. (1997) 'Critical Reflections on "Chinese Capitalism" as Paradigm', *Identities*, vol. 3, no. 3, pp. 303–30.

Dixit, J.N. (1996) *My South Block Years: Memoirs of a Foreign Secretary* (Delhi: UBPSD).

——(1998) *Across Borders: 50 Years of India's Foreign Policy* (Delhi: Picus Books).

Domínguez, J.I. and Fernández de Castro, R. (2001) *The United States and Mexico: Between Partnership and Conflict* (New York NY: Routledge).

Doornbos, M. (2001) ' "Good Governance": The Rise and Decline of a Policy Metaphor', *The Journal of Development Studies*, vol. 37, no. 6, pp. 93–108.

Downie, S. (2001) 'Cambodia', in P. Heenan and M. Lamontagne (eds), *The Southeast Asia Handbook* (Chicago IL: Fitzroy Dearborn), pp. 132–44.

Drifte, R. (1999) *Japan's Quest for a Permanent Security Council Seat: A Matter of Pride or Justice?* (London: Palgrave Macmillan).

Duffield, M. (1993) 'NGOs, Disaster Relief and Asset Transfer in the Horn: Political Survival in a Permanent Emergency', *Development and Change*, vol. 24, no. 1, pp. 131–57.

ECHO (n.d.) 'Echo's mandate', available at http://europa.eu.int/comm/echo/presentation/mandate_en.htm

ECLAC (UN Economic Commission for Latin America and the Caribbean) (2001) *Foreign Investment in Latin America and the Caribbean, 2000 Report* (New York NY: United Nations).

—— (2002a) *Panorama de la inserción internacional de América Latina y el Caribe, 2001–2002* (Santiago: ECLAC).

—— (2002b) *Anuario Estadístico de América Latina y el Caribe 2002* (New York NY: United Nations).

Economist Intelligence Unit (1991) *USSR: Country Profile 1991–1992* (London: EIU).

—— (1998–9) *Ghana Country Profile* (London: EIU).

El-Ghonemy, M.R. (1998) *Affluence and Poverty in the Middle East* (London: Routledge).

Elliott, L. (2001) 'Environmental Challenges', in D. Singh and A. Smith (eds), *Southeast Asian Affairs 2001* (Singapore: Institute for Southeast Asian Studies), pp. 68–81.

Ellman, M. and Kontorovich, V. (eds) (1992) *The Disintegration of the Soviet Economic System* (London: Routledge).

Elson, R. (1992) 'International Commerce, the State and Society: Economic and Social Change', in N. Tarling (ed.), *The Cambridge History of Southeast Asia: Volume Two, The Nineteenth and Twentieth Centuries* (Cambridge: Cambridge University Press), pp. 131–95.

Escobar, A. (1995) *Encountering Development: The Making and Unmaking of the Third World* (Princeton NJ: Princeton University Press).

Esping-Andersen, G. (1990) *Three Worlds of Welfare Capitalism* (Cambridge: Polity Press).

Esteva, G. (1992) 'Development', in W. Sachs (ed.), *The Development Dictionary: A Guide to Knowledge as Power* (London: Zed), pp. 6–25.

European Bank for Reconstruction and Development (2000) *Transition Report* (London: EBRD).

European Commission (2000a) *Operational Coordination between the European Community and the Member States of the European Union in the Field of Development Co-operation* COM(2000)108 final.

—— (2000b) *Working for the Regions*, Office for Official Publications of the European Communities, Luxembourg.

—— (2001) *The EU's relations with the Former Yugoslav Republic of Macedonia*, available at http://europa.eu.int/comm/external_relations/see/fyrom/index.htm

—— (2002) *Towards the Enlarged Union: Strategy Paper and Report of the European Commission on the Progress towards Accession by Each of the Candidate Countries* COM(2002)700 final, available at http://europa.eu.int/comm/enlargement/report2002/strategy_en.pdf

European Commission (2003) *Making Globalisation Work for Everyone: The European Union and World Trade*, Office for Official Publications of the European Communities, Luxembourg.

European Council (2000) *Presidency Conclusions: Santa Maria da Fiera European Council, 19 and 20 June 2000*, available at http://ue.eu.int/Newsroom/loadDoc.asp?max=1&bid=76&did=62050&grp=2587&lang=1

Evans, M.L. (2001) 'U.S. Drug Policy and Intelligence Operations in the Andes', *Foreign Policy in Focus*, vol. 6, no. 22, available at http://www.fpif.org/

Evans, P. (1995) *Embedded Autonomy: States and Industrial Transformation* (Princeton NJ: Princeton University Press).

——(1997) 'The Eclipse of the State? Reflections on Stateness in an Era of Globalization', *World Politics*, vol. 50, no. 1, pp. 62–87.

Ewing, W.A. (2003) 'Immigration Accord on Hold While Failed Border Enforcement Policies Continue', Policy Brief, Americas Program, Interhemispheric Resource Center, 13 June, available at http://www.americaspolicy.org

Farouk-Sluglett, M. and Sluglett, P. (1990) *Iraq since 1958* (London: I.B. Tauris).

Fauriol, G.A. and Weintraub, S. (2001) 'The Century of the Americas: Dawn of a New Century Dynamic', *The Washington Quarterly*, vol. 24, no. 2, pp. 139–48.

Fawcett, L. and Hurrell, A. (eds) (1995) *Regionalism in World Politics* (Oxford: Oxford University Press).

Fernández de Castro, R. and Rosales, C.A. (2000) 'Migration Issues: Raising the Stakes in US–Latin American Relations', in J.I. Domínguez (ed.), *The Future of Inter-American Relations* (New York NY: Routledge), pp. 237–58.

Fernández de Castro, R. and Rozental, A. (2003) 'El amor, la decepción y cómo aprovechar la realidad: La relación México-Estados Unidos 2000–2003', mimeo, Mexico City, July.

Fine, B. and Rustomjee, Z. (1995) *The Political Economy of South Africa* (London: C. Hurst).

Fine, B., Lapavitsas, C. and Pincus, J. (eds) (2001) *Development Policy in the Twenty-first Century: Beyond the Post-Washington Consensus* (London: Routledge).

First, R. (1983) *Black Gold: The Mozambican Miner, Proletarian and Peasant* (Hemel Hempstead: Wheatsheaf/Harvester Press).

Forrest, T. (1995) *Politics and Economic Development in Nigeria* (Boulder CO: Westview Press).

Frost, F. (1990) 'Introduction: ASEAN since 1967 – Origins, Evolution and Recent Developments', in A. Broinowski (ed.), *ASEAN into the 1990s* (London: Palgrave Macmillan), pp. 1–31.

Fry, G.W. and Faming, M.N. (2001) 'Laos', in P. Heenan and M. Lamontagne (eds), *The Southeast Asia Handbook* (Chicago IL: Fitzroy Dearborn), pp. 145–56.

Funabashi, Y. (1993) 'The Asianization of Asia', *Foreign Affairs*, vol. 72, no. 5, pp. 75–85.

Gaddy, C. and Ickes, B. (1998) 'Russia's Virtual Economy', *Foreign Affairs*, vol. 77, no. 5, pp. 53–67.

Gambari, I. (1996) 'The Role of Regional and Global Organizations in Addressing Africa's Security Issues', in E. Keller and D. Rothchild (eds), *Africa in the New International Order: Rethinking State Sovereignty and Regional Security* (Boulder CO: Lynne Rienner), pp. 29–37.

Gamble, A.M. and Payne, A.J. (eds) (1996) *Regionalism and World Order* (London: Palgrave Macmillan).

——(1996) 'Conclusion: The New Regionalism', in A.M. Gamble and A.J. Payne (eds), *Regionalism and World Order* (London: Palgrave Macmillan), pp. 247–64.

Gangopadhyay, P. (1998) 'Patterns of Trade, Investment and Migration in the Asia-Pacific Region', in G. Thompson (ed.), *Economic Dynamism in the Asia-Pacific* (London: Routledge), pp. 20–54.

Gavin, B. (2003) 'The Role of the European Union in Global Financial Governance', United Nations University/College of Europe, Bruges, mimeo, available at http://europa.eu.int/futurum/forum_convention/documents/contrib/acad/0115_r_en.pdf

Gerber, H. (1987) *The Social Origins of the Modern Middle East* (Boulder CO: Lynne Rienner).

Gibb, R. (1998) 'Southern Africa in Transition: Prospects and Problems Facing Regional Integration', *Journal of Modern African Studies*, vol. 36, no. 2, pp. 287–306.

Giddens, A. (1990) *The Consequences of Modernity* (Cambridge: Polity Press).

Gilpin, R. (1975) *U.S. Power and the Multinational Corporation: The Political Economy of U.S. Foreign Direct Investment* (New York NY: Basic Books).

Gilson, J.A. (2002) *Asia Meets Europe: Inter-Regionalism and the Asia–Europe Meeting* (Cheltenham: Edward Elgar).

Gleason, G. (2001) 'Interstate Cooperation in Central Asia', *Europe–Asia Studies*, vol. 53, no. 7, pp. 1077–95.

Godement, F. (1998) *The Downsizing of Asia* (London: Routledge).

Goldman, M. (1983) *USSR in Crisis* (New York NY: W.W. Norton).

Gomez, E.T. and Jomo, K.S. (1999) *Malaysia's Political Economy: Politics, Patronage and Profits* (Cambridge: Cambridge University Press).

Goodin, R.E. (1992) *Green Political Theory* (Cambridge: Polity Press).

Goodin, R.E., Headey, B., Muffels, R. and Diren, H.-J. (1999) *The Real Worlds of Welfare Capitalism* (Cambridge: Cambridge University Press).

Goskomstat (2000) *Rossiiskii statisticheskii ezhegodnik* (Moscow: Goskomstat Rossii).

Goskomstat SSSR (1987) *SSSR v tsifrakh v 1987 godu* (Moscow: Finansy i Statistika).

Government of India (2003) 'Economic Survey 2001–2002' (New Delhi: Ministry of Finance), available at http://indiabudget.nic.in/es2001-02/welcome.html

Greider, W. (1997) *One World, Ready or Not: The Magic Logic of Global Capitalism* (New York NY: Simon & Schuster).

Griffith, I. (2000) 'Transnational Crime in the Americas: A Reality Check', in J.I. Domínguez (ed.), *The Future of Inter-American Relations* (New York NY: Routledge), pp. 63–86.

Grubb, M. with Vrolijk, C. and Brack, D. (1999) *The Kyoto Protocol: A Guide and Assessment* (London: Royal Institute of International Affairs).

Guhan, S. (1995) *The World Bank's Lending in South Asia* (Washington DC: Brookings Institution).

Haas, E.B. (1958) *The Uniting of Europe: Political, Social and Economic Forces, 1950–1957* (Stanford CA: Stanford University Press).

——(1964) *Beyond the Nation State: Functionalism and International Organization* (Stanford CA: Stanford University Press).

Hadiz, V. (1997) *Workers and the State in New Order Indonesia* (London: Routledge).

Haggard, S. (1990). *Pathways from the Periphery: The Politics of Growth in the Newly Industrializing Countries* (New York NY: Cornell University Press).

——(2000) *The Political Economy of the Asian Financial Crisis* (Washington DC: Institute for International Economics).

Hall, P. and Soskice, D. (eds) (2001) *Varieties of Capitalism: The Institutional Foundations of Comparative Advantage* (Oxford: Oxford University Press).

Halliday, F. (1979) *Iran: Dictatorship and Development* (London: Penguin).

Hamilton, C. (1986) *Capitalist Industrialism in Korea* (Boulder CO: Westview Press).

Harding, J. (1997) 'The Mercenary Business: "Executive Outcomes"', *Review of African Political Economy*, vol. 24, no. 71, pp. 87–97.

Harris, N. (1986) *The End of the Third World: Newly Industrialising Countries and the Decline of an Ideology* (London: I.B. Tauris).

Harrison, G. (2001) 'Post-Adjustment Politics and Administrative Reform: Reflections on the Cases of Uganda and Tanzania', *Development and Change*, vol. 32, no. 4, pp. 657–81.

——(2002) *Issues in the Contemporary Politics of Sub Saharan Africa* (London: Palgrave Macmillan).

Harriss-White, B. (2003) *India Working: Essays on Society and Economy* (Cambridge: Cambridge University Press).

Hartcher, P. (2001) 'From Miracle to Malaise: Southeast Asia goes South', *The National Interest*, Spring, pp. 76–85.

Hatch, W. (1998) 'Grounding Asia's Flying Geese: The Costs of Depending Heavily on Japanese Capital and Technology', *National Bureau of Asian Research Briefing Paper*, Seattle WA.

Hatch, W. and Yamamura, K. (1996) *Asia in Japan's Embrace: Building a Regional Production Alliance* (Cambridge: Cambridge University Press).

Hay, C. (2000) 'Contemporary Capitalism, Globalisation, Regionalisation and the Persistence of National Variation', *Review of International Studies*, vol. 26, no. 4, pp. 509–31.

Hay, C. and Marsh, D. (eds) (2000) *Demystifying Globalization* (London: Palgrave Macmillan).

Hay, C. and Rosamond, B. (2002) 'Globalization, European Integration and the Discursive Construction of Economic Imperatives', *Journal of European Public Policy*, vol. 9, no. 2, pp. 147–67.

Held, D., McGrew, A., Goldblatt, D. and Perraton, J. (1999) *Global Transformations: Politics, Economics and Culture* (Cambridge: Polity Press).

Henderson, J. (1999) 'Reassessing ASEAN', *Adelphi Paper no. 328* (New York NY: Oxford University Press).

Heron, T. (2004) *The New Political Economy of US–Caribbean Relations: The Apparel Industry and the Politics of NAFTA Parity* (London: Ashgate).

Herring, R. (1994) 'Explaining Sri Lanka's Exceptionalism: Popular Responses to Welfarism and the "Open Economy"', in J. Walton and D. Seddon (eds), *Free Markets and Food Riots: The Politics of Global Adjustment* (Oxford: Blackwell), pp. 253–87.

Hettne, B. (1993) 'Neo-Mercantilism: The Pursuit of Regionness', *Cooperation and Conflict*, vol. 28, no. 3, pp. 211–32.

——(1995) *Development Theory and the Three Worlds: Towards an International Political Economy of Development* (Harlow: Longman).

Hettne, B. and Inotai, A. (1994) *The New Regionalism: Implications for Global Development and International Security* (Helsinki: United Nations University World Institute for Development Economics Research).

Hettne, B., Payne, A.J. and Söderbaum, F. (1999) 'Rethinking Development Theory: Guest Editors' Introduction', *Journal of International Relations and Development*, vol. 2, no. 4, pp. 354–7.

Hewison, K. (1997) 'Thailand: Capitalist Development and the State', in G. Rodan *et al.* (eds), *The Political Economy of South-East Asia: An Introduction* (Melbourne: Oxford University Press), pp. 93–120.

——(2000) 'Resisting Globalization: A Study of Localism in Thailand', *The Pacific Review*, vol. 13, no. 2, pp. 279–96.

Hewitt, V.M. (1997) *The New International Politics of South Asia* (Manchester: Manchester University Press).

Hibou, B. (1999) 'The "Social Capital" of the State as an Agent of Deception', in J. Bayart, S. Ellis and B. Hibou, *The Criminalization of the State in Africa* (London: James Currey), pp. 69–114.

Higgott, R. (1994) 'International Political Economy', in A.J.R. Groom and M. Light (eds), *Contemporary International Relations: A Guide to Theory* (London: Pinter), pp. 156–69.

——(2000) 'The International Relations of the Asian Economic Crisis: A Study in the Politics of Resentment', in R. Robison *et al.* (eds), *Politics and Markets in the Wake of the Asian Crisis* (London: Routledge), pp. 261–82.

Hill, H. (1996) *The Indonesian Economy since 1966* (Cambridge: Cambridge University Press).

Hinnebusch, R. (2002), 'Introduction: The Analytical Framework', in R. Hinnebusch and A. Ehteshami (eds), *The Foreign Policies of Middle East States* (Boulder CO: Lynne Rienner), pp. 1–27.

Hinnebusch, R. and Ehteshami, A. (eds) (2002) *The Foreign Policies of Middle East States* (Boulder CO: Lynne Rienner).

Hiranuma, T. (2002) 'Sugu soko ni aru kiki, shitsugyo maneku kudoka wa koshite kaihi suru (How to Avoid a Hollowed Out Industry That Will Lead to Unemployment)', *Toyo Keizai*, 5 January.

Hirsch, P. and Warren, C. (1998) 'Introduction: Through the Environmental Looking Glass', in P. Hirsch and C. Warren (eds), *The Politics of Environments in Southeast Asia: Resources and Resistance* (London: Routledge), pp. 1–25.

Hirst, P. and Thompson, G. (1996) *Globalization in Question: The International Economy and the Possibilities of Governance* (Cambridge: Polity Press).

Ho, K.L. (2001) 'Rituals, Risks and Rivalries: China and ASEAN in the Coming Decades', *Journal of Contemporary China*, vol. 10, no. 29, pp. 683–94.

Hodges, T. (2001) *Angola: From Afro Stalinism to Petro-diamond Capitalism* (London: James Currey).

Holland, M. (2002a) *The European Union and the Third World* (London: Palgrave Macmillan).

——(2002b) 'When is Foreign Policy not Foreign Policy? Cotonou, CFSP and External Relations with the Developing World', *National Europe Centre Paper* no. 28, Australian National University.

——(2003) '20/20 Vision? The EU's Cotonou Partnership Agreement', *Brown Journal of World Affairs*, vol. 9, no. 2, pp. 161–75.

Hollerman, L. (1991) 'The Headquarters Nation', *The National Interest*, no. 25, pp. 16–25.

Hollingsworth, J.R. and Boyer, R. (eds) (1997) *Contemporary Capitalism: The Embeddedness of Institutions* (Cambridge: Cambridge University Press).

Hooghe, L. and Marks, G. (2001) *Multi-Level Governance and European Integration* (Lanham NJ: Rowman & Littlefield).

Hooglund, E. (1992) 'Iranian Populism and Political Change in the Gulf', in *Middle East Report*, no. 174, pp. 19–21.

Hoogvelt, A. (1997) *Globalization and the Postcolonial World: The New Political Economy of Development* (London: Palgrave Macmillan).

Hook, G. (1999) 'The East Asian Economic Caucus: A Case of Reactive Subregionalism?', in G. Hook and I. Kearns (eds), *Subregionalism and World Order* (London: Palgrave Macmillan), pp. 223–45.

Hook, G. and Kearns, I. (eds) (1999) *Subregionalism and World Order* (London: Palgrave Macmillan).

Hook, G., Gilson, J., Hughes, C. and Dobson, H. (2001) *Japan's International Relations: Politics, Economics and Security* (London: Routledge).

Hormeku, T. (n.d.) 'The New Era Option – Strategic Options for ACP Regions', *TWN Africa*, available at http://twnafrica.org/print.asp?twnID=182

Hornik, R. (2002) 'Who Needs Hong Kong?', *Fortune*, 2 May.

Hossain, M., Islam, I. and Kibria, R. (1999) *South Asian Economic Development: Transformation, Opportunities and Challenges* (London: Routledge).

Hou, J. (2002) 'China's FDI Policy and Taiwanese Direct Investment (TDI) in China', Centre for Economic Development Working Paper no. 0206, Hong Kong University of Science and Technology, Hong Kong.

Howe, H. (1998) 'Private Security Forces and African Stability: The Case of Executive Outcomes', *Journal of Modern African Studies*, vol. 36, no. 2, pp. 307–31.

Hughes, C. (2000) 'Japanese Policy and the East Asian Currency Crisis: Abject Defeat or Quiet Victory?', *Review of International Political Economy*, vol. 7, no. 2, pp. 219–53.

Huntington, S. (1991) *The Third Wave* (Norman OK: University of Oklahoma Press).

Hurrell, A. and Woods, N. (eds) (1999) *Inequality, Globalization and World Politics* (Oxford: Oxford University Press).

Husain, I. (1999) *Pakistan: The Economy of an Elitist State* (Karachi: Oxford University Press).

Hussain, A. (2001) 'Vietnam', in P. Heenan and M. Lamontagne (eds), *The Southeast Asia Handbook* (Chicago IL: Fitzroy Dearborn), pp. 121–31.

Hutchcroft, P.D. (1998) *Booty Capitalism: The Politics of Banking in the Philippines* (New York NY: Cornell University Press).

Hutzler, C. (2002) 'China's New Leadership Indicates Change of Focus', *Wall Street Journal*, 25 February.

Huxtable, P. and Villalon, L. (1998) *The African State at a Critical Conjuncture: Between Disintegration and Reconfiguration* (Boulder CO: Lynne Rienner).

IDB (Inter-American Development Bank) (2002) *Integration and Trade in the Americas, Periodic Note, December 2000* (Washington DC: IDB).

Iftekharuzzaman (1998) 'Bangladesh: A Weak State and Power', in M. Alagappa (ed.), *Asian Security Practice: Material and Ideational Influences* (Stanford CA: Stanford University Press), pp. 315–37.

Ikenberry, G.J. (1989) 'Rethinking the Origins of American Hegemony', *Political Science Quarterly*, vol. 104, no. 3, pp. 375–400.

Isacson, A. (2001) 'Militarizing Latin America Policy', *Foreign Policy in Focus*, vol. 6, no. 21, available at http://www.fpif.org/

Issawi, C. (1982) *An Economic History of the Middle East and North Africa* (London: Methuen).

—— (1995) *The Middle East Economy* (Princeton NJ: Markus Wiener).

Jackson, R (1990) *Quasi-states: Sovereignty, International Relations, and the Third World* (Cambridge: Cambridge University Press).

Jahan, R. (2003) 'Bangladesh in 2002: Imperilled Democracy', *Asian Survey*, vol. 43, no. 1, pp. 222–9.

Jalal, A. (1990) 'State-Building in the Post-war World: Britain's Colonial Legacy, American Futures and Pakistan', in S. Bose (ed.), *South Asia and World Capitalism* (Delhi: Oxford University Press), pp. 262–304.

Johnson, C. (1982) *MITI and the Japanese Miracle: The Growth of Industrial Policy, 1925–1975* (Stanford CA: Stanford University Press).

—— (1987) 'Political Institutions and Economic Performance: The Government–Business Relationship in Japan, South Korea, and Taiwan', in F.C. Deyo (ed.), *The Political Economy of the New East Asian Industrialism* (New York NY: Cornell University Press), pp. 136–64.

Johnson, L. and Archer, C. (eds) (1996) *Peacekeeping and the Role of Russia in Eurasia* (Boulder CO: Westview Press).

Johnson, O. (1991) 'Economic Integration in Africa: Enhancing Prospects for Success', *Journal of Modern African Studies*, vol. 29, no. 1, pp. 1–26.

Jomo, K.S. (1997) *Southeast Asia's Misunderstood Miracle: Industry Policy and Economic Development in Thailand, Malaysia, and Indonesia* (Boulder CO: Westview Press).

Jönsson, C., Tägil, S. and Törnqvist, G. (2000) *Organizing European Space* (London: Sage).

Jørgensen, K.E. and Rosamond, B. (2002) 'Europe: Regional Laboratory for a Global Polity?', in M. Ougaard and R. Higgott (eds), *Towards a Global Polity* (London: Routledge), pp. 189–206.

Joyce, E. (1999) 'Packaging Drugs: Certification and the Acquisition of Leverage', in V. Bulmer-Thomas and J. Dunkerley (eds), *The United States and Latin America: The New Agenda* (London: Institute of Latin American Studies), pp. 207–25.

Kalinichenko, L. and Semenova, N. (2001) 'The Economy of Kazakhstan', in A. Vassiliev (ed.), *Central Asia* (London: Saqi), pp. 55–78.

Kaplinsky, R. (2000) 'Globalisation and Unequalisation: What can be Learned from Value Chain Analysis?', *Journal of Development Studies*, vol. 37, no. 2, pp. 117–46.

Kapur, A. (2001) 'Pokhran II and After: Consequences of the Indian Nuclear Tests of 1998', in A. Shastri and A.J. Wilson (eds), *The Postcolonial States of South Asia: Democracy, Identity, Development and Security* (London: Curzon Press), pp. 326–44.

Karshenas, M. (1990) *Oil, State and Industrialisation in Iran* (Cambridge: Cambridge University Press).

Katz, J. (2000) 'El nuevo modelo económico latinoamericano: Aspectos de eficiencia y equidad que questionan su sustentabilidad de largo plazo', mimeo, Santiago de Chile.

Kedourie, E. (1992) *Politics in the Middle East* (Oxford: Oxford University Press).

Kelegama, S. (2001) 'Sri Lankan Economy in Turbulent Times: Budget 2001 and IMF Package', *Economic and Political Weekly*, vol. 36, no. 28, pp. 2665–73.

Kelly, J. and Romero, C.A. (2002) *The United States and Venezuela: Rethinking a Relationship* (New York NY: Routledge).

Keohane, R.O. (1984) *After Hegemony: Cooperation and Discord in the World Political Economy* (Princeton NJ: Princeton University Press).

—— and Nye, J. (1972) *Transnational Relations and World Politics* (Cambridge MA: Harvard University Press).

—— and Nye, J. (1977) *Power and Interdependence* (Boston MA: Little, Brown & Co.).

Kerr, D. (1996) 'Opening and Closing the Sino-Russian Border: Trade, Regional Development and Political Interest in North-east Asia', *Europe–Asia Studies*, vol. 48, no. 6, pp. 931–58.

Keyder, C. (1987) *State and Class in Turkey* (London: Verso).

Khadka, N. (1998) 'Challenges to Developing the Economy of Nepal', *Contemporary South Asia*, vol. 7, no. 2, pp. 147–65.

Khanna, J. (ed.) (1995) *Southern China, Hong Kong, and Taiwan: Evolution of a Subregional Economy* (Washington DC: Center for Strategic and International Studies).

Khor, M. (2001) 'WTO Sorely Lacking in Neutrality', available at http://thestar.com.my, 16 July.

Kindleberger, C.P. (1973) *The World in Depression 1929–39* (Berkeley CA: University of California Press).

Kivimäki, T. (2001) 'The Long Peace of ASEAN', *Journal of Peace Research*, vol. 38, no. 1, pp. 5–25.

Klein, W.F. (2000) *El MERCOSUR: Empresarios y sindicatos frente a los desafíos del proceso de integración* (Caracas: Editorial Nueva Sociedad).

Knodt, M. and Princen, S. (eds) (2003) *Understanding the European Union's External Relations* (London: Routledge).

Kochanek, S. (1993) *Patron–Client Politics and Business in Bangladesh* (New Delhi: Sage).

——(1996) 'The Rise of Interest Politics in Bangladesh', *Asian Survey*, vol. 36, no. 7, pp. 704–22.

Köhler, H. (2002) 'Japan and the IMF: 50 Years of Economic Progress and International Leadership', speech at Symposium to Commemorate 50th Anniversary of Japan's Membership in The International Monetary Fund and the World Bank, Tokyo, 10 September.

Kolko, G. (1997) *Vietnam: Anatomy of a Peace* (London: Routledge).

Korany, B. and Dessouki, A. (eds) (1991) *The Foreign Policies of Arab States* 2nd edn (Boulder CO: Westview Press).

Korhonen, P. (1997) 'Monopolizing Asia: The Politics of a Metaphor', *The Pacific Review*, vol. 10, no. 3, pp. 347–65.

Kornai, J. (1992) *The Socialist System: The Political Economy of Communism* (Oxford: Clarendon Press).

Kuzin, D. (1993) 'Rossiiskaya ekonomika na mirovom rynke: problema konkurentosposobnosti', *Obshchestvo in ekonomika*, no. 3, pp. 32–44.

Kuznetsov, A. (1994) *Foreign Investment in Contemporary Russia* (London: Palgrave Macmillan).

Kwa, A. (2001) 'WTO Agricultural Negotiations: A Sorry Tale of American Arrogance, European Hypocrisy and Developing Countries in Disarray', *Focus on Trade*, no. 65, August (Bangkok: Focus on the Global South), available at http://focusweb.org

Kwan, C. (1994) *Economic Interdependence in the Asia Pacific Region: Towards a Yen Bloc* (London: Routledge).

Laffan, B., O'Donnell, R. and Smith, M. (eds) (2000) *Europe's Experimental Union: Rethinking Integration* (London: Routledge).

Lall, S. (1999) 'India's Manufactured Exports: Comparative Structure and Prospects', *World Development*, vol. 27, no. 10, pp. 1769–86.

Leaver, R. (1989) 'Restructuring in the Global Economy: From the Pax Americana to Pax Nipponica?', *Alternatives*, vol. 14, no. 4, pp. 429–62.

Leaver, R. (1994) 'International Political Economy and the Changing World Order: Evolution or Involution?', in R. Stubbs and G. Underhill (eds), *Political Economy and the Changing Global Order* (London: Palgrave Macmillan), pp. 130–41.

Le Billon, P. (2001) 'Angola's Political Economy of War: The Role of Oil and Diamonds, 1975–2000', *African Affairs*, vol. 100, no. 398, pp. 55–81.

Leftwich, A. (1995) 'Bringing Politics Back In: Towards a Model of the Developmental State', *Journal of Development Studies*, vol. 31, no. 3, pp. 400–27.

Leggett, J. (2000) *The Carbon War* (London: Penguin).

Leifer, M. (1996) 'The Asean Regional Forum', *Adelphi Paper*, no. 302 (London: International Institute for Strategic Studies).

Leo, C. (1984) *Land and Class in Kenya* (Toronto: University of Toronto Press).

Lewis, B. (1998) *The Multiple Identities of the Middle East* (London: Methuen).

—— (2002) *What Went Wrong?* (London: Weidenfeld & Nicolson).

—— (2003) *The Crisis of Islam* (London: Weidenfeld & Nicolson).

Leys, C. (1996) 'The Crisis in "Development Theory"', *New Political Economy*, vol. 1, no. 1, pp. 41–58.

Linder, S. (1986) *Pacific Century: Economic and Political Consequences of Asian-Pacific Dynamism* (Stanford CA: Stanford University Press).

Lintner, B. (2001) 'Laos: Signs of Unrest', in D. Singh and A. Smith (eds), *Southeast Asian Affairs 2001* (Singapore: Institute for Southeast Asian Studies), pp. 177–86.

Linz, J. and Stepan, A. (1996) *Problems of Democratic Transition and Consolidation* (Baltimore MD: Johns Hopkins University Press).

Loungani, P. and Mauro, P. (2001) 'Capital Flight from Russia', *World Economy*, vol. 24, no. 5, pp. 689–706.

Love, R. (1994) 'Drought, Dutch Disease, and Controlled Transition in Botswana Agriculture', *Journal of Southern African Studies*, vol. 20, no. 1, pp. 71–85.

Loxley, J. (2003) 'Imperialism and Economic Reform: NEPAD', *Review of African Political Economy*, vol. 30, no. 95, pp. 119–28.

Luciani, C. (ed.) (1990) *The Arab State* (London: Routledge).

Luck, E.C. (1999) *Mixed Messages: American Politics and International Organization, 1919–1999* (Washington DC: Brookings Institution Press).

MacGaffey, J. (1991) *The Real Economy of Zaire* (London: James Currey).

Mahbub ul Haq Human Development Centre (HDC) (2001) *Human Development in South Asia 2001: Globalisation and Human Development* (Oxford: Oxford University Press).

Malaquias, A. (2001) 'Making War and Lots of Money: The Political Economy of Protracted Conflict in Africa', *Review of African Political Economy*, vol. 90, no. 28, pp. 521–36.

Malone, D.M. (2003) 'US–UN Relations in the UN Security Council in the Post-Cold War Era', in R. Foot, S.N. MacFarlane and M. Mastanduno (eds), *US Hegemony and International Organizations* (Oxford: Oxford University Press), pp. 73–91.

Mamdani, M. (1995) 'Democratization and Marketization', in K. Mengisteab and B. Logan (eds), *Beyond Economic Liberalization in Africa* (London: Zed), pp. 17–21.

—— (1996) *Citizen and Subject* (London: James Currey).

Manet, P. (2001) 'Doha Confirms the WTO's Ultraliberal Ideology', ATTAC Press Release, 15 November, available at http://attac.org/fra/asso/doc/doc75en.htm

Mann, M. (1997) 'Has Globalization Ended the Rise and Rise of the Nation-state?', *Review of International Political Economy*, vol. 4, no. 3, pp. 472–96.

Manners, I. (2002) 'Normative Power Europe: A Contradiction in Terms?', *Journal of Common Market Studies*, vol. 40, no. 2, pp. 235–58.

Marcella, G. (2003) 'The United States and Colombia: The Journey from Ambiguity to Strategic Clarity', North–South Center Working Paper Series, no. 13, March, pp. 1–43.

Marks, G. (1993) 'Structural Funds and Multilevel Governance in the EC', in A. Cafruny and G.G. Rosenthal (eds), *The State of the European Community Volume II* (Boulder CO: Lynne Rienner), pp. 391–410.

Marsh, D. (1995) 'The Convergence between Theories of the State', in D. Marsh and G. Stoker (eds), *Theory and Methods in Political Science* (London: Palgrave Macmillan), pp. 268–87.

Martin, P.L. and Teitelbaum, M.S. (2001) 'The Mirage of Mexican Guest Workers', *Foreign Affairs*, November/December, online version, pp. 1–9.

Mastanundo, M. (2000) 'Models, Markets and Power: Political Economy and the Asia-Pacific, 1989–1999', *Review of International Studies*, vol. 26, no. 4, pp. 493–507.

Mathou, T. (2001) 'Bhutan in 2000: Challenges Ahead', *Asian Survey*, vol. 41, no. 1, pp. 131–7.

McCord, W. (1996) *Dawn of the Pacific Century: Implications for Three Worlds of Development* (New York NY: Transaction Books).

McGowan, W. (1993) *Only Man is Vile: The Tragedy of Sri Lanka* (London: Picador).

McKinnon, R. (1993) *The Order of Economic Liberalization*, 2nd edn (Baltimore MD: Johns Hopkins University Press).

McMichael, P. (2000) *Development and Social Change: A Global Perspective* (Thousand Oaks CA: Pine Forge Press).

Menon, R. and Spruyt, H. (1998) 'Possibilities for Conflict and Conflict Resolution in Post-Soviet Central Asia', in B. Rubin and J. Snyder (eds), *Post-Soviet Political Order: Conflict and State Building* (London: Routledge), pp. 104–27.

Michalopoulos, C. (1998) *The Participation of the Developing Countries in the WTO*, Policy Research Working Paper no. 1906, World Bank, New York.

Ministry of Finance (MOF) (Japan) (1998) 'A New Initiative to Overcome the Asian Currency Crisis – New Miyazawa Initiative', official statement, available at http://www.mof.go.jp/english/if/e1e042.htm

Mistry, P. (2000) 'Africa's Record of Regional Co-operation and Integration', *African Affairs*, vol. 99, no. 397, pp. 553–75.

Mittelman, J.H. (2000) 'Globalization: Captors or Captive', *Third World Quarterly*, vol. 21, no. 6, pp. 917–29.

Mkandawire, T. (1999) 'Crisis Management and the Making of "Choiceless Democracies"', in R. Joseph (ed.), *State, Conflict, and Democracy in Africa* (Boulder CO: Lynne Rienner), pp. 119–36.

Mody, A. and Negishi, S. (2001) 'Cross-border Mergers and Acquisitions in East Asia: Trends and Implications', *Finance & Development*, vol. 38, no. 1 (IMF on-line publication).

Mohtadi, H. (1998), 'Environmentally Sustainable Development in the Middle East and North Africa', in N. Sahfik (ed.), *Prospects for Middle Eastern and North African Economies* (London: Palgrave Macmillan), pp. 262–87.

Moody-Stuart, G. (1997) *Grand Corruption* (Oxford: World View).

Moore, M. (1990) 'Economic Liberalization versus Political Pluralism in Sri Lanka?', *Modern Asian Studies*, vol. 24, no. 2, pp. 341–83.

——(2001) 'Political Underdevelopment: What Causes "Bad Governance"', *Public Management Review*, vol. 3, no. 3, pp. 358–418.

Mosley, P., Harrigan, J. and Toye, J. (1991) *Aid and Power: The World Bank and Policy Based Lending* (London: Routledge).

Motyl, A.J. (2001) *Imperial Ends: The Decay, Collapse, and Revival of Empires* (New York NY: Columbia University Press).

Mshomba, R. (2000) *Africa in the Global Economy* (Boulder CO: Lynne Rienner).

Mudimbe, Y.V. (1998) *The Invention of Africa: Gnosis, Philosophy, and the Order of Knowledge* (London: James Currey).

Muñoz, H. (2001) 'Good-bye USA?', in J.S. Tulchin and R.H. Espach (eds), *Latin America in the New International System* (Boulder CO: Lynne Rienner), pp. 73–90.

Narine, S. (1998) 'ASEAN and the Management of Regional Security', *Pacific Affairs*, vol. 71, no. 2, pp. 195–214.

Naughton, B. (1997) 'The Emergence of the China Circle', in B. Naughton (ed.), *The China Circle: Economics and Electronics in the PRC, Taiwan, and Hong Kong* (Washington DC: Brookings Institution), pp. 3–40.

Navlakha, G. (2003) 'Nepal: From Battle of Arms to Battle of Ideas', *Economic and Political Weekly*, vol. 38, no. 11, pp. 1032–3.

Neher, C.D. (1994) *Southeast Asia in the New International Era* (Boulder CO: Westview Press).

——(2001) 'Burma', in P. Heenan and M. Lamontagne (eds), *The Southeast Asia Handbook* (Chicago IL: Fitzroy Dearborn), pp. 157–64.

Nesadurai, H. (2002) 'The Political Economy of the ASEAN Free Trade Area (AFTA): An Attempt at Developmental Regionalism', paper for Conference on 'Running on Empty? Politics, Markets and Southeast Asian Regionalism', City University of Hong Kong, 17–18 January.

Noman, O. (1990) *Pakistan: A Political and Economic History since 1947* (London: Kegan Paul).

Nugent, N. (1996) *Vietnam: The Second Revolution* (Brighton: Inprint).

Odén, B. (2000) 'The Southern African Region and the Regional Hegemon', in B. Hettne, A. Inotai and O. Sunkel (eds), *National Perspectives on the New Regionalism in the South* (London: Palgrave Macmillan), pp. 242–64.

O'Donnell, R. (1997) 'Irish Policy in a Global Context: From State Autonomy to Social Partnership', *European Planning Studies*, vol. 5, no. 4, pp. 545–58.

O'Dowd, L. (2002) 'The Changing Significance of European Borders', *Regional and Federal Studies*, vol. 12, no. 4, pp. 13–36.

OECD (2002) *Aid and Statistics: Donor Aid Charts* (Paris: OECD/DAC).

Oh, J.K-C. (1999) *Korean Politics: The Quest for Democratization and Economic Development* (New York NY: Cornell University Press).

Ohmae, K. (1995) *The End of the Nation State* (New York NY: Free Press).

Oman, C. (1994) *Globalisation and Regionalisation: The Challenge for Developing Countries* (Paris: Organization for Economic Cooperation and Development).

Osborne, M. (2000) *Southeast Asia: An Introductory History*, 8th edn (London: Allen & Unwin).

Overholt, W. (1994) *The Rise of China – How Economic Reform is Creating a New Superpower* (New York NY: Norton).

Owen, R. and Pamuk, S. (1998) *A History of Middle East Economies in the Twentieth Century* (London: I.B. Tauris).

Page, J. (1998) 'From Boom to Bust – and Back? The Crisis of Growth in the Middle East and North Africa', in N. Sahfik (ed.), *Prospects for Middle Eastern and North African Economies* (London: Palgrave Macmillan), pp. 133–58.

Pantojas-García, E. (2001) 'Trade Liberalization and Peripheral Postindustrialization in the Caribbean', *Latin American Politics and Society*, vol. 43, no. 1, pp. 57–77.

Paterson, M. (1996) *Global Warming and Global Politics* (London: Routledge).

Payne, A. (1996) 'The United States and its Enterprise for the Americas', in A.M. Gamble and A.J. Payne (eds), *Regionalism and World Order* (London: Palgrave Macmillan), pp. 93–129.

——(1998) 'The New Politics of "Caribbean America"', *Third World Quarterly*, vol. 19, no. 2, pp. 205–18.

——(1999) 'The Association of Caribbean States', in G. Hook and I. Kearns (eds), *Subregionalism and World Order* (London: Palgrave Macmillan), pp. 117–37.

Payne, A.J. and Gamble, A.M. (1996) 'Introduction: The Political Economy of Regionalism and World Order', in A.M. Gamble and A.J. Payne (eds), *Regionalism and World Order* (London: Palgrave Macmillan), pp. 1–20.

Pempel, T.J. (1999) *The Politics of the Asian Economic Crisis* (New York NY: Cornell University Press).

——(2000) 'International Finance and Asia Regionalism', *The Pacific Review*, vol. 13, no. 1, pp. 57–72.

Pérez-López, J.F. (1999) 'The Cuban External Sector in the 1990s', in V. Bulmer-Thomas and J. Dunkerley (eds), *The United States and Latin America: The New Agenda* (London: Institute of Latin American Studies), pp. 267–85.

Petiteville, F. (2003) 'Exporting "Values"? EU External Co-operation as a "Soft Diplomacy"', in M. Knodt and S. Princen (eds), *Understanding the European Union's External Relations* (London: Routledge), pp. 127–41.

Phar Kim Beng (2002) 'Is Hong Kong irrelevant?', *Asia Times*, 28 November.

Philip, G. (1999) 'The Dilemmas of Good Governance: A Latin American Perspective', *Government and Opposition*, vol. 34, no. 2, pp. 226–42.

Phillips, N.J. (2003a) 'Hemispheric Integration and Subregionalism in the Americas', *International Affairs*, vol. 79, no. 2, pp. 257–79.

——(2003b) 'The Rise and Fall of Open Regionalism? Comparative Reflections on Regional Governance in the Southern Cone of Latin America', *Third World Quarterly*, vol. 24, no. 2, pp. 217–34.

——(2004a) *The Southern Cone Model: The Political Economy of Regional Capitalist Development in Latin America* (London: Routledge).

Phillips, N.J. (2004b) 'Regionalising Multilateralism?: The New Politics of Trade in the Americas', in D. Kelly and W. Grant (eds), *The Politics of International Trade: Actors, Issues, Regions* (London: Palgrave Macmillan).

Picard, E. (1990) 'Arab Military in Politics', in C. Luciani (ed.), *The Arab State* (London: Routledge), pp. 189–219.

Pieterse, J.N. (1996) 'The Development of Development Theory: Towards Critical Globalism', *Review of International Political Economy*, vol. 3, no. 4, pp. 541–64.

Polidano, C. (2001) 'An Exocet in a Red Box: Parliamentary Accountability in the Sandline Affair', *Public Administration*, vol. 79, no. 2, pp. 249–74.

Pollack, M. (1995) 'Regional Actors in an Intergovernmental Play', in C. Rhodes and S. Mazey (eds), *The State of the European Union Volume 3* (Boulder CO: Lynne Rienner), pp. 361–90.

Popov, V. (2000a) 'Shock Therapy versus Gradualism: The End of the Debate (Explaining the Magnitude of Transformational Recession)', *Comparative Economic Studies*, vol. 42, no. 1, pp. 1–57.

——(2000b) *The Political Economy of Growth in Russia* (Washington DC: Center for Strategic and International Studies PONARS Working Paper Series no. 17).

Potter, R.B. (2001) 'Progress, Development and Change', *Progress in Development Studies*, vol. 1, no. 1, pp. 1–4.

Prodi, R. (2000) 'Europe and Global Governance', speech to the 2nd COMECE Congress, Brussels, 31 March, available at http://europa.eu.int/comm/external_relations/news/03_00/speech_00_15.htm

Qu, G.P. (1990) 'China's Environmental Policy and World Environmental Problems', *Environmental Affairs*, vol. 2, no. 2, pp. 103–8.

Randall, V. and Theobald, R. (1998) *Political Change and Underdevelopment: A Critical Introduction to Third World Politics* (London: Palgrave Macmillan).

Ravenhill, J. (2003) 'The New Bilateralism in the Asia Pacific', *Third World Quarterly*, vol. 24, no 2, pp. 299–318.

Reno, W. (1995) 'Reinvention of an African Neopatrimonial State: Charles Taylor's Liberia', *Third World Quarterly*, vol. 16, no. 1, pp. 109–21.

——(2000) 'Africa's Weak States: Nonstate Actors and the Privatization of Inter-state Relations', in D. Rothchild and J. Harbeson (eds), *Africa in World Politics: The African State System in Flux* (Boulder CO: Westview Press), pp. 286–308.

Review of African Political Economy (*ROAPE*) (1995) 'Banana Wars in Somalia', vol. 22, no. 64, pp. 274–5.

Richards, A. and Waterbury, J. (1990) *A Political Economy of the Middle East* (Boulder CO: Westview Press).

Richelle, K. (2003) 'The European Community Development Policy', The EU Current Agenda for Development Policy, Copenhagen, 12 March, available at http://europa.eu.int/comm/development/body/richelle/speeches/richelle_20030312_en.ctm

Rix, A. (1993) 'Japan and the Region: Leading from Behind', in R. Higgott, R. Leaver and J. Ravenhill (eds), *Pacific Economic Relations in the 1990s: Cooperation or Conflict?* (Boulder CO: Lynne Rienner), pp. 62–82.

Robinson, N. (1999a) 'The Global Economy, Reform and Crisis in Russia', *Review of International Political Economy*, vol. 6, no. 4, pp. 531–64.

——(1999b) 'The Commonwealth of Independent States as an International Institution', in P. Heenan and M. Lamontagne (eds), *The CIS Handbook* (Chicago IL: Fitzroy Dearborn), pp. 16–27

——(2002) *Russia: A State of Uncertainty* (London: Routledge).

Robinson, W.I. (1998) '(Mal)Development in Central America: Globalization and Social Change', *Development and Change*, vol. 29, no. 3, pp. 467–97.

Rodan, G. (1989) *The Political Economy of Singapore's Industrialisation* (London: Palgrave Macmillan).

Rogers, P. (1997) 'International River Basins: Persuasive Unidirectional Externalities', in P. Dasgupta *et al.* (eds), *The Economics of Transnational Commons* (Oxford: Clarendon Press), pp. 35–76.

Rosamond, B. (2002) 'Imagining the European Economy: Competitiveness and the Social Construction of Europe as an Economic Space, *New Political Economy*, vol. 7, no. 2, pp. 157–77.

——(2003) 'The Europeanization of British Politics', in P. Dunleavy, A. Gamble, R. Heffernan and G. Peele (eds), *Developments in British Politics 7* (London: Palgrave Macmillan), pp. 39–59.

——(2004) *Globalization and the European Union* (London: Palgrave Macmillan).

Rose, C. (1998) *Interpreting History in Sino-Japanese Relations: A Case Study in Political Decision Making* (London: Routledge for the Nissan Institute).

——(2000) ' "Patriotism is not Taboo": Nationalism in China and Japan and Implications for Sino-Japanese Relations', *Japan Forum*, vol. 12, no. 2, pp. 169–81.

Rose, R. (1996) *What is Europe? A Dynamic Perspective* (New York NY: HarperCollins).

Rosenau, J. (1997) *Along the Domestic–Foreign Frontier: Exploring Governance in a Turbulent World* (Cambridge: Cambridge University Press).

Ross, M. (1999) 'The Political Economy of the Resource Curse', *World Politics*, vol. 51, no. 1, pp. 297–322.

Rowley, C. and Lewis, M. (eds) (1996) *Greater China, Political Economy, Inward Investment and Business Culture* (London: Frank Cass).

Roxborough, I. (1979) *Theories of Underdevelopment* (London: Palgrave Macmillan).

Rozental, A. (2003) 'Mexico under Fox: The Foreign Policy Agenda', mimeo, Mexico City, July.

Ruggie, J.G. (1996) *Winning the Peace: America and World Order in the New Era* (New York NY: Columbia University Press).

Ruigrok, W. and Tulder, R. van (1995) *The Logic of International Restructuring* (London: Routledge).

Rutland, P. (1999) 'Mission Impossible? The IMF and Market Transition in Russia', *Review of International Studies*, vol. 25, special issue, pp. 183–200.

Sachs, J.D. (1997) 'IMF Orthodoxy isn't what Southeast Asia Needs', *International Herald Tribune*, 4 November, p. 8.

Said, E. (1992) *Culture and Imperialism* (London: Chatto & Windus).

Sakwa, R. and Webber, M. (1999) 'The Commonwealth of Independent States, 1991–1998: Stagnation and Survival', *Europe–Asia Studies*, vol. 51, no. 3, pp. 379–415.

Salame, G. (1989), 'Political Power and the Saudi State', in B. Berberoglu (ed.), *Power and Stability in the Middle East* (London: Zed), pp. 70–89.

Salazar-Xirinachs, J.M. (2001) 'The FTAA, the OAS and the New Pact in the Americas', Organization of American States, Trade Unit, February, available at http://www. sice.oas.org/tunit/STAFF ARTICLE/jmsx pact e.asp.

Sasuga, K. (2002) 'The Dynamics of Cross-Border Micro-Regionalisation Between Guangdong, Taiwan and Japan: Sub-national Governments, Multinational Corporations and the Emergence of Multi-Level Governance', unpublished PhD thesis, University of Warwick.

Sayigh, Y. (1992) *Arab Military Industry: Capabilities, Performance and Impact* (London: Brasseys).

Schatz, S. (1994) 'Structural Adjustment in Africa: A Failing Grade so Far', *Journal of Modern African Studies*, vol. 32, no. 4, pp. 679–92.

Schmidt, V.A. (2002) *The Futures of European Capitalism* (Oxford: Oxford University Press).

Scholte, J.A. (1997) 'Global Capitalism and the State', *International Affairs*, vol. 73, no. 3, pp. 427–52.

——(2000) *Globalization: A Critical Introduction* (London: Palgrave Macmillan).

Schraeder, P. (2000) *African Politics and Society* (New York NY: St Martin's Press).

Schuurman, F.J. (ed.) (1993) *Beyond the Impasse: New Directions in Development Theory* (London: Zed).

Scott, J. (1995) *Development Dilemmas in the European Community* (Buckingham: Open University Press).

Sedelmeier, U. and Wallace, H. (2000) 'Eastern Enlargement: Strategy or Second Thoughts?', in H. Wallace and W. Wallace (eds), *Policy-Making in the European Union*, 4th edn (Oxford: Oxford University Press), pp. 427–60.

Sen, A. (1999) *Development as Freedom* (Oxford: Oxford University Press).

Serrano, M. (2000) 'Transnational Crime in the Western Hemisphere', in J.I. Domínguez (ed.), *The Future of Inter-American Relations* (New York NY: Routledge), pp. 87–110.

Shambaugh, D. (ed.) (1995) *Greater China: The Next Superpower?* (Oxford: Oxford University Press).

Sharma, S.D. (1999) *Development and Democracy in India* (Boulder CO: Lynne Rienner).

Shearman, P. and Sussex, M. (2001) 'Foreign Policy Making and Institutions', in N. Robinson (ed.), *Institutions and Political Change in Russia* (London: Macmillan – Palgrave), pp. 151–72.

Sheean, D. (2001) 'More Power to the Powerful', *Far Eastern Economic Review*, 1 February, pp. 16–20.

Simon, D. (ed.) (1997) *The Emerging Technological Trajectory of the Pacific Rim* (New York NY: M.E. Sharpe).

—— (2001) 'The Bitter Harvest of War: Continuing Social and Humanitarian Dislocation in Angola', *Review of African Political Economy*, vol. 90 no. 28, pp. 503–20.

Smith, A. (1998) 'The Sub-regional Level: The Key Battleground for the Structural Funds?', in P. Le Galès and C. Lequesne (eds), *Regions in Europe* (London: Routledge), pp. 50–67

Smith, M.L. and Jones, D.M. (1997) 'Asean, Asian Values and Southeast Asian Security in the New World Order', *Contemporary Security Policy*, vol. 18, no. 3, pp. 126–56.

Smith, P. (2000) *Talons of the Eagle: Dynamics of U.S.–Latin American Relations*, 2nd edn (New York NY: Oxford University Press).

Söderbaum, F. (2001) 'Turbulent Regionalization in West Africa', in M. Schulz, F. Söderbaum and J. Öjendal (eds), *Regionalization in a Globalizing World* (London: Zed), pp. 61–81.

Soesastro, H. (1995) 'ASEAN and APEC: Do Concentric Circles Work?', *The Pacific Review*, vol. 8, no. 3, pp. 475–93.

Solnick, S. (1997) *Stealing the State: Control and Collapse in Soviet Institutions* (Cambridge MA: Harvard University Press).

Stamps, J. (2001) 'Russia's WTO Accession: Many Hurdles Remain', *International Economic Review*, July/August, pp. 7–15.

Stark, D. (1996) 'Recombinant Property in East European Capitalism', *American Journal of Sociology*, vol. 101, no. 4, pp. 993–1027.

Statkomitet SNG (2000) *Sodruzhestvo Nezavisimykh Gosudarstv v 1999 godu. Statisticheskii ezhegodnik* (Moscow: Statkomitet SNG).

Stevens, C. (2000) 'Trade with Developing Countries: Banana Skins and Turf Wars', in H. Wallace and W. Wallace (eds), *Policy-making in the European Union*, 4th edn (Oxford: Oxford University Press), pp. 402–26.

Stiglitz, J. and Yusuf, S. (eds) (2001) *Rethinking the East Asian Miracle* (New York NY: Oxford University Press for the World Bank).

Strange, S. (1970) 'International Economics and International Relations: A Case of Mutual Neglect', *International Affairs*, vol. 46, no. 2, pp. 304–15.

Strange, S. (1995) 'Political Economy and International Relations', in K. Booth and S. Smith (eds), *International Relations Theory Today* (Cambridge: Polity Press), pp. 154–74.

Stubbs, R. (2000) 'Signing on to Liberalization: AFTA and the Politics of Regional Economic Cooperation', *The Pacific Review*, vol. 13, no. 2, pp. 297–318.

Suárez-Orozco, M.M. (1999) 'Latin American Immigration to the United States', in V. Bulmer-Thomas and J. Dunkerley (eds), *The United States and Latin-America: The New Agenda* (London: Institute of Latin American Studies), pp. 227–44.

Tan, A. (2000) *Intra-Asean Tensions*, Discussion Paper no. 84 (London: Royal Institute for International Affairs).

Taneja, N. (2001) 'Informal Trade in SAARC Region', *Economic and Political Weekly*, vol. 36, no. 11, pp. 959–64.

Tavares de Araujo, J. Jr (1998) 'FTAA: Risks and Opportunities for Brazil', Organisation of American States Trade Unit, March, pp. 1–42.

Therborn, G. (2001) 'Europe – Super Power or Scandinavia of the World?', in M. Telò (ed.), *European Union and New Regionalism: Regional Actors and Global Governance in the Post-Hegemonic Era* (London: Ashgate), pp. 227–43.

Tilly, C. (1991) 'War and State Power', *Middle East Report*, no. 171, pp. 38–40.

Toye, J. (1987) *Dilemmas of Development: Reflections on the Counter-Revolution in Development Theory and Policy* (Oxford: Basil Blackwell).

Tsie, B. (1996) 'States and Markets in the Southern African Development Community (SADC): Beyond the Neoliberal Paradigm', *Journal of Southern African Studies*, vol. 22, no. 1, pp. 75–99.

Tussie, D. (1998) 'Multilateralism Revisited in a Globalizing World Economy', *Mershon International Studies Review*, no. 42, pp. 183–93.

——(2002) 'On Shifting Ground: The Crossroads of Regional and Sectoral Associations', in D. Tussie (ed.), *Trade Negotiations in Latin America: Problems and Prospects* (London: Palgrave Macmillan), pp. 1–16.

Ui, J. (ed.) (1992) *Industrial Pollution in Japan* (Tokyo: United Nations University Press).

Underhill, G.R.D. (2002) 'Global Integration, EMU and Monetary Governance in the European Union: The Political Economy of the Stability Culture', in K. Dyson (ed.), *European States and the Euro: Europeanization, Variation and Convergence* (Oxford: Oxford University Press), pp. 31–52.

United Nations (1997) *Sharing Asia's Dynamism: Asian Direct Investment in the European Union* (New York NY: United Nations).

United Nations Development Programme (2001) 'Moldovan Development Indicators', available at http://www.un.md/moldova/living_conditions_report.html

——(2002) *Arab Human Development Report 2002* (New York NY: United Nations).

United Nations Industrial Development Organization (1992–3) *Industry and Development: Global Report* (New York NY: United Nations).

US Census Bureau (2002) 'The Hispanic Population in the United States: March 2002', document P20-545, available at http://www.census.gov/prod/2003pubs/p20-545.pdf

US Department of Homeland Security, Bureau of Citizenship and Immigration Services (2002) *Fiscal Year 2002 Yearbook of Immigration Statistics*, available at http://www.immigration.gov/graphics/shared/aboutus/statistics/IMM02yrbk/IMM2002list.htm

US Department of State (2001) 'White House Reviews Progress on Stemming Hemisphere's Drug Trade', 15 May, available at http://usinfo.state.gov

US Department of State, Bureau for International Narcotics and Law Enforcement Affairs (2003) 'Fiscal Year 2004: International Narcotics and Law Enforcement Budget Justification', June, available at http://www.state.gov/g/inl/rls/rpt/cbj/fy2004/

USTR (Office of the United States Trade Representative) (2003) *2003 Trade Policy Agenda and 2002 Annual Report of the President of the United States on the Trade Agreements Program*, available at http://www.ustr.gov/reports/2003.html

US White House, International Office of National Drug Control Policy (2002) *Fact Sheet: Certification for Major Illicit Drug Producing and Transit Countries*, available at http://www.whitehousedrugpolicy.gov/publications/international/factsht/certification.html

Vale, P. and Maseko, S. (1998) 'South Africa and the African Renaissance', *International Affairs*, vol. 74, no. 2, pp. 271–87.

Vanaik, A. (1998) 'India's Place in the World', in P. Chatterjee (ed.), *Wages of Freedom: Fifty Years of the Indian Nation-State* (Delhi: Oxford University Press), pp. 61–88.

Van de Walle, N. (2000) 'Africa and the World Economy: Continued Marginalization or Re-engagement?', in D. Rothchild and J. Harbeson (eds), *Africa in World Politics: The African State System in Flux* (Boulder CO: Westview Press), pp. 263–86.

VanGrasstek, C. (1998) 'What is the FTAA's Role in the USA's Global Strategy?', *Capítulos del SELA*, no. 54, pp. 163–73.

Van Ham, P. (2001) 'The Rise of the Brand State: The Postmodern Politics of Image and Reputation', *Foreign Affairs*, vol. 80, no. 5, pp. 2–6.

Van Houtum, H. (2002) 'Borders of Comfort: Spatial Economic Bordering Processes in and by the European Union', *Regional and Federal Studies*, vol. 12, no. 4, pp.37–58.

Van Onselen, C. (1976) *Chibaro: African Mine Labour in Southern Rhodesia, 1900–1933* (London: Pluto).

Varshney, A. (1995) *Democracy, Development, and the Countryside: Urban–Rural Struggles in India* (Cambridge: Cambridge University Press).

Vassiliev, A. (2001) 'Russia and Central Asia', in A. Vassiliev (ed.), *Central Asia* (London: Saqi), pp. 7–30.

Wade, R. (1990) *Governing the Market: Economic Theory and the Role of Government in East Asian Industrialization* (Princeton NJ: Princeton University Press).

Wai-chung Yeung, H. (1999) 'Under Siege? Economic Globalization and Chinese Business in Southeast Asia', *Economy and Society*, vol. 28, no. 1, pp. 1–29.

Wallace, H. (2000) 'The Institutional Setting: Five Variations on a Theme', in H. Wallace and W. Wallace (eds), *Policy-Making in the European Union*, 4th edn (Oxford: Oxford University Press), pp. 3–37.

Wanner, B. (1999) 'Uproar Over JDA Official's Remarks Raises Questions About Japanese Attitudes Toward National Security', *Japan Economic Institute Report* no. 45A, Washington DC.

Washbrook, D. (1990) 'South-Asia, the World System, and World Capitalism', *Journal of Asian Studies*, vol. 49, no. 3, pp. 479–508.

Waterbury, J. (1993) *Exposed to Innumerable Delusions* (Cambridge: Cambridge University Press).

Weber, S. (2001) 'Conclusion', in S. Weber (ed.), *Globalization and the European Political Economy* (New York NY: Columbia University Press), pp. 273–93.

Weeks, J. (1996) 'Regional Cooperation and Southern African Development', *Journal of Southern African Studies*. vol. 22, no. 1, pp. 99–119.

Weidenbaum, M. and Hughes, S. (1996) *The Bamboo Network: How Expatriate Chinese Entrepreneurs are Creating a New Economic Superpower in Asia* (Riverside NJ: Simon & Schuster).

Weinbaum, M.G. (1999) 'Pakistan: Misplaced Priorities, Missed Opportunities', in S.S. Harrison, P.H. Kreisberg and D. Kux (eds), *India and Pakistan: The First Fifty Years* (Cambridge: Cambridge University Press), pp. 89–104.

Weiss, L. (1997) 'Globalization and the Myth of the Powerless State', *New Left Review*, no. 225, pp. 3–27.

Wendt, A. (1992) 'Anarchy is What States Make of It: The Social Construction of Power Politics', *International Organization*, vol. 46, no. 2, pp. 335–425.

Wendt, A. and Duvall, R. (1989) 'Institutions and International Order', in E.-O. Czempiel and J.N. Rosenau (eds), *Global Change and Theoretical Challenges: Approaches to World Politics for the 1990s* (Lexington NJ: Lexington Books), pp. 52–73.

White, G. (1987) *Development in East Asia* (New York NY: St Martin's Press).

Whitman, R. (2002) 'The Fall, and Rise, of Civilian Power Europe?', *National Europe Centre Paper* no. 16, Australian National University.

Wickremeratne, L.A. (1977) 'Planning and Economic Development', in K.M. De Silva (ed.), *Sri Lanka: A Survey* (London: C. Hurst), pp. 144–71.

Williams, D.G. (1996) 'Governance and the Discipline of Development', *The European Journal of Development Research*, vol. 8, no. 2, pp. 157–77.

Wilson, A.J. (1979) *Politics in Sri Lanka, 1947–1979* (London: Palgrave Macmillan).

Winters, J.A. (1996) *Power in Motion: Capital Mobility and the State* (New York NY: Cornell University Press).

——(2000) 'The Financial Crisis in Southeast Asia', in R. Robison *et al.* (eds), *Politics and Markets in the Wake of the Asian Crisis* (London: Routledge), pp. 34–52.

Wolf, M. and Luce, E. (2003) 'India's Slowing Growth: Why a Hobbled Economy Cannot Meet the Country's Needs', *Financial Times*, 4 April 2003.

Woo, W.T., Sachs, J. and Schwab, K. (eds) (2000) *The Asian Financial Crisis: Lessons for a Resilient Asia* (Boston MA: MIT Press).

Woodruff, D. (1999) *Money Unmade: Barter and the Fate of Russian Capitalism* (New York NY: Cornell University Press).

Woods, N. (2000) 'The Challenges of Multilateralism and Governance', in C.L. Gilbert and D. Vines (eds), *The World Bank: Structures and Policies* (Cambridge: Cambridge University Press), pp. 132–56.

——(2003) 'The United States and the International Financial Institutions: Power and Influence Within the World Bank and the IMF', in R. Foot, S.N. MacFarlane and M. Mastanduno (eds), *US Hegemony and International Organizations* (Oxford: Oxford University Press), pp. 92–114.

Woolcock, S. (2000) 'European Trade Policy: Global Pressures and Domestic Constraints', in H. Wallace and W. Wallace (eds), *Policy-Making in the European Union*, 4th edn (Oxford: Oxford University Press), pp. 373–99.

World Bank (1981) *Accelerated Development in Sub Saharan Africa: An Agenda to Action* (Washington DC: World Bank).

—— (1989) *Sub-Saharan Africa: From Crisis to Sustainable Growth: A Long Term Perspective Study* (Washington DC: World Bank).

—— (1993) *The East Asian Miracle: Economic Growth and Public Policy* (New York NY: Oxford University Press for the World Bank).

—— (1995) *Workers in an Integrating World* (Oxford: Oxford University Press).

—— (1997) *The State in a Changing World* (Oxford: Oxford University Press).

—— (1998–9) *Knowledge for Development* (Oxford: Oxford University Press).

—— (2000) *African Development Indicators* (Washington DC: World Bank).

—— (2001a) *Attacking Poverty* (Oxford: Oxford University Press).

—— (2001b) *Global Development Finance-Building Conditions for Effective Development Finance* (New York: World Bank).

—— (2002) *Building Institutions for Markets* (Oxford: Oxford University Press).

World Bank Group (n.d.) 'The World Bank's Role in EU Enlargement', available at http://lnweb18.worldbank.org/eca/europeanintegration.nsf

Wyatt, A. (2002) 'Reconsidering India's Economic Nationalism', unpublished paper presented at the Political Studies Association Annual Conference, University of Aberdeen, 5–7 April.

Xiang, B. (2002) 'Ethnic Transnational Middle Classes in Formation – A Case Study of Indian Information Technology Professionals', unpublished paper presented at the Political Studies Association Annual Conference, University of Aberdeen, 5–7 April.

Young, A.R. (2002) *Extending European Cooperation: The European Union and the 'New' International Trade Agenda* (Manchester: Manchester University Press).

Young, T. (1999) 'The State and Politics in Africa', *Journal of Southern African Studies*, vol. 25, no. 1, pp. 155–63.

Zaprudnik, J. and Urban, M. (1997) 'Belarus: From Statehood to Empire?', in I. Bremmer and R. Taras (eds), *New States, New Politics: Buildings the Post-Soviet Nations* (Cambridge: Cambridge University Press), pp. 276–315.

Zartman, W. (ed.) (1995) *Collapsed States: The Disintegration and Restoration of Legitimate Authority* (Boulder CO: Lynne Rienner).

Zhang Y.J. (1998) *China in International Society since 1949* (London: Palgrave Macmillan).

Zon, H. von (2000) *The Political Economy of Independent Ukraine* (London: Palgrave Macmillan).

Zubaida, S. (1989) *Islam, the People and the State* (London: Routledge).

—— (2003) *Law and Power in Islam* (London: I.B. Tauris).

Zysman, J. (1983) *Governments, Markets, and Growth: Financial Systems and the Politics of Industrial Change* (New York NY: Cornell University Press).

—— (1996) 'The Myth of the Global Economy: Enduring National Foundations and Emerging Regional Realities', *New Political Economy*, vol. 1, no. 2, pp. 157–84.

Index